READINGS IN ANCIENT
MEDIEVAL PHILOSOPHY

JAMES COLLINS received his A.B., A.M., and Ph.D. degrees in philosophy from The Catholic University of America in Washington, D.C., and was for a time a Research Fellow at Harvard University. Since 1945 he has been teaching philosophy at St. Louis University, where he is at present a full professor in his field. Dr. Collins is a member of the International Phenomenological Society and the American Catholic Philosophical Association; he was in 1954 the president of the latter organization. Dr. Collins is an Associate Editor of the philosophical journal, *The Modern Schoolman,* and has been appointed area editor for the history of Renaissance, modern, and contemporary philosophy for *The New Catholic Encyclopedia.* He is the author of *The Thomistic Philosophy of the Angels* (1947), *The Existentialists* (1952), *The Mind of Kierkegaard* (1953), *God in Modern Philosophy* (1959), and is a contributor to several journals of philosophy and to encyclopedias.

Readings in Ancient and Medieval Philosophy

Selected with Introduction and Commentary

by JAMES COLLINS, Ph.D.
Professor of Philosophy
Saint Louis University

THE NEWMAN PRESS • WESTMINSTER, MARYLAND

1960

Nihil obstat: EDWARD A. CERNY, S.S., S.T.D.
Censor Librorum
Imprimatur: FRANCIS P. KEOUGH, D.D.
Archbishop of Baltimore

June 3, 1960

The *nihil obstat* and *imprimatur* are official declarations that a book or pamphlet is free of doctrinal and moral error. No implication is contained therein that those who have granted the *nihil obstat* and *imprimatur* agree with the opinions expressed.

Contents

114, 332

Part Two

MEDIEVAL PHILOSOPHY

V. PATRISTIC THOUGHT

VI. CHRISTIAN PHILOSOPHIES FROM ST. ANSELM TO ST. BERNARD

VII. ARABIAN AND JEWISH PHILOSOPHIES

VIII. THIRTEENTH-CENTURY MASTERS: GROSSETESTE TO AQUINAS

Introduction

This collection of readings is designed for use in the college introductory courses in the history of ancient and medieval philosophy. The aim of such courses is not only to describe the basic lines of development but also to acquaint us with some of the sources and historical studies. The more we can make a first-hand acquaintance with these writings, the more authentic and intimate will be our understanding of philosophy as a historical process that constantly grows and engages in self-criticism. The student finds his introductory framework in the lectures and text-books, but he needs to begin doing some personal reading in the great philosophers and the well-trained historians. The purpose of the present selection is to encourage this study of the best historical work being done in the fields of ancient and medieval philosophy. Some source materials are included, but a special effort is made to meet the need for a convenient collection of twentieth-century historical studies of some major thinkers in the Western philosophical tradition extending from Thales to Cusanus.

As a distinct discipline using the techniques and resources of modern historical research, the historical study of philosophy is barely a century-and-a-half old. It received its first great impetus from Hegel and Schelling, whose lectures on the history of philosophy brought out the importance of understanding the past developments in philosophy and giving them a definite critical interpretation. But their pioneer labors also revealed the need for numerous specialized studies in the various areas, so that the philosophical interpretation and assimilation could rest upon a sound and broad basis in knowledge of all the relevant sources. The leading histories of philosophy and the majority of special monographs and articles published during the nineteenth century were written from the standpoint of German idealism. For a long while it seemed as though this philosophy had captured the history of philosophy and established a monopoly over its speculative use. It seemed as though only the doctrines of absolute idealism were able to profit from a historical study of the sources.

During our own century, however, the situation has gradually, yet radically, changed in the direction of terminating the dominance of the idealist conception of the history of philosophy, including its ancient and medieval phases. This is due partly to the internal decline of idealism itself to the point where it is on the defensive regarding its own fundamental principles of interpretation. In part, it is also due to the fact that the leading representatives of other philosophical positions are becoming increasingly sensitive to the need for making careful historical studies, both for their own sake and for what they can contribute toward the understanding and resolution of present-day philosophical issues. Another factor encouraging a broader participation in the history of philosophy is the advance made generally in the history of ideas and in the particular histories of the academic disciplines other than philosophy. A more concrete and realistic approach to the history of philosophy is suggested by the many lines of interconnection and convergence traceable between the main philosophical movements and the broader setting in religion, science, literature, and social life. Whole regions in the history of philosophy are being rescued from obscurity and arbitrary presentation through a more accurate study of the philosophical texts and a more perceptive consideration of the cultural matrix for the philosophical systems in every age.

These tendencies favoring a more faithful approach toward our philosophical heritage have proven to be specially beneficial in the areas of ancient and medieval Western philosophy. Scholars have been encouraged to read the Greek sources without the preoccupation of trying to fit the results into some pre-cast idealistic categories. What the Greek and Roman thinkers said is being weighed as testimony about the ancient Western venture in philosophy, taken for its own sake and not merely as a forerunner of the modern types of thought culminating in idealism. Medieval philosophy has benefited even more vastly from the changed climate in historical studies. Two generations of scholars have now concentrated their research upon the great medieval sources in philosophy and theology, supported by excellent research in the other aspects of medieval culture. It is no longer possible to make merely vague references to these ages of Christian philosophy as a torpid interlude or as a somewhat boring concentration upon the problem of the universals or even as a theological era in which no intrinsic interest in the philosophical problems was permitted to develop. Such substitutes for historical understanding are no longer tolerated, because we now have at our disposal numerous reliable editions and translations of the medieval sources together with some excellent historical surveys of the several phases in medieval philosophical speculation.

Everyone concerned about intellectual issues has gained by this quickening of historical studies in the philosophical field. Today, as at no previous time in Western life, we are aware of the importance of the historical factor involved in philosophical work. This awareness is not of the over-ripe Alexandrine sort, which presages a decline in speculative vigor, but rests on a deliberate assessment of the intellectual resources needed for our creative advances. Philosophy, along with every other intellectual sphere of endeavor, is quickened rather than deadened by being able to draw upon a reliable fund of historical knowledge and vision.

Through the history of philosophy, one learns the discipline of making an honest, careful, and initially sympathetic inspection of the reasoned positions taken by great men concerning the main issues. It teaches us the rockbottom intellectual habit of understanding what a philosopher is saying before we attempt to weigh and criticize his views. Unless we first sit at his feet for a certain while and listen to his discourse, we cannot hope to know his mind and make an estimate of it which is at once relevant to his position and effective for the growth of truth. This kind of intellectual formation is indispensable, not only for learning how to share in the intellectual life of philosophy, but also for learning how to participate in the discussions within a pluralist society. A careful study of the history of philosophy is one definite means whereby college students can prepare themselves for meeting the diversity of philosophical standpoints in contemporary America, as well as for contributing their personal share to the discussions and practical decisions which shape our common life.

One of the marked differences between the condition of Christian philosophies at the time of Leo XIII's call for the restoration of the full wealth of the Christian philosophical tradition (in *Aeterni Patris,* 1879) and today lies in the present emphasis upon historical investigations and their incorporation into the college program. We can now see why it is unwise to concentrate the philosophical component in a liberal education exclusively upon the systematic or purely analytic approach. It is indispensable to have the systematic courses, which are usually organized around the doctrines of Aristotle and St. Thomas. But the philosophical curriculum is impoverished and defective in its responsibility toward the students, if it aims at achieving a complete insulation from the cross currents in the history of philosophy. Although they were not historically minded in our sense of the term, both Aristotle and St. Thomas displayed lively interest in the views of other men. They kept the windows of inquiry open at all times to a conscientious study of the main teachings of other men. There is no other way of genuinely preparing oneself for the intellectual problems and discussions of life than by examining the major philosophical systems in their sources and with the guidance of reliable scholars in the field. The need to study the history of philosophy is particularly urgent for college students today, since they are bound to be confronted directly or indirectly with quite divergent philosophical opinions drawn from the historical materials. The student is well advised to begin his study of the various philosophies during his college years and in conjunction with his other academic work.

In order to maintain a broad correlation between these readings and the courses in the history of philosophy as they are actually given, I have paid attention to the organization and treatment in some of the standard histories of ancient and medieval philosophy. These include the textbooks of Copleston, Owens, Brady, and Gilson. Their divisions of the various periods and their emphasis upon the basic problems provide a rough framework within which to fit our selected texts. This arrangement permits an orderly relation to be established between class work and independent reading assignments. Yet I have tried to choose materials which do not simply repeat the content of the textbooks now in use, but which make an independent approach to the sources and thus furnish a challenge to the student. In many cases the selections are also mentioned in the bibliographies of these textbooks, thus making such bibliographical suggestions more meaningful and practical for readers.

The internal organization of the readings involves a certain amount of interpretation of the movement of philosophical thought. Thus Plato and Aristotle are regarded as the high points in the ancient period, so that separate sections are devoted to them. And within each of these sections, the readings are intended to underline the fact that Plato and Aristotle owe their pre-eminent position partly to their systematic investigation of problems in all the areas of philosophy, ranging from theory of knowledge and scientific method to metaphysics and ethics. Only a sampling is possible from the great variety of doctrines elaborated during the pre-Socratic age and the period of Hellenistic speculation in the later Greek and Roman worlds. The selections from the several systematic fields illustrate, however, the breadth of interest which enabled the philosophers of the ancient world to lay the permanent foundations for all of our subsequent philosophical inquiries.

Medieval philosophy is understood in a broad way to include the Christian thought of the Patristic period and the contributions of Arabian and Jewish writers, in addition to the work done by the Latin Christian minds of the middle ages. In the earlier phase, St. Augustine looms up as the most important thinker and the fountainhead for much of the later speculation. Our selections from the middle ages accentuate the doctrines of the thirteenth-century writers and seek to convey something of the rich complexity of their age. This emphasis is not intended to detract from the value of studying the thought of the earlier Christian doctors or of tracing out the pattern of speculation during the fourteenth and fifteenth centuries, when medieval and Renaissance strains of thought are intermingled. Inevitably in attempting such a wide coverage, I have been unable to include many worthy representatives of medieval philosophy. Among the outstanding omissions are St. John Damascene, Scotus Erigena, the School of Chartres, and the later writers in scientific and political areas. It is hoped, however, that the selections from the men actually included here will whet the reader's interest to look into other aspects of their thought and to branch out into a study of the people I have had to omit.

In view of the fact that there are several available anthologies and longer translations devoted exclusively to the ancient and medieval sources, the present collection is drawn mainly from reliable secondary studies published in English. Some translations of primary sources are included for all the main periods, but there is a preponderance of articles and chapters written by competent historians of philosophy. Copies of the original publications are usually too few to permit their practical classroom assignment in the periodical or book form. There are no selections made directly from the four greatest minds in the periods under consideration: Plato and Aristotle, Augustine and Aquinas. A partial exception is made in the case of one Platonic dialogue, where the student will be able to examine the way in which a key text and an expert commentary thereon are combined. These four major sources are usually represented quite adequately in college libraries, as well as in other volumes in the Newman Press College Readings Series. Hence I have taken the opportunity to concentrate, in their case, upon some historical studies which inspect various aspects of their doctrine. In the instance of St. Thomas, however, even the historical literature is fairly well covered in several other collections, so that Maritain's essay on Thomistic humanism is offered here as a thoughtful example of a unified interpretation stressing the present significance of Aquinas. Nevertheless, a number of the other selections deal with him by way of making comparisons between his thought and that of other medieval authors.

In the case of primary sources, a choice is made wherever possible of men who make a vigorous and clear presentation of their own views. It is always best to become acquainted with a philosopher in his strongest aspects. This removes the temptation to deal only with straw men or to study only those elements in a system which are most obviously open to objection. Why a thinker can attract other minds is unintelligible to us, until we consult him in his most lucid and convincing passages. As an aid to critical thinking on such texts, the introductory comments suggest some brief points of evaluation, together with the requisite background information.

Among the translations of primary sources included here the reader will notice the presence of several kinds of philosophical writing. Plato is the classic representative of the dialogue form, whereas Epicurus presents us with an instance of the familiar philosophical letter (which is historically complicated by being conveyed to us through the medium of another author, Diogenes Laertius). In St. Gregory of Nyssa, we can feel the close relationship between reflective religious meditations and a reasoned view of God and man. The account of the various positions on the problem of the universals given to us by John of Salisbury is a good instance of on-the-spot reporting done in the philosophical order, and done during a time when philosophical disputes were treated as prime topics of cultivated conversation. We find in the selection from Duns Scotus a prime instance of the medieval Question, which is one of the most supple and effective tools ever devised for philosophical inquiry. Abelard and Cajetan agree at least in a certain dryness of style, whereas the passage from Cusanus compares with the earlier text from Parmenides for its use of imagination and analogy.

Some fruitful comparisons can also be made among the materials taken from the historians of philosophy. Anyone interested in the technique of commenting upon a single key passage and drawing out its many implications will find it well developed in the analyses made respectively of the skeptical attitude and St. Albert's definition of the soul. There is a wide variety of ways in which historians achieve their criticism in the midst of faithful exposition of thought. This can be observed in the essay on Plato's dyadic theory of being, where the internal difficulties of the position are quietly shown to pile up. An implicit type of criticism is achieved in the very reserve with which the Aristotelian theory of movers is explained, with the caution that we should not read into it the sharper views of Christian theism. Another mode of criticism is that of pointing out some consequences of a doctrine for the later history of thought, a method followed in the articles on Avicenna and Ockham. Sometimes the aim of the historian is to defend his source from misinterpretation, as we can see in the discussion of Plato's political ideas and of Averroes' position on personal immortality.

Other questions are worth asking, when the student feels that he can begin to look at the materials in a comparative way. For instance, he may want to know how far the biographical data are significant in the history of philosophy, and for this purpose he can compare the portrait of Socrates given here with the account of St. Augustine's studies in neo-Platonism. Another interesting point concerns the connections which historians of philosophy establish between the philosophical order and other cultural elements. This preoccupation is noticeable in the approach taken to the pre-Socratic views on justice as seen in the light of the medical tradition, as well as in the initial account of the partial conflict between early Greek religion and philosophy. That this influence of extra-philosophical factors on the course of philosophical speculation continues to be a cardinal theme, can be seen in the description of Philo Judaeus as being dependent on revelation for some central ideas. The very fact of our inclusion of readings on the Arabian and Jewish thinkers is a further indication of how necessary it is to gauge the effect of cultural cross influences.

Finally, the history of philosophy brings home to us in a concrete way the observation that there are some persistent core questions facing men in every age. We notice the theme of practical knowledge and moral choice in Aristotle and the Stoics, in Augustine and Boethius, in St. Bernard and Abelard. The problem of God is with us all the way from Xenophanes to Cusanus, with the impact of revelation being felt in this area in the approaches of Clement of Alexandria, St. Anselm, and Moses Maimonides. Man as the image of God is a guiding thought for St. Gregory of Nyssa, and it helps to determine the two chief types of

Christian humanism in Bonaventure and Aquinas. That the general problem of knowledge is constant for philosophers can be verified by consulting the Platonic dialogue, the report on the universals, and the analysis of Ockham. Various meanings for "science" are traceable, if one compares Aristotle with Robert Grosseteste and Roger Bacon. Our selections also remind us about the persistence of certain special issues, such as the question of the world's eternity (Aristotle, Averroes, Siger of Brabant) and that of the cosmic import of light (Plotinus and Grosseteste).

The editorial policy followed here with regard to omissions from the text should be clearly set forth. The guiding consideration has been to achieve the maximum of relevant materials for reading and classroom discussion. For that purpose, most of the footnotes in the original publications are omitted, although some citations and explanations are retained. I have added an occasional note, but all editorial footnotes are enclosed within square brackets. An effort has been made to keep the main text as an integral whole wherever that is practically possible, either by using an entire chapter or article or by using a continuous division or section within the chapter or article. Omissions which are made in the main body of the text are not indicated there typographically, but the fact of there being such omissions is furnished in the first footnote accompanying every selection. For the sake of smoothness, introductory sentences have been slightly modified in some instances, but without changing the meaning of the original text. There are also some modifications of paragraphing and punctuation to suit the present format. Since complete bibliographical information is furnished for every selection, the original publication can always be consulted. Readers who are attracted to the issues under discussion will naturally want to do some further work in our sources.

In three instances, it was found advisable to have essays specially written for this book. For their prompt and expert cooperation, I am indeed grateful to the following contributors of original papers: Dr. Charles Fay, Assumption University, Windsor, on Boethius; Rev. Clifford Kossel, S. J., Mount St. Michael's, Spokane, on Aristotle; Rev. Peter Nash, S. J., Jesuit Seminary, Toronto, on Giles of Rome. This collection of readings could not have been assembled without the generous support of Rev. William Wade, S. J., Director of the Philosophy Department at St. Louis University. In gathering the materials from many books and periodicals, I was also aided considerably by the staff of the Pius XII Library of St. Louis University.

JAMES COLLINS

Normandy, Missouri
May, 1960

PART ONE

Ancient Philosophy

I. Early Greek Philosophy

Western philosophy had its birth in the cosmic and moral speculations of the Greek thinkers of the sixth and fifth centuries before Christ. The sages at Miletus went beyond the ordinary perception of things and the mythical stories in search of a reasonable account of nature, considered in its change, order, and unity. They looked for some basic element or pattern, by reference to which the conflict and harmony of things could become meaningful and ordered. The Pythagoreans explored the formal proportions of number and harmony in both the greater cosmos and the smaller one of human society, whereas the Eleatics were fascinated by the paradoxes of change and the correlation between mind and being. In all these inquiries into nature, the pre-Socratic philosophers were animated negatively by a profound dissatisfaction with the account of things given in the popular religious stories and poetic elaborations. Historians of thought have disagreed, however, about the precise relations of the philosophical doctrines to the religious outlook as a whole. Opinions have ranged from attributing to the philosophers a theoretical and religious pantheism, in which nature itself is divine, to regarding them basically as anti-religious materialists bent upon replacing the gods by visible elements.

This is the problem to which Werner Jaeger addresses himself in the book from which Selection (1) is taken. With his customary balance, he shows that the undoubted antagonism between philosophy and popular religious practice does not entail a rejection of the divine principle and of every religious attitude. Yet there is no need of taking a view at the other extreme, which sees a prefiguring of philosophical pantheism and its religious correlate in the pre-Socratic awareness of the presence of the divine. The conflict between the philosophers and the older poets, such as Homer and Hesiod, is an explicit theme in the poems of Xenophanes of Colophon. In a somewhat groping way, he realizes that among all the gods there is a supreme one who moves things by the thought of his mind. This is sufficient to supply a basis for the criticism and purification of prevailing religious notions. There is a strong reaction against a *particularistic, anthropomorphic, and morally degrading conception of the divine. Even though philosophical speculation is not yet in possession of a definite doctrine on the immaterial and transcendent God, it does recognize the impropriety of many popular and poetic descriptions of the gods. Jaeger quotes Aeschylus, however, to show that paideia or education can be a joint responsibility of poets and philosophers in leading a people toward a more exalted religious conception.*

One reason why there are scholarly disagreements about the precise import of the pre-Socratic writings is that the texts usually survive only in a fragmentary condition. Often our only record is a statement by Plato or Aristotle. These major philosophers are vitally concerned with the thought of their predecessors, whom they regard as posing the basic problems and at least pointing in the direction where a solution is to be found. The surviving passages have been gathered together in a Greek-German edition by H. Diels: The Fragments of the Pre-Socratics. *Selection (2) is taken from the English translation by Kathleen Freeman which is outstanding for its close fidelity to the original. From a careful study of her version, one can appreciate not only something of the early Greek way of philosophizing but also the reason for the difficulties which have beset interpreters ever since Plato's day. The words which the translator italicizes and puts within parentheses are intended to clarify or explain a sentence, but there remain many doubtful readings.*

Selection (2) contains the heart of Parmenides' great poem, setting forth the ways of truth and opinion. Retaining the imaginative framework, Parmenides describes in the prologue how a chariot bore him to the presence of the goddess. The main text, given here, is her instruction to the inquiring philosopher concerning the two paths of inquiry. The way of being and truth is open to him who follows reason or logos to the point of grasping the one, continuous whole, in its self-identity and immobility. Opposed to this is the path of opinion, taken by those who rely upon sense perception and accept the perpetual flux of Heraclitus as real. Arguments are advanced against admitting the truth of becoming and multiplicity, but the reasoning is more informal than in the logical paradoxes proposed by Parmenides' pupil, Zeno of Elea. However, the goddess does not want the reasonable man to remain ignorant of how things seem to the senses, and how an organized set of opinions can be developed concerning a world of changing opposites and natural necessities. One problem in interpretation concerns how there can be any thought and expression about nonbeing and becoming. The doctrine on opinion must be related to that on truth, in such fashion that the well-instructed man can know the former without disturbing the exclusive claim of the latter and his certainty in it. The device of the goddess and her descriptions is somewhat analogous to that of a contemporary meta-language, which permits a descriptively true report about the names used in the realm of opinion and yet avoids confusing its content with the truth of being.

In this poem, the inviolate whole of being is compared to a well-rounded sphere, uniformly related to its limit. By contrast with the subsequent view of the Christian theologians, the Greek mind regards the unbounded or infinite as something defective and incomplete, lacking the perfection of a definite form. The references in Parmenides to justice and necessity as binding down being to a motionless whole are puzzling. They indicate the presence of some intellectual influences which cannot be reduced simply to a logical reaction against the partisans of flux. In Selection (3), Gregory Vlastos suggests that there is indeed a common pattern of thought embracing, in certain respects, not only Parmenides and Heraclitus but also such "physiologists" or philosophers of nature as Anaximander and Empedocles. He seeks a clue in the medical tradition, which stands in very intimate relation with philosophical thought throughout ancient philosophy and beyond. The rational theory of health and climate rests upon the idea of counterpoised powers and a mixture of equal forces. This suggests a broader basis for justice than is usually supposed, since the notion of a cosmic harmony of equilibrated powers provides an objective assurance of measure, harmony, and justice in things as well as in human actions.

Vlastos' essay is an excellent example of how the historian of philosophy profits by the history of science, and also of how he employs the comparative type of argument. The analysis moves reversely to the chronological order, since the author seeks to account for the absence of the term "justice" in Empedocles by analyzing a similar strain of reasoning in Parmenides, where that term does occur in conjunction with views on equality and wholeness. Vlastos then exploits his interpretation of equality in these men in order to contest Burnet's view (Early Greek Philosophy) of one of the earliest Ionian thinkers, Anaximander, and to remove an ambiguity in Aristotle's account of the boundless. The relation between the political practice of rotation in office and the general theory of equality through cosmic rotation is mentioned, but is not fully worked out. Like most historical investigations, this one culminates in a properly philosophical conclusion. If the basic consideration is cosmic equality, then there is a naturalization of the concept of justice and a view of nature as an immanent whole, within which all powers are contained.

It is likely that Socrates challenged this supposition about the foundational role of cosmic equality in determining the nature of justice, since it would make our moral life depend upon something which does not accord any decisive importance to human insight and choice. Not much can be said about the historical Socrates since we are entirely dependent for information about him upon the early dialogues and Apology of Plato, together with the more prosaic reports in Xenophon and Aristotle. Nevertheless, the figure of Socrates has always inspired men as a noble model. His unpretentious and persistent mode of inquiry, his fearless examination of received opinion, and his personal commitment to the search after the moral good, are traits which permanently belong to the philosophical mind. In Selection (4), Xavier Zubiri meditates upon the essential heritage of Socrates and his role as precursor for Plato and Aristotle. He emphasizes that our chief debt to Socrates is not for some special doctrine or even an abstract methodology, but rather for his concrete example of how to live reflectively and bring the inquiring mind to bear upon human affairs, so as to discover the human significance of everyday things and everyday talk.

1

XENOPHANES' DOCTRINE OF GOD [1]

XENOPHANES was an intellectual revolutionary. The earlier philosophers had presented their new conceptions of reality to their contemporaries as a plain, well-rounded whole. But Xenophanes was a man of an altogether different sort, who perceived the devastating novelty of their approach and loudly proclaimed that it was irreconcilable with the traditional views. The dominant intellectual and moral tradition of the time had no more distinguished representative than Homer, by whom, as Plato remarks, all Hellas had been educated. Xenophanes thought the same: to him Homer was the man

From whom all men have learned since the beginning.

1 [From Werner Jaeger, *The Theology of the Early Greek Philosophers* (Oxford: Clarendon Press, 1947), pp. 41-50. Reprinted by permission. Notes are omitted.]

These words reveal a clear awareness of Homer's overpowering authority throughout the realm of Greek culture. And it was precisely because of this awareness that Xenophanes felt compelled to attack Homer as the mainstay of the prevailing errors. At this moment the latent antagonism between the new philosophical thinking and the old world of myth, which had dominated the earlier achievements of the Greek spirit, broke into open conflict. The clash was inevitable. While the pioneer thinkers of the new philosophy had not marshalled their discoveries polemically, Xenophanes made the world of myth a focal point for his opposition. It was not unreasonable that he, the poet, should be the one to see in this situation implications which spelled disaster for all previous poetry. It seemed to him self-evident that the poet is the one real educator of the people, and his work the only genuinely responsible authority of *paideia*. And so it was with Xenophanes that the work of deliberately transfusing the new philosophical ideas into the intellectual blood stream of Greece began.

It is characteristic of the effect of Ionian philosophy upon the most enlightened contemporary minds that the problem of God is central for Xenophanes. This is the best evidence of the extent to which the new doctrines of the origin of the world had encroached upon the domain of religion. Naturally, Anaximander must have sensed his own opposition to the traditional anthropomorphic deities when he boldly asserted the Boundless to be the Divine, and thus refused to let divine nature take the form of distinct individual gods; but it is Xenophanes who first declares war on the old gods with the impressive words:

> . . . One god is the highest among gods and men;
> In neither his form nor his thought is he like unto mortals.

By this negation the poet gives his newly discovered knowledge a fixed direction and propulsive force which it hitherto lacked. These are words which catch men's fancy far more easily than those of Anaximander, despite the genius with which he first expressed this knowledge. For not only did Xenophanes choose to put his message in poetical form; he also consciously applied his philosophical insight to the whole world of the anthropomorphic gods of Homer and Hesiod—a world which had previously counted as plain historical fact, but which now was collapsing. In these two lines the bearing of the new knowledge upon the old divinities is made explicit for the first time, not only in its positive aspects, but also negatively and critically. The philosophical intuition of a single world-ground, of course, involves new riddles more difficult than those for which it provides an answer. Xenophanes himself points out in another context that even when one sees the truth, this knowledge can never give its possessor complete assurance of its validity; about the highest questions there must always be widespread doubt. This insight, which, though tinged with resignation, is still far removed from the thoroughgoing skepticism of later centuries, inevitably appears whenever man starts to reason about these problems. But one thing at least is certain for Xenophanes: the human mind is an inadequate form through which to comprehend that infinite, all-governing unity which the philosophers have recognized as the principle of all things. It never occurs to Xenophanes to suggest that God may be without form altogether. It is significant that in all the time that the Greeks gave their philosophical attention to these matters, the problem of the form (*morphē*) of the Divine was one that never lost its importance. It always remained an essential part of the problem *de natura deorum,* and in the Stoic philosophy it acquired new impetus in the doctrine of God's immanence in the world, which was represented as a sphere. But Xenophanes does not express his views of the divine form in positive terms. He does not say that the world is God, so that God's form is merely the world's form; for Xenophanes is not to be dismissed with the word pantheist. He merely makes way for a philosophic conception by denying that God's form is human.

In other respects he retains the conventional Greek pluralism. For understandable reasons Christian writers have always tended to read their own monotheism into Xenophanes' proclamation of the One God; but while he extols this God as more than human, he also describes him explicitly as "the greatest among gods and men." This manner of speaking, with its polar juxtaposition of gods and men, follows the old epic formulas; nevertheless, it still makes it perfectly clear that besides the One God there must be others, just as there are men. On the other hand, it would be wrong to conclude that these must be the anthropomorphic gods of the epic, which would rank side by side with the one highest God and would enable Xenophanes to compromise with the popular religion. It is more plausible to think of the dictum of Thales that all things are full of gods, or of Anaximander's doctrine of the one divine primal ground and the innumerable gods (that is, the innumerable worlds) that have come into being, even if we have no right to ascribe to Xenophanes any specific dogma of this sort. In any case the one all-embracing God is so far superior to all the other lesser divine forces that he alone could really seem important to Xenophanes.

But Xenophanes goes even further in draining off the residue of anthropomorphism from his conception of the One God. He writes that God "sees as a whole, thinks as a whole, hears as a whole." Thus God's consciousness is not dependent upon sense organs or anything comparable. On the other hand, Xenophanes' God is unquestionably represented as a conscious, personal being, a fact which distinguishes him from what Anaximander calls the Divine. The philosophical attempt to divest the gods of their forms, which Stenzel sees in Anaximander's conception, is quite foreign to Xenophanes. The fact that he speaks very definitely of the One God who is more than all others is hardly to be explained as a mere reversion to traditional poetic language. One would not be likely to say of Anaximander's "Boundless" that it sees as a whole, thinks as a whole, hears as a whole. Moreover, Anaximander, unlike Xenophanes, does not attack the gods in order to supplant them with his own divine Being. But no one can doubt that Xenophanes actually prays to his God; we could be sure of this even if we did not have his banquet elegy to show us how seriously and directly he puts his religious ideas into practice.

These ideas, however, continue to unfold in sharp opposition to the prevailing faith, just as if they were intended to become a prevailing faith themselves. God, says Xenophanes:

> ... ever abides
> In the selfsame place without moving; nor is it fitting
> For him to move hither and thither, changing his place.

Here Xenophanes is again criticizing the Homeric representation. In Homer the gods' quickness of movement is construed as a veritable token of the divine power. Xenophanes, however, demands that his God be immobile, for he sees in this a mark of the highest dignity, as is clear from the words: "Nor is it fitting for him to move." (We meet the same religious intuition again in the contemporary statues and paintings which represent the gods as sitting in full majesty upon thrones, though naturally the artists had to express this insight in anthropomorphic terms.) Furthermore, the idea of God's absolute calm and immobility leads inevitably to an altered conception of his manner of acting upon things:

> But effortlessly he sets all things astir
> By the power of his mind alone.

This conjunction of omnipotence and repose is of tremendous importance in paving the way for the idea of God that we meet in later years. We think at once of the Aristotelian unmoved mover, an idea which really originates here in Xenophanes. Aristotle's doctrine attempts, by adopting the Platonic formula: "it produces motion as being loved," to give greater plausibility to this noble conception of divine action upon the world. In Aeschylus we find much earlier evidence of the power and vigor of the idea, particularly in the great prayer to Zeus in *The Suppliants*. The poet depicts the divine dominion in a way that reveals not only the critical significance of Xenophanes' pioneering for a purer conception of God, but also its positive religious significance for his own time. The notion that God can sway the world merely by the power of his mind is shifted from the cosmic to the ethical sphere.

> Down from their high-towered hopes
> He flings poor, wretched mortals,
> Donning no armour of might.
> For gods act without effort:
> High from their hallowed seats
> They somehow make their own thinking
> Come all at once to pass.

Aeschylus' expressive but almost prosaic "somehow" (*pōs*) shows that he is moved by a great and difficult idea which is readily perceptible to his religious feeling, though his reason cannot grasp the "how" of this activity. This is not the only place in which the poet reveals that he has been directly influenced by contemporary philosophical thought and scientific discoveries. When he imagines the divine powers dwelling on high, he still clings to the old conception of the gods as throned in heaven; but we must bear in mind that even Xenophanes, as Aristotle rightly declares, conceived his idea of the One God by "looking up at the sky," thus bringing the divine unity before his very eyes.

According to Auguste Comte, the metaphysical stage, which follows the mythical stage of intellectual development and is itself superseded by positive science, is the critical crucible through which the mythical consciousness must pass. We need not discuss the value of Comte's whole system as a contribution to intellectual history; but it does at least help us to formulate the relation between mythical religion and Xenophanes' metaphysical thought in a manner quite consistent with his own genius. In Xenophanes the critical side of the new philosophical theology becomes fully conscious. The idea of an omnipotent Being, transcending all the other powers in the world, even the gods themselves, was one which the later epic-writers had already associated with their highest god. In the eighth book of the *Iliad,* for example, the poet makes Zeus say to the other gods:

> ... And if
> You should try to dangle a cable of gold from the sky,
> And hang on it, all you goddesses and all you gods,
> You could not drag great Counsellor Zeus from his heaven
> Down to the plain, no matter how mighty your straining.
> But I—were I once of a mind to lift, I'd pull
> The whole pack of you up, with all the land and the ocean,
> And fasten the cable to one of the peaks of Olympus,
> And leave you swinging.

Aristotle cites this passage as the first intimation of the power of the unmoved mover in the early history of Greek thought. But the all-too-human form of this conception would have struck Xenophanes as childish. In his century thinking men had not yet learned to hunt for their primitive forbears. Xenophanes' God has no need to nod his head like the Homeric Zeus to make Olympus quake with terror. Only the phrase: "effortlessly he sets all things astir by the power of his mind alone," betrays the unconscious persistence of the old Homeric tendency to humanize the sublime.

The fragments reveal further characteristic evidence of Xenophanes' critique of anthropomorphism. He finds his task easiest in the realm of ethics, where the way has already been prepared, largely by the progressive moralization of the gods during the sixth century.

> ... Homer and Hesiod say that the gods
> Do all manner of things which men would consider disgraceful:
> Adultery, stealing, deceiving each other.

Godhead must certainly be free from any moral weakness which even men consider blameworthy: this is a point on which Xenophanes and all his more thoughtful contemporaries would agree. But he is not content with so easy a victory. He launches another attack at the very root of the epic theogonies:

> ... But mortals suppose that the gods undergo generation;
> They dress them with clothes like their own, as well as with voices
> And figures.

The idea of the un-becoming and the unending, with which Anaximander characterized his divinity, the *apeiron*, put an end to such notions. Xenophanes merely works out some of the consequences of this philosophy in detail, a process which must have brought him up against the problem of the origin of anthropomorphism:

> ... But if cattle and horses had hands, and were able
> To paint with their hands, and to fashion such pictures as men do,
> Then horses would pattern the forms of the gods after horses,
> And cows after cows, giving them just such a shape
> As those which they find in themselves.

Then there would be theriomorphic gods as well as anthropomorphic ones. Apparently Xenophanes was not aware that there were already just such animal-gods in Egypt, and man-made at that; but he would have found this only a little disturbing to his theory, which he proceeds to develop with further ethnological details:

> ... The gods of the Ethiopians are black with snub noses,
> While those of the Thracians are blond, with blue eyes and red hair.

Thus each race apotheosizes its own type. The gods of the Greeks, to be sure, are more beautiful; but this does not give them any better claim to be regarded as the only true gods. They, too, are merely copied after one particular human race, and so they confirm the words of the poet [Goethe]:

> That everyone calls God, indeed *his* God,
> The best thing that he knows.

Xenophanes was the first to formulate that religious universalism which, both in later antiquity and more especially in the Christian era, was deemed to be an essential feature in the idea of God, indispensable to any true religion. This does not mean, of course, that its opposite, religious particularism, was ever a conscious article of faith even in the earlier mythical stage of Greek religion; Homer himself thought of his Greeks and Trojans as praying to the same gods, despite the division of their sympathies between the two warring parties. Since Homer's time, however, the Greeks had come to recognize how various the ideals of the gods were among individual nations; and this realization could only lead them to deduce, from the very fact of this particularism, the vanity of all such distinctions between gods, however naturally they may have come about. In the western world, universalism began neither with the Christians nor with the prophets of Israel, but with the Greek philosophers. When St. Augustine in his *De civitate Dei* speaks of Greek philosophy in this connection as the precursor of the Christian religion, he is giving a thoroughly correct account of the historical relationship between the two.

In this development Xenophanes was not an isolated phenomenon. He merely brought to the full light of consciousness the inevitable consequences of the philosophical revolution in religious faith to which the Ionian theories of nature led; from his time on, universalism had a place in the theology of all the Greek thinkers as one of their basic assumptions, whether or not they took the trouble to express it. True, the time was not yet ripe for the new conception to play any decisive role in the history of Greece as a nation. The public status of the *polis*-gods in the Greek city-states was as yet unimpaired, although a personage like Xenophanes had already broadcast his criticism of them far and wide. Even Xenophanes still thought of his own refined conception of God in connexion with the *polis* and the problem of its legal order. This fact is clear from an elegy that has come down to us in its entirety, where he praises the cultivation of the intellect (*sophië*). Xenophanes considered himself uniquely equipped to propagate *sophië* in his new home in the west of the Greek world; and it was only because he saw in it the highest political virtue that he considered his own efforts justified. Not until the fourth century, when the gods of the *polis* had died and the *polis* itself was losing its identity in the world-empire of Alexander, did the universalistic theology come into its own and emerge from the background of philosophy to cushion the impending collapse of all established authority.

We have already pointed out that while Xenophanes' utterances presuppose the new and profoundly disturbing experience of the Anaximandrian cosmology, they also contain something peculiarly his own. Anaximander's conception of the Divine was deduced by pure speculation about the idea of an absolute beginning, from which it acquired its attributes—its boundlessness and its property of never having become. But in Xenophanes we find a new motif, which is the actual source of his theology. It is nothing that rests on logical proof, nor is it really philosophical at all, but springs from an immediate sense of awe at the sublimity of the Divine. It is a feeling of reverence that leads Xenophanes to deny all the finite shortcomings and limitations laid upon the gods by traditional religion, and makes him a unique theological figure, despite his dependence on the views of the natural philosophers. Only as a theologian, indeed, can he really be understood. His religious motif—the demand for utter sublimity in the Godhead—is expressed with particular clarity in the assertion that it is not seemly for God to move hither and thither. Unrest is not appropriate to the divine majesty. The word *epiprepei,* which Xenophanes uses here, is not, as a matter of fact, repeated in any of the other fragments; but it reveals the criterion on which his entire criticism of anthropomorphism is based: all these human frailties are out of keeping with God's essential nature. The misdeeds of the Homeric and Hesiodic gods are incompatible with the moral elevation of the Divine; nor are clothing, speech, human form, and birth any more appropriate. In the concept of the appropriate, which here appears for the first time in the Greek tradition, we strike one of the distinctive aspects of Greek genius, the significance of which for later ages is incalculable. It originates in that feeling for harmony and proportion which is peculiarly characteristic of the Greek artistic temper. But it is no less important in the realm of ethics and politics and in the theoretical approach to reality. In the history of this basic attribute of the Greek spirit a special chapter (and a particularly important one in the light of its enormous influence) should be devoted to its application to the problem of God—the problem of what things befit the divine nature and what things do not.

2

PARMENIDES: THE TWO WAYS OF SEARCH [1]

THOU shalt inquire into everything: both the motionless heart of well-rounded Truth, and also the opinions of mortals, in which there is no true reliability. But nevertheless thou shalt learn these things (*opinions*) also—how one should go through all the things-that-seem, without exception, and test them.

Come, I will tell you—and you must accept my word when you have heard it—the ways of inquiry which alone are to be thought: the one that IT IS, and it is not possible for IT NOT TO BE, is the way of credibility, for it follows Truth; the other, that IT IS NOT, and that IT is bound NOT TO BE: this I tell you is a path that cannot be explored; for you could neither recognise that which IS NOT, nor express it.

For it is the same thing to think and to be.

Observe nevertheless how things absent are securely present to the mind; for it will not sever Being from its connection with Being,

[1] [From *Ancilla to the Pre-Socratic Philosophers*, edited and translated by Kathleen Freeman (Oxford: Basil Blackwell, 1948), pp. 42-45. Reprinted by permission. Some notes are omitted.]

whether it is scattered everywhere utterly throughout the universe, or whether it is collected together.

It is all the same to me from what point I begin, for I shall return again to this same point.

One should both say and think that Being Is; for To Be is possible, and Nothingness is not possible. This I command you to consider; for from the latter way of search first of all I debar you. But next I debar you from that way along which wander mortals knowing nothing, two-headed,[2] for perplexity in their bosoms steers their intelligence astray, and they are carried along as deaf as they are blind, amazed, uncritical hordes, by whom To Be and Not To Be are regarded as the same and not the same, and (for whom) in everything there is a way of opposing stress.

For this (view) can never predominate, that That Which Is Not exists. You must debar your thought from this way of search, nor let ordinary experience in its variety force you along this way, (namely, that of allowing) the eye, sightless as it is, and the ear, full of sound, and the tongue, to rule; but (you must) judge by means of the Reason (Logos) the much-contested proof which is expounded by me.

There is only one other description of the way remaining, (namely), that (What Is) Is. To this way there are very many signposts: that Being has no coming-into-being and no destruction, for it is whole of limb, without motion, and without end. And it never Was, nor Will Be, because it Is now, a Whole all together, One, continuous; for what creation of it will you look for? How, whence (could it have) sprung? Nor shall I allow you to speak or think of it as springing from Not-Being; for it is neither expressible nor thinkable that What-Is-Not Is. Also, what necessity impelled it, if it did spring from Nothing, to be produced later or earlier? Thus it must Be absolutely, or not at all. Nor will the force of credibility ever admit that anything should come into being, beside Being itself, out of Not-Being. So far as that is concerned, Justice has never released (Being) in its fetters and set it free either to come into being or to perish, but holds it fast. The decision on these matters depends on the following: IT IS, or IT IS NOT. It is therefore decided—as is inevitable—(that one must) ignore the way as unthinkable and inexpressible (for it is no true way) and take the other as the way of Being and Reality. How could Being perish? How could it come into being? If it came into being, it Is Not; and so too if it is about-to-be at some future time. Thus Coming-into-Being is quenched, and Destruction also into the unseen.

Nor is Being divisible, since it is all alike. Nor is there anything (here or) there which could prevent it from holding together, nor any lesser thing, but all is full of Being. Therefore it is altogether continuous; for Being is close to Being.

2 I.e., "in two minds."

But it is motionless in the limits of mighty bonds, without beginning, without cease, since Becoming and Destruction have been driven very far away, and true conviction has rejected them. And remaining the same in the same place, it rests by itself and thus remains there fixed; for powerful Necessity holds it in the bonds of a Limit, which constrains it round about, because it is decreed by divine law that Being shall not be without boundary. For it is not lacking; but if it were (spatially infinite), it would be lacking everything.

To think is the same as the thought that It Is; for you will not find thinking without Being, in (regard to) which there is an expression. For nothing else either is or shall be except Being, since Fate has tied it down to be a whole and motionless; therefore all things that mortals have established, believing in their truth, are just a name: Becoming and Perishing, Being and Not-Being, and Change of position, and alteration of bright colour.

But since there is a (spatial) Limit, it is complete on every side, like the mass of a well-rounded sphere, equally balanced from its centre in every direction; for it is not bound to be at all either greater or less in this direction or that; nor is there Not-Being which could check it from reaching to the same point, nor is it possible for Being to be more in this direction, less in that, than Being, because it is an inviolate whole. For, in all directions equal to itself, it reaches its limits uniformly.

At this point I cease my reliable theory (Logos) and thought, concerning Truth; from here onwards you must learn the opinions of mortals, listening to the deceptive order of my words.

They have established (the custom of) naming two forms, one of which ought not to be (mentioned): that is where they have gone astray. They have distinguished them as opposite in form, and have marked them off from another by giving them different signs: on one side the flaming fire in the heavens, mild, very light (in weight), the same as itself in every direction, and not the same as the other. This (other) also is by itself and opposite: dark Night, a dense and heavy body. This world-order I describe to you with all its phenomena, in order that no intellect of mortal men may outstrip you.

But since all things are named Light and Night, and names have been given to each class of things according to the power of one or the other (Light or Night), everything is full equally of Light and invisible Night, as both are equal, because to neither of them belongs any share (of the other).

You shall know the nature of the heavens, and all the signs in the heavens, and the destructive works of the pure bright torch of the sun, and whence they came into being. And you shall learn of the wandering works of the round-faced moon, and its nature; and you shall know also the surrounding heaven, whence it sprang and how Necessity brought and constrained it to hold the limits of the stars.

3

EQUALITY AND JUSTICE IN EARLY GREEK COSMOLOGIES [1]

THE early Greek notion of justice lends itself with seductive ease to application far beyond the bounds of politics and morals. To respect the nature of anyone or anything is to be "just" to them. To impair or destroy that nature is "violence" or "injustice." Thus, in a well-known instance, Solon speaks of the sea as "justest" when, being itself undisturbed by the winds, it does not disturb anyone or anything. The law of the measure is scarcely more than a refinement of this idea of one's own nature and of the nature of others as restraining limits which must not be overstepped.

Cosmic justice is a conception of nature at large as a harmonious association, whose members observe, or are compelled to observe, the law of the measure. There may be death, destruction, strife, even encroachment (as in Anaximander). There is justice nonetheless, if encroachment is invariably repaired and things are reinstated within their proper limit. This is the vantage-point from which the commentators have generally interpreted cosmic justice in the pre-Socratics. It is perfectly sound. But it leaves out the additional postulate of equality; for, clearly, it is quite possible to think of harmony and nonencroachment as a relation between unequals. Solon so thought of it. But the founders of Greek scientific thought generally made the opposite assumption: they envisaged harmony in terms of equality. Cosmic equality was conceived as the *guaranty* of cosmic justice: the order of nature is maintained *because* it is an order of equals. To my knowledge, this has never been established. I propose to review the relevant evidence and interpret briefly its historical significance.

I. MEDICAL THEORY

Greek medical thought offers two well-known formulas of equalitarian harmony: Alcmaeon's definition of health as "equality (*isonomia*) of the powers" and the conception of temperate climate as equality (*isomoiria*) of the hot and the cold, the dry and the moist. *Isonomia* and *isomoiria* here render explicit the equalitarian assumption implicit in the first

[1] [From Gregory Vlastos, "Equality and Justice in Early Greek Cosmologies," *Classical Philology*, 42 (1947), 156-178. Reprinted by permission of the University of Chicago Press. Notes, Greek phrases, and a few sentences of English text are omitted. The "Fragments" to which internal reference is made can be located in Kathleen Freeman, *Ancilla to the Pre-Socratic Philosophers*.]

principles of medical theory, *dynamis* and *krasis*. The original meaning of *dynamis*, as Peck observes, is not "a substance that has power" but rather "a substance which *is* a power, which can assert itself, and by the simple act of asserting itself, by being too strong, stronger than the others, can cause trouble." Its strength must, therefore, be "taken away" and thus "moderated." And this is to be done not through repression by a superior but through counterpoise against an equal. This is the heart of the doctrine of *krasis*. Alcmaeon's *isonomia* of the powers is no more than its earliest-known statement at a time when interest still centered in the fact of equilibrium itself rather than in the specific nature of the equilibrated powers.

The kind of equality here envisaged can best be gauged from the methodology of "Hippocratic" medicine. Observation, for all its acuteness, is mainly directed toward qualitative data, with only the vaguest quantitative base. No effort is made to measure individual "powers," generalize their observed values, and construct therefrom an equation, however crude. The existence of the equation is rather an outright assumption. If there is health, it is assumed that the constituent powers must be (1) in equilibrium and therefore (2) equal to one another, much as opposing parties in an evenly matched contest are assumed to be equal. This is exactly the sense in which equality figures in the medical treatises and, indeed, as we shall see, in the whole development of early cosmological theory from Anaximander to Empedocles. Powers are equal if they can hold one another in check so that none can gain "mastery" or "supremacy" or, in Alcmaeon's term, "monarchy" over the others. Medical theory assumes this kind of equality even when it conceives *krasis* not as the equipoise of pairs of physical opposites (hot-cold, dry-moist, etc.) but as a many-valued blend of powers; for here, too, the purpose of blending is to insure that "no individual power is displayed." Should any power escape this blending and "stand by itself," it would be ominously "strong" and thus create the "monarchy" which constitutes disease.

When we come to the *"krasis* of the seasons" we move directly into the area of cosmic justice; for medical thought is not content with the empirical fact that some climates are better suited than others (and thus more "just") to human nature. It goes further to explain the harmony of human nature to its environment through an absolute cosmic fact, i.e., the harmony of the environmental forces with one another. This is, in turn, construed as an equilibrium of opposites. But there is a difference. This *isomoiria*, unlike that of the body, can be grounded in an observable equation which is capable of strict quantitative expression—the equinox, when (1) day is equal to night, (2) all the hours throughout the day and night are equal to one another, and (3) the sun rises at a point midway between the northernmost and the southernmost risings of the year (i.e., the summer and winter solstices). That climatic *isomoiria* should be attended by these astronomical equalities was so impressive that the relation between the two was taken as one of causal implication. Thus the Island of Iambulus in Diodorus ii. 56. 7 is endowed with a year-round equinox to validate its claim to the most temperate of climates.

But if *isomoiria* belongs to the equinoctial seasons, a way must be found somehow to bring the rest of the year within the framework of equalitarian harmony. This was done through the idea of rotation in office, or "successive supremacy" among the powers. As in the democratic *polis* "the demos rules by turn," so the hot could prevail in the summer without injustice to the cold, if the latter had its turn in the winter. And if a similar and concurrent cycle of successive supremacy could be assumed to hold among the powers in the human body, then the *krasis* of man and nature would be perfect.

Man's body has always all of these [*sc.* four humors]; but as the seasons revolve they [*sc.* the humors] become now greater, now lesser, each in turn and in accordance with nature. . . . At one time of the year winter is strongest; next spring; then summer; then autumn. So too in man at one time phlegm is strongest; next blood; next bile, first yellow, then the so-called black [Frag. 7. 48-52 and 61-66].

II. EMPEDOCLES

Empedocles is our best bridge from medicine to philosophy proper. His thought was so congenial to the medical theorists of his time that, by all accounts, his influence upon them was enormous. Even in the Aegean it was strong enough to draw the fire of the author of *Ancient Medicine*. In his system man's flesh and blood is made up of the four world-components on the pattern of *isomoiria;* where this equality is imperfect, we get the deviations from perfect health and wisdom in man. But in the cosmos the "roots" are strictly equal among themselves, and, since each of them is, like Parmenides' Being, eternally equal to itself, cosmic justice is perpetually sure. Even at the zenith of the ascendancy of Strife, when each of the four "roots" would be "unmixed" (Frag. B35. 15) and thus, by Hippocratic norms, a "strong substance," no harm could result, for none would be stronger than any of the rest. Thus, even when Strife rules the World, equality is a sufficient preventive of "injustice."

Much has been written on what Empedocles really meant by the "equality" of his elements. In one argumentative passage (*De gen. et cor.* 333 a 19-34) Aristotle professes to be in the dark as to whether equality in volume or in "power" was meant; in another (*Meteor.* 340 a 14) he gives himself away, assuming the latter as a matter of course. Aristotle's quandary in the first passage, even if only rhetorical, shows well enough that the distinction had not been settled by Empedocles. The second passage suggests just as well that "power" was, nevertheless, uppermost in Empedocles' mind, as it certainly was for the medical writers. Empedocles is not averse to spatial categories: Love is "equal in length and breadth." But, when he formally declares that the roots are equal, he immediately goes on to say that (1) they are of equal age, (2) each has its peculiar honor but (3) they rule in turn (Frag. B17. 27-29). Could we ask for more conclusive proof that not mere extension but "power" (with its associated concept of "honor") is uppermost? Points 2 and 3 state the principle of "successive supremacy," whose significance in medical theory has just been explained; and they are introduced by Point 1, which rules out flatly the possibility that any of them could claim permanent supremacy in virtue of seniority rights. Because of 1 the universe cannot be "monarchy," for no power within it possesses the qualifying primogeniture. Because of 2 and 3 the universe must be an *isonomia,* for it conforms to the democratic principle of rotation of office.

Thus Empedocles builds a universe to the specifications of Alcmaeon's formula of health; and in so doing he levels ancient inequalities which had been fixed by religious tradition. Zeus, heretofore "king of kings, of all the blessed the most blessed, over all the mighty sovereign in might" (Aesch. *Suppl.* 524-26) is now merely one of the roots, on a par with the "unheard-of" divinity, Nestis, so inconsequential that its very identity remains in doubt. And as for Strife—"unseemly," "dreadful," "evil," "mad"—every impulse of sentimental justice would urge its subordination to the power that makes all "have thoughts of love and work the works of peace" (Frag. B17. 23), "queen Cypris," who in the golden age ruled alone in place of Zeus (Frag. B128). But equalitarian justice rules otherwise. Were not Harmony matched with its perfect equal in Strife, there would be no created world, only the non-descript mixture of the *Sphairos.* It is only the strictly reciprocal power of Strife to undo the work of Harmony and "prevail in turn" (Frag. B17. 29) that makes a cosmos possible. And, this equality once assured, the process works just as well backward as forward: whether Harmony or Strife has supremacy, the other will be "rising up to [claim] his prerogatives" (Frag. B30. 2), and a world will be born and destroyed in either case.

A lacuna in the argument so far is the apparent absence of any explicit reference to justice in the fragments; the word *dikē* is never mentioned. My answer is that the reference to justice is nonetheless present; Empedocles' surviving words, if carefully examined, contain expressions which are charged with the imagery and notion of justice. Consider Fragment B30 once again: Strife "rose up to [claim] his prerogatives in the fulness of alternate time set for them [*sc.* Love and Strife] by the mighty oath. . . ." (Burnet's translation). The fragment breaks off abruptly. But we hear of "mighty oaths" again in Fragment B115, where they "seal" the "decree of the gods." Here "oaths" represent the binding, inviolate, *necessary* character of that decree, which is an "oracle of *Anankē.*" But we know that in Parmenides *Anankē* and *Dikē* perform the same function of holding Being fast "in the bonds of the limit." We may thus infer that "mighty oath" in Empedocles, like "strong *Anankē*" in Parmenides, alludes to the orderliness of existence conceived under the aspect of justice. This inference is confirmed by three other terms in the fragment:

1. *"The 'prerogatives' of Strife."*—This tells us that the dominance of Strife is not lawless self-assertion but duly established right or "office"; it is its "rightful share" or "just portion."

2. *"In the fulness of time"*—"Time" here is no abstract measurement of the passage of events. It is the proper time-span allotted to Strife (as also to Love) in the cosmic order; it is a "measure" whose observance is of the essence of justice.

3. *"Alternate time."*—"Alternate time" specifies what kind of justice this is: the equalitarian justice of rotation of office.

III. PARMENIDES

In Parmenides' Being the reference to justice is more explicit, and there is a stronger accent on its compulsiveness. There may be injustice among men, for they can overstep the limit of their own nature. There can be no injustice in Being, for its limit is an unbreakable "chain" (Frag. B8. 26 and 31) or "fetter" (Frag. B8. 14) which "holds it fast." Justice or Necessity is thus spoken of as an active force. But it is immanent in Being, since Being is all there is. What is there, then, about Being which accounts for this necessary justice? It is its self-identity or, as Parmenides thinks of it, its homogeneity or "self-equality." "It is all alike"; "it is equal to itself on all sides."

For the historical source of this conception we should look to Anaximander's theorem that the earth owed its stability to its all-around equality. Aristotle's paraphrase of the theorem leaves us uncertain as to which of the words, if any, are Anaximander's own. But taking the text at its face value, the similarity is striking:

PROBLEM

ANAXIMANDER: Why the earth is stationary.
PARMENIDES: Why Being is stationary.

SOLUTION

ANAXIMANDER: Because it "is set at the center and is equably related to the extremes."
PARMENIDES: Because it is "like the bulk of a well-rounded sphere, equally poised from the center in every direction."

Anaximander is thinking of the earth, moving with the whirl, yet keeping its place. The circumference of the eddy moves, the center also moves, yet the center is stationary with respect to the circumference. Let us abstract from Anaximander's cosmological detail; keep only the part of the design which insures the paradoxical triumph of stability over motion by virtue of equality; allow for the fact that equality will be no longer an external relation and that the "extremes" are now the "limits" of Being itself; then what is left will be "like a well-rounded sphere, equally poised from the center in every direction."

Deprived of its cosmological application, the sphere is merely vestigial. It is only a simile; the round shape as such is irrelevant to Parmenides' thought: he is concerned only with the formal property of all-around equality. In *this* sense the sphere makes a perfect vehicle for his conception of Being as "all alike," without distinction of "greater" and "lesser" or of more and less complete, a whole whose parts are all equal among themselves, so that none can dominate any other. Thus absolute homogeneity means an internally secure equilibrium; and, since it is also secure against external disturbance, Being cannot move. It is "held fast" by its own "all-around equality."

The same property, applied to Truth, defines a perfectly "just" universe of discourse, for Truth, like Being, is "well-rounded"—a term which we must interpret in line with Parmenides' own conception of the sphere as a whole whose parts are all equal among themselves. This is not a bad way to describe the purely deductive system which is Parmenides' norm of truth: in such a system (to use the language of a later logic) every proposition expresses an equivalence, and every difference masks an identity. This implies a perfectly coherent universe, without rifts or gaps. Here inference can pass securely from the given to the not-given. Here the starting-point becomes a matter of indifference: as on a circle, one can traverse the same line of truth from any starting-point whatever. In such a world, thought is perfectly "just," i.e., in full accord with its own nature and the nature of Being. Outside this world, thought is "forced" to utter the unutterable and think the unthinkable. It thus attempts the impossible, in defiance of the just necessity (*chreōn*) of thought and Being. This cannot injure Being, for it is "all inviolable." But it can and does injure thought, foredooming it to "blindness," "wandering," and "helplessness."

A final confirmation of the present thesis—that Parmenidean justice is grounded in equality—may be found in the cosmological appendix to the world of Truth and Being, which makes sense of the quasi-truth and quasi-being of the world of "mortal opinion." It is no use glossing over the harsh contrast between the two worlds: the first is Truth, the second opinion; the first is "unshaken" in its "trustworthiness," the second "deceitful" at its very best; the first is "all alike," the second a mixture of two absolutely *un*like powers. Nevertheless, Parmenides' account of the second is not a systematization of current error. It is original physical inquiry, attempting the same task to which the Ionians had addressed themselves, using their own categories and reaching results which are confidently proclaimed superior to theirs. The general formula of this cosmology is defined with astonishing precision, and it is formally identical with that of Empedocles: (1) each of the opposites is, like Parmenides' Being, absolutely self-identical; (2) neither is, like Heraclitus' opposites, identical with its own opposite; (3) both are equal. On the meaning of equality here our best clue is in Parmenides himself, who, as we have seen, elsewhere uses "equal" as an alternate for "equally poised"; and this agrees perfectly with medical and Empedoclean usage. In the equipoise of opposite powers Parmenides finds the next best thing to the internal equipoise of Being itself. That is why the mock world of Light and Night is, in its own way, not chaos but cosmos and falls, like Being itself, under the sway of Just Necessity.

IV. HERACLITUS

Just as the self-identity of Truth and Being *is* justice for Parmenides, so the "strife" of Becoming *is* justice for Heraclitus. Here, too, we find, among the mediating concepts, necessity (*chreōn*) and measure: "The earth is poured out as sea, and is measured according to the same *logos* as before it becomes earth" (Frag. B31). "Strife" *is* justice because, through the very conflict of the opposites, the measure will be kept. This means (1) that in every transformation the fire which is "exchanged" remains constant and (2) that the distribution of fire among the opposites is also constant: "The way up and down is one and the same" (Frag. B60), which I take to mean that the sum total of "upward" changes in the universe equals the "downward" ones, so that the middle term, water, is exactly divided between the two ways, half of it "turning" to earth and the other half to fire.

Much could be said of the similarities of this design to the Empedoclean. Both are inspired by the principle of the "hidden" harmony (Frag. B54) of Harmony itself with its own opposite, Strife, achieved in both systems by assuming that these, like all other opposites, balance. But there are important divergences both in structure and in intention; and these are material to the role of equalitarian justice in the two cosmologies. The structural differences are mainly two: (1) the universe has not yet been parceled out into six separate sets of Parmenidean being; nor (2) has its history been marked off into separate epochs of successive supremacy. Because of (1) it would be useless to look for the formal equation of physical roots. Everything in Heraclitus' world is in process; instead of equality between substantives of permanence, we find reciprocity between verbs of change. For everything "turning" one way, something else is "turning" the opposite way: "cold things grow hot, the hot grows cold; the moist grows dry, the dry grows moist" (Frag. B126). Because of (2) the world is not made and unmade in alternate eons; generation and destruction are concurrent and constant, hence the form of the world is also constant. Fire, "kindled" by "gathering" into its own substance a measure of fuel, is also "extinguished" by "scattering abroad" the same measure of light. This measured give-and-take accounts for the permanence of the world which "was and is and is to be."

But there is another difference which may well be intentional: the words "equal" and "equality" never occur in the fragments. To express the harmony of the opposites Heraclitus does not say that they are equal but that they are one; to express their equivalence he says that they are "the same thing." This is no verbal accident. It is true to a pattern of thought which separates him from Anaximander (as well as from Empedocles) and brings him closer to Anaximenes: the physical opposites are all explained as modifications of one of them; they are thus literally "the same thing." This One is the "common" thing throughout the universe. And, since it defines the measure of every process (Frag. B90), Heraclitus thinks of it as the "one divine law," all-powerful, all-sufficient, all-victorious (Frag. B114). It is the "thought which governs all things through all things" (Frag. B41).

Should this doctrine of the One "governor" of the universe be interpreted in line with the "aristocratic" politics with which Heraclitus is commonly credited in the textbooks? It is clear enough that he was a misfit in Ephesian politics. This is in striking contrast to Anaximander, Parmenides, and Empedocles, all of whom seem to have held posts of authority and influence in their respective states. But from this we cannot jump to the conclusion that Heraclitus was a partisan of aristocracy in its relevant, historical sense. His tirades against the "many" follow logically enough from his basic conviction that they are philosophically benighted. But the philosopher's contempt for the folly of the crowd is not peculiar to Heraclitus. Parmenides shared it; and so did Empedocles, whose loyalty to democracy is well attested. What is peculiar to Heraclitus is, rather, the doctrine of the "common": truth is the "common"; the world is "common"; and in the state, law is the "common."

This concept of the state as a community, united by a common stake in a common justice, is perfectly compatible with democratic politics. Early in the sixth century it had inspired the Solonian reform program. It survived throughout the fifth century and into the fourth as a cherished doctrine of Athenian democracy. Thus the doctrine of law as "common" remains constant throughout a period of sweeping change *within* the democratic tradition. The vital choice in democratic politics in Heraclitus' day was whether to press forward toward the radical equalitarianism of the lot and "ruling in turn" or else adhere to the earlier democracy, predicated, as in Solon, not on equal dignity but on common justice. If our meager evidence permits any hypothesis concerning Heraclitus' political sympathies, it would be that he favored the limited democracy of the past. This is in line with his known admiration for Bias of Priene, who figures in the tradition as an early democratic statesman. Indeed, Heraclitus' saying, "the many are bad" (Frag. B104), is also traditionally ascribed to Bias. And Heraclitus' doctrine that the city "strengthens" itself through the law has an obvious affinity to Bias' reputed saying that "the strongest democracy is the one wherein all fear the law as their master."

From this perspective we should interpret those fragments in Heraclitus which exalt the "one" against the "many." The core of his politics is the supremacy of the "common" law. "And it is law, too, to obey the counsel of one" (Frag. B33) can only mean: the will of "one" is law only when it expresses the "common" to which all (including the "one") are subject. So, too, we must think of the cosmic supremacy of fire in Heraclitean physics, not as the predominance of a single power but as the submission of all powers to a single law. For if we think of fire as itself one of the powers, then it must keep its equal place among the rest. Thus water is absolutely impartial as between fire and earth, its two neighbors (and enemies) on the way up and down: it dies into earth as much as into fire; it lives from fire as much as from earth. Or if, conversely, we think of fire not as one of the many but as the One which *is* the many, then fire is not a separate power lording it over the rest; its justice is simply the common measure in all the powers. If everything is fire, then the "government" of fire in the cosmos is cosmic self-government.

V. ANAXIMANDER

We must reckon, finally, with the oldest and most controversial text in pre-Socratic philosophy, Anaximander's Fragment 1:

And into those things from which existing things take their rise, they pass away once more, "according to just necessity [*chreōn*]; for they render justice and reparation to one another for their injustices according to the ordering of time."

Any responsible interpretation of these words calls for justification; and this involves unavoidably the evaluation of certain Aristotelian texts which form our most important collateral evidence. I have left this last so as to approach it in the light of Heraclitus, Parmenides, Empedocles, and the medical writers: their thought-forms are safer guides to Anaximander than are the categories of Aristotelian physics. Yet, even so, we must respect what we know of the development of pre-Socratic thought and guard against reading into Anaximander atomic physics or Parmenidean logic.

A. *Equality of the Opposites*

Aristotle writes:

Some people make not air or water the infinite, but this [*sc.* "something distinct from the elements"] in order that the other elements may not be destroyed by the element which is infinite. They are in opposition to one another—air is cold, water is moist, fire hot. If one were infinite, the others would have been destroyed by now. As it is, the infinite is something other than the elements, from which they arise [*Phys.* 204 b 24-29].

Anaximander is not named here. But the identification is made in Simplicius, and there is no good reason to question it. What the argument aims to prove is fortunately clear enough from independent evidence. We know that the first generation or two of Ionian thought *did* turn one of the opposites into the boundless source of everything else. This is obvious for Anaximenes' air. In the case of Xenophanes, we have his own words, off-hand, untechnical, and all the more valuable on that account: the earth has its upper limit just where you see it, "next to your feet"; as for its lower limit, there is none, "it goes on endlessly" (Frag. B28). Thales' water, too, must have been as endless as Xenophanes' earth and in the same sense: it must "go on endlessly," for it supports the earth, while no provision is made for its being supported, in turn, by anything else. Thus, in denying infinity to any of the opposites, Anaximander was going against the general trend. He could only have done so for a good reason. The argument in *Phys.* 204 b 24-29 supplies the reason: to safeguard the equilibrium among the opposites.

That the main components of the universe are equal was an old tradition in popular cosmology. In *Iliad* xv it is implied that the heavens, the sea, and "the murky darkness" are equal, since their respective lords are equals in "rank" and "portion." In Hesiod earth and heavens are declared equal (*Theog.* 126); and the distance between heavens and earth is equal to that between earth and Tartarus (*ibid.* 719-25). Such ideas are mainly without even a semblance of physical justification. They boldly read into the universe that feeling for symmetry and balance which makes the *Odyssey* speak of a well-made ship as "equal" and of a wise, balanced mind also as "equal." Anaximander's own cosmology is designed with just such a sense of aesthetic symmetry, with equality as the main motif: the intervals between each of the infinite worlds are equal; the intervals between earth, fixed stars, moon, and sun are also equal; earth and sun are equal; the two land-masses of the earth—Asia and Europe—are equal, and the two great rivers in each are equal and divide the regions through which they flow into equal parts. To cap all this with the equality of the opposites which constitute this world would be in fine harmony with the whole design. The argument in *Phys.* 204 b 24-29 takes us beyond this aesthetic presumption into physical reasoning: If one of the opposites were boundless, it would not only mar the architectonic elegance of the cosmology but would positively "destroy" the other opposites. Why so? Because—as we know from Fragment 1—the opposites are constantly encroaching upon one another. If one of them were limitless, there would be no stopping it by the rest, singly or in combination, for they are all limited. Its encroachment would continue until the rest were destroyed.

B. *Justice in the Boundless*

We may now settle accounts with the older interpretation of Fragment 1: that the very existence of the cosmos is itself an injustice against the Boundless, to be expiated by reabsorption. This was the general view before the restoration of the words "to one another" in the second clause; thereafter, it was left without firm foothold in the text and has been largely abandoned. What still gives it a measure of plausibility is the suggestion in the first clause that "reparation" is somehow connected with "passing away"; how can things "render justice and reparation *to one another*" in a process which destroys their very existence? Unless this paradox can be resolved, we shall find ourselves drifting back into the older view, even after formally abandoning it; we shall be constantly tempted to think of the Boundless itself as the payee of the "damages" and, consequently, as itself the victim of the original injustice.

We may approach the answer by way of the little-noticed fact that the fragment refers *in the plural* to the matrix from which all things arise and to which they all return. This is strange, for the reference is obviously to the Boundless; and this is plainly singular. The shift to the plural can mean only that in this context the Boundless is explicitly thought of as a plurality. This is in line with what Aristotle tells us in *Phys.* 187 a 20-22, where he speaks of Anaximander's opposites as being "contained in" the "one" and issuing from it by a process of "separation." Burnet ruled against this statement as "not even a paraphrase of anything Anaximander said." [2] But this objection to Aristotle's word for "contained in" as "unhistorical"—his only definite reason for the sweeping condemnation of the text—is completely unfounded. The same word occurs frequently in the pre-Socratics and the medical literature with the very sense required in the present context, i.e., the relation of any ingredient to the compound of which it forms a part. As for the other terms used here by Aristotle—"separation" and "oppositions"—both refer to characteristic concepts of Ionian medicine and physics and accord perfectly with what we know of Anaximander's system. The "opposites" are obviously "the hot, cold, dry, moist, and the rest" (Simpl. *Phys.* 150. 24), which are the main components of his cosmology. "Separation" is the basic cosmogonic category of Ionian thought, the process by which "the heavens and all the infinite worlds" are formed in Anaximander.

There is, nonetheless, a residual problem here: If the *apeiron* is a compound of opposites, why should Aristotle think of it as "one" and contrast it as such with the "one and many" of Empedocles' *Sphairos* and Anaxagoras' primitive mixtures? The answer is surely that Empedocles and Anaxagoras both thought of their original compound as made up of Parmenidean bits of Being, eternally self-identical in the mixture as in the world which issues from it. This is just what we cannot ascribe to Anaximander without anachronism: he thought of his Boundless as "one" in a far more intimate sense than would have been possible for a physicist schooled in Parmenidean logic. That logic compelled Empedocles to revise the basic concept of *krasis* and to think of it as a mere juxtaposition of minute particles. For the unreformed doc-

2 [John Burnet, *Early Greek Philosophy* (4th ed.; London: Black, 1948), p. 57, n. 1.]

trine of *krasis* we may look to the anti-Empedoclean statement which speaks of a compound in *krasis* as "one and simple." This seems to be our best clue to the sense in which Anaximander's Boundless is "one": it does "contain" the "opposites"; but these are so thoroughly mixed that none of them appears as a single, individual thing. This would explain why Aristotle and his school commonly refer to Empedocles' principles (*archai*) as six and to Anaxagoras' as infinite in number, while they invariably speak of Anaximander's principle as one. And it would further explain what we must understand by the Aristotelian term "indeterminate" as applied to Anaximander's Boundless. Just as in a Hippocratic compound in *krasis* the individual opposites are "not apparent," so neither are they in Anaximander's Boundless: no part of the compound, no matter how minute, being either hot or cold or dry or moist, etc., the whole is just what Aristotle would call "indeterminate."

On this interpretation we can explain the strictly reciprocal nature of injustice and reparation in Fragment 1. The Boundless itself, being perfectly blended, must be a state of dynamic equilibrium. In no portion of it can any power dominate another and thus commit "injustice." Only when the world-forming segregation occurs can separate powers show up. Thereafter, whatever one of these is strong enough to encroach upon another, "injustice" will result. When the world is, in due course, reabsorbed into the Boundless, the opposites are *not* destroyed. They do *not* cease to exist. They are only blended once again, and their equilibrium is perfectly restored. And this must entail a process of "reparation," where unjust gains are disgorged and unjust losses fully made up. Thus at no time is there either injustice against the Boundless or reparation to it. Reabsorption into the Boundless is only the process which insures full reparation among the opposites themselves; the damages are paid not to the Boundless but to *one another*.

C. *Justice in the World*

But what of the interval between generation and dissolution? Are we to suppose that the life-history of the world is a series of encroachments, unchecked until a judgment day at the very end? Such a supposition would go against every canon of pre-Socratic physics. If becoming were a theater of injustice without reparation, it would be not cosmos but chaos, and the elegant pattern of balanced equalities in Anaximander's world would collapse. But such a possibility is precluded by the structural elements of Anaximander's own cosmogonic process. The opposites, balanced in the Boundless, issue from it *together* in balanced proportions. It follows that the hot in a given world will be no stronger than the cold, and so for the other opposites. Moreover, since the world is "encompassed" by the Boundless, nothing can enter or depart to upset the balance fixed upon the opposites in the process of generation. Thus the Boundless "governs" the world throughout its growth and decline.

This is never a matter of direct action by the Boundless upon the inner structure of the world, for the whole of the cosmology is delineated in terms of the interaction of the opposites themselves upon one another. The Boundless "governs" by "encompassing," i.e., by safeguarding the original equality of the opposites with one another.

If this equality is maintained, justice is assured, for no opposite will be strong enough to dominate another. When encroachment occurs, it will be compensated by "reparation," as, e.g., in the seasonal cycle the hot prevails in the summer, only to suffer commensurate subjection to its rival in the winter. We have already met this ordered sequence of "successive supremacy" in the medical writers and Empedocles. And, although our evidence is not sufficient to establish it conclusively in the case of Anaximander, we can impute it to him with considerable likelihood. In any case we can assume with perfect confidence that, while reabsorption into the Boundless would be the complete and absolute end of all injustice, nevertheless over-all justice is preserved throughout the life-process of the world despite the occurrence of injustice; and this by the equation of reparation to encroachment, which is itself assured through the invariant equality of the opposites.

Every student of Greek science must feel how profound was the debt of subsequent cosmology to Anaximander. His were the seminal ideas of the whirl, the infinite worlds, the unsupported earth, the conception of sun and stars as huge, freeswinging masses rather than fixtures on a copper dome. Yet more important than these and his other physical hypotheses was his philosophical concept of nature as a self-regulative equilibrium, whose order was strictly immanent, guaranteed through the fixed proportions of its main constituents. Once established, this idea becomes the common property of classical thought. It is shared by minds as diametrically opposed as Lucretius, on the one hand, and the pious author of the *De mundo,* on the other. In Anaximander we can trace it back to its source in the political assumption that justice was an affair between equals and that its settlement involved an equation of compensation to injury.

VI. THE NATURALIZATION OF JUSTICE

When Parmenides speaks of *Dikē-Anankē* holding Being fast in the bonds of the limit, his words echo Hesiod and Semonides, who speak of fate as a "bond of unbreakable fetters"; but his thought is far from theirs. In Hesiod and Semonides the source of the compulsion is external to the thing compelled. In Parmenides the compulsion is immanent. The first is a nonrational concept of *anakē:* the determining agency remains hidden from human reason. The second is so thoroughly rational that *anankē* merges with *dikē,* and *dikē* with logicophysical necessity: the order of nature is deducible from the intelligible properties of nature itself. We may speak of this transition, the work of Anaximander and his successors, as the naturalization of justice. Justice is no longer inscrutable *moira*, imposed by arbitrary forces with incalculable effect. Nor is she the goddess *Dikē*, moral and rational enough, but frail and unreliable. She is now one with "the ineluctable laws of nature herself"; unlike Hesiod's *Dikē*, she could no more leave the earth than the earth could leave its place in the firmament.

Thus the naturalization of justice transformed her status and added immeasurably to her stature. But it also transformed nature. These "ineluctable laws of nature," what were they prior to Milesian physics? Behind the massive stability of heaven and earth had lurked a realm of arbitrariness and terror. The uniform motions of sun and moon could be inexplicably broken by an eclipse; the fertility of earth and womb might mysteriously fail; children could be born "unlike those who begat them, but monsters"; these and a thousand other things could be thought of as lesions in natural order, special interventions of Zeus and his instruments, vindicating the authority of the supernatural by suspending or reversing the ordinary course of nature. The adventurous reason of Ionian science charted this realm of magic, detached it from the personal control of supernatural beings, and integrated it into the domain of nature. All natural events, ordinary and extraordinary alike, were now united under a common law.

The equality of the constituents of this new commonwealth of nature was of the essence of the transformation, for it meant the abolition of distinctions between two grades of being—divine and mortal, lordly and subservient, noble and mean, of higher and lower honor. It was the ending of these distinctions that made nature autonomous and *therefore* completely and unexceptionably "just." Given a society of equals, it was assumed, justice was sure to follow, for none would have the power to dominate the rest. This assumption, as we have seen, had a strictly physical sense. It was accepted not as a political dogma but as a theorem in physical inquiry. It is, nonetheless, remarkable evidence of the confidence which the great age of Greek democracy possessed in the validity of the democratic idea—a confidence so robust that it survived translation into the first principles of cosmology and medical theory.

Of the four *physiologoi* we have studied, Heraclitus alone appears estranged from democratic politics. His interest in the current belief in equality is not so much to vindicate as to qualify and correct it. It is therefore significant that there should be no mention of equality in his physical fragments. The equalitarianism of his physics, such as it is, seems imposed upon the author as a structural necessity rather than as a conscious choice. Order he must have, and he knows of no other way of getting it than by enforcing the equal submission of all powers to the "common" law. Thus Heraclitus in his own way remains within the general framework of equalitarian physics; certainly, he makes no effort to break with that tradition. The attempt first comes with Anaxagoras' doctrine of *nous*, which, unlike Heraclitus' fire, is "mixed with nothing, but is alone, itself by itself," and has therefore absolute, one-sided dominion over the "mixed" forces of nature. But this revolt proved abortive. It was Plato, the bitter critic of Athenian democracy, who carried through the intellectual revolution (or, more strictly, counterrevolution) to a successful conclusion; and Aristotle followed, though with hesitations and misgivings. In their systems we find at last the explicit and thoroughgoing negation of Anaximander's equalitarian universe.

The attributes of divinity are now reserved to one set of superior entities, which alone are perfect, "prior," sovereign, ageless, incorruptible. Nature is no longer a single mechanical system, composed throughout of the same stuff, ordered throughout by the same laws of motion. It breaks apart into a "hither" and a "yonder."

4

SOCRATIC WISDOM AS ETHICS [1]

WHATEVER the positive contribution of Socrates in the sphere of philosophy may have been, it was predetermined by the position he assumed. Was he or was he not an intellectual? An unequivocal answer cannot be given. To us, that is to the generations that have followed him, he was. But to his epoch and probably to himself—for we all to some extent judge ourselves from the standpoint of our world— he was not.

To his epoch he was not, because he did not devote himself to any of the pursuits which in his time were deemed intellectual. He did not occupy himself with cosmology, nor with the traditional problems of philosophy. He was not, of course, the inventor of the concept nor of the definition. Aristotle's remarks need not necessarily be taken in the strictly technical sense which they later acquired. As a matter of fact, Aristotle only said that Socrates sought to know what things are in themselves, not with reference to circumstances; and that he tried to concentrate upon the meaning of words, in order not to be carried away by the sheer brilliance of speeches. Neither is it very probable that Socrates made great ethical discoveries; at least it is not evident that he was concerned with aught else than public and private virtue in its various aspects. How could he have been regarded as an intellectual? The intellectual of his times was an Anaxagoras or an Empedocles, a Zeno, or, perhaps, a Protagoras. Socrates was nothing of the sort, nor did he seek to be. On the contrary he preferred not to be.

Was he then simply a just man, a man of perfect morals? We are not

[1] [From Xavier Zubiri, "Socrates and Greek Wisdom," *The Thomist*, 7 (1944), 45-52. Reprinted by permission.]

absolutely certain what morality he professed, nor even are we acquainted in detail with his life. Furthermore, politics has helped, with its errors, to create great historical figures in the imagination of citizens. At all events, his unquestionable moral eminence would not have justified his influence on philosophy. And yet it was decisive. All the historical criticism in the world cannot dispel this fact, whose details may be confused, but whose magnitude remains unchangeable.

To put it baldly, Socrates did not create science; he created a new type of intellectual life, of wisdom. His disciples harvested the fruits of that new life. And as happened with Parmenides and Heraclitus in their day, so did it with Socrates. When a new life dawns, it is at first understood in the light of the old day. Hence to some Socrates was but another Sophist; to others, a good man. To those who followed him, he was an intellectual. Actually, he simply inaugurated a new kind of *sophia*. Nothing more, but nothing less.

One might view this new wisdom only in the negative light of Socrates' withdrawal from the intellectual life which was in vogue, his emphatic rejection of it. Socrates kept aloof from public life, withdrawn into his own private existence. He cast aside rhetoric in order to ponder seriously on Being and Thought. But it would be an error to suppose that his withdrawal meant that he adopted an attitude of total isolation. Socrates was not a solitary thinker.

That a life be private is not the same as that it be isolated. On the contrary, there is the danger that the solitary man will find his isolation to be a form of notoriety and, therefore, of publicness. That some of his disciples thus misinterpreted Socrates' attitude is well known. It is not a question of this, nor of what solitude meant to Descartes, for example. The "Solus recedo" of Descartes, solitary communion with himself and his thoughts, is a far cry from the position of Socrates, for the simple reason that there never was a Greek who adopted such an attitude. Socrates returned to his home, to a life like that of anyone else, without giving himself over to the novelty of a progressive conception of life, as did the Athenian élite, but also without allowing himself to be impressed by the sheer power of the past. He had his friends and talked with them. For every true Greek the words "to talk" are as closely associated with "to think," as for the Semite the words "to pray" are with "to recite." The prayer of the Semite is an *oration;* something in which his *os* (mouth) participates. For the Greek, speech does not occur isolated from thought; his *logos* is at one and the same time both things. The Greeks always have understood thought as the soul's silent dialogue with itself; and dialogue with others was, to them, audible thought. Socrates was a good Greek; he thought while talking, and talked while thinking. And incidentally, he was the first to employ dialogue as a method of thinking.

But how did Socrates live? At least, how did he *understand* that one should live? This is the essential point for us.

In the first place, one should live with *nous* or *mens*. Aristotle tells us that Socrates exercised his thought, his *dianoia*. However, there was some confusion on this point. Traditional philosophy had grown out of the *mens* and had drawn its sustenance from it, both in the soul of the philosopher and in his expression through the *logos*. Nevertheless, in this, perhaps the most critical moment of pre-Socratic philosophy, the *mens* was being applied to Nature, to that which men were wont to call "the Divine." The common world was thrust aside together with the things of the world, men and their major vicissitudes; and these were thrust aside, not in a random fashion, not by a simple preterition, but in a much more absolute fashion, that is to say, they were judged unworthy on the grounds of being mere *doxa,* and were excluded from the world of being, as things that seek to be, but do not have true being. It was for this reason that Socrates called those philosophers demented. Actually, the generations which immediately followed the Persian Wars reacted vigorously; but what triumphed in the field of intelligence was what led to the rational science of natural things. The first ones to elaborate it, Empedocles and Anaxagoras, still too closely resembled Parmenides and Heraclitus. On the contrary, those men whose endeavors subsequently established science firmly, had for the most part scarcely seen the light of day in Socrates' time. Therefore Socrates could not center his attention exclusively on them. And Empedocles and Anaxagoras, if we consider them to be scientists, were little more than embryonic. Because of their affinities with classical wisdom, they were incapable, as it were, of satisfactorily coming into touch with the things of daily life. Protagoras alone sought to make things his point of departure, yet even he took them, not in the sense of natural things, *onta,* but in that of usual things, *chrēmata*.

And so Socrates is in this regard a typical representative of his generation. We can understand why he was mistaken for a Sophist. He tried to think and talk of things as they appear directly in daily life, not in public life, in the realm of *doxa,* but, on the contrary, taking them as they are in themselves, that is, as they really are, independent of circumstance. Socrates situated himself momentarily in private life. Public life was to come later. Only a good man can be a good citizen, and only a good citizen can be a good statesman. So Socrates applied his mind to the ordinary things of life, without rhetoric, but with *mens*. Before Socrates, the *mens* had been applied only to "the Divine," to Nature, to the cosmos, or to the rational investigation of the nature of things. Now it concentrated, by a curious paradox, on the modest things of daily life. This was the radical innovation of Socrates. The grave defect of traditional philosophy was, in his opinion, that it had disdained daily life and had disqualified it as an object of Wisdom, and then had sought to control it with considerations drawn from the clouds and the stars.

Socrates meditated on common things, and on what man does with them in life. Moreover, he meditated on the *technai*. But the *technai* on which he meditated were, therefore, not only the ones which were established as sciences, but also every branch of "knowing-how-to-do" in life: the crafts, such as carpentry and healing; that is to say, all the skills which man acquires in his intercourse with things. This is the Greek conception of *aretē,* or virtue, which intrinsically is wholly devoid of any primarily moral sense. "Is" once again entered into philosophy, although not the "is" of Nature, but the "is" of those things which are within the reach of man and upon which his life depends. I believe that Xenophon is sufficiently explicit on this point.

Let us immediately rise to meet a false interpretation. The fact that Socrates meditated upon the things of daily life does not mean that he meditated only upon man and his actions. Commonly the testimony of Aristotle is taken to mean this. Nevertheless, the Greek word *ēthos* has an infinitely broader meaning than the one we now give to the word "ethics." The ethical embraces primarily man's attitudes towards life, his character, his customs, and, naturally, the moral element. Actually the word could be translated as "way or manner of life," in the fullest sense of the word, in contrast to the single meaning of "manner." And so Socrates adopted a new way of life: meditation upon what the things of life are. Consequently, the "ethical" element lay not primarily in what he *meditated upon,* but in the very fact that he *lived in meditation.* The things of life are not man, but they are the things which are encountered in his life and on which he depends.

To make man's life depend on meditation upon these things is not to choose the moral in contrast to the natural as a subject of meditation; it is simply to make of meditation the supreme *ēthos.* In other words, Socratic wisdom does not *center upon* the ethical, it *is* in itself ethical. That actually he centered his meditation by preference on civic virtue is something wholly secondary. The essential fact is that the intellectual man ceased to be a vagabond who lived among the stars, and became a wise man. *Wisdom as ethics:* this was the contribution of Socrates. Basically it was a new intellectual life.

This new ethics, the ethics of meditation upon the things of life, led inevitably to a specific intellection of them. With traditional philosophy, Nature is that whence all emerges; and when wisdom took the form of rational science, things appeared before the *mens* with their own *physis.* "Nature" gave way to "the nature of each thing." Socrates was far removed from this for the time being. When, in order to establish things as a basis for life, he focused his *mens* and his meditation upon things as they present themselves in life, *einai*—the fact that things "are"—took on a new value. It was not, at the outset, anything alluding to the nature of things, nor does this mean that Socrates discovered the concept. For that we must wait for Aristotle and Plato. But the Aristotelian concept is nothing but the theory of the *quid,* of the nature of each thing, of its *ti.* What the *mens* of Socrates achieved by concentrating upon the things of daily life was to see the "what" of the things of life. Wisdom as ethics led, therefore, to something decisive with respect to the understanding of things, something so significant that it was the root of all the new philosophy, and allowed philosophy to find anew, by new paths, the themes of traditional philosophy which, for the moment, had been put aside.

Let us follow the development of Socratic meditation on the "what" of things. To begin with, it developed as Socrates thought and talked with his friends. But conversation was no longer dispute. It could not now be a matter of defending pre-existing opinions, because there were no opinions to be defended and therefore it would have been idle to expound them. Talking of things, from the standpoint of things, was now what took place. Conversation ceased to be dispute and became dialogue, a calm and peaceful movement among things which permitted one to steep himself in them. It was a form of talk in which man, rather than speaking himself, allowed things to talk; it was almost as though things themselves spoke within us. Socrates doubtless recalled that for Parmenides and Heraclitus man's infallible knowledge of things issued from something that man has within him and which to them seemed something divine, *nous* and *logos*. Socrates sought to eliminate all excessive allusion to a superhuman wisdom. Man's wisdom, for Socrates, was nothing divine, *theion;* he was satisfied to call it modestly *daimonion.*

To attain such wisdom he held in suspension that feeling of assurance and certainty with which man reposes upon the things of life. He made it evident that in daily life one does not know what he holds in his hands; the very thing which makes life usual is precisely this ignorance. To recognize it is to establish oneself in the life of wisdom. Thereupon things, and along with them life itself, become problems. It is the wisdom of ignorance, of "not knowing whereof you speak." Only at this price does man capture a new kind of certainty. When we talk with a sick man, we take into consideration his sickness, and even share his misfortune. But if we put aside our vital relationship with him, and consequently if we ignore this relationship of man to man which attains its fullest development in the totality of the circumstances and situations in which it takes place, then the sick man vanishes from before our eyes and we are left face to face with his sickness, and the sickness is no longer an object of compassion or grief, it is simply an ensemble of characteristics which the sick man possesses—a *quid*. And this shift of attention from the sick man to his sickness, which for the time being leaves the man to one side, becomes paradoxically a new, firmer, and surer way of "treating the sick." This was the source of the universality of the Aristotelian definition and of that singular change of the notion of "what" to the notion of "why." Socrates himself did not even dimly discern this. But it could be achieved only by Socratic reflection.

In this way, by this "irony," by interrupting the course of wisdom and establishing it on firmer and more readily accessible ground, namely the things of daily life, Socrates saved in principle the truth discovered by traditional wisdom. But only in principle, for the full development of *sophia* as a way of knowing was the achievement of Plato and Aristotle.

Was Socrates a philosopher? If by philosopher we mean one who has a philosophy, he was not. If we mean one who is searching for a philosophy, perhaps not, either. But he was something more. Actually his life was a philosophic existence, an existence rooted in a philosophic *ēthos*, which, in a world strangled by public life, opened up to a private group of friends the realm of an intellectual life and of a philosophy, and established it upon new bases, launching it in a new direction, perhaps without realizing too clearly whither it was headed. Philosophy found its constitution in Socratic reflection. The life of Athens offered Socrates a limited number of choices: to project himself into public life as a virtuoso of oratory and thought, like Protagoras and his disciples; to busy himself with the new branches of knowledge from which later were to come the sciences; to sink himself in the amorphous mass of citizens absorbed in the rounds of daily life; to re-enter the flow of contemporary life—not simply to let himself be carried along by it but to guide it by meditation based upon what the things of life "are." Socrates unhesitatingly chose the last of these courses. And his decision made possible the existence of philosophy.

The actual content of his activity is of little consequence, and his personal life of even less. The majority of his disciples took his attitude, his *ēthos* as a *tropos,* a manner and no more. They tried, with more or with less mental baggage—baggage and nothing else—to *imitate* Socrates. Assuredly this was for him the bitter irony of his life. Out of this imitation grew the small Socratic schools.

A few sought to do something more, sought to adopt his *ēthos*, to approach things Socratically, to live Socratically the problems which things pose for the intelligence, and things rewarded them with new *sophia*—the "philo-sophy" of the Academy and the Lyceum.

II. Plato

Since a much larger proportion of the writings of Plato and Aristotle has survived than that of any other Greek philosophers, we are able to follow their complex inquiries in considerable detail and depth. Plato's thought underwent a steady development, from the early Socratic investigations into the definition of virtue to the dialectic of forms and the vision of the good, which marked the middle dialogues, and thence to the final period of self-questioning about the nature of being and knowing. The texts presented here are concerned mainly with this last phase, when Plato was facing the full force of the antinomy between a monism of being and a monism of becoming, and was striving courageously to retain a balanced theoretical and practical outlook. Even though the golden dream of an essential view of the good could not be made actual in philosophy and society, there was still the task of marking out some areas of certainty concerning aspects of knowledge and reality, as well as some social plans which could be carried out.

The essay on Socrates (4) has already brought out the close connection in the Greek mind and language between thinking and speaking, dialectic and dialogue. Plato is the consummate master of the dialogue form of philosophical inquiry. Yet, for all their apparently effortless flow, the Platonic dialogues contain many complex and baffling statements, calling forth a long tradition of commentaries over the centuries. Selection (5) is a relatively simple example of the interweaving of text and commentary. F. M. Cornford makes his own translation of the original and places it within the setting of an analytic and comparative explanation. The Theaetetus *belongs in a group of later dialogues, in which Plato is reconsidering the nature and conditions of knowledge. In the earlier sections of the* Theaetetus, *he has pointed out that the extreme positions of Parmenides and Heraclitus on the reality of becoming have their epistemological ramifications. The leading sophist, Protagoras, is only working out the noetic implications of Heraclitus' doctrine of universal flux, when he maintains that man is the measure of all things and that we have knowledge only of sense appearances. (As Selection [3] showed, the historical Heraclitus subordinated process to the balanced tension of opposites, constituting a cosmic unity and moral wisdom.)*

Plato criticizes this view, since it dissipates every stable object of knowledge and reduces the individual to his private, transient impressions. In Selection (5), he then considers the opinion of the young Theaetetus that perception is true knowledge. Cornford gives a lucid account of the two stages in the examination of this position. Plato's conviction that mind is distinct in nature from the senses and every corporeal organ is a permanent part of his philosophy. He appeals to the common terms in discourse, the act of judging and comparing, and the formal grasp of existence (ousia) and unity, as indicative of the presence in man of some suprasensuous cognitive power. Nevertheless, the conclusion that sense perception has no part in knowledge does not follow rigorously from the evidence presented here. As Cornford observes, it depends upon the general Platonic doctrine on the intelligible forms as the genuine objects of knowledge.

That Plato discovers rifts and internal difficulties in his own general theory of forms, is established by Leonard Eslick in Selection (6). He makes a circumstantial study of the Sophist, *another dialogue of Plato's later years which brings to a climax the investigations of the* Parmenides *and the* Theaetetus *into being and knowing. Plato's deep involvement in the earlier Greek discussion of motion and manyness is visible here, along with his characteristic refusal to separate the questions of knowledge and reality. Thus, if one accepts the pure flux of Heraclitus, things are dissolved into their relations and there is no essential unity of structure which can serve as the object of knowledge. Yet a thing cannot be sheer unity and nothing else, for then it will be isolated from the rest and incapable of sustaining the relations and predications of knowledge. Parmenides saves the unity of being at the cost of extinguishing all rational discourse about it.*

The Platonic solution in the Sophist *is to insist upon the thoroughly dyadic character of reality: the basic constituents of the real are both unity and the other, both being and nonbeing. Some unsatisfactory consequences of this complex view of the real, as a whole containing parts, are nevertheless inescapable. The forms are interwoven and sustain relations, but they do so, not in virtue of their own essence or unity, but only in virtue of the factor of otherness and nonbeing present in them. Hence the resultant knowledge is purely relational. It provides no real basis for bringing either the forms or the one within the scope of true knowledge and essential discourse. Eslick suggests that this disappointing outcome prompted Aristotle to locate the real differences within being itself, and hence to exchange a generic conception of being for an analogous one.*

Selection (7) is drawn from Ronald Levinson's book, In Defense of Plato. *This book offers a spirited and well-grounded challenge to the attacks made upon Plato's personal character, as well as his moral and political doctrines, by Warner Fite* (The Platonic Legend), *Karl Popper* (The Open Society and Its Enemies), *and R. H. Crossman* (Plato Today). *These authors regard Plato as a totalitarian political thinker, who despaired of the ordinary man, placed his entire hope in an aristocracy of birth and wealth, and advocated establishing its rule through a violent revolution. In the passage included here, Levinson is concerned mainly with Crossman's interpretation of Plato's trips to Syracuse. During his dozen years of travelling after the execution of Socrates, Plato visited Sicily and became friendly with Dion, brother-in-law to Dionysius I, the tyrant of Syracuse. Even after his return to Athens, Plato retained the friendship of Dion. From the probably authentic Seventh and Eight Letters of Plato, we learn that, in his sixties, he accepted an invitation from Dion to return to Syracuse after the accession of Dionysius II. The purpose of this second trip was to instruct the new tyrant in philosophy and secure the establishment of just laws. After a brief initial success in interesting Dionysius in the life of the mind, Dion was banished and Plato left the scene. His third and final visit was also fruitless so that, after a short period of house arrest, Plato withdrew permanently from this practical mission. Aided by some of Plato's pupils, Dion was able to drive out Dionysius and set himself up as ruler, but in a short while he himself was assassinated. It was under these circumstances that Plato composed the Seventh Letter, for the guidance of Dion's followers.*

Levinson challenges the assumption that the Republic *was written with an eye to carrying out its provisions in Syracuse. This leads him to suggest a more flexible relationship between the ideal state outlined in that dialogue and the practical plans set forth in Plato's* Laws *and the* Letters. *In the practical as well as the speculative order, Plato's thought continues to develop and struggle with real conditions, right up to the end. Finally, Levinson points out the discrepancies between the picture of Plato as a paleo-fascist and the actual content of his political advice to friends in Syracuse. The author agrees with G. R. Morrow (Studies in the Platonic Epistles) that, in modern terms, the practical political intent of Plato is the establishment of a mixed, constitutional rule.*

5

PLATO'S CRITICISM OF PERCEPTION [1]

PLATO now considers the claim of perception to be identical with knowledge. This claim, as advanced by Theaetetus, strictly implies not only that perception is knowledge, but that it is the whole of knowledge. The following refutation proves (I) that perception cannot be the whole of knowledge, for a great part of what is always called knowledge consists of truths involving terms which are not objects of perception; and (II) that, even within its own sphere, the objects of perception have not that true reality which the objects of knowledge must possess. Hence, so far from being co-extensive with knowledge, perception is not knowledge at all.

(I) *Perception is not the whole of knowledge.*—The first argument does not depend on the details of Plato's theory of sense-perception. Such a theory, he would hold, can never be more than a probable account which might need amendment. But even if it be not accepted, he can still show that perception, in the strict sense which is taken to exclude judgment, cannot be the whole of knowledge.

184B. SOCR. Well then, Theaetetus, here is a point for you to consider. The answer you gave was that knowledge is perception, wasn't it?
THEAET. Yes.
SOCR. Now suppose you were asked: "When a man sees white or black things or hears high or low tones, what does he see or hear with?" I suppose you would say: "With eyes and ears."
THEAET. Yes, I should.
C. SOCR. To use words and phrases in an easygoing way without scrutinizing them too curiously is not, in general, a mark of ill breeding; on the contrary there is something lowbred in being too precise. But sometimes there is no help for it, and this is a case in which I must take exception to the form of your answer. Consider: is it more correct to say that we see and hear *with* our eyes and ears or *through* them?
THEAET. I should say we always perceive through them, rather than with them.
D. SOCR. Yes; it would surely be strange that there should be a number of

[1] [From F. M. Cornford, *Plato's Theory of Knowledge* (London: Routledge and Kegan Paul, 1935), pp. 102-109. Reprinted by permission. The text of Plato is: *Theaetetus*, 184B-186E. Most of the notes are omitted.]

senses ensconced inside us, like the warriors in the Trojan horse, and all
these things should not converge and meet in some single nature—a mind,
or whatever it is to be called—*with* which we perceive all the objects of
perception *through* the senses as instruments.

THEAET. Yes, I think that is a better description.

SOCR. My object in being so precise is to know whether there is some part
of ourselves, the same in all cases, with which we apprehend black or
white through the eyes, and objects of other kinds through the other
E. senses. Can you, if the question is put to you, refer all such acts of apprehension to the body? Perhaps, however, it would be better you should
speak for yourself in reply to questions, instead of my taking the words
out of your mouth. Tell me: all these instruments through which you perceive what is warm or hard or light or sweet are parts of the body, aren't
they?—not of anything else.

THEAET. Of nothing else.

SOCR. Now will you also agree that the objects you perceive through one
185A. faculty cannot be perceived through another—objects of hearing, for instance, through sight, or objects of sight through hearing?

THEAET. Of course I will.

SOCR. Then, if you have some thought about both objects at once, you
cannot be having a perception including both at once through either the
one or the other organ.

THEAET. No.

SOCR. Now take sound and color. Have you not, to begin with, this thought
which includes both at once—that they both *exist?*

THEAET. I have.

SOCR. And, further, that each of the two is *different* from the other and
the *same* as itself?

B. THEAET. Naturally.

SOCR. And again, that both together are *two,* and each of them is *one?*

THEAET. Yes.

SOCR. And also you can ask yourself whether they are *unlike* each other
or *alike?*

THEAET. No doubt.

SOCR. Then through what organ do you think all this about them both?
What is common to them both cannot be apprehended either through
hearing or through sight. Besides, here is further evidence for my point.
Suppose it were possible to inquire whether sound and color were both
brackish or not, no doubt you could tell me what faculty you would use—
C. obviously not sight or hearing, but some other.

THEAET. Of course: the faculty that works through the tongue.

SOCR. Very good. But now, through what organ does that faculty work,
which tells you what is common not only to these objects but to all
things—what you mean by the words "exists" and "does not exist" and
the other terms applied to them in the questions I put a moment ago?
What sort of organs can you mention, corresponding to all these terms,
through which the perceiving part of us perceives each one of them?

THEAET. You mean existence and non-existence, likeness and unlikeness,
sameness and difference, and also unity and numbers in general as ap-
D. plied to them; and clearly your question covers "even" and "odd" and

all that kind of notion. You are asking, through what part of the body our mind perceives these?

SOCR. You follow me most admirably, Theaetetus; that is exactly my question.

THEAET. Really, Socrates, I could not say, except that I think there is no special organ at all for these things, as there is for the others. It is clear
E. to me that the mind in itself is its own instrument for contemplating the common terms that apply to everything.

SOCR. In fact, Theaetetus, you are handsome, not ugly as Theodorus said you were; for in a discussion handsome is that handsome does. And you have treated me more than handsomely in saving me the trouble of a very long argument, if it is clear to you that the mind contemplates some things through its own instrumentality, others through the bodily faculties. That was indeed what I thought myself; but I wanted you to agree.

186A. THEAET. Well, it is clear to me.

In this argument, for the first time, we go behind the earlier account of sense-perception, which regarded the subject as no more than a bundle of distinct sense-organs, and sense-perception as a process occurring between organ and external object. That account stands; but it is now added that, behind the separate organs, there must be a mind, centrally receiving their several reports and capable of reflecting upon the data of sense and making judgments. In these judgments the thinking mind uses terms like "exists," "is the same as," "is different from," which are not objects of perception reaching the mind through the channel of any special sense, but are "common" to all the objects of sense. The mind gains its acquaintance with the meaning of such terms through its own instrumentality, not by the commerce between bodily organs and objects.

These terms are called "common" (*koina*) in contrast with the "private" (*idia*) or "peculiar" objects of the several senses. "Common" means no more than that. They are not to be confused with the "common sensibles" which Aristotle regarded as the objects of a common sensorium seated in the heart, namely objects perceptible by more than one sense, such as motion, shape, number, size, time. Plato does not speak of a "common sense" (*koinē aisthēsis*), but on the contrary insists that his common terms are apprehended, not by any sense, but by thought. The judgments involving them are made by the mind, thinking by itself, without any special bodily organ. The terms are "common," not in Aristotle's sense, but in the sense in which a name is common to any number of individual things. Thus "exists" is "applied in common to all things" (*koinon epi pasi*, 185C); it can occur in a statement about any subject you like. Existence, we are presently told (186A), "attends on" or "belongs to" all things. These common terms are, in fact, the meanings of common names—what Plato calls "Forms" or "Ideas." The instances given here correspond to the instances given by Socrates in the *Parmenides* (129D), where he says that Zeno's dilemmas could be escaped by "separating apart by themselves Forms such as likeness and unlikeness, plurality and unity, rest and motion and all such things." The terms there mentioned happen to be those which occurred in Zeno's arguments against plurality and motion; Socrates adds later (130B) the moral Forms "beautiful, good, and all such things," just as he will presently add them here (186A). In the *Theaetetus* Plato is determined to say as little as possible about the Forms, and he here avoids using the word; but that these "common" terms simply are Forms should be obvious to anyone who has read the *Parmenides*. The avoidance of the word has misled many critics into asserting that the Forms are not mentioned in the *Theaetetus*, and miscalling these common terms "categories."

Plato could not press the argument further in this direction without openly discussing the Forms as the true objects of knowledge. But the inference is clear: that percepts cannot be the only objects of knowledge, as the identification of knowledge with perception implied. Any statement we can make about the objects of perception, and therefore any truth, must contain at least one of these common terms. Therefore all knowledge of truths, as distinct from immediate acquaintance with sense-data, involves acquaintance with Forms, which are not private objects of perception, not individual existents, not involved in the Heraclitean flux. The reader can now draw the first conclusion: Perception is not the whole of knowledge.

The argument next proceeds to the second conclusion: (II) *Perception, even within its own sphere, is not knowledge at all.*

186A. SOCR. Under which head, then, do you place existence? For that is, above all, a thing that belongs to everything.

THEAET. I should put it among the things that the mind apprehends by itself.

SOCR. And also likeness and unlikeness and sameness and difference?

THEAET. Yes.

SOCR. And how about "honorable" and "dishonorable" and "good" and "bad"?

THEAET. Those again seem to me, above all, to be things whose being is considered, one in comparison with another, by the mind, when it reflects

B. within itself upon the past and the present with an eye to the future.[2]

SOCR. Wait a moment. The hardness of something hard and the softness of something soft will be perceived by the mind through touch, will they not?

THEAET. Yes.

SOCR. But their existence and the fact that they both exist, and their contrariety to one another and again the existence of this contrariety are things which the mind itself undertakes to judge for us, when it reflects upon them and compares one with another.

2 Theaetetus seems to be thinking of the recent argument against Protagoras, turning on the question of judgments about the comparative goodness or badness of future effects, and what *will* seem honorable (laudable) or dishonorable customs to a State. Socrates stops him short and applies his statement to the contrasts of sense qualities. Touch can show us that this is hard, that soft; but it is thought, not sense, that reflects upon the contrast of hard and soft.

THEAET. Certainly.

SOCR. Is it not true, then, that whereas all the impressions which penetrate to the mind through the body are things which men and animals alike

C. are naturally constituted to perceive from the moment of birth, reflections about them with respect to their existence and usefulness only come, if they come at all, with difficulty through a long and troublesome process of education?

THEAET. Assuredly.

SOCR. Is it possible, then, to reach truth when one cannot reach existence?

THEAET. It is impossible.

SOCR. But if a man cannot reach the truth of a thing, can he possibly know that thing?

D. THEAET. No, Socrates, how could he?

SOCR. If that is so, knowledge does not reside in the impressions, but in our reflection upon them. It is there, seemingly, and not in the impressions, that it is possible to grasp existence and truth.

THEAET. Evidently.

SOCR. Then are you going to give the same name to two things which differ so widely?

THEAET. Surely that would not be right.

SOCR. Well then, what name do you give to the first one—to seeing, hearing, smelling, feeling cold and feeling warm?

E. THEAET. Perceiving. What other name is there for it?

SOCR. Taking it all together, then, you call this perception?

THEAET. Necessarily.   ..

SOCR. A thing which, we agree, has no part in apprehending truth, since it has none in apprehending existence.

THEAET. No, it has none.

SOCR. Nor, consequently, in knowledge either.

THEAET. No.

SOCR. Then, Theaetetus, perception and knowledge cannot possibly be the same thing.

THEAET. Evidently not, Socrates. Indeed, it is now perfectly plain that knowledge is something different from perception.

Such is the final disproof of the claim of perception to be knowledge. Though admitted to be, in a sense, infallible, perception has not the second mark of knowledge: it cannot apprehend existence and truth. There is a certain ambiguity about the words "existence" (*ousia*) and "truth" (*alētheia*): both are commonly used by Plato to mean that true reality which he ascribes to Forms and denies to sensible objects. If we keep to the sense suggested by the previous context, the statement should mean that the simplest judgment, such as "Green exists here," is beyond the scope of perception proper, our immediate awareness of green. The faculty of perception has no cognizance of the meaning of the word "exists"; and, since only judgments or statements can be true, all truths are beyond its scope.

To the Platonist, however, who is familiar with the associations of "reality" and "truth," the passage will mean more than this. The statement that reflections on the existence or usefulness of our sense-impressions come only, if at all, after a long and troublesome education seems at first sight to conflict with the argument for Recollection in the *Phaedo,* where it was asserted that from the time when we first begin to use our senses we make judgments involving Forms, which we must therefore have known before birth. All judgments involve the use of some common term; and Plato cannot mean to deny here that uneducated people make judgments. Plainly he means that they have not such knowledge of Forms as the dialectician gains by the long process of education described in *Republic* vii. And the *Phaedo* may only mean that, though children do make judgments such as "This is like that" and mean something by them, they have only a dim and confused apprehension of Forms such as likeness. The advance to knowledge is a gradual recovery of clear vision, possible only by a training in dialectic.

The conclusion suggested earlier was that perception cannot be the whole of knowledge because there are other objects—the common terms —which the mind must know if it is to reflect at all. If we now take account of the Platonic sense of "reality and truth," we can add a further influence. Even my direct perception of my own sense-object cannot be called "knowledge," because the object is not a thing which is unchangingly real, but only something that becomes and is always changing. Some might say that they are more certain of the sensations and perceptions they have at any moment than they are of anything else; and to deny the name of knowledge to such direct acquaintance is, in a sense, a matter of terminology. But to Plato knowledge, by definition, has the real for its object, and these objects have not true and permanent being. This point, however, cannot be elaborated without entering on an account of the intelligible world. Hence a certain ambiguity is allowed to remain about the meaning of "reaching truth (reality) and existence."

6

THE DYADIC CHARACTER OF BEING IN PLATO [1]

I

IF BEING is conceived in a univocal way, so that it cannot admit of intrinsic essential differences, then all being is one. The classic exponent of pure univocity of being is Parmenides of Elea. To make being univocal is to make it a genus. No genus can contain its *differentiae* in act within itself without being made self-contradictory. Its differences must therefore lie outside of it and be extrinsic to it.

1 [From Leonard Eslick, "The Dyadic Character of Being in Plato," *The Modern Schoolman*, vol. 31 (1953-54), pp. 11-18. Reprinted by permission.]

A genus is not predictable of its differences. Consequently, if being is a genus, it could be differentiated only by nonbeing. But for Parmenides of Elea, nonbeing is unthinkable and cannot exist. It follows with rigorous necessity, therefore, that multiplicity, formal diversity, and change are all ultimately unreal. Being is a simple, homogeneous, unchanging unity.

The doctrine of the great Eleatic is a pure position, and like many such positions in the history of philosophy, it is intolerable. To Plato, confronted with the stubborn facts of multiplicity and change, a revolutionary development in the very notion of being was necessary. As Plato, speaking through the Eleatic Stranger in the *Sophistes,* puts it:

> We shall find it necessary in self-defence to put to the question that pronouncement of Father Parmenides, and establish by main force that what is not, in some respect, has being, and conversely that what is, in a way is not.[2]

For Plato, therefore, the problem of the one and the many demands for its solution something quite inadmissible to Parmenides—the existence of nonbeing.

Such a doctrine was surely strange and unknown in Elea, and it is put by Plato into the mouth of an Eleatic *stranger*. Nevertheless, it is important to note that the stranger who leads the discussion in the *Sophistes* is still *from* Elea. The starting point of Plato's revolutionary development of the notion of being is an Eleatic starting point. In beginning in this way, Aristotle tells us that Plato was posing the problem of the one and the many in "an obsolete form." [3] There will be no hint in Plato of the *analogical* character of being which Aristotle was first to propose. Plato will be no more willing than Father Parmenides to admit of *intrinsic* essential differences within being itself. But however the Platonic doctrine of the dyadic character of being is to be finally judged, it is one of the most extraordinarily subtle and powerful positions in the history of thought and one of the least well understood. It will be the task of this paper to determine some of the exigencies which led Plato to it, and some of the consequences following upon it.

II

For Plato, to *be* is to be *one*. But this does not in the least imply that being and unity are convertible, as they are in Aristotle. It is equally true for Plato that to be is to be *other* than one. The Platonic principles of participation and of separation (*chorismos*) are both operative. As the second hypothesis of the *Parmenides,* concerning the one which *is,* as distinguished from unity taken simply in itself, makes clear, an existing unit is a composite of *two* distinct elements, unity *and* being. Unity taken strictly in itself, as we learn from the first hypothesis of the *Par-*

2 *Sophistes* 241D.
3 *Metaphysics* 1088b35.

menides, is absolutely simple and indivisible, and as such it can be the subject of no predication whatsoever. But every being—that is, every existing unit—is something other than simple, indivisible unity, though that is indeed its ultimate essence. The Platonic principle of separation operates to divide a being from its own essence, from its own unique *inseity.* If it were *only* simple, indivisible unity, it could not enter into participation and the relations of discourse. It would be completely and utterly devoid of any relationship to anything else whatsoever. An existing unit, however, is always composite, a differentiated whole of parts. Unity itself cannot be a divisible whole of parts. Nothing, for Plato, could *be* unless it were in some sense an indivisible unit, separate from all others, a stable and unique term not constituted by its relations. As Plato tells us in the *Theaetetus,* it is necessary to separate the Forms, for if there are no absolute self-existents, no being which has its being unto itself, then being must be altogether abolished.[4] In other words, if, as the description of perception outlined in the *Theaetetus* has it, beings are constituted to be what they are entirely by the relations into which they enter, the whole of reality becomes a flux. Knowledge is destroyed, for it is without any stable enduring object. But on the other hand, for Plato nothing could be if it were *only* an indivisible unit, if it were in no sense also a whole of parts and consequently a many, really related to the others. As the *Sophistes* puts it, "the complete separation of each thing from all is the utterly final obliteration of all discourse." [5] These two demands, therefore, give rise to Plato's doctrine of the dyadic character of being. Being must somehow be *both* indivisible static unity and a divisible, dynamic whole of parts. It must be *both in itself* and *in relation.*

III

The great dialogue, the *Sophistes,* begins in earnest when the meaning of the term "being" is called into question. Since we have seen that the task for Plato is to discover existing nonbeing, there is no way to do it except by a careful investigation of being. The dialectical method is applied diligently; using discourse, Plato must analyze the exact meaning of the term "being" as it is used by all the previous philosophers.

What results from an investigation of the dualists? They say that two principles, like hot and cold, are the ultimates of the universe. What do they mean by saying both and each *are*? They must mean being is a third over and above the two principles, but then they contradict themselves. Or they must mean that the two will resolve into one, being, and again there is a contradiction.

The Eleatic answer is not much better. Those philosophers apply *two* names to the oneness of all: being and one. But to apply two names

4 157B.
5 259E.

while affirming the absolute unity of reality seems to Plato ridiculous.[6] Either being is a whole of parts, and, being not being unity itself, there will be plurality, or being is not a whole of parts. In this latter case, there are two possibilities. If wholeness exists, then being does not exist. Hence there will be plurality. If wholeness does not exist, then being cannot come into being as a complete, determinate number. In any case, there will be plurality, in contradiction to the Parmenidean one. Indeed, in the last case, according to Plato there will be infinite plurality.

The investigation of the dualists and the Eleatics has revealed that being is itself a complexity to be grasped and that it is not as evidently understood as was first thought. When we are shown the arguments of a purified materialism and of idealism, a similar conclusion becomes manifest.

At this point in the *Sophistes* Plato advances a new conception of being. He proposes "as a sufficient mark of real things the presence in a thing of the power of being acted upon or of acting in relation to however insignificant a thing." [7] What this famous doctrine of being as *dynamis* means is simply that no being is wholly self-enclosed and separated in complete isolation from all others. Nothing can *be* unless it exists in relation to others. Clearly being is to be viewed as able to become other than itself. No being, therefore, is totally and absolutely immobile.

But what of those "friends of the Forms" who hold that the Forms are static? This position, which seems to have been Plato's own in his earlier period, leads to grave difficulties about knowledge and discourse. Neither change, life, soul, nor understanding have any place in being so conceived. We can know nothing about that which is completely cut off from all other things, as the first hypothesis of the *Parmenides* had made abundantly clear. For the Forms to enter into predication in any way it is necessary that they have the power of interparticipating—that they be divisible wholes of parts, something radically impossible for that which is *only* indivisible unity. All of our discourse, as Plato says, "owes its existence to the weaving together of the Forms." [8]

On the other hand, in order to have a world of true being which can be the proper object of knowledge, the separation and self-existence of the Forms is necessary. Since the Forms are immutable, they are the proper object of knowledge rather than sensible things, which are always in flux and becoming. But the separation of the Forms, which is necessary if they are to be true beings, seems to conflict with their knowability. Plato therefore considers it necessary to establish a new position which is neither Eleatic nor Heraclitean.

On these grounds, then it seems that only one course is open to the philosopher who values knowledge and the rest above all else. He must refuse to accept from the champions either of the one or of the many Forms the doctrine that reality

6 *Sophistes* 244D.
7 *Ibid.*, 248C.
8 *Ibid.*, 259E.

is changeless; and he must turn a deaf ear to the other party who represents Being as everywhere changing. Like a child begging for "both," he must declare that Being or the sum of things is both at once—all that is unchangeable and all that is in change.[9]

The crux of this argument is knowledge, the saving of which is certainly Plato's goal, just as it was to be the goal of Kant. Knowledge is a given, knowledge demands both. If reality were one in an absolute unity knowledge becomes impossible, for knowledge is discourse, and discourse involves predicating one thing of another. If reality were becoming, absolute change, knowledge likewise becomes radically impossible, for every term would resolve into its relations. In order, therefore, to save true knowledge, it becomes necessary for Plato to show both how the Forms can be separate and yet at the same time interweave and participate in one another. How is this possible?

If being is both at rest and in motion, both changeless and changing, then Plato must face the same question which he posed to the dualists. They were asked to explain how being is predicated of hot and cold without contradiction being involved. Why isn't the thesis that being is both motion and rest open to the same charge of contradiction? There remains only one thing to do: use the method of dialectic to see what is meant.

Clearly motion and rest are opposed to each other, yet both are real. The existence of both is necessary to account for discourse, the existence of which is taken as given. Motion is, but it is not rest; and rest is, but it is not motion. It follows, therefore, that being is both at rest and in motion and yet is _neither_. The genus, taken in itself, is in Platonic logic _other_ and separate from the species which participate in it. Being is neither motion nor rest; nor is motion rest, or rest motion. When we come, therefore, to speak of these things, how should we proceed? Only three possibilities are open: (1) either none of the Forms combine and are related or (2) all combine with all or (3) some have relations to others and some not.

If the first alternative is accepted, all thought is destroyed. The Forms can only be named and cannot enter into predication. It upsets all theories of being—the Eleatic, the doctrine of the "friends of the Forms," dualism, and flux.[10] This supposition must be rejected.

The second alternative must likewise be rejected, for if it were true, motion in participating in rest would stop, while rest, sharing in motion, would be in movement.[11]

Only the third is left, namely, that some Forms participate in others, but never all in all. One of the recurring metaphors in the later Platonic dialogues is suggested by this alternative—the metaphor of the alphabet, for here too some letters cannot be combined with others. Just as an art

9 _Ibid.,_ 249D.
10 _Ibid.,_ 251E-52A.
11 _Ibid.,_ 252D.

of grammar is needed to combine letters, so some art is needed to combine those Forms which participate and to divide those which do not. This art is true dialectic, which is now applied to the problem of being, motion, and rest.

Up to this point we have seen that these are three, that two will not blend with each other, and that being can be blended with both. Now each form is *other* than the others, and yet the *same* in relation to itself. Motion and rest, however, cannot be either *other* or the *same, for if either motion or rest be identical with anything that is said in common of the two, motion would be rest and rest motion*. Nonetheless, motion and rest do participate in *same* and *other,* for we have admitted that motion is the same as itself and other than rest, and likewise for rest. What of being and *same,* and being and *other?* They must be different. If being were identified with *same,* then motion and rest would also be identical, since they both participate in being. In regard to being and *other,* Plato's text is of capital importance in establishing the dyadic character of being on the joint foundation of separation and participation:

Must we think of Other and Being as two names for a single kind? Perhaps. But I suppose you admit that, among things that exist, some are always spoken of as being what they are just in themselves, others as being what they are in reference to other things. Of course. And what is other is always so called with reference to another thing, isn't it? That is so. It would not be so, if Being and Other were not very different things. If Other partook of both characters as Being does, there would sometimes be within the class of different things, something that was different not with reference to another thing. But in fact we undoubtedly find that whatever is different, as a necessary consequence, is what it is with reference to another. . . . Then we must call the nature of Other a fifth among the Forms we are singling out.[12]

There is some evidence that the question of whether it is strictly proper to refer to the other as a *Form* at all was hotly debated in the Academy in Plato's lifetime. For the Forms, as true beings, must have the dyadic character of existing both in themselves and in relation, whereas the other is distinct from all beings precisely in the fact that it is quite literally nothing in itself. It has no essence of its own. Perhaps this is the origin of the question about whether there can be Forms of relations, of which Aristotle speaks in the *Metaphysics.* But in any event, the other *exists* for Plato and this is precisely the existence of nonbeing which was considered necessary to advance beyond the absolute monism of Father Parmenides.

What are some of the consequences of this position? Every Form is one in itself. By essence every Form is identical, for every Form is a unity. Unity is the principle by which the Form has existence. Yet each Form, although *a* unity, is not *the* one, but is a reflection of the one in

12 *Ibid.,* 255C-E.

the Platonic material principle, which is called "the other" in the *Sophistes*, "the unlimited" in the *Philebus*, "the receptacle" in the *Timaeus*, and "the indeterminate dyad" in the oral discourses. This can only mean that the other when intermingled with the one produces many images of the one. Now, part of these imitations of the one is nonbeing itself. It is this part of the other in each Form which accounts both for the fact of their being other than the one and other than each other. There are, therefore, for Plato no intrinsic differences between beings in the *essential* order. The essence of a being, which is simply indivisible unity, can in no way be the foundation of its differences from, and relations to, other beings. That which makes it to be other than the others is itself distinct from the Form in itself. The Spinozist maxim that all determination is negation is a supreme principle of Platonic dialectic.

It also follows, as Aristotle makes abundantly clear,[13] that the ultimate subject of Platonic predication is nonbeing, rather than substance or *ousia*. The one is the essence of all of the Forms; but to say what the one is, is impossible, as the *Parmenides* had made plain. Knowledge, therefore, as Plato tells us in the *Seventh Epistle*,[14] in its attempt to penetrate into the essence attains instead only a description of qualities—that is, of the relative nonbeing of the thing. Any attempt to give a real account of any Form must necessitate giving an explanation of its relations to every other Form. Ultimate truth, in the order of essence, can never be attained because the real one never can be manifested in rational discourse.

13 *Metaphysics* 988a7-14.
14 341-44D.

7

PLATO'S POLITICAL VENTURE IN SICILY [1]

IT IS instructive to consider the actual program that Plato and Dion attempted to set up in place of the existing tyranny in Sicily. And here we confront our basic disagreement with Crossman. We cannot follow him in his belief that it was Plato's hope and expectation, after a period of preparation lasting perhaps (Crossman does not specify) no more than a decade or so, to see rising from the reform of the tyranny the whole shining fabric of the *Republic,* complete with the communism of the ruling class and the dictatorship of a philosopher in the person of the converted Dionysius II.

1 [From Ronald Levinson, *In Defense of Plato* (Cambridge, Mass.: Harvard University Press, 1953), pp. 374-383, 390-393. Reprinted by permission. The notes are omitted. Criticism is directed against R. H. Crossman, *Plato Today* (New York: Oxford University Press. 1939).]

We cannot accept the notion that the *Republic* bears clear traces of having been written with any such application in view. Syracuse, like Athens, and in even higher degree, was extremely ill-fitted for conversion into the compact, ordered, and austere city of the *Republic*. And as to Dionysius II, nothing in the record could have suggested to Plato that he possessed that extraordinary endowment of intellect and moral genius by which the philosopher kings had been defined, and on the basis of which they were to have been selected from among the most promising members of their generation. It must be remembered, too, that those exalted beings were to have been trained and protected from all untoward influences from earliest childhood; the environment of the court had supplied Dionysius, who was already some thirty years old at his accession, with an education opposed to this at all points. Judging from the *Republic* alone, then, it appears probable that Plato's initial program for Syracuse, so far as he permitted himself to have one in advance, would have been far less ambitious than the creation of the ideal city, with Dionysius as philosopher king.

An inspection of the letters themselves will reveal, however, the difficulty of arriving at certainty regarding Plato's political objectives in Syracuse, and will show how it is possible for highly responsible observers to reach opposing interpretations; how Crossman can hold his view, while Morrow can argue forcefully that the aim was never other than the establishment of a constitutional monarchy.[2] We shall seek to marshal first the reasons for this latter view, as derived from the Seventh Letter.

Letter VII is an open letter, or pamphlet, purporting to be written by Plato, shortly after the death of Dion, to Dion's friends and supporters in Syracuse, in response to their request for advice concerning the settlement of Sicilian political affairs. It combines a few paragraphs of this advice with a brief account of the development of Plato's own political principles, leading into a more detailed record of his entire relationship to Sicily, particularly to Dionysius II and to Dion.

As to the making of Dionysius into a fit person to serve as enlightened ruler of Sicily, the letter contains no evidence that Plato had been led to expect in Dionysius any very unusual gifts of mind or spirit; none had been asserted of him by Dion in his initial appeal to Plato (327 E-328 A). The young tyrant had come to feel, Dion had reported, a longing for philosophy and education; and Dion had thought it possible that he might become sufficiently inspired with a desire for the virtuous life to cooperate in establishing good government, in accord with Plato's political principles, in Syracuse. Thus the tyranny would be abolished "without massacres and murders" and the other evils of civil strife (372 D). Accordingly, we are not surprised to hear of Plato's and Dion's efforts, undertaken on Plato's arrival, to convert Dionysius from his dis-

2 [There is general agreement between Levinson and Glenn Morrow, "Studies in the Platonic Epistles," *Illinois Studies in Language and Literature*, vol. 18, nos. 3-4 (1935).]

solute way of life, employing every resource of the teacher and moralist and holding out to him an alluring picture of the fruits of reform: troops of friends upon whom he could depend as loyal supporters of his rule, and by whose aid he could hope to extend his power against the Carthaginians (331 E). The attempted conversion failed; but Plato expresses his conviction that if it had succeeded, or if Dion's later attempt himself to establish a government of laws in Syracuse had been successful, the highest interests of philosophy and of mankind throughout the world would have been served;

for if ... philosophy and power had really been united in the same person, the radiance thereof would have shone through the whole world of Greeks and barbarians, and fully imbued them with the true conviction that no state or any individual man can ever become happy unless he passes his life in subjection to justice combined with wisdom, whether it be that he possesses these virtues within himself or as the result of being reared and trained righteously under god-fearing rulers in their ways (335 D).

Noticeable in all this is that though the ruler is to possess philosophy, the primary stress is laid upon moral goodness and the transforming effect of the sovereign's virtue (and of the good laws, which, as we are told in the case of Dion, he would have established) upon public morals, with the resulting benefit to all.

In mentioning law as a feature of the Syracusan government-to-be, we have touched upon a recurring theme in the Seventh Letter. On the opening page we read the declaration that Dion's opinion from the very first (and Plato's own, for he had derived it from Plato) had been that "the Syracusans ought to be free and dwell under the best laws" (324 B). Again in his advice to the friends of Dion, Plato announces as his third repetition of the doctrine, the advice he had urged first upon Dion and then upon Dionysius: "Neither Sicily, nor yet any other State . . . should be enslaved to human despots but rather to laws" (334 C). Dion, who had accepted this teaching, would have brought "freedom" to Syracuse, and would then have endeavored "to set the citizens in order by suitable laws of the best kind" (336 A). Dion, we hear again near the end of the letter, aimed only to establish "a moderate government" (*politeia*) "and the . . . justest and best of laws" (351 C). To be noted in passing is the vehement rejection of any intention to redistribute property, either by violent seizure or by popular decree (351 B).

This repeated assertion of the primacy of law, coupled with the idea of an exemplary ruler, implies, it would seem, the establishment of what we should call constitutional monarchy. We shall see, when we come to examine the Eighth Letter, that Plato approved highly the voluntary relinquishment by a king of a large part of his power for the good of the state. And we need not doubt that Plato had originally expected to superintend this relinquishment and, relying on his own experience and insight as moral and educational expert, with the help of

Dion as the expert in Sicilian affairs, himself to take the major part in the drawing up of the new constitution. In the light of these considerations, it is not unlikely that Plato intended the function of the ruler, once he had employed his power to instate the government of laws, to be chiefly that of setting the moral tone and standard of the state, and expected him to relegate the actual conduct of affairs, with certain specified exceptions, to the magistrates, himself remaining thenceforth, like all others in the realm, subject to the laws.

The resettling of the Sicilian cities is viewed from the standpoint of Plato's usual concern for the preservation of the values of Hellenic culture against barbarian encroachment (336 A). These cities were to be resettled, equipped with codes of "equal laws" (*isonomia*) (336 D), and linked to one another and Syracuse in bonds of friendship by "laws and constitutions" (332 E).

From the Third Letter, if we may trust it, we hear (316 A) that Plato labored, during the early months of his stay at the court of Dionysius II, in constructing "preludes" to laws, those moralizing and persuasive little prefaces which were Plato's own invention and of which we hear so much in the *Laws*. This occupation, if shared with Dionysius, or if the preludes were presented to him for examination and approval as they were composed, would seem to have been well suited to the elementary instruction of the royal pupil in the principles of morals and legislation, and implies that the promulgation of laws was at the heart of Plato's plan for Syracuse from the beginning.

We have assembled from the Seventh Letter the principal evidence which suggests that Plato's original plan for the reform of Syracuse was the more moderate one of constitutional monarchy. But we are not at liberty to brush aside Crossman's assumption to the contrary, which must be allowed to possess a considerable initial plausibility.

(1) In support of the view that the ideal Republic was to be attempted, the Seventh Letter provides, as its second repeated theme, the coupling of the notions of philosophy and political power. We have already quoted one such passage. There is also the impressive reassertion, included in Plato's brief account of his own intellectual history, of the familiar central sentence of the *Republic* stating the necessity that philosophers shall become rulers, and conversely (326 A-B). Dion, too, in urging Plato in the first instance to come to Syracuse and attempt to win over Dionysius II, had urged that this was the long-awaited opportunity to combine in the same persons philosophy and the rule over great cities (328 A). These expressions undoubtedly suggest, at first blush, that the realization of the ideal city was definitely intended. Dion's prediction of the unbounded happiness throughout Sicily (327 C, D), which was to result from the new philosophical regime, points in the same direction, and recalls that "cessation of evils" promised on the same terms in the *Republic*.

(2) At a later point in the letter, Plato has occasion to disparage attempts to expound in writing ultimate metaphysical principles, as Dionysius has purported to do, in a book which he has published; and in this connection Plato mentions the prerequisites to grasping these principles: love of wisdom, disposition to sober living, long application in association with a master, or, later on, independently (340 C-D). Presently Plato adds the all-essential precondition to any degree of success in the enterprise: the candidate must have natural goodness of soul, kinship to the objective goodness of which he is in search, as well as the necessary intellectual powers; without these, "Lynceus himself could not make him see" (344 A). It would be open to Crossman to argue that the educative ideals here under discussion are essentially those of the ideal rulers of the *Republic,* and that Plato's association of them with his own attempts to promote the education of Dionysius proves that Plato had all along, up to the moment of ultimate failure, been grooming Dionysius for the office of philosopher king in the full sense. Also lending support to this view is the passage in the third letter (319 C) which records that Plato had prescribed for Dionysius the study of geometry as a preliminary to the carrying out of legal reforms.

(3) One other sentence in the letter lends support to Crossman's view. Plato, it will be remembered, is offering advice to the friends of Dion as to the settlement of Sicilian affairs, now that Dion has passed from the scene. He has recommended the summoning of a legislative commission to draw up laws for Syracuse and the lesser cities of the island. But in the sentence in question (337 D) he declares that such an arrangement is only the "second" best, in contrast to what he had hoped to accomplish in association with Dionysius, the "first" or truly best plan, "good things common to all." This latter phrase, standing in loose connection with the rest of the sentence, is commonly interpreted as a brief description or identification of the first plan. The sentence, then, can be understood to mean that the "first," or truly best, is identical with the basic pattern of the *Republic,* and can be read as Plato's explicit statement that his original intent at Syracuse was the establishment of the ideal city. The chief support of this interpretation is found in the *Laws* (739 A-E), where, referring to the constitution of the *Republic,* or to one that differs from it only by going further in the same direction of communism, Plato puts it "first," in contrast to the type of city aimed at in the *Laws,* which is "second in point of excellence."

We must now weigh, one against the other, the two interpretations of Plato's plan for Syracuse, beginning with the part assigned to Dionysius. In the face of the evidence, it cannot be denied that Plato originally hoped, on the strength of Dion's recommendation, to turn Dionysius into a philosopher or lover of wisdom, in some sense of that adjustable word. Absolute power, or so Plato believed, lay already in his hand; and thus he would fulfill the requirement of the combination of power with philosophy. But here we must not be led into accepting a choice between the rival errors of "all" or "none," with no permission to accept a modest intermediate "some," in respect to the degree of philosophic wisdom required. It is no doubt true that Plato would have been delighted to carry Dionysius as "high as metaphysic wit could fly," had that young man exhibited the requisite strength of wing; later on, on his second visit to the young monarch, Plato did make trial of his fitness for the higher flights, and found him wanting. No doubt, also, Plato was well aware of the long and arduous discipline the candidate would have to endure in order first to overcome his moral miseducation, and then to acquire the minimum intellectual grounding for exemplary virtue, and for this purpose he may well have considered geometry a useful study. Yet it is very unlikely that Plato felt it a necessary condition for the substantial success of his venture that Dionysius should complete a program of studies in all branches of mathematics and in dialectics, culminating in the immediate vision of the Good, such as that sketched in the *Republic* for the higher education of the guardians.

Our contention may be enforced by reference to the case of Dion. Plato's confidence in him was apparently unlimited, and his death, Plato pronounced in the Seventh Letter, was as great a blow to the cause of philosophic rule as the refusal of Dionysius II to enter upon the life of philosophy. Dion, though not himself in the strategic position of ruler, had been able to spread the right appraisal of values among some of the young men of the Syracusan court, with Plato's full approval (327 B-D); we even hear of his having imparted some knowledge of philosophical doctrines (338 D). Yet Dion, to all appearances, had enjoyed only a very limited opportunity to pursue philosophy into its more advanced and technical reaches. True, there is every reason to suppose that he had eagerly read and pondered Plato's dialogues as they successively appeared, and had in the process developed fuller insight into the principles of the Platonic philosophy. But his claims to be a "philosopher" appear to have reposed for Plato, who so styles him (336 B) in the Seventh Letter, primarily upon his noble enthusiasm for virtue and his steadfast subordination of all opposing claims to those of justice. No more than this, possibly less, is what Plato would have felt it necessary to achieve in the education of Dionysius. And this would be much; for should this be realized, then Plato could hope that power joined to the wisdom of virtue, accompanied by the promulgation of good laws, and resulting in the morality and happiness of a nation, would stand as a beacon for the illumination of "the whole world of Greeks and barbarians" (VII, 335 D, 336 B). Herein is contained explicit indication of awareness and concern on Plato's part, if the Seventh Letter is genuine, for that wider community of mankind for which Popper was unable to detect in him anything but hostility.[3]

3 [See Karl Popper, *The Open Society and Its Enemies.* Vol. I: *The Spell of Plato* (London: Routledge, 1945), p. 134.]

We have not yet met the argument derived from the parallelism between the prerequisites to philosophical insight as described in Letter VII and that combination of qualities and pursuits exacted of the candidates for the highest office in the *Republic*. What in my view goes far to turn the force of this argument is the context of the passage in the letter, which is nonpolitical. Plato is talking epistemology and metaphysics. The question is how a knowledge of first principles can be reached, such as would be requisite for describing them in a treatise like that which Dionysius was reported to have written (an attempt that Plato deprecates in any case). Plato is describing something far above that minimum "love of wisdom" which he would have felt necessary for any sort of philosophic ruler, even assuming him to be assisted by skilled and philosophically trained advisers, as Dionysius would have been by Dion and Plato. Nor is he describing the basic level of conceptual competence which the beginning study of geometry was intended to promote—if the third letter and Plutarch are correct in reporting that this formed part of Plato's curriculum for Dionysius.

What we are here arguing, in short, is the perhaps somewhat uncustomary view that Plato, in speaking of his great hope that a true love of philosophy should arise among the mighty, was willing if necessary to accept in such exalted persons an equipment less than maximum, if only the king in question was amenable to instruction and was himself virtuous, and to adjust accordingly the type of political organization which should be adopted. A sort of symbiosis of the ruler and his philosophic advisers was tacitly assumed for at least the period during which the new constitution was being shaped and imposed. The future course of affairs was left vague, possibly on the assumption that the ruler, having submitted himself to the laws, would withdraw so far as his duties permitted into those more delightful occupations of the spirit of which in the *Republic* Plato speaks with such conviction. Thus in time he might come to possess in his own right philosophic insight. Plato has not confided to us his plans or expectations in this respect. But he may consistently with his principles have believed that such a king would by his blameless and disinterested conduct so win the esteem of the citizens that, as occasion arose, he would be consulted in national crises, and so would continue to exert a beneficent influence despite his abandonment of absolute power.

There remains in support of the view that we are maintaining what is, I think, our least disputable piece of evidence. We are offered in the *Laws* (711 E ff.) a brief sketch of the cooperative relationship between a young tyrant, who is "temperate, quick at learning, with a good memory, brave, and of a noble manner," who is also "fortunate . . . only in this, that in his time there should arise a praiseworthy lawgiver, and that, by a piece of good fortune, the two of them should meet"; from such a conjunction there arises, more quickly and easily than in any other way, the best state. And this is effected primarily by the example and influence of the monarch, who distributes honor and dishonor, reward and degradation, in accord with the true and valid standards of "reason's dictates, called by the name of 'law' " (713 E).

It is possible to see in this Plato's retrospective comment on his Sicilian experience, his reassertion that what he had hoped to accomplish was still highly desirable and, in a favorable case, possible. We are also, on this assumption, given a clue to exactly what it was which to Plato's mind was responsible for the failure with Dionysius: the tyrant must possess temperance, not of the philosophic kind which is identical with wisdom, but that "ordinary kind . . . which by natural instinct springs up at birth in children and animals, so that some are . . . continent, in respect to pleasures" (710 A). It seems to be plain from this passage that Plato did not expect the young tyrant to supply from within himself the necessary wisdom, at least in the early stages; though it is provokingly obvious, also, that Plato does not draw so precise a line as could be wished between the respective functions of the partners in the association.

But if Dionysius was expected to acquire only a limited philosophical insight, there is no longer any reason to suppose that Plato would have sanctioned a code of laws which left such a ruler in possession of absolute power. That is to say, once the supposition is abandoned that Dionysius was to become in his own person the completely trained lawgiver, we may revert to our earlier stated view, and take in its obvious sense Plato's statement that Syracuse must be enslaved not to men but to laws. The aim of Plato was to abolish the tyranny as such, and from his repeated coupling of the contemplated government that was to replace it with the "rule of law," we feel justified in rejecting any identification of Plato's plan for Syracuse with a program in which law was overshadowed by the benevolent omniscience of its idealized rulers, and in concluding, as we have said above, that constitutional monarchy, with the right of hereditary succession, was the intended form of rule.

This view is reinforced by a consideration which Crossman has not confronted: if the *Republic* was to have been realized at Syracuse, an absolute prerequisite would have been the voluntary renunciation by Dionysius of all right to transmit his power to his descendants, and the handing over the authority to choose future rulers of Syracuse to a self-perpetuating group of philosopher-guardians, which, if we follow Crossman, would have been set up under Plato's direction by selection of candidates from among the sons of the nobility or members of the court circle of Syracuse. The abdication of Dionysius himself would also have been entailed, had the scheme been carried out consistently, as soon as among the crop of new philosophers one or more should be found who were his superiors. To have proposed to a reigning tyrant any such idea would certainly have been wildly unrealistic; and there is, in fact, no hint that either Dion or Plato ever included it in his most distant plans.

If, then, we assert that Dionysius was not expected to become, in the full sense, a philosopher king, and that the new government of Syracuse was to be a constitutional, hereditary monarchy, it may be felt that we have still not sufficiently accounted for Plato's and Dion's predictions of "unbounded felicity" for Sicily; it may be argued that the author of the *Republic* could have anticipated so happy a result only if the reformed government of Syracuse were to correspond closely with the particular institutional arrangements of his ideal state. Crossman, as we have seen, relying apparently on the sentence in Letter VII describing Plato's original plan as "first" in excellence, and particularly on the phrase "good things common to all," takes it for granted that Plato expected this pattern to be established in some detail, and that at no distant date. Yet this supposition is not so solidly grounded as at first appears. The phrase "good things common to all" has been plausibly rejected by Morrow as an intrusion into Plato's text of a marginal gloss by some early commentator. If this view be accepted, we are no longer required to believe that the "first" or best plan included the distinctive social institutions of the *Republic*. Had it done so, surely we might have looked for extensive indications, both earlier and later in the Sicilian letters, that Plato intended making so remarkable an alteration in the social landscape; but apart from the disputed sentence, they maintain an unbroken silence.

The notion that Plato's reforming imagination was inseparably attached to the particularities of the *Republic* is further weakened by a second consideration. The concluding section of the *Politicus,* a dialogue written some time after Plato's first visit to Dionysius II, sketches institutions markedly divergent from the scheme of the *Republic*. The account is short and by no means explicit, but it is clear that there is no separation of the citizens into three classes, nor is there any mention of communism of property or of wives. And yet, as truly as we so term the Republic, it is an ideal state, designed and supervised by the Statesman in person. Again, how very different are the institutions of the *Laws,* a state of Plato's mind only once removed from ideality. The conclusion of the matter would seem to be that Plato reserved the right to employ in his political planning as much or as little of the pattern of the *Republic* as the fitness of the occasion might suggest, keeping always to the principle that the laws and institutions of a state, in proportion to its excellence, must be so devised as to place power at the service of wisdom, embodied either in ideal rulers or in good laws, and to issue in the maximum attainment by its citizens of the whole of virtue, and of the highest degree of mutuality and harmony. The constitution of Syracuse might therefore, under its Platonic reformation, approximate the pattern of any state which should embody this principle. And in anticipating such a consummation, Plato and Dion might well have felt cause for rejoicing.

The Eighth Letter purports to have been written during the three-cornered civil war between the party of Dion and that of the exiled

Dionysius, with the advocates of a restored democracy taking the field against both. The recommendation of a legislative commission is made and a constitution briefly outlined (356 C-357 A). There are to be three kings, the respective heads of the three factions, but their powers are more symbolic than substantial; they are denied the right to exile, banish, or put to death citizens. For the rest, what we are told of the constitution strikingly resembles that of the *Laws*, upon which Plato was supposedly working at the time. This is the system to which Crossman refers as that of "cabinet responsibility to a popular assembly." It is to be a mixed or balanced government, with power divided between a board of Law-wardens, a council, and an assembly of the citizens. There are to be popular courts, but all capital cases are to be decided by a higher court composed of Law-wardens and exmagistrates. And this constitution is averred (357 A) to be that which Dion, after his capture of power, had intended to institute.

Plato retains his interest in the resettlement of the Greek cities of Sicily; his philhellenism is still in full flood (357 A-B). Meanwhile he urges immediate cessation of internecine conflict and a policy of conciliation (352 E ff.). There is much talking down of the importance of wealth (355 A-C), again in conformity with many passages in the *Laws*. And throughout, the utmost importance is attached to the rule of law, which is to exercise "despotic sway over the kings themselves as well as the rest of the citizens" (335 E). Of great interest to us for the backward light it throws upon Plato's present advice is that it is the same as "the counsel I gave of old. And now also my word of advice to every despot would be that he should shun the despot's title and his task, and change his despotism for kingship" (354 A).

By the aid of these statements regarding Plato's and Dion's earlier intentions we are enabled, by stages, to infer our way back to the general nature of the original plan. The finally proposed constitution is declared to be the same, with minor exceptions, as the program that Dion would have carried out after the expulsion of Dionysius; in the Seventh Letter, as we have reported, Plato had declared that what Dion would have accomplished under these same circumstances would have contributed as much to the cause of philosophy and to the benefit of mankind as could have been achieved had Dionysius proved capable of all that Plato hoped. We must, of course, not mistake these substantial similarities for outright identities. The final plan was, admittedly, a dilution of a second plan (the one in which Dion was central), which was itself an unwelcome alternative to the original, which revolved about Dionysius. But enough remained to determine an important measure of agreement. There was, in any case, to be a constitution, which would impose substantial limitations upon the power of the king. The powers thus lost would necessarily have been transferred to certain other legally established authorities. The Seventh Letter did not tell us how these other authorities were to be constituted, but from the assertions of the

Eighth Letter, quoted above, it is a reasonable inference that the framework of kings, Law-wardens, council, popular assembly, and courts of appeal was part of the original scheme, with the single structural difference that, in the first and second versions, there would have been but one king. If these inferences are sound, the conclusion that no attempt to reproduce the Republic was ever under view, needs no further proof, and it is clearly the framework of the city of the *Laws,* with the addition of a philosophically virtuous monarch, which Plato's original plan for Syracuse had more closely resembled. And now, from this he had been obliged to accept a reduction and again a further reduction.

It is plain to see how the two "second-best" plans for Sicily represent an abatement from Plato's ideal of the practicable best. In the first place, while Plato was by no means willing, as Crossman has said he was, that "the best of the existing aristocracy should become dictators," it appears that he was willing to concede, as a practical expedient and part of the "second-best" plan, that they should serve as legislative commissioners. As we have seen, Plato believed, not without some justification in the actual social conditions of his day, that effective intelligence was more likely to be found among the wealthy, who could afford the luxury of leisure and education, and believed also, apparently, that a distinguished family was a fairly reliable index of human quality as judged at a distance. Presumably he also thought that wealth would render the commissioners proof against the influence of bribes, and that their lineage would lend prestige to the results of their labors.

We can regret that Plato failed to see, as we so clearly discern, that fifty men of property, chosen neither as social philosophers nor as philanthropic saints, however disinterested they might be in relation to persons and to local issues, would be very likely to legislate in favor of their own economic class. As at least a partial offset to this tendency, however, we may remember that the Eighth Letter (and perhaps the Seventh Letter intended to do the same) makes it a basic requirement that in the framing of the constitution the interests of the democratic principle shall be conserved. And he plainly saw the interval between these laymen and the intellectually trained and practically experienced legislator, with eyes fixed on the harmony and virtue of the whole state, whose place he and Dion might have supplied. His second point of concession was the substitution for the originally intended, highly moralized monarch, of the three kings, one of them in the tarnished person of the philosopher *manqué,* the no longer young Dionysius II. And of course it was necessary for Plato to forego all mention of those educational, sociological, and economic innovations characteristic of the theoretic city of the *Laws,* which it would have been pedantically unrealistic to introduce into such a context.

On the opposite side of the ledger, Plato was able to declare his faith in the following principles: (1) The necessity of tempering aristocratic rule by a moderate recognition of the democratic principle, or conversely.

This idea, to which we find Plato giving full and emphatic expression in the *Laws,* was none the less sincere despite the fortunate circumstance that in the context of the Silician situation he was able to advocate the offering of it as a concession to the partisans of democracy. On occasion, a philosopher also can be a diplomat. (2) The prime necessity of putting an end to civic division and turmoil, and the constitutional safeguarding of all citizens against summary violence and oppression. (3) The subordination of the concern for wealth to higher values. (4) And, finally, the principle upon which we have found him constantly laying the greatest stress, subservience, equally binding on all classes and factions in the state, to the rule of law.

The application of these four principles in the imperfect form alone possible in the face of the factional division that had developed, could not have seemed to Plato the full equivalent of what he and Dion had originally hoped to procure for the Sicilian realm, or even of what Dion alone might have accomplished; yet the resulting polity would have been in its degree acceptable and consonant with his ideals. Syracuse, so strikingly like Athens as to have prompted Thucydides to compare the two in mentality and outlook—a great maritime, commercial city, and thus liable, as was Athens on Plato's view, to all the resulting moral infections—and, moreover, a city undoubtedly actual, not theoretically existing only—was thus to be provided with a constitution resembling in general outline that of Solon. It seems probable, therefore, that this would also have been his minimum plan for the reformation of Athens, with the solemn proviso that it must be achievable without bloodshed.

III. Aristotle

One aim of Richard McKeon's Selection (8) is to situate Aristotle with respect to his predecessors. The Aristotelian scientific method includes a correction of the two extreme positions of Plato and Democritus concerning the nature of the real and hence concerning science. Plato admits forms and principles, but keeps them separate from sensible things; Democritus' atomism gives speculation a basis in the material world, but fails to provide any adequate account of generality, specific differences, and causality. Aristotle's "middle method" combines the foundation in sensible fact with the formal structure and the causal principles. Furthermore, it maintains a certain order of inquiry, such that we begin with the sensible things which are best known to us, and proceed to the forms and causes which are most intelligible in themselves but which are known by us through demonstration. When facts are seen in their universal significance, and forms in their particular embodiment, then the conditions of a human science are realized and demonstration can be made in certain areas. The Aristotelian theory of scientific inquiry is oriented toward this synthesis of sensible data and formal structures and causes, at least to the extent that it can be achieved within the given limitations of our kind of sensible world and our kind of sensuous-and-rational knowledge.

McKeon underlines another fact of analytic balance and differentiation in Aristotle. There need be no rivalry between the special sciences and the most general explanations of logic and metaphysics. Each of the sciences is constituted by its own problems, subject matter, and formal method of inquiry. These distinctive factors are never cancelled out or rendered deductively superfluous in the wake of the search for common first principles of thought and being, since no attempt is made to derive all facts and theories a priori from some overarching logical formula or metaphysical agency. In the Organon or group of logical treatises dealing with the method of scientific and dialectical inquiry, Aristotle's native caution is displayed in two ways, both of which effectively set off his philosophy from any thoroughgoing rationalism. First, his distinction be-

tween the evidence for the intrinsic validity of a principle and the evidence for its applicability in a particular case shows that one cannot simply invoke the certainty of a general principle to resolve the particular issue. *The human mind never dispenses with the need for constant observation of the factual situation* and the special formal considerations in each field. In the second place, Aristotle insists upon *the difference between the order of being and the order of knowing*, as far as human speculative knowledge is concerned. The way in which natural things come to be is not the same as the way in which we come to know them or to demonstrate their connection. *Hence there cannot be any simple identification of the logical connections and the real relations, even though the former are designed ultimately to lead us to the latter* and elucidate them for us.

The hazard of overlooking these points and thus of transforming Aristotle into the image of some later philosophies is noted by Father Joseph Owens. In Selection (9), he addresses himself to the thorny question of the unmoved movers, as presented in Book Lambda of the Metaphysics. *The main interpretation under fire here is an idealistic view that the Aristotelian movers are not intended as existent beings,* but are only ideal goals entertained in the minds of the agents which animate the heavens. But Owens also warns against equating the first unmoved mover unqualifiedly with the Judaeo-Christian God and then reducing the other movers either to a lower plane of being or to a subjective status. The noble way in which Aristotle describes the inner life of thought belonging to the first mover, has certainly encouraged this identification or at least has predisposed the theistic reader to find the full perfection of the Godhead in this mover. *But the treatment of a being's nature cannot be divorced from that of its existence*, especially in the case of beings which we can come to know only through inferential means. When these two aspects of the doctrine on the first mover are kept together, there are certain difficulties which militate against accepting either of the above explanations of the movers of the heavens.

Owens exhibits the primary effort of the historian to understand a philosophical text within its own intellectual horizon, and to refrain at least temporarily from viewing it in reference to its subsequent influence and one's own position on the subject. Within the context of Aristotle's metaphysics, *there is no good ground for attributing to him the notion that the heavenly movers are only generalized conceptions of desirable perfections which are being sought by the celestial souls.* Each mover must be an individual, actual, causing, and thinking substance—traits which make it independent of being a valuational ideal in the mind of a celestial soul. The relation between the first unmoved mover and the God of Christian theism is a much more complex problem, and the literature dealing with it is vastly beyond the possibility of giving it definitive treatment in an article. The question is complicated by the analysis which would have to be made of the movers in the Physics and of Aristotle's conception of efficient causality. Nevertheless, Owens establishes some significant points concerning the line of discussion in the Metaphysics. *The unmoved movers are many and not unique;* they are all separate formal acts, on *the same level of being with the first mover;* apart from their difference as forms, the movers are otherwise unrelated and self-sufficient; they exercise only final causality. Aristotle does speak of a single general or ruler, but his scientific methodology requires him to have many independent movers *because of the observed fact of several irreducible heavenly motions.* From the standpoint of an experiential and realistic theism, the difficulty does not lie in the fact that the Stagirite employs an a posteriori type of demonstration, but rather in the *limitation of the inquiry to the final cause of a given sensible motion as motion.*

Aristotle's logical and metaphysical studies did not blunt his mind to the distinctive nature of ethical inquiry. In the Nicomachean Ethics, he exemplified his own methodological rule about adapting oneself to the subject matter and the available means for knowledge. *He drew that matter for ethics from the individual moral choices, along with all the elements of desire and knowledge affecting those choices.* In his analysis of the moral judgment, Father Clifford Kossel concentrates Selection (10) upon the center of gravity for Aristotelian ethics. Through his account of moral judgment, *the Stagirite was able to avoid the extremes of a conventional theory and a purely rationalistic one.* Moral choice is not simply the expression of social pressure and individual passion, powerful as these influences are. The moral man tries to choose a reasonable course, *one that will fulfill his natural inclination toward a humane sort of happiness. He cannot isolate the particular act from the general moral truths, and yet he cannot deduce the practical conclusion from general premises alone.* The problem of moral judgment is thus unavoidably complex, since it *involves a discernment of the mutual relevance of the ultimate end, the practical principle for some area of conduct, and the particular action in view.*

All of these factors must be seized upon by the thoughtful agent, not in their separate structures but precisely in their practical convergence for the concrete moral act. That is why Aristotle lays such stress upon the training of appetite by laws and customs, by instruction from men of practical wisdom, and by one's own habits and experience gained through previous moral choices. Kossel notes the distinctive sort of knowledge obtained by the responsive mind, operating under the best conditions in the moral order. When Aristotle calls this knowledge an "opinion," he does not intend to classify it as a likely conjecture or always as probability. Moral conviction can be certain knowledge, but its concern with the particular and the contingent prevents it from meeting the Aristotelian requirements for scientifically demonstrated knowledge.

8

ARISTOTLE'S SCIENTIFIC METHOD OF ANALYSIS [1]

FOR Aristotle, the inquiry into the nature of things depends on divesting from thought and statement all elements that might be due to the peculiarities of thinking and formulation and on bringing them to as close conformity as possible, in whole and part, with the nature of things of which the statement is true. With respect to form and essence, it is important to consider the relation of the parts of the formula to the parts of the thing, for the parts of the form are parts of the concrete thing and they are sometimes prior, sometimes posterior to the whole. With respect to matter and potentiality, matter is in itself unknowable, and potentiality can be grasped, not by definition or formula, but only by induction and analogy. Finally, the nature of the first mover raises problems concerning divine thought which are solved by the recognition that in some cases knowledge and the thing are identical; for in the productive sciences, if matter be disregarded, the substance or the essence of artificial things is the object of knowledge, while in the theoretical sciences the formula or the act of thinking is the object, and in both cases the thing and knowledge are identical.

If the movement of inquiry in metaphysics is from predicates to the discovery of the subjects which exist independently and underlie the predicates attributed to them and the qualities that inhere in them, the movement of inquiry in logic is from the subjects to the characteristics

---

[1] [From Richard McKeon, "Aristotle's Conception of the Development and the Nature of Scientific Method," *Journal of the History of Ideas*, vol. 8 (1947), pp. 34-44. Reprinted by permission. Many notes are omitted.]

of predicates as unitary independent terms, or as parts of propositions, or as middle terms in arguments, or finally as related to their respective subjects in the premisses of arguments. Inquiry into statement and proof requires translation into symbolic or linguistic terms of the meanings attached to words, and that inquiry takes the form of determining the unity of the term, the proposition, the argument, and the premiss; and the grounds of unity for each are found sometimes in verbal formulations, sometimes in characteristics which language shares with thought but not with things, sometimes in criteria determined by the nature of things. The importance of the problem of symbolic unity is marked vividly by the recurrent use which Aristotle makes of the example of the unity of the *Iliad* as a collection of words in contrast to the unity of a definition or a proposition which is not verbal or artificial but depends on the nature of things external to the statement; and the isolation of marks of unity in each case leads, as do similar inquiries into what is prior in knowledge and what is prior in being, to differentiation of kinds of discourse and marks of the various functions to which language may be put.

The transition to questions of discourse and argument raises the characteristic questions of Aristotle's scientific method, for whereas the subject matters of the natural sciences are natural things and the processes of knowledge are natural processes, the meanings and uses of words are conventional. Yet when words are used to express meanings, or to state what is conceived to be true, or to infer from one statement to another, they are defined, or delimited, by their functions relative to things, ideas, and other terms. So defined, the regress of terms in discourse, like the regress of cause in nature, must be finite: there is a limited number of kinds of terms distinguished by their characteristics into categories; there is a limited number of relations which terms may have to each other which differentiate the quantity, quality, and modality of predication; there is a limited number of figures and modes of syllogistic inference; finally there is a limited number of premisses dependent on a limited number of terms which extend from the ultimate subject, which is the individual thing, to the attribute, which is predicable of a subject but not itself a subject, through a finite number of intermediate terms. Unless predications have a downward limit in the descent to particularity and an upward limit in the ascent to universality, as well as a finite number of steps between these two extremes, scientific demonstration is impossible; but that limitation in turn depends on the knowability of essential nature and the differentiation of accidental from "natural" predication. Scientific demonstration, therefore, depends on first premisses in which first essential predicates are asserted of their subjects. The immediate premisses on which demonstration depends are known immediately by intellect or intuition, because there are no prior premisses on which they may be made to depend and there are no middle terms by which to prove the connection of their subjects and predicates.

The first principles of demonstration coincide with what is first and best known in nature and with the first principles of things.

The scientific method of Aristotle is essentially a method of differentiation. The name which he liked to use to set forth the central devices of proof and to distinguish demonstration from other manners of proof was "analytics," and the statement of scientific method or demonstration depends on differentiating the part played by the use of symbols, the processes of thought, and the nature of things in resolving problems. The objective sought in science, the statement of truth, is possible because of coincidences in the structures of the three, while statements of opinion and fallacy mark their deviations. In a sense, only concrete substances exist, but the nature of concrete substance consists most truly in its essence, which is universal, not in the aggregate of accidents which inhere in it. What we perceive by the senses is therefore the particular, yet we know the particular only in its principles and causes. Science is of the universal, yet a science which does not account for concrete phenomena is empty or erroneous. All science depends on knowledge of first principles which are known immediately and indubitably; and yet all knowledge, including knowledge of first principles, is derived from experience, and it is extremely difficult to be sure when we have knowledge.

These are paradoxes only if the distinctions which Aristotle struggled to enforce are forgotten. They have continued to seem paradoxes because ironically the dialectical distinctions by which Aristotle moved away from the doctrines of his predecessors have been used as the currency of philosophic discussion, and he has been held to a standard set by choice between distinctions which he originated to serve as signs of incompleteness. The differentiation between things better known to us and things better known in nature, was intended to correct the one-sidedness of theories that sought truth exclusively in thought or in sense; but this distinction has been used in the study of his works to separate them into an early "rationalistic" or Platonic portion and a later "empirical" or scientific portion. Aristotle argued that first philosophy or metaphysics was necessary as a separate science, in part to correct the errors of philosophers who made ideas things or who, conversely, reduced all processes to matter, for a separate science of first principles is impossible in either a system of universal dialectic or an all-embracing science of atoms; yet the discussion of metaphysics has since Aristotle's time divided doctrines primarily into idealism and materialism. His logic, finally, in which terms conventional in significance are related in their functions to the thoughts they express and the things they signify for the purpose of setting up a scientific demonstration which follows from principles at once of proof and of things, has been treated and criticized as a "formal" logic; or alternatively its elementary distinctions, like the categories, the predicables, and the "common-places," have been transformed into metaphysical principles.

Yet the content and construction of Aristotle's scientific achievements and the methodological presuppositions on which they are based can be understood only if the application of this middle method to facts and phenomena is kept mid-way, as he sought to keep it in the formulation of his scientific conclusions, between the extreme of materialistic, empirical nominalism and the extreme of idealistic, rationalistic realism. These distinctions were, in a sense, Aristotle's invention for a simplified dialectical description of the doctrines of Democritus and Plato, but they have been used by philosophers as keys to the understanding of Aristotle and as marks of his deficiencies. When Aristotle treats of principles he is easily taken for a forgetful or timid Platonist; and therefore portions of the *Metaphysics* and of the *Organon* have been separated from less "Platonic" portions by scholars who argue that almost any concern for principles must belong—when the two "periods" are not too obviously intermingled —to the period of Aristotle's early prescientific apprenticeship to the Academy. When he treats of scientific questions, on the other hand, his enthusiasm for phenomena and facts is taken as a likeness to Democritus, for he attributes a similar scientific enthusiasm to the atomists; and then he is critized chiefly for holding the vestiges of philosophical ideas whose absence he deprecated in Democritus. The oppositions which Aristotle formulates in terms of the doctrines of Democritus and Plato, therefore, have prevented rather than facilitated the shift which it was Aristotle's purpose to make from the dialectical consideration of principles in relation to what men have thought to their scientific consideration in relation to what the facts are.

Aristotle's scientific method, considered in relation to things, is a method of differentiation and analysis rather than of reduction and analogy, and therefore particular sciences are distinguished from each other in such fashion that each science has its proper subject matter, principles, and method. His metaphysics is not constructed as a universal explanation suited to solve all problems and explain all phenomena, nor is his logic a deductive system in which all sciences are derived ultimately from a few principles, but rather both grow out of the effort to formulate particular theories and to examine particular problems. He thought of sciences in the plural, each science consisting of a homogeneous set of problems, concerned with a single genus of things, possessed of principles peculiar to it and a method adapted to its proper investigations. But to recognize peculiar principles in individual sciences is to recognize the need for common first principles by which to distinguish and relate the sciences. The problems of metaphysics are problems of first principles and things; the problems of logic are problems of first principles and proof. Both are concerned with the double problem involved in relating principles to individual circumstances. In logic the pair of problems turns, first, on the grounds on which those first or common principles, which are subject to no direct demonstration, may be alleged, and, second, on the significances of statements and terms, whether or not they are constructed into demonstration dependent on first principles.

In application to the particular sciences, scientific method depends on particular principles and is applied to a limited class of subjects. Metaphysical questions concerning the nature of being as such, the justification of principles, or the demonstration of the existence of the subject matter of the sciences are not proper problems to any of the particular sciences. The physicist need not pause to consider whether or not Being is fundamentally one and motionless, and the geometer need not refute the man who denies the principles of his science. Problems of logic, on the other hand, are involved in the very material of science, and scientific inquiry and proof are the illustration of logic, while logic, in the Aristotelian tradition, is an "instrument" of science. The three sets of distinctions bearing on subject matter, principles, and form of inference, which have been observed in Aristotle's dialectical statement of his scientific method in counter-distinction to the methods of Democritus and Plato, serve to mark the characteristics of his method which make possible the translation of its operation into terms and propositions: his deference to facts, his demand for principles, and his reduction of data and theories to terms of formal analysis.

The effort in any scientific analysis is to proceed from the facts of sense experience to those things better known in nature which may serve as principles for general scientific proof. The possibility of scientific demonstration depends on knowledge of first principles, which is more certain than the scientific demonstration which follows from it and which is, therefore, once achieved, indubitable. Yet the certainty of such knowledge is not inconsistent with the recognition that it is only rarely achieved and difficult to recognize. In any case of conflict between theory and empirical data, formal preconceptions must be abandoned in favor of adherence to facts. Not only are the principles of all sciences derived originally by induction from experience, but they are checked ultimately by their adequacy to account for phenomena, and Aristotle therefore pauses from time to time, as he does for example in discussing the generation of bees, to point out insufficiencies in observation and to assert the dependence of theory finally on improved observation.

> This seems to be the manner in which the generation of the bees occurs, both according to argument and according to what seems to take place among the bees. What takes place, however, has not yet been explored sufficiently, but if it ever is, then credit must be given to sensation rather than arguments, and to arguments only if they accord with the observed phenomena.[2]

The error of some of the older philosophers consisted precisely in disregarding sense-perception on the ground that one ought to follow the argument. What is to be sought in general is accord between facts

---

[2] *On the Generation of Animals* iii. 10. 760ᵇ27-33.

and arguments, and theories are acceptable only if the consequences which follow from them are verifiable in the facts of sense perception. In the practical sciences, likewise, the opinions of the wise are consulted and their agreement lends force to arguments, even when the wise disagree with most men, who perceive only externals and therefore judge by them, but ultimately the resolution of moral and political problems depends on reference to the facts.

So the opinions of the wise seem to be in agreement with our arguments. But while even such considerations carry some conviction, the truth in practical matters is judged from operations and life, for the decisive factor is to be found in them. We must therefore examine what we have already said by bringing it to the test of operations and life, and if it is in harmony with those operations we must accept it, but if it disagrees with them we must suppose it to be merely arguments.[3]

Arguments, however, differ from sensation and observation and depart from their minuteness and accuracy of detail.

The success of any scientific analysis, on the other hand, depends not only on fidelity to fact, but on isolating true principles and causes; for, in the first place, principles and causes separate essential from accidental relations among the attributes observed in experience; and, in the second place, after essential natures have been defined, principles and causes are the source of explanation of the inherence of other attributes in the thing. We are said to know truly only when we know the principles and causes of things; and the infinity of irrelevant facts can be separated from those which are susceptible of scientific explanation, and the facts and relations pertinent to scientific inquiry can be differentiated with respect to the particular sciences and their problems only by use of principles and causes. The chief difficulty with scientific principles does not arise in questions of their self-evidence or certainty, but in questions of their relevance; and errors result not only from following the lead of preconceptions without taking sufficient account of the facts of observation, but also from assuming falsely that we know because we have applied true principles to particular things without noting whether or not the principles are applicable to that kind of subject matter or that genus of thing.

It is difficult to know whether one knows or not, for it is difficult to know whether one knows from the principles of the particular things or not, and this is the essence of knowing. We think that we have scientific knowledge if we have reasoned from some true and first premisses; but that is not the case, for it is necessary that the terms of the proof be of the same genus as the first principles.[4]

The problems in the particular sciences consist in the special principles of those sciences, not in appeal beyond the science to common principles of several or all sciences. Such problems fall outside the scope

3 *Nicomachean Ethics* x. 8. 1179ᵃ16-22.
4 *Posterior Analytics* i. 9. 76ᵃ26-30. Cf. *ibid.* 75ᵇ37-76ᵃ3.

of the scientist; he should assume both the existence of his subject matter and the fundamental principles involved in it, and he should take
as his task the demonstration that his principles are connected with the
class of facts on which his inquiry turns and that they do explain those
facts. Thus in his discussion of the sterility of mules, after refuting the
doctrines of Empedocles and Democritus, Aristotle entertains the possibility that a more dialectical or, as he calls it, "logical" proof might
be more plausible, justifying his use of the expression "logical proof"
because "the more universal it is the further removed it is from the special and proper principles." The dialectical alternative to the theory
of Democritus is rejected precisely because of its departure from proper
principles.

> For this argument is too universal and empty, for arguments which are not
> based on proper [i.e., special] principles are empty, and only seem to pertain to
> the things, but do not really. For as geometrical arguments are based on geo-
> metrical principles, so also in the other sciences; that which is empty may seem
> to be something, but is really nothing.[5]

The special principles irrelevant to one subject matter may sometimes
be more proper to other subjects within the same science; or they may require mention in a science, although their subject matter is proper to
another science; or in the course of generalization it may turn out that
phenomena explained by principles proper to them may also be explained by more universal principles when the phenomena share their
essential characteristics with a larger class of phenomena.

In logic as in other inquiries there are appropriate arguments and
problems, and the translation of problems of knowledge and nature into
problems of inquiry and proof is a translation of facts and principles
into their expression in symbols and terms. All inquiry is a search for
middle terms, and although neither the facts which are investigated nor
the principles which are indemonstrable are subjects of logic, except insofar as they are in some manner subject to analysis or indirect proof,
both affect the structure of logical problems, since there is a single scientific knowledge of each single thing qua single, and the terms and
arguments of scientific proof, no less than the particulars that fall under
them, must be proper to and of the same genus as the principles. Principles and demonstrations are both analyzable into terms, and since
terms are expressive of the attributes—real, probable, or problematic—of
things, the problems of method, scientific or dialectic, may be reformu-
lated as a search for terms.

The method is the same in all instances, in philosophy, in any art, and in
learning. We must look for the attributes and subjects of both our terms, and
we must supply ourselves with as many of them as possible, and we must inquire
into them by means of the three terms—refuting in one way, confirming in another; starting from premises in which the terms are arranged in accordance

[5] *Ibid.* 748[a]7-11.

with truth when the proofs are by the standard of truth, and from probable premisses in dialectical proofs. . . . Most of the principles, however, in any particular science are peculiar to it. Consequently it is the function of experience to supply the principles pertinent to each science. I mean, for example, that astronomical experience is the source of astronomical science, for once the phenomena had been grasped sufficiently, the demonstrations of astronomy were discovered. It is the same in any other art or science. Consequently if we grasp the attributes of the particular thing, it will readily be in our power to set forth the demonstrations; for if none of the true attributes of the things has been omitted in accordance with history [i.e., such accumulations of data as are assembled in natural history, the history of animals, etc.], we shall be able, in the case of everything that admits of demonstration, to discover it and demonstrate it, and in the case of everything which does not admit of proof, to elucidate it.[6]

When the method has reached the point at which it is stated as a search for terms and the arrangement of terms in principles and proofs, the method is the same for all inquiries and studies, all arts and sciences, however diverse the subject matters to which the terms apply or the investigations by which they are isolated, or the principles by which they are related.

The method of Aristotle is not based on the assumption either that the mind will discover truth if it is reoriented toward the source of truth or that it will find truth within itself if the distractions of sense are removed, and therefore the method is not constructed to reproduce the stages of thought as they are normal to the human mind freed from the intrusion of error or the characteristics of things as they exist and evolve apart from the intrusion of the mind. A science, as Aristotle conceives sciences, may be treated in terms of its subject matter, or in terms of the ideas which guide the inquiry of the scientist and are compounded and analyzed in his proofs, or in terms of the symbols and propositions in which his problems and demonstrations are stated. What the scientist is concerned about is his subject matter; but he can treat his subject matter, in discovery or proof, only by means of the concepts that have been evolved relative to it; and he can exhibit to others, as the results of his labors, neither the things themselves nor his ideas about them, but only propositions and proofs in which he seeks to embody and communicate what he thinks true about the nature of things. When the exposition and proof are successful there is an identity between what is proved, what is known, and what is the case, but the events by which what is actual came about do not parallel the processes by which we know, and the methods of proof, even when efforts are made to be historical and empirical, are distinct from both the sequences of things and those of thought. When differences arise about the interpretation of things or the formulation of ideas, those differences are resolved in discussion of the statements expressive of what is thought to be true of things. The method by which what is expressed in statements is validated leads to

[6] *Prior Analytics* i. 30. 46ª3-27; cf. *Metaphysics* iv. 3. 1005ᵇ8-11.

the differentiation of sciences according to subject matter, principles, and method; and the examination of the method, in turn, depends for its success on a differentiation of the uses of terms—in themselves, in propositions, in syllogisms, and in principles. The working out of that differentiation is the task of the logical treatises now assembled in Aristotle's works under the title the *Organon*.

The differentiation of uses of terms depends on and reinforces the differences of the sciences. For if there were no difference between mathematical and physical definitions and methods of proof, there would be no need to differentiate the causes, and therefore no basis for separating physics, logic, or metaphysics from mathematics. The Aristotelian analysis of sciences depends on the differentiation of mathematics from physics and on the consequent separation of scientific method from metaphysical analysis. The use of the causes to differentiate truth from probability, error, and ignorance as a means of setting up criteria for scientific method is the other side of the use of the causes to differentiate the characteristics of being qua being from accidental, mental, or verbal qualifications of being as a means of setting up distinctions among the sciences and among the principles of things. The failures of earlier attempts to frame definitions and to employ method were due to inadequate analyses of the causes as well as to deficiencies of the dialectic of inference in mathematical or operational manipulations. The analysis of logic and scientific method depends on a like differentiation of parts and functions in statement and proof, and it encounters a like danger, for as each of the sciences which Aristotle differentiated may be—and has been—made into the basis and model for the unification of all sciences on theoretic, practical, or artistic grounds, so each of the parts of his analysis of symbols, as terms, statements, inferences, and principles, may be made the basis for an analysis which sweeps aside his distinctions and revolutionizes logic, while retaining his technical terms and devices so that logic, despite revolutions, was thought by philosophers as recent as Kant to have been without history from the time when he instituted it.

9

THE REALITY OF THE ARISTOTELIAN
SEPARATE MOVERS [1]

I

THE separate substances of the Aristotelian *Metaphysics* have received an amazing variety of interpretations in the modern era. A glance over the commentaries, monographs and periodical literature of the present century makes the wide divergence of opinion abundantly evident.

These substances have been considered in recent times, as in traditional interpretation, to be identical with the immobile Movers of the *Physics*. Both *Physics* and *Metaphysics* refer to the same *separate* substances. On the other hand, the immobile Movers of the *Physics* have been identified with the *immanent* souls of the Heavens, and so sharply distinguished from the separate substances of the *Metaphysics*. Then, in the opposite extreme, the Movers of the *Metaphysics* have been completely identified with the celestial souls. Or again, the first only of the Movers has been declared separate, and the others identified with the different sphere-souls, among which is the first Mover of the *Physics*. In still another interpretation the first Mover alone is separate, but the other immobile Movers are held to be the divine thoughts, identical with the first Mover. Even the first Mover has been interpreted as a thought in the mind of some other Being, as merely an ideal or standard of goodness which does not imply—though it need not exclude—any corresponding existent reality in the Aristotelian universe. [2]

The separate substances have further been explained as species of a genus. But such a genus has been held inadmissible, and the Movers have been related in the "prior and posterior" manner of the Platonic Ideal Numbers. The first Mover has been distinguished from the others as immobile both *per se* and *per accidens,* while the other Movers are of a nature that is immobile *per se* only. On the other hand, this verbal distinction in the text has been seen as making no essential difference whatever in the Movers. The plurality of these Movers has been declared

[1] [From Joseph Owens, C.Ss.R., "The Reality of the Aristotelian Separate Movers," *The Review of Metaphysics,* vol. 3 (1949-1950), 319-337. Reprinted by permission. Most of the notes and several paragraphs are omitted.]

[2] B. A. G. Fuller, "The Theory of God in Book *Lambda* of Aristotle's Metaphysics," *Philosophical Review,* vol. 16 (1907), p. 180; T. M. Forsyth, "Aristotle's Concept of God as Final Cause," *Philosophy,* vol. 22 (1947), 112-123; G. A. Lindbeck, "A Note on Aristotle's Discussion of God and the World," *Review of Metaphysics,* vol. 1 (1947-1948), 104-106.

an open contradiction to a supposed "monotheism" of the Stagirite, or explained historically as a different phase in the chronological development of his thought.

Needless to say, various nuances and interlockings of these interpretations complicate the situation still further. Many of the difficulties, it is true, arise from the deepest problems in Aristotelian thought, and have busied the commentators for centuries. But in the traditional controversies, the unmoved Movers were always looked upon as real and independently existing entities. There was difference of opinion about the precise level of reality to be assigned to them, but that they required no subsistent reality at all is something comparatively new. The view that an unmoved Mover could be merely a thought of some other Being, in the sense of an ideal or standard, is distinctly modern and invites a fresh consideration of the texts from this standpoint.

But can the topic be isolated for a short treatement without delving too deeply into the exhausting problems of the Aristotelian Primary Philosophy?

To a certain extent, probably sufficient for present purposes, it can. Some fundamental doctrines, however, will have to be accepted on appeal to the obvious meaning of the text. Other important tenets may be considered as admitted. In this way the discussion may be kept within reasonable bounds.

That an immobile Mover of the *Metaphysics* can function *only* as a final *cause,* and that its causality requires the Aristotelian Heavens to be animated, may be taken as admitted in this question, and indeed should now be beyond controversy. Both these tenets, in fact, are emphasized in a recent thought-provoking article which goes on to conclude "that on Aristotle's grounds, it is superfluous to assign existence to God." [3] Also, there is obviously no doubt that Aristotle himself considered his immobile Movers to be living Beings, enjoying the highest and fullest type of life. The text is clear and precise on this point, and is not disputed in the present context. But the question is whether the Stagirite's reasoning justifies this conclusion. Would not a standard or ideal that has no existence outside the thought of the one who strives after it suffice to fill the role of an Aristotelian immobile Mover? Does the Stagirite's explanation of the universe actually require a separate Mover or Movers which have their reality and existence—and in this sense "substantiality"—independently of the thought of the Beings which strive to imitate their perfection?

II

In its opening sentence, Book *Lambda* of the *Metaphysics* professes to be dealing with substance. It distinguishes three substances. Two of these are sensible (one eternal, the other perishable), and the third is im-

[3] G. A. Lindbeck, *op. cit.,* p. 105.

mobile. Sensible substance is changeable. It is considered as evident, and as evidently plural. It is treated by natural philosophy.

Immobile substance, on the other hand, is tentatively assigned to a different science. It is not seen as immediately evident. One has to show, first that there is such a substance, and secondly to determine whether it is unique or plural.

That there is such a substance is demonstrated by one argument only. This argument is based on the act and potency seen in sensible movement. It is developed in three stages.

The first stage proves that there must be some eternal substance. This initial conclusion follows from two premisses. The first premiss is that substances are prior to all other Beings—namely, to quality and quantity, etc., and to movement. This doctrine had already been established in the opening chapter of *Lambda*. The second premiss is that motion and time are eternal, time being either identical with or following upon movement. No proof is offered. The doctrine seems to be accepted from the *Physics*. From these two premisses it follows that there must be some eternal substance; for motion always presupposes substance, and if motion is eternal, the substance presupposed must be equally eternal. The unicity or successive plurality of such substance does not affect the argument at this stage. All that is required is that there always be some substance prior by nature to the movement.

The second stage of the argument shows that this substance has to be something *acting*. If it is only *able* to cause motion, motion need not follow; for it is possible that something which merely has the *power* to cause motion may not actually be causing it. The eternal substance in question, then, must actually be causing motion.

For this reason the Platonic eternal substances, the Forms, are not sufficient, unless there is in them a principle able to cause motion. Even this is not sufficient, or any other (Platonic) substance besides the Forms. If the substance is not actually causing motion, the eternal motion of the Heavens will not follow. Here the Platonic Forms are considered as merely potential, and not having of themselves the actuality required to cause the celestial motion.

The final stage proves that the cause required must not merely be actually causing motion, but that its very substance must be act. For if it were potential, i.e., if it were equally able to be or not be, it would still be possible for it not to be, and so the motion need not be eternal. Such substances (here the plural is used), therefore, can have no matter. Matter, as had already been shown, means *potency* for change.

Such is the reasoning of the Stagirite. The Mover so reached is something which is eternally acting, in a sense that requires its very substance to be the *acting*. There can be no element or aspect in it which is merely *able* to act. It can have no potency or matter. Only that kind of actual Being can account for the eternal motion of the Heavens.

Could a thought produced by a celestial soul have that type of actuality?

According to those who propose this interpretation, such a thought is reached by universalizing the notions of goodness, or Being, or act. Now such a universal, at least on Aristotelian principles, is always something potential. Actual thought, as well as what it immediately attains, is always a "this" (tode ti), something individual. For the same reason no universal could be substance in the context of the Primary Philosophy, nor a cause of individual generation in Book Lambda. The Platonic Ideas, which in this respect are equated with the universals, are in consequence described as potential. A universal, though hypostatized, remains in its nature something potential. Clearly, then, no standard or ideal formed on the basis of a universal has the type of actuality required by the Aristotelian argument.

But even though such a thought were reached by some other process which would allow it to be actual in the sense demanded by the Stagirite's reasoning, it would by that very actuality be immediately identified with the substance held to be producing it. It could not be a thought that is at all *able* to be produced by anything else, for it could not have potentiality in its nature. It would have to be a *thinking* of itself, and and so would be substance in its own right, with no dependence whatsoever upon the celestial soul.

Aristotle's reasoning, therefore, demands that the first cause of celestial motions be substance in its own right, and in no way dependent upon anything else for production or Being. In this sense it is separate from sensible things, even eternal sensible things. The Stagirite's principles, accordingly, fully justify his conclusion: "That there is then a substance eternal and immobile and separate from sensible things, is clear from what has been said." [4]

III

A further question asked is whether this substance is unique or plural.

The Stagirite answers that the number of immobile Movers has to be equal to the number of original motions observable in the Heavens. Each motion which cannot be reduced to the motion of the first Heaven must have a distinct immobile Mover as its cause. A plurality of such distinct motions is observable to the astronomers. There is consequently a corresponding plurality of immobile Movers.

Aristotle goes on to show that this number of the immobile Movers cannot be further multiplied through the supposition of many distinct universes, specifically the same but numerically different. The reason is that the *first* Mover cannot be multiplied, since it has no matter, and the movement which it causes is unbroken. There can accordingly be

[4] Metaphysics, 1073a 3-5.

only the one universe, and so there can be only the one set of separate Movers.

This reasoning establishes a plurality of immobile Movers, distinguished as first and second according to the order of the celestial motions. No other basis of distinction is provided by the argument.

What type of reality is to be accorded to each of these Movers?

In the first chapter of Book *Lambda,* sensible substance was looked upon as admitted by all. Plants and animals were mentioned as examples. Sensible substance, accordingly, is evident and is evidently plural. That is a matter of immediate observation. Immobile substance, on the other hand, had to be demonstrated. Only its effects were observable. These indicated that there was immobile substance, and that, like sensible substance, it was plural. The plurality in each case follows upon observation, in the one case immediate, in the other case through demonstration from observable effects. In neither case is there any attempt to deduce unicity or plurality *a priori* from the nature of either sensible or immobile substance, and in neither case may the Greek use of the singular with the article in introducing the theme be taken to preclude the supposition of plurality.

What type of *form* does this reasoning imply?

It is quite evidently a form which is "a this." It is something individual as such, though without being a singular of a species. Such a form is not reached by a process of universalization or abstraction. It is the individual form seen in each sensible thing. This form in sensible things is the actualization of a potency. It is of its very nature distinct from other forms—the form of a plant is different as form from the form of an animal. Only when the specifically same form is multiplied is a *per se* unintelligible principle (i.e., matter) required, which can be added to the form without making any formal difference which would change the species. An Aristotelian form, accordingly, is of its own nature individual and distinct from all other forms. It allows no further principle, such as matter, to account for this difference. Individual sensible motion, according to the Aristotelian analysis, requires individual act and potency in the mobile thing, and everything which has matter is mobile. But motion also requires, as its ultimate cause, a correspondingly individual act which has no potency, and so is individual form without matter, and entirely immobile.

Such a form is conceived, not as a universal, but after the manner of an individual sensible form, minus the relation to matter. Because it is actual, it cannot be a universal. Like the forms involved in sensible motion, it has to be individual and definite in its own nature. It is distinct as such from any other form. It is of itself a different nature. The universals and the Platonic Forms, on the contrary, are of the same nature as the singulars which share them. Platonic Forms are only sensible natures plus the characteristic of "eternal." But an Aristotelian separate form, because it is not the form of a matter, is of a different *nature* from any sensible form, and because it is a *form* it is different from any other separate form.

The Aristotelian separate form, accordingly, is not reached by any process of abstraction. It is not something common. It is *ousia*, which no common attribute—not even Being and Unity—can ever be. It is therefore not the hypostatized concept of goodness or actuality. It is a definite act, an individual form. It is "a this" in its own right. There is no more reason why there cannot be many such forms than why there could not be many specifically different sensible forms. That there are in fact many such different sensible forms is a matter of direct observation. That there are many supersensible forms is a deduction from observable celestial motions.

The difficulty encountered in the question lies partly in the use of the one Aristotelian term *eidos* to denote both the individual *form* and the universal *species*. *Eidos* is an equivocal. It denotes something which is actually individual but potentially universal. This is one of the recognized Aristotelian types of equivocity—equivocity by act and potency. And because the argument from motion requires that the ultimate Mover be actual, the meaning of *eidos* here can be only the actual, individual sense.

The reality of all the separate Movers, reached in this way, will be of the same level as that of the first. Each, it is true, is a different form. But there is no reason in the Aristotelian argument for placing the first of these Movers on any higher level of Being than the others. They are all forms without matter, distinct only by the fact of being different forms; and even this distinction is known to men only through the order of the heavenly motions.

Not only the first Mover but also each of the others, accordingly, has to be a substance existing in its own right and independently of being thought by another substance. The other separate Movers cannot be the thoughts of the first.

IV

A number of vexing queries at once arise in the mind of the present-day critic when confronted with this doctrine.

What relation, for example, have these separate Movers to one another?

Apparently they have none, except the negative one of being different. Each separate substance is fully self-sufficient in its own actuality.

Why does the first Heaven desire only one Mover, the first, while other heavenly bodies desire several? How is each Mover known by the respective sphere-souls? No answer is to be found in the extant text of the Stagirite. Does each heavenly body, like man, possess a passive mind which somehow is illumined by a corresponding Mind which is in act (i.e., a separate Mover)?

The texts give hardly enough data to deduce Aristotle's answer to these questions. Accordingly, all these considerations about the relations of the Aristotelian separate Minds to souls, whether human or celestial, must remain highly controversial. They serve, however, as a guard against over-simplifying the Aristotelian problem through the use of later categories. It is difficult for the modern student, in the wake of so many centuries of Jewish, Christian, and Moslem thought, to keep from approaching the separate substances in terms of God, angels, and immortal human souls. These form three different levels of Being. But in Aristotle the level seems exactly the same. It is that of Mind, which is separate and actual, form without matter. On this one level all the problems of the relations of sensible Beings to the supersensible have to be solved.

V

With regard to the immediate problem, however, the answer is clear enough. The Aristotelian argument requires a plurality of substantial Movers, each of which is actual and separate, in the sense of depending on no prior substance for its Being. None of these Movers can have the status of a mere standard or ideal which is produced in the thought of a celestial soul, or in a Mind different in any way from the very thinking of that thought.

The difficulties brought against this doctrine seem to arise from two sources. Either an Aristotelian separate substance is expected to conform to the notion of the Christian God, and when it is found lacking in the efficiency and unicity and infinity of Being which go with that notion, it is denied all reality; or else the separate substance is conceived as an hypostatized universal, the universal of act or goodness or Being, which requires no reality and admits no multiplicity.

But if Aristotle's reasoning is followed in its own context, it leads to the acceptance of really and independently existent separate substances. The argument is firmly based upon observed sensible movement. The Stagirite's analysis of that movement may have been sadly incomplete, both from the metaphysical and the physical viewpoints, as later centuries of investigation have shown. But if the observational process and metaphysical analysis be frozen at the point which they had reached with Aristotle, and the philosophical reasoning be built upon the data so required, the argument seems flawless. The sensible motion so observed and analyzed has inevitably to be caused by a plurality of independently existent, actual, living separate substances.

10

ARISTOTLE ON THE ORIGIN AND VALIDATION OF THE MORAL JUDGMENT [1]

IN THE fifth and fourth centuries B.C., there became current in Greece certain ethical and social views which erected the distinction between nature (*physis*) and law (*nomos*) into a basic opposition. *Nomos* was held to include not only what we call civil laws but all social conventions and customs, society itself and its constitutions, just and unjust, right and wrong—at least so far as the latter involved a socially sanctioned moral code. Many Sophists, for instance, maintained that these were all against nature, being mere human conventions and contracts or even conspiracies imposed by some men to control others.

Since these things are the product of human reason in its effort to construct society and culture, nature was inevitably reduced to irrational, instinctive impulse and desire, and more especially to the drives for power, prestige, wealth, and pleasure. It was held that nature is good and law is evil, although the latter may at times be a necessary evil. The strong, natural man ignores law when he dares, and employs it as a shield of respectability when he cannot violate it with impunity. These positions, in their crude and refined forms, are admirably described in Books I and II of Plato's *Republic*.

Such views were contrary to the more persistent Greek belief in the social good, and to the major philosophical tradition in which reason and law belonged in some way to the stuff of nature and were a measure of the just and good. Socrates, Plato, and Aristotle defended the tradition and met the challenge of the new views by their effort to manifest that society, morals, and all the works of human ethical and social reason are in continuity with nature, as its genuine completion. Speaking for tradition, Plato says that the man who disparages justice does not know what he is doing, and so we must reason gently with him.

We will ask him on what grounds conduct has come to be approved or disapproved by law and custom. Is it not according as conduct tends to subdue the brutish parts of our nature to the human—perhaps I should rather say to the divine in us—or to enslave our humanity to the savagery of the beast? (*Republic*, IX, 589)

Aristotle might not agree with some of the peculiarly Platonic connotations in this passage, but he would certainly go along with the gen-

1 [Written especially for this volume by Clifford Kossel, S.J. Internal references to *Ethics* refer to Aristotle's *Nicomachean Ethics*.]

eral view that the aim of society and good conduct is to make man more manly, to develop fully the potentialities of human nature. All his ethical and political writings tend to show what he says explicitly in the *Politics:* that man is by nature a political animal; that we cannot rightly know man until we see him in his final state, the state of full and self-sufficient activity, which is attained only in the final and self-sufficient community, the city-state (*Politics,* I, 1-2; cf. *Ethics,* I, 7, 1097b8 ff.; IX, 9; X, 9).

Again, Aristotle assures us that there is a natural object of wish, and that along with conventional or legal justice there is also a natural justice (*Ethics,* V, 7). But he also grants that the very starting points of political inquiry, of which ethics is a part, are subject to such variety and fluctuation of opinion as easily to give rise to the view that morality is purely conventional (*Ethics,* I, 3). We rightly ask, then, whether Aristotle's position is merely the noble faith of a good man, or whether he believes that his position can be justified rationally and how he goes about doing it.

At first sight Aristotle's *Nicomachean Ethics* seems quite complicated, but continued examination reveals that the many aspects necessary to an understanding of moral decision converge to a view which can be formulated briefly, but can be understood only through patient examination of moral experience. We cannot, of course, discuss every ethical judgment proposed by him, but we will use typical problems to illustrate his methodology. Nor will we discuss separately the problem of origin and that of validation or justification. Even if space permitted, the two are so intimately connected as hardly to allow of separate treatment. As a guide, we will first formulate the general view of moral choice.

All moral decision results from the interplay of reason and appetite; moral equilibrium and truth are attained when reason is conformed to right appetite by affirming what it seeks and negating what it flees. Moral decision is guaranteed to be fully human and infallibly good when the following three conditions are realized: the most determinable element of man's nature, his appetites, have been trained under the guidance of another's reason to seek what is truly good and to avoid evil; by reflection on his appetites and experience, the agent himself has gradually elicited from these particular judgments of good their relationship to an over-all human good and end; finally, through added experience, reflection, and continued training of the appetites, he has developed the capacity to grasp each concrete situation in its proper relation to the over-all end of human life and readily to choose in accord with this, because appetite now seeks what reason affirms. We may add that if the latter capacity is developed not only in regard to one's personal good but with regard to the good of the city, we have Aristotle's ideal of the fully mature and good man. Nature, through reason, has fully realized the form of man (*Ethics,* VI, 5).

Now to fill out some of these points. In Book VII of the *Ethics,* Aristotle uses the logical device of the syllogism to manifest the elements involved in moral choice. Eliminating some of the complications, a moral syllogism would go about like this:

> All just acts are good and to be done;
> But paying back now the money I borrowed from this man
>   is a just and good act;
> So I should pay him now.

As we shall see, this is not a strict deductive syllogism at all. The major and minor premises simply stand for two different inductive judgments which are present in the mind and which will govern the conclusion, which is about choice and action, if bad appetite does not prevent the seeing of the relation between them by suggesting an alternative to the major or minor or both.

The major expresses some general end or good, either the over-all end of life or some special aspect of it, as in the present case. The minor presents a particular action or situation, which is either a means to this end or a partial realization of it. Since the minor and conclusion are singulars, this cannot be a strict scientific deduction, for there is no demonstrative passage from the universal to the singular. There is only insight or perception that the singular is an instance of the universal. Aristotle's ethical doctrine, then, revolves around two kinds of principles or ultimates (archai), the end, which is the mainspring of action, and the particulars in which these ends can be achieved (Ethics, VI, 11). If we see how Aristotle attains and validates knowledge of the ends and of the particulars as instances of the ends, we will see his essential methodology.

Now there are two moments in the grasp of the particular good. One precedes the explicit formulation of general ends, and the other is concomitant with or succeeds it. When in Book I of the Ethics Aristotle proposes to determine the ultimate end, he insists that, for ethical discussion to be profitable, the auditors must already have had moral experience and be well trained. By habit, they will be in control of their appetites, which means that they will be acting according to a rational rule. But they do not have to know this "reason"; it is enough that they recognize that such and such actions are good and such and such are bad (Ethics, I, 3-4).

This is that incomplete moral virtue (Ethics, VI, 13) which seeks and knows the good, without the reason. Such students have been properly directed by another's reason (that of parents and legislators) to seek and judge the particulars, although they do not grasp its implications. But because they do judge rightly in the particular, they are open to see the reason implied in it. With long experience they may inductively arrive at the connection by themselves, but they may also be aided by the mature reflection of another, a teacher, to find the unity in the multiplicity of good moral judgements.

In his effort to discover the end of human life, Aristotle holds that this question, along with all other ethical investigations, begins from opinion, proceeds by dialectic, and terminates in opinion. The Greek word *doxa,* translated by the English "opinion," did not necessarily involve the connotation of weakness and tentativeness of the English word. It is rather any knowledge *that* such and such is the case, without a precise grasp of a necessitating reason. Scientific knowledge in the strict sense manifests a necessary relationship between an attribute and a subject, through a medium which reveals the exact cause of the relation. Opinion knows the connection of attribute and subject in some other way—by perception, induction, or analogy, for instance. The state of mind in *doxa* ranges from lightly held, even erroneous opinion (in the English sense) to a true judgment, with complete conviction and certitude. Hence, if Aristotle says that something is opinion, this does not mean that he holds it as either untrue or uncertain, but only that it is "inexact," i.e., does not come up to what he requires for scientific demonstration in the *Posterior Analytics.*

Scientific knowledge, then, will have as its objects only relationships which are necessary; whatever is contingent, which can be other than it is, will be the object of opinion. Hence ethical matters, which involve not only the contingency of matter and circumstance but that of choice, can be the object only of opinion based on dialectic (*Ethics,* I, 3, 4, 7). For Aristotle, dialectic means the method of discovering, testing, and defending truth, where scientific demonstration is impossible or not available in the circumstances of the discussion. It has many variations, but the one which interests us here is that which proceeds from "common-places," i.e., from generally admitted views or from the judgments propounded by experts. This is Aristotle's first way of discovering the final end.

It is clear from the *Ethics* that this is not a mere counting of noses. Dialectic always retains its connotation of dialogue; it is a questioning, probing, analytic method. Starting with moral opinions, it tests them, manifests their implications, shows their deficiencies by comparison with other opinions or with common experience, and so finally aims to elicit the truth found in some or all. It was Aristotle's firm conviction, based on his view of the finality of nature, that what "people say" and what experts or men of mature reflection say, has some truth in it. It is foolish, for instance, to deny that pleasure is a good, when practically everyone actually seeks it and affirms it to be good (*Ethics,* I, 8; VII, 8; X, 1).

That is why the student of ethics must already have made good particular judgments, before he turns to analysis. He will not deny that pleasure is good, but he will be led easily to see that this is not the whole story. One can appeal, for instance, to his firm judgment that adultery is evil, although it is pleasant. But the student who is habitually dominated by passion will be unable to see that justice is good, if, in general, it means paying one's debts, and right now means that he must not use for some pleasurable purpose this money which he owes to another, even if he could do so with impunity. Passion prevents his seeing the end which is the reason and measure (*Ethics,* VI, 5, 1140b12-19).

Aristotle supports his "opinion-analysis" by another dialectical argument, this one from analogy. As every art and profession and every natural being has a proper function, there must be one for man. Since the only thing that differentiates man from other things and man as a whole from his particular aspects is the life of reason as a whole, man's proper function must lie in the excellent activity of reason. These are not scientific demonstrations, but Aristotle certainly considers them conclusive. They match the facts, as including all the elements which men actually desire in seeking the end or the good life.

Now, for Aristotle, the final good of life is not some transcendent object, something separate from human existence. It is a certain kind of living, a continuous virtuous activity measured by reason (*Ethics,* I, 6, 7, 10; VI, 2). In fact, it is the very activity of reason itself in both the theoretical and practical spheres. Hence, life cannot be divided simply into an end and the means. A particular action may be considered as a means to a particular or a general end. This is the aspect Aristotle takes, when he describes the process of deliberation. But in a truer sense, the particular actions which are most pertinent, those which can in themselves be designated as good or evil, are not mere means; they are themselves partial fulfillments of the end; they are the end realized here and now. These are the things which are especially represented by the minor of the moral syllogism, which should carry the mind to the conclusion.

This is why the end itself is a matter of opinion; it is always incarnated in a series of contingent particulars. So we come back to the question: How do we recognize the end-in-the-particular? Here is the place of that virtue of virtues, practical wisdom or prudence (*phronēsis*). It is the habit of good deliberation, a virtue of the intellect. It presupposes appetites well trained in moral habit. But it raises the appetitive virtues to the full state of virtue, because it not only makes them accord with reason but makes reason present in them (*Ethics,* VI, 13). Hence, Aristotle sometimes says that moral virtue makes the aim right, and prudence provides the means. This does not mean that prudence does not know the end, but only that such knowledge depends on the presence of good appetite. But knowing the universal (the end) is not what makes it prudence; it is its grasping the end *in* the particular, the ability to weigh properly all the elements in a given situation and judge rightly how to achieve the end here and now.

In the last analysis, this is a perception, not a mere sense perception, but an intellectual insight into the intelligible moral relationships in the situation presented through the senses. This can only be acquired by careful observation of long experience, which includes the experience of others, for the prudent man also knows enough to listen to well-trained men. The young do not have this moral experience or well-balanced judgment, and the old may have it without formal study or proof (*Ethics,* VI, 8, 11). But the more clearly the end is defined and understood, granted the presence of right moral habits and experience in the individual, the more excellent and competent will be his prudence.

Both the origin and validation of moral judgment, then, are in training and reflection. Only the good man will recognize the genuine good, as the healthy man recognizes wholesome food. And Aristotle supposes that most men are morally healthy, or at least have sufficient natural inclination to moral health so that they can be led in the right way. If one is so utterly morally sick as not to recognize any good, he can only be controlled by the pure coercive force of law.

The capacity for the good life is in every man (except, perhaps, the "natural slave," a matter we cannot discuss here). Its realization through good moral judgments is a natural development of natural potentialities, but one for which both the individual and society (by training) are responsible (*Ethics,* I, 9; II, 1; III, 5; X, 9). Because Aristotle holds that form or nature always tends to realize itself as end, and will for the most part achieve this end in some degree, he believes that training through social tradition and reflection on individual and social experience will yield a knowledge of true ends, along with a proportionate capacity to achieve those ends in a creative way.

This is not to say that every element in every tradition is good and to be retained. Rather, it means that, in spite of periods of decline, in spite of confusions of ends and means, and in spite of perversities of appetite, in the long run the form of man does reveal itself to the observant eye for what it is, in its finality as a reasoning being. Aristotle would certainly maintain that it is far better that a youth have the tradition of parental teaching and the legal institutions of a good city graven on his soul through moral training than that he attend even Aristotle's own lectures on ethics.

But there is a place for ethics. Aside from the natural tendency of the mind to reflect and examine, it is a defensive and creative discipline. Precisely owing to the confusions and mixtures of error and superstition in social tradition, even noble-minded young men may lose their way, or through frustration in the face of evil give themselves over to the Sophists' "natural" drives. If through the fine instruments of philosophical analysis, they can be brought to see, in outline at least, what the good is and its basis in reason, their conviction and stability will be bolstered (*Ethics,* I, 2; X, 9). Moreover, with a knowledge of both the universal and the singular, they will be better equipped to implement their good will in the constant creative endeavor which both personal and social morality requires. For the sake of themselves, their children and their city, they will also make themselves capable of being legislators.

IV. Hellenistic Philosophies

The four main philosophical schools of the so-called Hellenistic age were the Epicurean, the Stoic, the skeptical, and the neo-Platonic. Although the emphasis of the first two schools was placed upon moral philosophy, they also made important contributions to logic and natural philosophy. Most of our biographical information about Epicurus, as well as so many other Greek philosophers, comes from the gossipy and not always reliable book by Diogenes Laertius, Lives and Opinions of Eminent Philosophers, compiled toward the beginning of the third century of our era. Along with personal stories, this source also supplied three epistles summarizing the Epicurean doctrine on physics, meteorology, and ethics. The ethical teaching was set forth in the Letter of Epicurus to Menoeceus, printed here as Selection (11).

A direct reading of the text quickly alerts us to the discrepancy between the dictionary meaning for "epicurean" and the actual teaching of Epicurus. He does not deny the existence of the gods, but he does insist that they have no concern for men (except, perhaps, by way of recognizing kinship with the good and alienation from the bad). Although he argues that any relation with the turbulence of human affairs would destroy the gods' blessed state, his basic reason for denying providence and immortality is to relieve the human mind of any troubling fears arising from the thought of a future reckoning at the hands of the gods. Epicurus maintains that his theory about pleasure as the highest good does not lead to gross sensuality or the lack of discrimination. Yet it is the very insistence upon choosing the better pleasures of the mind which involves his hedonism in difficulties. Epicurus oscillates between defining the pleasant life negatively as the absence of bodily pain and mental trouble, and positively in terms of a certain prudent and measured use. But he leaves in obscurity the real ground for the degrees and kinds of pleasures, as well as the obligatory reason for choosing the more refined ones. To do so, he would have to state what our actions are free for, as well as free from, and this would entail a distinction between pleasure as a concomitant good and the directly specified goods or ends of human action.

A wide historical sweep is achieved by E. V. Arnold in Selection (12), since he describes Stoicism not only in its Greek origins but also in its later Roman expressions, especially Cicero and Seneca. Arnold not only explains the Stoic doctrine but advocates it in its best form. He helps to remove the misconceptions that Stoic ethics is self-founded and that it gravitates around the isolated individual agent. Both of these common errors arise from overlooking the decisive role of physics or philosophy of nature in this system. Because the human individual is regarded as a microcosm or little world, his nature and moral standard can only be understood through his reference to the macrocosm or larger universe. The unity of the whole cosmos is established in a monistic way, by breaking down any ultimate distinction between the divine being and the creative fire or primal stuff of the universe, as well as between soul and body. Because mind in man shares in the divine reason immanent in the universe as its controlling principle, we have the primary duty of conforming with the nature of things. This is a social obligation, binding us to all men in the worldwide community, precisely because of our common sharing in the divine reason. This Stoic view of the natural moral law has to be kept distinct from a theistic doctrine of natural law, however, because of the total immanence of the divine reason and its identity with the stuff of the universe. Where God is regarded as being other than the universe and the human spirit, conformity with the internal rational pattern of the cosmos is not a precise and adequate statement of the ultimate ground of moral obligation and the moral aim. Moreover, the theistic conception of virtue requires that it be ordained beyond a resignation to the necessities of the universal whole.

In neither the Epicurean nor the Stoic system does the choice of spiritual goods lead to a transcendence of matter and the finite world. These philosophies regard spirit as a more refined and harmonious portion of the common stuff of the universe, but not as a type of being which is distinct in kind from the "monism of stuff." Hence their ethical precepts concerning a preference for the goods of mind and spirit rest upon purely immanent considerations of tonality and measure. They do not express a conformity of the wholly immaterial principle in man to the transcendent spiritual reality and goodness of God.

Out of the subjectivism of Protagoras and the other sophists, a skeptical standpoint was evolved by Pyrrho of Elis. His chief arguments, as well as the modifications introduced by the New Academy, were reported in detail by Sextus Empiricus. His Outlines of Pyrrhonism *pro-*

vided not only a definitive summary for the closing phase of ancient philosophy but also a major sourcebook for Montaigne and the modern skeptics. Venant Cauchy's analysis of this book in Selection (13) illustrates two paths sometimes followed by the historian of philosophy: the close explanation of a key text, and the criticism based upon internal problems. A circumstantial account is given of every phrase in Sextus' descriptive definition of the skeptical way. That it is an attitude of mind, rather than a strict doctrinal commitment, follows from the skeptical repudiation of the claim to have knowledge. Nevertheless, Cauchy points out, by way of internal criticism, that the shift from doctrine to a way of thinking entails its own problems of consistency. There is a capital difference between suspending one's judgment as the result of difficulties encountered in an unending search for truth, and suspending it as a matter of settled policy, by logical techniques, and with the proviso that there will be no future discovery of truths.

Cauchy makes one quotation from St. Augustine's Answer to Skeptics *(Contra Academicos). This acute and beautiful dialogue is based on actual conversations which Augustine had with his son and other friends. It was written at the villa at Cassiciacum, shortly after his conversion. The intellectual circumstances of that conversion will be described in Selection (18), but this dialogue can be recommended here for its searching analysis and critique of the skeptical attitude. Through his reading of Cicero, Augustine was thoroughly familiar at least with the Academic variety of skepticism. From an examination of verisimilitude, probability, and the ideal of the wise man, as well as the truths in mathematics and ethics, he shows concretely how the mind can gradually discover the reasonableness of overcoming the skeptical suspension of judgment. At the end of the discussion, Augustine adds characteristically that "we are impelled toward knowledge by a twofold force: the force of authority and the force of reason"* (Answer to Skeptics, *III, 20, 43). Thus his debate with the skeptics is a prelude to the twofold search for wisdom through faith and reason which marked not only his personal speculation but also the entire millenium of philosophy which followed in his wake.*

In a still unfinished series of works ranging from Philo to Spinoza, H. A. Wolfson has been exploring the impact of Jewish thought upon the history of philosophy. Philo is a cardinal figure in his account, since in Philo there is a confluence of the two currents of Old Testament revelation and Greek philosophy. The doctrinal instance used here as

Selection (14) concerns the two divine attributes of unnamability and incomprehensibility. Wolfson shows how the emphasis in Exodus upon the hidden and ineffable God shaped Philo's ideas, and may well have affected his interpretation of Plato and Aristotle. This is a problem in reconstructing the genesis of a philosopher's thought out of the given elements and influences. There is a certain risk involved in this logical type of reconstruction of an individual's system, since the historical indications are not always present and must be supplied for by a certain amount of conjecture. As an instance of this method and as a Jewish contribution to the question of reason and revelation, this study of Philo is instructive. Whatever the precise way whereby Philo reached his position, it bears the indelible marks of a mind deeply schooled in revelation. Western philosophical speculation about God was transformed by the grafting of the Judaeo-Christian factor of reverence for the mystery and personal majesty of the unknown God.

Even Plotinus qualifies his dialectic of the union of mind with the one, in ways which show his respect for the latter's transcendence. Perhaps just as fundamental to his philosophy as the question of the return to the one, however, is that of the original process of emanation of mind and the rest of the universe from the one. In Selection (15), A. H. Armstrong approaches this issue at its most critical angle, namely, the use made of the metaphor of light streaming from the sun. He notes the previous use of this metaphor from Plato's reference to the sun of the intelligible world down to the Stoic creative fire and the Hermetic writings. Plotinus feels a need to make light noncorporeal, yet also to keep it at the frontier of matter and spirit. But when a physical agency is removed from the account of the procession of things from the one, the heart is taken out of emanation, in so far as it is intended to support a necessary and eternal efflux of power throughout the single, organic universe.

This internal criticism is important, not only for assessing the philosophy of Plotinus, but also for recognizing the ambiguity surrounding the light-metaphor in its subsequent uses. It will figure prominently in many medieval and modern philosophies, usually in support of either a theistic or a pantheistic theory of the universe's emanation from God. Yet of itself, it cannot determine precisely what kind of participation and causal activity are involved in this origin of things from God. There are several kinds of emanation theories, and the import of the light-

metaphor can only be determined by reference to the total doctrinal context in the individual system. Metaphorical thinking is inevitable and sometimes useful in philosophy, but it is not by itself demonstrative and does require an interpretative reference to the guiding intellectual judgments and methods of inference at work.

11

A DOCTRINAL LETTER FROM EPICURUS TO MENOECEUS [1]

EPICURUS to Menoeceus, greeting.

Let no one be slow to seek wisdom when he is young nor weary in the search thereof when he is grown old. For no age is too early or too late for the health of the soul. And to say that the season for studying philosophy has not yet come, or that it is past and gone, is like saying that the season for happiness is not yet or that it is now no more. Therefore, both old and young ought to seek wisdom, the former in order that, as age comes over him, he may be young in good things because of the grace of what has been, and the latter in order that, while he is young, he may at the same time be old, because he has no fear of the things which are to come. So we must exercise ourselves in the things which bring happiness, since, if that be absent, all our actions are directed toward attaining it.

Those things which without ceasing I have declared unto thee, those do, and exercise thyself therein, holding them to be elements of right life. First believe that God is a living immortal and blessed, according to the notion of a god indicated by the common sense of mankind; and so believing, thou shalt not affirm of him aught that is foreign to his immortality or that agrees not with blessedness, but shalt believe about him whatever may uphold both his blessedness and his immortality. For verily there are gods, and the knowledge of them is manifest; but they are not such as the multitude believe, seeing that men do not steadfastly maintain the notions they form respecting them. Not the man who denies the gods worshipped by the multitude, but he who affirms of the gods what the multitude believes about them is truly impious. For the utterances of the multitude about the gods are not true preconceptions but false assumptions; hence it is that the greatest evils happen to the wicked and the greatest blessings happen to the good from the hand of

---

1 [From *Diogenes Laertius: Lives of Eminent Philosophers,* translated by R. D. Hicks ("Loeb Classical Library," 183 [Cambridge, Mass.: Harvard University Press, 1950]), vol. II, pp. 649-659. Reprinted by permission.]

the gods, seeing that they are always favourable to their own good qualities and take pleasure in men like unto themselves, but reject as alien whatever is not of their kind.

Accustom thyself to believe that death is nothing to us, for good and evil imply sentience, and death is the privation of all sentience; therefore a right understanding that death is nothing to us makes the mortality of life enjoyable, not by adding to life an illimitable time, but by taking away the yearning after immortality.[2] For life has no terrors for him who has thoroughly apprehended that there are no terrors for him in ceasing to live. Foolish, therefore, is the man who says that he fears death, not because it will pain when it comes, but because it pains in the prospect. Whatsoever causes no annoyance when it is present, causes only a groundless pain in the expectation. Death, therefore, the most awful of evils, is nothing to us, seeing that, when we are, death is not come, and, when death is come, we are not. It is nothing, then, either to the living or to the dead, for with the living it is not and the dead exist no longer. But in the world, at one time men shun death as the greatest of all evils, and at another time choose it as a respite from the evils in life. The wise man does not deprecate life nor does he fear the cessation of life. The thought of life is no offense to him, nor is the cessation of life regarded as an evil. And even as men choose of food not merely and simply the larger portion, but the more pleasant, so the wise seek to enjoy the time which is most pleasant and not merely that which is longest. And he who admonishes the young to live well and the old to make a good end speaks foolishly, not merely because of the desirableness of life, but because the same exercise at once teaches to live well and to die well. Much worse is he who says that it were good not to be born, but when once one is born to pass with all speed through the gates of Hades. For if he truly believes this, why does he not depart from life? It were easy for him to do so, if once he were firmly convinced. If he speaks only in mockery, his words are foolishness, for those who hear believe him not.

We must remember that the future is neither wholly ours nor wholly not ours, so that neither must we count upon it as quite certain to come nor despair of it as quite certain not to come.

We must also reflect that of desires some are natural, others are groundless; and that of the natural some are necessary as well as natural, and some natural only. And of the necessary desires some are necessary if we are to be happy, some if the body is to be rid of uneasiness, some if we are even to live. He who has a clear and certain understanding of these things will direct every preference and aversion toward securing

---

[2] [This argument supposes that every act of life and morally responsible judgment depends intrinsically upon the presence of the organism and its sense perception. But the question of immortality concerns the continued existence of an immaterial principle which, even after death, can retain knowledge of moral distinctions and responsibility for moral actions. (Editor's note.)]

health of body and tranquillity of mind, seeing that this is the sum and end of a blessed life. For the end of all our actions is to be free from pain and fear, and, when once we have attained all this, the tempest of the soul is laid; seeing that the living creature has no need to go in search of something that is lacking, nor to look for anything else by which the good of the soul and of the body will be fulfilled. When we are pained because of the absence of pleasure, then, and then only, do we feel the need of pleasure. Wherefore we call pleasure the alpha and omega of a blessed life. Pleasure is our first and kindred good. It is the starting point of every choice and of every aversion, and to it we come back, inasmuch as we make feeling the rule by which to judge of every good thing. And since pleasure is our first and native good, for that reason we do not choose every pleasure whatsoever, but ofttimes pass over many pleasures when a greater annoyance ensues from them. And ofttimes we consider pains superior to pleasures when submission to the pains for a long time brings us as a consequence a greater pleasure. While therefore all pleasure because it is naturally akin to us is good, not all pleasure is choiceworthy, just as all pain is an evil and yet not all pain is to be shunned. It is, however, by measuring one against another, and by looking at the conveniences and inconveniences, that all these matters must be judged. Sometimes we treat the good as an evil, and the evil, on the contrary, as a good. Again, we regard independence of outward things as a great good, not so as in all cases to use little, but so as to be contented with little if we have not much, being honestly persuaded that they have the sweetest enjoyment of luxury who stand least in need of it, and that whatever is natural is easily procured and only the vain and worthless hard to win. Plain fare gives as much pleasure as a costly diet, when once the pain of want has been removed, while bread and water confer the highest possible pleasure when they are brought to hungry lips. To habituate one's self, therefore, to simple and inexpensive diet supplies all that is needful for health, and enables a man to meet the necessary requirements of life without shrinking, and it places us in a better condition when we approach at intervals a costly fare and renders us fearless of fortune.

When we say, then, that pleasure is the end and aim, we do not mean the pleasures of the prodigal or the pleasures of sensuality, as we are understood to do by some through ignorance, prejudice, or wilful misrepresentation. By pleasure we mean the absence of pain in the body and of trouble in the soul. It is not an unbroken succession of drinking-bouts and of revelry, not sexual love, not the enjoyment of the fish and other delicacies of a luxurious table, which produce a pleasant life; it is sober reasoning, searching out the grounds of every choice and avoidance, and banishing those beliefs through which the greatest tumults take possession of the soul. Of all this the beginning and the greatest good is prudence. Wherefore prudence is a more precious thing even than philosophy; from it spring all the other virtues, for it teaches that we cannot lead a life of pleasure which is not also a life of prudence, honour, and justice; nor lead a life of prudence, honour, and justice, which is not also a life of pleasure. For the virtues have grown into one with a pleasant life, and a pleasant life is inseparable from them.

Who, then, is superior in thy judgment to such a man? He holds a holy belief concerning the gods, and is altogether free from the fear of death. He has diligently considered the end fixed by nature, and understands how easily the limit of good things can be reached and attained, and how either the duration or the intensity of evils is but slight. Destiny, which some introduce as sovereign over all things, he laughs to scorn, affirming rather that some things happen of necessity, others by chance, others through our own agency. For he sees that necessity destroys responsibility and that chance or fortune is inconstant; whereas our own actions are free, and it is to them that praise and blame naturally attach. It were better, indeed, to accept the legends of the gods than to bow beneath that yoke of destiny which the natural philosophers have imposed. The one holds out some faint hope that we may escape if we honor the gods, while the necessity of the naturalists is deaf to all entreaties. Nor does he hold chance to be a god, as the world in general does, for in the acts of a god there is no disorder; nor to be a cause, though an uncertain one, for he believes that no good or evil is dispensed by chance to men so as to make life blessed, though it supplies the starting point of great good and great evil. He believes that the misfortune of the wise is better than the prosperity of the fool. It is better, in short, that what is well judged in action should not owe its successful issue to the aid of chance.

Exercise thyself in these and kindred precepts day and night, both by thyself and with him who is like unto thee; then never, either in waking or in dream, wilt thou be disturbed, but wilt live as a god among men. For man loses all semblance of mortality by living in the midst of immortal blessings.

12

THE STOIC VIEW OF MAN AND MORALITY [1]

THE way in which the Stoics approach the individual man, in his nature and moral conduct, depends mainly upon their conception of the universe as a single whole. Thus it follows from the monistic standpoint that man is not ultimately an "individual" or unit of the universe; for the universe itself is the only true unit, and a man

[1] [From E. V. Arnold, *Roman Stoicism* (Cambridge: the University Press, 1911), pp. 238-244, 273-275, 281-285, 292-293. Reprinted by permission. The notes and some sentences in the main text are omitted.]

is a part of it which cannot even for a moment break itself off completely from the whole. It is therefore only in a secondary and subordinate sense, and with special reference to the inculcation of ethics, that we can treat Zeno or Lucilius as separate and independent beings. Again, when we say that man "consists of body and soul," we are merely adopting popular language; for body and soul are ultimately one, and differ only in the gradation of spirit or tone which informs them. Then we learn in dialectics that the highest power of man is that of "assent" or free choice, which is displayed in every exercise of reason; and the same power, though in a different aspect, is at work in every moral act. The doctrine of the universe is based upon the postulate that it is a living rational being on the largest scale; and it follows that each man is a "microcosm," and contains in himself a complete representation of the universe in miniature. Lastly, we see that man takes his place in the universe, a little lower than gods and daemons, and as greatly higher than animals as these in their turn surpass plants and inanimate objects; and that his nature, considered as composite, includes all the varying gradations of spirit to which these orders correspond within the universe. In all his parts alike the divine element is immanent and it binds them together in a coherent unity (*sympatheia tōn merōn*). It remains for us to put together from these and like points of departure a complete picture of human nature.

I. THE KINGDOM OF THE SOUL

To indicate the general trend of Stoic thought on this subject we propose the title "the kingdom of the soul." Starting with the popular distinction between body and soul, we find that the biologist and the physician alike are preoccupied with the study of the body, that is, of physiology. Only as an afterthought and supplement to their work are the functions of soul considered; and they are treated as far as possible by the methods suggested by the study of the body. All this is reversed in the Stoic philosophy. The study of the soul stands in the front, and is treated by methods directly suggested by observation of the soul's functions. The body is not entirely ignored, but is considered of comparatively small importance. Further, the soul itself is manifold, and is likened to a State, in which all is well if the governing part have wisdom and benevolence proportionate to its power, and if the lower parts are content to fulfill their respective duties; but if the balance of the State is upset, all becomes disorder and misery. Lastly, this kingdom is itself a part of a greater whole, namely of the Cosmopolis or universal State. By the comparison with a kingdom we are also directed towards right moral principle. For as the citizen of Corinth or Sparta ought not to repine because his city is of less grandeur than Athens, so no man should be anxious because his external opportunities are limited. He has a kingdom in his own mind and soul and heart. Let him be content to find his happiness in rightly administering it.

The doctrine that man is a representation or reflection of the universe is of unknown antiquity. It seems to be clearly implied by the teaching of Heraclitus, in so far as he lays it down that both the universe and man are vivified and controlled by the Logos. The technical terms "macrocosm" and "microcosm" are employed by Aristotle. But even if we suppose that this conception is a commonplace of Greek philosophy, it is in Stoicism alone that it is of fundamental importance, and knit up with the whole framework of the system. And accordingly we find that all the Stoic masters laid stress upon this principle. The words of Zeno suggest to Cicero that "the universe displays all impulses of will and all corresponding actions just like ourselves when we are stirred through the mind and the senses." Cleanthes used the dogma of the soul of the universe to explain the existence of the human soul as a part of it. Chrysippus found a foundation for ethics in the doctrine that man should study and imitate the universe. Diogenes of Babylon says boldly that God penetrates the universe, as soul the man; and Seneca that the relation of God to matter is the same as that of the soul to the body. It is little wonder therefore if by Philo's time the analogy had become a commonplace, and philosophers of more than one school were accustomed to say that "man is a little universe, and the universe a big man." God is therefore the soul of the universe; on the other hand the soul is God within the human body, a self-moving force encased in relatively inert matter, providence at work within the limitations of natural necessity.

Ultimately, soul and body are one; or, in the language of paradox, "soul is body." This follows not only from the general principles of our philosophy, but also specifically from observation of the facts of human life. "The incorporeal," argued Cleanthes, "cannot be affected by the corporeal, nor the corporeal by the incorporeal, but only the corporeal by the corporeal. But the soul is affected by the body in disease and in mutilation, and the body by the soul, for it reddens in shame and becomes pale in fear: therefore the soul is body." And similarly Chrysippus argues: "death is the separation of soul from body. Now the incorporeal neither joins with nor is separated from body, but the soul does both. The soul therefore is body." This doctrine is commonly adduced as evidence of the "materialism" of the Stoics: yet the Stoics do not say that "soul is matter," and (as we shall see) they explain its workings upon principles quite different to the laws of physics or chemistry. The essential unity of body and soul follows also from the way in which we acquire knowledge of them. For we perceive body by the touch; and we learn the workings of the soul by a kind of touch, called the inward touch (*entos haphē*).

Having realized that the division of man into soul and body is not ultimate, we may more easily prepare ourselves to make other divisions.

A division into three parts, (i) body, (ii) soul or life (*psychē, anima*), and (iii) mind (*nous, animus*), was widely accepted in Stoic times, and in particular by the school of Epicurus; the mind being that which man has, and the animals have not. The Stoics develop this division by the principle of the microcosm. Mind is that which man has in common with the animals; growth (*physis, natura*), that which he has in common with the plants, as for instance is shown in the hair and nails. Man also possesses cohesion (*hexis, unitas*) but never apart from higher powers. Further, these four, mind, soul, growth, and cohesion, are not different in kind, but all are spirits (*pneumata*) which by their varying degrees of tension (*tonos, intentio*) are, to a less or greater extent, removed from the divine being, the primal stuff. In this sense man is not one, nor two, but multiple, as the deity is multiple.

The soul in its substance or stuff is fire, identical with the creative fire which is the primal stuff of the universe. But the popular conception, according to which the soul is air or breath, and is seen to leave the body at death, is also not without truth. There is a very general opinion that the soul is a mixture of fire and air, or is hot air. By this a Stoic would not mean that the soul was a compound of two different elements, but that it was a variety of fire in the first stage of the downward path, beginning to form air by relaxation of its tension: but even so this form of the doctrine was steadily subordinated to the older doctrine of Heraclitus, that the soul is identical with the divine fire. Formally, the soul is defined, like the deity himself, as a "fiery intelligent spirit"; and in this definition it would seem that we have no right to emphasize the connection between the word "spirit" (*pneuma*) and its original meaning "breath," since the word has in our philosophy many other associations. It is further a Stoic paradox that "the soul is an animal," just as God is an animal. But the soul and the man are not on that account two animals; all that is meant is that men and the brutes, by reason of their being endowed with soul, become animals.

II. THE LAW FOR HUMANITY

The department of Ethics contains two divisions: ethics (in the stricter sense) which is concerned with the action of the individual; and politics, which has to do with the order of the State. It has been maintained that in Stoicism the latter is altogether subordinated, and that the central aim of this philosophy is to erect a shelter for the individual. The truth of this view is more than doubtful. Stoic ethics are not based on the needs of the individual, but on the demands of the supreme Law. "If there is a universe, then there is a universal law, bidding us do this and refrain from that." "If there are gods, there is virtue." Thus it is noteworthy that Zeno's earliest work was "on the State," and that it is an attempt to show how a state can be ordered by wise laws. The whole theory of the Logos leads up to the same point. The same eternal Wisdom through which the primal stuff took shape is, in another function, the Right Rule (*orthos logos, vera ratio*) which commands and forbids. Right Rule and Common Law (*koinos nomos, lex communis*) are terms of identical meaning, by which a standard of supreme authority is set up; State law and conventional morality, though always of narrower range, and often of inferior purity, are yet a reflection of universal Law. The moral law must therefore first be studied in its bearings on man as a political and social animal.

The root-principle of the Stoic State is that it is world-wide, a Cosmopolis. This title arose from the practice, attributed to Socrates and Diogenes (as well as others), of replying to the current question "Of what city are you?" by the answer "Of the universe." We must therefore regard ourselves as members not of a clan or city, but of a world-wide society. In this society all distinctions of race, caste and class are to be subordinated to the sense of kinship and brotherhood. This principle is equally opposed to the nationalist prejudices which rank Hellene above barbarian, to philosophical theories (such as that of Aristotle) which distinguish intelligent peoples fitted by nature to rule and others only fitted to obey, and to ideal states (such as that of Plato) in which a ruling class is to be developed by artifice and schooling. Only the brute animals are excluded from this community, for they are not possessed of reason; they have therefore no rights, but exist for the service of men. All human beings are capable of attaining to virtue, and as such are natural-born citizens of the Cosmopolis. Loyalty to this state, however, in no wise hinders a due loyalty to existing states which may be regarded as partial realizations of it. Socrates submitted to the laws of Athens even when they bade him die; Zeno and Cleanthes declined the citizenship of that famous city, lest they should be thought to hold cheap the places of their birth; and amongst the Romans Seneca frequently insists that every man is born into two communities, the Cosmopolis and his native city.

The world-state is not held together either by force or by statecraft, but by goodwill. We must be able to say "Love is god there, and is a helpmate to make the city secure." This feeling of love and friendship grows up naturally between wise men, because they partake in the reason of the universe; so that we may equally well say that the bond of the State is the Logos (*ratio atque oratio*). Since reason and the universal law exist in the community from the beginning, law does not need to be created; it exists of itself, and by natural growth (*physei*). The writing down of laws is only a stage in their development.

For the individual man the ethical problem is to bring himself, a part of nature, into harmony with the whole. Whether we think of destiny, of providence, of the gods, or of the state, success for the individual is to agree and to cooperate; to struggle and to rebel is to fail. This success is the end (*telos*) for which man exists, the supreme good (*summum bonum*), the ultimate good (*ultimum bonorum*), that towards which all other right action works, whilst it works itself for no other end. Its name in the individual is virtue (*aretē, virtus*), and it is an active and firmly-established disposition of the soul. It follows from the monistic principle that the end for man is one, and that virtue is one; but nevertheless each is capable of being regarded in many respects. The harmony of the ethical end with other parts of the Stoic philosophy is marked by such phrases as "life according to nature," the rule "keep company with God," and the identification of virtue and reason.

Because virtue is one thing and not many, it makes a man's life one consistent whole, and stands in sharp contrast to the changing and undecided ways of the crowd. Virtue is therefore frequently defined as consistency in life, an even, steady course of action, self-consistency, a principle in agreement with its applications. The opposite of virtue is the unending restlessness and indecision of the man in the crowd. Accordingly we are told that the earliest Stocis thought it a sufficient definition of wisdom or virtue that it was something simple; and similarly Zeno said that the end of life was "to live consistently." To this short definition the words "with nature" were soon added, whereby the distinctiveness of the original definition was diminished: for all the philosophical schools are agreed that the right life must be guided by nature (*physei*), not by convention (*thesei*).

From the time of Chrysippus the relation of right living to nature was further analyzed. Chrysippus defined the "nature" referred to as "universal and human nature," thereby further approximating to the teaching of rival schools; but on the other hand he gave this new and more characteristic explanation "to live virtuously is to live according to scientific knowledge of the phenomena of nature, doing nothing which the Universal Law forbids, which is the Right Reason which pervades all things, and is the same as Zeus, the Lord of the ordering of this world." Diogenes of Babylon introduced the words "to take a reasonable course in choosing or refusing things in accordance with nature." Antipater's definition is "to live with preference for what is natural, and aversion to what is against nature," thus throwing the stress on the doctrine of the "things of high degree." Panaetius made a distinct step forward when he admitted the claims of universal nature to be supreme, but (subject to them) held that each man should follow the pointings of his individual nature. This teaching, however, comes rather near to naming a twofold end. Cicero follows Panaetius in his *De Officiis,* but in the *De Finibus* adheres more closely to Chrysippus, and Seneca agrees with him in laying stress on the need of scientific knowledge of natural events. In the main, therefore, "life according to nature" means to the Stoics life in accordance with the general movement of the universe, to which the particular strivings of the individual must be subordinated.

From the religious standpoint virtue is willing cooperation with the deity, in preference to that unwilling cooperation to which even evil doers are forced. This conception, first set forth by Cleanthes in a poem, is also enforced by Seneca and Epictetus in varying phrases. "I do not obey God," says Seneca, "I agree with him. I go with him heart and soul, and not because I must." With a slight change of language this leads us to the paradox that "obedience to God is liberty." "I have placed my impulses," says Epictetus, "in obedience to God. Is it his will that I shall have fever? It is my will too. Is it his will that I should obtain anything? It is my wish also. Does he not wish it? I do not wish it." The personal bent of Epictetus leads him to develop this idea in the direction of suffering rather than of acting. "If the good man had foreknowledge of what would happen, he would cooperate towards his own sickness and death and mutilation, since he knows that these things are assigned to him in accordance with the universal arrangement." The proof that this must be so rests on the unity of the Divine and individual purposes: "Good cannot be one thing, and that at which we are rationally delighted another thing."

It is not perhaps quite so clearly stated that the virtue of the individual is that disposition which will make him the best possible member of society, that is, the best possible citizen of the Cosmopolis. Yet this is everywhere implied. In the first place the wise man will take part in the life of the community, he will marry and bring up children. In the second place the virtue of man differs from the corresponding quality in the animals in that man is formed by nature for social union; hence his reason only comes into play simultaneously with the recognition that he is a member of a community, and as such bound to prefer the good of the whole to that of a part. "Nature," says Panaetius, "through reason unites man to man, so that they have a common bond in conversation and life; it induces men to approve and take part in public gatherings and festivals, and to collect the materials for a social and cultivated life for themselves, their children, and all whom they hold dear."

The doctrine of the sufficiency (*autarkeia, sufficientia*) of virtue was consistently taught by the Stoics of all periods, though in ever-varying phraseology. Zeno adopted the Cynic phrase "virtue is sufficient for happiness" or in other words "virtue needs but herself for a happy life." Chrysippus maintains that there are only three logical views as to the supreme good, that it is virtue or pleasure or both, and for himself he chooses the first. Happiness therefore is not made greater if advantages are added to virtue; or rather, virtue does not permit addition (*accessio*). In the transition period Antipater of Tarsus is said to have faltered, and to have attributed a little importance, though very little, to external advantages; but his definition of the supreme good is in full accord with the general teaching of the school. Panaetius and Posidonius held to the orthodox doctrine both in word and deed, if we may trust the direct statements of Cicero; nevertheless, they were so anxious to assimilate their expressions to those of ordinary life, that the conclusion could easily be drawn that in their hearts they too attached importance to external goods. One authority indeed states that they held health, strength, and estate to be "needful" for happiness, thus abandoning the sufficiency of virtue; but in the absence of direct quotation we shall hardly be willing to accept this statement as implying anything different from the distinction of Chrysippus, viz. that "the wise man *needs* nothing, but *has use* for everything."

But any faltering shown by the transition writers was more than made good by the zeal of the teachers under the principate. Seneca enforces the paradox in a score of phrases; in the form of a proverb, "virtue is its own reward"; in rhetorical exuberance, "virtue can defy death, ill fortune, and tyranny"; it is "independent even of the deity"; and "no circumstances can increase or impair its perfection." Epictetus often dwells on the same theme, and the whole work of Marcus Aurelius is a meditation upon it. Nor is the dogma merely scholastic; the teachers of the Roman period lay special emphasis on the practical importance of upholding the ideal of virtue, as alike single and complete in itself.

13

THE SKEPTIC ATTITUDE [1]

THE history of philosophy offers us an interesting field in which to observe the workings and development of the human mind. Nowhere does this hold more truly than in the radical forms of thought which compel man by sheer force of logic to contradict facts as a result of an uncritical acceptance of pseudo-evidences.

A clear example of this is found in the skepticism of Sextus Empiricus. If we represented the entire history of philosophy by a straight line, skepticism would constitute one end and realism the other, with all the intervening systems attempting an impossible compromise between the two attitudes, some nearer, some further from one or the other, but ever failing in their hopeless ventures.

An objective study of the skeptic attitude in its most logical exponent, Sextus Empiricus, sheds light on the doctrines which fall short of realism. We observe there the difficulties which must be overcome in order to obtain a true knowledge of reality and the numerous bypaths which lead away from truth. We come to realize that the greatest danger to realism lies in realists themselves, in their shallow understanding of their

[1] [From Venant Cauchy, "The Nature and Genesis of the Skeptic Attitude," *The Modern Schoolman*, vol. 27 (1949-50), pp. 203-213. Reprinted by permission. Most of the notes are omitted.]

own system, their sense of inferiority in the face of a hostile world, and their lack of confidence in the perpetual originality of the mind.

DEFINITION OF THE SKEPTIC ATTITUDE

The first book of the *Outlines of Pyrrhonism* presents a thorough description of the Pyrrhonian attitude. Sextus distinguishes Pyrrhonism from all the other systems which have arisen in the development of thought. Human search for truth, our writer contends, may achieve three possible results: either one attains the objects of the investigation, or one concludes to the impossibilty of ever knowing truth, or lastly one continues in endless search. All brands of dogmatists fall under the first category; they devise theories which are presented as certain knowledge of reality. The Academy, with Carneades and Clitomachos, teaches, however, that the mind can never attain the object of its investigation. The skeptics alone keep on searching without giving in to dogmatic rashness or Academic prejudice.

Thus Sextus really distinguishes two types of dogmatism. The first affirms the possibility of knowing reality with certitude; its numerous adherents are called Stoics, Epicureans, Peripatetics, to mention only the main schools of the Roman Empire. The other type of dogmatism masquerades as a form of skepticism; it denies the possibility of knowing reality, and as such cannot be more than a negative dogmatism. Skepticism stands out against these two extremes. Skeptics refrain from affirming anything whatsoever: even the expressions or the words they use serve as false fronts which they would gladly destroy along with the dogmatic systems.

Throughout his works, Sextus aims at defining skepticism in such a way as to distinguish it from all dogmatic tendencies. Let us consider for the moment the definition proposed in the first book of the *Outlines:*

> Skepticism is an ability, or mental attitude, which opposes appearances to judgments in any way whatsoever, with the result that, owing to the equipollence of the objects and reasons thus opposed, we are brought firstly to a state of mental suspense and next to a state of "unperturbedness" or quietude.[2]

Sextus goes on to explain the different parts of his definition. He warns against taking the word "ability" in a subtle sense; there is no need to stretch its meaning. Skepticism is primarily an ability, a tendency, a power of the mind. By the word "appearance," our skeptic designates the sensible qualities (*aisthēta*) as opposed to the intelligible (*noēta*). The expression "in any way whatsoever" may be related (a) to ability, thus emphasizing the very general meaning of the word; (b) to the opposition between phenomena and noumena, in order to indicate that the skeptic opposes phenomena and noumena in every conceivable way; (c) or again to phenomena and noumena taken as present participles.

---

[2] *Outlines of Pyrrhonism,* i, 8; Vol. I of *Sextus Empiricus,* translated by R. G. Bury (4 vols.; Cambridge, Mass.: Harvard University Press, 1933-1949), vol. I, p. 7.

In the latter case the skeptic manifests a complete indifference in the choice of phenomena and noumena: he accepts everything that comes to him and for this reason may dispense with the useless work involved in determining a theory of cognition.

Sextus emphasizes this atmosphere of indefiniteness by his explanation of the expression "objects and reasons thus opposed." By "opposed," he does not only mean the opposition existing between affirmation and negation, but any incompatibility between propositions. Skepticism is a militant attitude; it does not adopt a position, but must constantly be on guard to ridicule and destroy the dogmas of its adversaries. The skeptic attitude has no claim to objectivity; on the contrary, it is entirely enclosed in the subject. Theoretically, the skeptic never leaves his shell, even if he seems at times to take a dogmatic stand in order to pull apart the dogmas of his enemies. "Epuipollence" ("equal value of opposed theses"), affirms Sextus, does not imply a factual equality between propositions, but expresses the bewilderment of the mind faced with conflicting arguments of equal force. This equality, Sextus tells us, does not imply a contact with things, but merely results from a subjective process. Suspension of judgment (*epochē*), which follows upon equipollence, is defined as a state of mind according to which the skeptic neither denies nor affirms anything. Quietude (*ataraxia*) is the serenity and peace of mind which result from suspension of judgment. As we shall see later, autosuggestion plays an important part in the formation of the skeptic attitude; the skeptic strives with all his heart to achieve suspension of judgment and the tranquillity which follows upon it, in much the same way as the sages of India yearn for their identification with the supreme and impersonal Self.

SKEPTICISM AS AN ATTITUDE

The skeptic, as we may conclude from a study of his phenomenalism, does not claim to know the nature of things. The unstable phenomena which come from without cannot serve as a basis for speculative assent. Even the choice of a definite rule of conduct is incompatible with Pyrrhonian doubt; for, in the end, one must always trace it back to some type of speculative affirmation. But if all thought, speculative or practical, is rejected from skepticism, it can be nothing more than an attitude, an orientation of the mind; herein lies one aspect of the basic contradiction of skepticism. No one believes that the skeptic can free himself so easily from all speculation, but nonetheless he would reject from his attitude any speculative implication. He sees himself as the opponent of all who lay claim to a knowledge of reality.

Many texts appear to identify skepticism with the skeptic attitude. In other schools, the attitude affords the general atmosphere, the mental background in which the doctrines are set. But in the Pyrrhonian school, systematic thought is willfully destroyed and nihilism itself seems doomed to a regress ad infinitum which even foregoes the possibility of a purely negative philosophy.

The definition of skepticism gives us precious information concerning the intimate relationship between the skeptic way (*agōgē*) and the attitude. Indeed the word *ability*, which defines skepticism, may be construed as identical with attitude or as flowing directly from it. Skepticism is not a philosophy, but a practical attitude. The skeptic stands out among others in that he inquires constantly without ever attaining the object of his inquiry.

In the definition, the adjective *skeptic* does not qualify *ability* but *way*, which is the subject of the preceding sentence. But what is the exact meaning of *way*, and why should Sextus use it instead of *philosophy* or some other expression? There is a very simple reason: Sextus wishes to shun from the very beginning any word which might present skepticism in the false light of speculative systems. The word *way* guards against this danger; it implies action and change. Sextus must have recourse sooner or later to expressions which resemble speculative principles; but we must never forget that he considers these expressions in a context of *way*, and thus averts the danger of appearing to dogmatize. We can attach no other meaning to his warning in the opening lines of the *Outlines*. The skeptic expressions represent efforts to follow a road whose term one can never hope to attain.

This view of skepticism as a mere attitude may be drawn from the outline given by Sextus at the beginning of his skeptic books. The first book, where he thoroughly defines his attitude, is indicated with its main subdivisions. Although the remainder occupies eight times as much space as the first book of the *Outlines*, Sextus merely refers to it as a special part in which he proposes objections to each section of dogmatic philosophy. In fact, the other books (the remainder of the *Outlines*, *Against the Logicians*, *Against the Physicists*, and *Against the Ethicists*) simply make use of the skeptic attitude, as determined in the first book, to destroy the theories of the dogmatists. One will find in these protracted catalogues of objections, valid or sophistical, minor confirmations, but nothing essential to skepticism that has not been set forth in the first book of the *Outlines*. Sextus himself refers to them as commentaries.

We do not deny, of course, the inherent contradiction of an attitude rejecting speculative implications. It is quite another task, however, to explain how and why this came to be. This we will attempt by an intrinsic criticism of the skeptic attitude as defined in the works of Sextus Empiricus.

DUAL CHARACTER OF THE SKEPTIC ATTITUDE

The skeptic attitude implies a basic duality which we must determine before we can understand the nature of skepticism. At the beginning of his *Outlines*, Sextus shows the thinker bewildered by the confusion prevalent in knowledge; the opposition of the different systems which claim a knowledge of reality increases his perplexity. His difficulties force him to contiune his investigation without ever attaining truth. We call this the first phase in the formation of the skeptic attitude. The other phase seems to follow naturally from the permanence of the problems; it is marked by a satisfaction or a crystallization of the mind in instability. The two phases may be found not only in Pyrrhonian skepticism, but in all types of skepticism. Thus, when Cicero speaks of the difficulties encountered in searching for a criterion of truth, he stays in the first phase; he faces a real problem. But no sooner has he enunciated his principle: "it is possible for a false presentation to occur that has the same character as a given true one" (*Academica*, II, xxxi), than he neglects the difficulty to adopt a position of instability. These two phases in the development of skepticism remain present in the final stage. At this point, they could be designed as the contradictory aspects of the skeptic attitude, but we still refer to them as the two phases of skepticism in view of their role in the elaboration of the attitude.

First Phase

One may distinguish in Sextus a spontaneous and a crystallized or systematic doubt. The spontaneous, which is characteristic of the first phase, results from the real difficulties encountered in our investigation of the world. We can hardly describe the process of knowledge; we cannot even hope that such a description will ever express adequately the complexity of our operations. Erroneous opinions constantly remind us of our limitations, and, when left without solution, prepare the mind for universal doubt.

We refer to this phase of spontaneous doubt whatever nobility, anguish, or sincere inquiry may be uncovered in the skeptic attitude. The decision to suspend judgment is a consequence of the difficulties which confront the mind; it is not the cause of the attitude considered under its aspect of spontaneity.

For the Skeptic, having set out to philosophize with the object of passing judgement on the sense-impressions and ascertaining which of them are true and which false, so as to attain quietude thereby, found himself involved in contradictions of equal weight, and being unable to decide between them suspended judgement.[3]

At the beginning of the second book of the *Outlines,* Sextus tries to base the skeptic search for truth on a professed ignorance of the nature of things:

For to continue the investigation of problems is not inconsistent in those who confess their ignorance of their real nature, but only in those who believe they have an exact knowledge of them.[4]

3 *Outlines of Pyrrhonism*, 1, 26 (Bury, I, 19).
4 *Ibid.,* ii, 11 (Bury, I, 157, 159).

The skeptics like to consider their attitude under this aspect of spontaneity. What is more natural, indeed, than to resent the rashness of the solutions proposed by the dogmatists to the most difficult problems? The ridiculous dogmas of many philosophical systems gain nothing but contempt from thinkers seriously preoccupied with knowing the truth, and we find here reason enough to grant the skeptic a certain amount of sincerity. This spontaneity appears somewhat in the refutations: the skeptic does not make as much use as he could of the objections advanced in previous refutations. He considers each dogmatic thesis, destroying even the solutions offered by the dogmatists to the skeptic difficulties. Sextus would not have us look upon skepticism as a system of universal negation or relate the negation found in the refutations to an intention derived from his attitude; on the contrary, the skeptic admits the strength of dogmatic arguments; but he does not fail to attribute as much strength to the opposite theses. Skepticism thrives on irreducible oppositions and lack of precision.

The first phase of the attitude appears even in the names attributed to the Pyrrhonians. The word *skeptic* (from *skeptesthai*, "to observe," "to reflect") does not imply primarily a systematic rejection of assent, but the thorough examination of facts necessary before adopting a position. The skeptics are also called "zetetics" (from *zētein*, "to search"), to indicate that they seek the truth, and "aporetics" (from *aporein*, "to doubt," "to have problems"), because their attitude is a result of the difficulties encountered in the knowledge of reality. The name "ephectics" (from *epechō*, "to retain," "to stop," "to suspend judgment"), however, can hardly be explained in a context of spontaneous doubt. In Sextus' account of this name, we detect the contradiction prevailing between the two phases of the skeptic attitude; after affirming that the skeptic (as opposed to the dogmatists and Academics) searches constantly for truth, he speaks of suspension of judgment as a state of mind which comes after the search.

Second Phase

Sooner or later the skeptic achieves a systematic state of mind. In reaction against the immoderate affirmations of the dogmatists, the spontaneous doubt of the first phase slowly develops into a crystallized or systematic doubt. The skeptic, filled with contempt for dogmatic assertions and unable to unravel for himself the problems of knowledge, inclines by contrast to consider his doubt as a value; there lies the precise origin and the radical vice of skepticism, its capitulation to self-satisfaction. He looks for tranquillity in the possession of science, but, deterred by supposedly unsolvable difficulties, resorts to suspension of judgment. By a stroke of luck tranquillity follows upon suspension of judgment. This awareness of skepticism as a value affords a smooth transition from the first phase to the second.

The second phase consists in abandoning in fact the search for truth. The skeptics invent their principle of equipollence, according to which one may oppose to any given thesis a contradictory proposition of equal value. In the first phase, skepticism appears as an evolution in the direction of truth; in the second, it crystallizes in willful suspension of judgment. "If nothing can be known and if opinion is most disgraceful, then a wise man ought never to accept anything as certain," writes Augustine in his account of Academic skepticism (*Answer to Skeptics*, II, v, 11). We must place here an arbitrary intervention of the will, for a state of uncertainty and anguish can never lead of itself to stability in the possession of an end. In the light of this second phase, the systematic nature of the tropes and the dogmatic character of the skeptic principles receive their full import. Skepticism becomes a sort of cynical nihilism railing at and despising all forms of assent. By a gradual process of autosuggestion, the principle of equipollence is substituted for the investigation of truth. Peace of mind, which stimulated inquiry as a distant goal, is found to result unexpectedly from suspension of judgment.

The skeptic does not *intend* to suspend judgment, but in the face of innumerable problems, he cannot do otherwise; there is no reason for accepting or refusing one solution rather than another. Unable to distinguish true from false, he abstains from judging; this action brings him the peace of mind he sought as the end of his inquiry. At this point, the second phase makes its appearance. Henceforth this new factor takes its place within the skeptic attitude; instead of trying to find truth in one of two contradictory conclusions, the skeptic strives to show the equal strength of the contradictory arguments. This a priori decision brings him peace of mind. By pronouncing judgment on the goodness or badness of things, writes Sextus, one is exposed to unnecessary disturbances. For if one possesses the good, the mind is disturbed by the fear of losing it; if one does not possess it, the privation causes much sadness. The skeptic, on the contrary, affirms nothing about the natures; he takes things and events as they come and does not pursue goods or flee evils, for he does not claim to know what is good or bad.

Sextus illustrates the formation of the skeptic attitude by a striking example taken from the life of a painter named Apelles. One day, the artist was vainly trying to represent foam around a horse's mouth. Irritated by the inadequacy of his work, he threw a sponge at the painting. The sponge, striking the picture, accomplished what he had been trying in vain to achieve. The skeptic searches constantly for truth, but without success. Misled by failure, he willfully renounces assent and resorts to equipollence and suspension. After this decision has been forced upon him by the problems of philosophy, the skeptic unexpectedly finds himself in possession of his end (*ataraxia*). But we can readily discern the great differences between the painful suspension forced on the mind by the difficulties of nature and the self-satisfied suspension which leads to tranquillity. No amount of Pyrrhonian explanation can obscure the contradictory character of suspension (*epochē*) considered under both aspects. And only a clear distinction between the two phases mentioned above affords us a thorough insight into the nature of the skeptic attitude.

PERMANENCE OF BOTH PHASES IN
THE SKEPTIC ATTITUDE

We noticed how smoothly the skeptic effected his transition to the second phase; he sincerely believes that he has relinquished none of the advantages implied in spontaneous doubt. In the skeptic mind, the second phase does not replace the first; on the contrary, skepticism holds fast to the characteristics of spontaneous doubt. The skeptic attempts to show that sincerity and spontaneity still dominate his attitude. He introduces himself as the nemesis of dogmatic exaggerations. If his language appears too dogmatic at times, he hastens to repudiate such an interpretation. When he wishes to explain the skeptic attitude in itself, he emphasizes the spontaneous aspect; he seems to feel that there alone his attitude may claim an inkling of dignity.

The two phases are not separated in the works of Sextus; they are confused in what the skeptic believes to be a perfectly legitimate unification. One or the other phase prevails according to his different preoccupations. While entering into the second phase, the skeptic reflects on the first; he still claims to inquire after truth, but renounces all hope of ever attaining it, or even of going towards it in any way whatsoever.

This concomitance of the two phases explains the basic difficulties involved in a correct interpretation of the skeptic attitude. Historians have tried more or less to judge Sextus Empiricus and Pyrrhonism as another system in the thought of ancient times. Baffled by numerous inconsistencies, they have either accused Sextus of being a poor exponent of Pyrrhonism or examined for the most part questions of secondary importance relating to the life or medical affiliation of Sextus. No sooner have we isolated a characteristic of the second phase than we find a text emphasizing the first phase and contradicting our previous conclusion. Such is the inevitable penalty for considering Pyrrhonism as a system. The characteristics of the first phase are closely related to those of the second phase in a background of confusion and ignorance. The two phases are constantly present in the skeptic attitude; they constitute the two poles of influence which may be found more or less in any systematic departure from the principles of realism.

The two phases may be clearly distinguished in their extreme manifestations. But there lies a region of indeterminacy in the transition from one phase to the other. Most of the skeptic states of mind partake of both phases. This confusion does not warrant a rejection of the theory;

on the contrary, the theory affords us with the only means of explaining the basic reasons for this confusion.

One may rightfully inquire how the skeptics can maintain such an attitude. Sextus and his predecessors were aware of the contradiction, but this was no problem for them from the viewpoint of speculation. Sextus, however, attempts to conciliate the two phases by explaining and correcting the dogmatic appearance of his principles. Time and time again, he shows his concern over the negative dogmatism implied in the second phase. He feels vaguely the insurmountable difficulty involved in a conciliation of spontaneous and systematic doubt. The first phase presents skepticism as a *fieri;* the second crystallizes this *fieri,* and should logically destroy the progressive character of spontaneous doubt.

The skeptic is not a philosopher; he despises those who glory in this title. His mind thrives on voluntary ignorance and indetermination. We already noted this characteristic in the definition of skepticism. The Pyrrhonian does not attribute any value to apprehension; he rejects definition, which is the cornerstone of science. He does not admit any contact with reality and his phenomenalistic theory of knowledge serves merely as a precaution against the attacks of the dogmatists. The two phases always pervade the skeptic attitude; and no explanation of the skeptic states of mind is complete without situating them in this dual context.

14

THE UNNAMABLE AND INCOMPREHENSIBLE GOD OF PHILO JUDAEUS [1]

PHILO's denial of a distinction of genus and species in God must have led him to a denial of the possibility of defining God, for definition, as may be gathered from his definition of man as being either a "rational mortal animal" or a "hopeful animal," consists, according to him, as it does according to Aristotle, of the combination of genus and species. And since God cannot be defined, no concept can be formed of his essence, for the concept of the essence of a thing is formed by its definition. Philo therefore maintains that "it is wholly impossible that God according to his essence should be known (*katanoēthēnai*) by any creature," for God is "incomprehensible." Together with the incomprehensibility of God he speaks also of the unnamability and ineffability

1 [From Harry A. Wolfson, *Philo: Foundations of Religious Philosophy in Judaism, Christianity, and Islam* (revised second printing, 2 vols., Cambridge, Mass.: Harvard University Press, 1948), vol. II, pp. 110-126. Reprinted by permission. Several paragraphs and the notes are omitted.]

of God, for God, he says, "is unnamable (*akatonomastou*) and ineffable (*arrhētou*) and in every way incomprehensible (*akatalēptou*)." By "incomprehensible" he does not mean that God is not comprehended by the senses but rather, as he explicitly says elsewhere, that "he is not comprehended by the mind."

Now, neither Plato nor Aristotle definitely says that God according to his essence cannot be known or is incomprehensible or cannot be envisaged even in mind. In Plato indeed the ideas are like the God of Philo "incorporeal," "invisible and imperceptible by the sense," "immovable" and "immutable" and similarly of God, whether he is the idea of the good or something distinct from the ideas, he says that he is simple (*haploun*) and is unchangeable, and still the ideas as well as God are considered by him as knowable. With regard to the ideas he says that "being" (*ousia*), that is, the totality of the ideas, is known by the intelligence (*gnōsis*) and that after proper preparation we can ultimately arrive at a knowledge of "what the essence of beauty is" (*ho esti kalon*), and with regard to that which is "ever unchangeably real," evidently including both God and the ideas, he says that it is "comprehensible (*perilēpton*) by the mind with the aid of reason." He admits of course, that "we do not sufficiently know the good" and that "in the world of knowledge the idea of the good appears last of all and is seen only with an effort," but this does not mean that it is unknowable.

Similarly in Aristotle, God is described as one and incorporeal and simple and indivisible. If that simplicity and indivisibility excluded the distinction of genus and species in God, then, of course, God could not be defined and hence God could not be known. But Aristotle never says explicitly that the simplicity of God excludes the distinction of genus and species and that God cannot be defined and cannot be known. Quite to the contrary, on the basis of an analysis of his own statements, it can be shown that, according to him, God's simplicity does not exclude from his essence the distinction of genus and species.

And just as Plato and Aristotle do not definitely say that God is unknowable so do they not definitely say that God cannot be named or spoken of. Indeed Plato says that "the Maker and Father of this All it is a hard task to find and having found him it is impossible to declare him to all men." The meaning of this passage, however, is not that God cannot be *declared,* that is, described, but rather that He cannot be declared to *all men,* because, according to Plato, it requires certain specific preparations to arrive at a knowledge of the ideas, and by the same token also at a knowledge of God, which preparations are not common to all men. It was not until later, on their becoming acquainted with Philo's view of the unknowability and ineffability of God, that the Church Fathers raised the question whether Plato meant by his statement that God was ineffable or not. Clement of Alexandria takes this passage as meaning that God is ineffable, "for," he asks, "how can that be effable (*rhēton*) which is neither genus, nor difference, nor species, nor individual, nor number?" So was also the interpretation of this passage of Plato by Celsus. In opposition to Celsus, however, Origen argues that from the wording of Plato's statement it is to be inferred that "he does not speak of God as ineffable (*arrhēton*) and unnamable (*akatonomaston*); on the contrary, he implies that he is effable and that there are a few to whom he may be declared."

In view of all this, when Philo derives from the principle of the simplicity of God the principle of the unknowability and unnamability of God, he has given expression to a view which must have been meant by him to be either a new interpretation of Plato and Aristotle or in opposition to them. Indirectly, from the fact that Plato's statement with regard to the difficulty of finding God and the impossibility of declaring him to others is taken by Philo quite definitely to refer to the existence of God, it may perhaps be inferred that he believed Plato to have held that as for the essence of God it is even impossible to find it and not merely to declare it to others. But, as against this, there is the passage in which he tries to show how "all Greeks and barbarians," that is, all Greek and barbarian philosophers, acknowledge the existence of a God "whose nature is not only invisible by the eye but also hard to guess by the mind." It will be noticed that with reference to the eye he says here that God's nature is "invisible" (*ahoratos*) and not merely "hard to see" (*dyshoratos*), whereas with reference to the mind he says that it is only "hard to guess" (*dystopastos*) but not "unguessable" (*atopastos*) or "incomprehensible" (*akatalēptos*). Is it not possible that his choice of words here was deliberate, because, to him, while philosophers have indeed the conception of a God whose nature is "invisible" and "hard to guess," they have no conception of a God whose nature is absolutely "incomprehensible"? But, however that may be, Philo was either giving new emphasis to a view which he considered as being implicit in the views of philosophers or else he was giving utterance to an entirely new view. In either case, we must probe for the reason of his new view, or of his new emphasis upon a view of which he thought to have found corroboration in the teachings of the philosophers.

The explanation, we shall now try to show, is suggested by Philo himself in two passages.

In one of these passages Philo shows how, starting with the philosophic principle of the incorporeality of God, which to him was also a scriptural principle, he arrives by the aid of scriptural verses at the principles of the unknowability and unnamability of God. The passage is a homily on the verse "And the Lord was seen by Abraham and said to him, 'I am thy God.'" Commenting upon this verse, he first tries to disabuse the reader of the thought that God was seen by Abraham in the literal sense of the term. "Do not suppose," he says, "that the vision was presented to the eyes of the body, for they see only the objects of sense and those are composite, brimful of corruptibility, while the divine is uncompounded and incorruptible." The vision of God here means, he argues, a mental vision, for "it is natural that an intelligible object can be apprehended only by the mind." Up to this point, it will be noticed, his interpretation of the verses contains nothing which is not in complete harmony with philosophic reasoning. For, given a God who is incorporeal and uncompounded, he cannot be perceived by the senses. Whatever conception one forms of it must be only in the mind. Plato and Aristotle and others have said that much.

But then Philo goes further and maintains that God cannot be apprehended by any man, not only as an object of sense but even as an object of intelligence, "for we have in us no organ by which we can envisage it, neither in sense, for it is not perceptible by sense, nor yet in mind." This is quite evidently going beyond what is warranted by purely logical reasoning from the philosophic principle of the incorporeality of God. No philosopher, as we have seen, ever said so explicitly. Philo himself seems to have been conscious of the fact that he was going here beyond philosophy or, at least, beyond the explicit statements of philosophers, and so he hastens to support his view by scriptural verses. The scriptural verses which he quotes are "Moses went into the thick darkness, where God was" and "Thou shalt see what is behind me, but my face thou shalt not see." From these verses he infers that God "by his very nature cannot be seen," by which he means that God cannot be comprehended by the mind. Once he has established the incomprehensibility of God by these verses, he derives therefrom the impossibility of naming God, for "it is a logical consequence that no proper name even can be appropriately assigned to the truly existent," and in proof of this he says: "Note that when the prophet desires to know what he must answer to those who ask about his name he says 'I am he that is,' which is equivalent to 'My nature is to be, not to be spoken.'" Another proof-text quoted by him is the verse "I appeared to Abraham, Isaac and Jacob as their God, but my name Lord I did not reveal to them." And once he has established the unnamability of God by these verses, he derives therefrom the incomprehensibility of God, arguing that "indeed, if he is unnamable, He is also inconceivable and incomprehensible."

One may perhaps find a sort of circle in his reasoning here. Starting first with scriptural verses which he interprets to mean that God is incomprehensible, he derives therefrom that God is also unnamable. Then, supporting his logical conclusion that God is unnamable by a verse which explicitly says that the name of God was not revealed to those to whom He appeared, he derives therefrom that God is also incomprehensible. Probably what Philo means to say is that the incomprehensibility and the unnamability of God are logically implied in one another and that both of them rest primarily upon scriptural verses. As for these scriptural verses, it will be noticed that the ones which serve him as a proof-text for the unnamability of God are more explicit than the one which serves him as a proof-text for the incomprehensibility of God, and, consequently, even though the latter verse is quoted by him first, it is the former verse, that about the unnamability of God, which may be considered as the primary basis of his view about the incomprehensibility of God.

But once he has found the implication of the principle of the incomprehensibility of God in the scriptural teaching as to the unnamability of God, he comes to find the same implication also in the scriptural teaching as to the unlikeness of God, though in its primary sense, as we have seen, it implies only that God is incorporeal. Thus, commenting upon the verse "How dreadful is this place," he says that the verse refers to the question of the whereabouts of God, and he mentions two views on the subject. "Some say that everything that subsists occupies some space, and of these one allots to the Existent One this space, another that, whether inside the world or a space outside it in the interval between worlds. Others maintain that the Uncreated resembles nothing among created things, but so completely transcends them that even the swiftest understanding falls far short of apprehending him and acknowledges its failure." Here then the principle of the unlikeness of God, which is a scriptural principle, is taken as the basis of the principle of the incomprehensibility of God.

But there is more than that to this passage. The exponents of the first view which he mentions are the Stoics and Epicureans. Consequently the exponents of the view which he opposes to that of the Stoics and Epicureans must also be some Greek philosophers. Now, as we have seen, no Greek philosopher before Philo has ever said explicitly that God is incomprehensible. But it is possible, as we have suggested, that Philo has read into those philosophers, such as Plato and Aristotle, who believed in the incorporeality and simplicity of God, his own belief, derived by him from Scripture, as to the unlikeness and the incomprehensibility of God. Or, it is possible that in his reference here to philosophers who maintain that "The Uncreated is like nothing among created things" Philo had in mind specifically the statement reported in the name of Antisthenes to the effect that "God does not become known from an image, nor is He seen with eyes; He is like no one. Wherefore no man can come to the knowledge of Him from an image."

But it will be noticed that this statement of Antisthenes by itself does not say that, because of His unlikeness to anything corporeal, God cannot be comprehended even by the mind. All he says is that "no man can come to the knowledge of Him from an image," which may merely mean that God cannot be adequately described in terms borrowed from corporeal objects. Philo's additional inference in the statement quoted that, because of his unlikeness to any created being, God is incomprehensible even to the mind is a view at which he has arrived, as we have been trying to show, by reasoning from his own combination of the scriptural principle of the unlikeness of God with the scriptural principle of the unnamability of God.

In the light of all that we have said, we can reconstruct the mental processes by which Philo must have arrived at the view of the unnamability and unknowability of God. From philosophic sources he derived the belief that God is incorporeal and hence indivisible and simple. With this philosophic belief he identified the scriptural teaching of the unlikeness of God. Now this principle of incorporeality would on purely philosophic grounds explicitly exclude only such compositions in the divine nature as philosophers would call (a) body and soul, (b) the four elements, (c) substance and accident, and (b) matter and form. It would not of itself exclude the distinction of genus and species, and hence it would not exclude definition and hence also it would not of itself lead to the indescribability and unknowability of God.

But in Scripture Philo has found (a) statements to the effect that God has not revealed his name to those to whom He appeared and also (b) laws prohibiting (1) mention of the proper name of God, (2) taking in vain any other name of God and (3) treating lightly the word "God" in general. Scripture thus teaches the doctrine of the unnamability of God. This scriptural doctrine of the unnamability of God logically led him to the doctrine of the indefinability of God and the indefinability of God logically led him to the doctrine of the incomprehensibility of God; and once he arrived at the incomprehensibility of God, he found corroboration for it, by means of interpretation, in the verse "Moses went into the thick darkness, where God was." Then, having arrived at the doctrine of the incomprehensibility of God, he is led to extend the meaning of the scriptural doctrine of the unlikeness of God to include also his incomprehensibility; but, inasmuch as the scriptural doctrine of unlikeness has already been identified by him with the philosophic principle of incorporeality and simplicity, he is thus also led to ascribe the principle of the incomprehensibility of God to all those Greek philosophers who believed in God's incorporeality and simplicity.

15

PLOTINUS ON *NOUS* AS EMANATION [1]

PLOTINUS' doctrine of *Nous* is the fullest expression in his system of the universal later Hellenic belief in a totally unified cosmic order. It is also the means by which he tries to bring the absolute, transcendent One into the organic unity of such a cosmos. *Nous* is the first stage in the emanation or procession of the universe from the One; and in Plotinus' account of it are to be found such attempts as he makes to

[1] [From A. H. Armstrong, *The Architecture of the Intelligible Universe in the Philosophy of Plotinus* (Cambridge: the University Press, 1940), pp. 49-61. Reprinted by permission. Some paragraphs of the main text and the notes are omitted.]

supplement or improve upon the concept of emanation. The connection between the One and *Nous* is the most vital point in the structure of Plotinus' system. We have already considered it from the point of view of the One. Now we must turn to consider it from the point of view of *Nous,* and must also consider the relation of *Nous* to what comes after it, Soul and the visible universe. In doing this we shall have to go into the question of what Plotinus really meant by "emanation" and what are the origins of the conception.

Nous in Plotinus has clearly become something far more complex and important than the "second mind" or "second god" of the Middle Platonist tradition, of Numenius and Albinus. Its different aspects may be summarily classified as follows: (i) It is a radiation, or efflux from the One, like light from the sun. (ii) In a few passages it is conceived as the first unfolding of the potentialities of the One, which is a seed holding all things in potency. (iii) It is the highest phase of intellect, both human and universal, which, directly contemplating the One, apprehends it in multiplicity. (iv) With this last is closely connected the idea that *Nous* proceeds from the One as a potency and is actualized by returning upon it in contemplation. (v) It is the Intellectual Cosmos, a world-organism which contains the archetypes of all things in the visible universe. As such it possesses to the full that organic unity which the later, "Posidonian" Stoics had predicated of the visible, for them the only, cosmos, but which Plotinus had denied to it in any full or real sense. (vi) This aspect is to some extent connected with the psychological side of *Nous* by considering it as a universe of interpenetrating spiritual beings, each containing all the others organically united in its contemplation. These six aspects may be grouped under three general headings, *Nous* as Emanation, *Nous* as Mind, and *Nous* as Universe.

I shall here examine the genuine conception of emanation which is bound up with the "positive" conception of the One and is expressed in metaphors of light.

It is fairly clear what Plotinus means to express in his account of emanation. *Nous* and *Psyche* are produced by a spontaneous and necessary efflux of life or power from the One, which leaves their source undiminished. The relation between the One and *Nous* is described as being like that of the sun and its light, or in similes from the "radiative" effects of fire, snow, or perfumes. The difficulty is to give the conception any philosophical meaning. It is not easy to see what the significance of this conception of emanation or radiation can be when applied to two spiritual beings, and in particular how, if the process is necessary and eternal, the one can be inferior to the other or essentially different in character. The metaphor does not really work when applied to the peculiar relationship which must exist between the One and *Nous*. We must, I think, admit if we read the passages in question that Plotinus is really trying to give an explanation of this relationship; he is not content simply to say that the One "produces" *Nous* in some mysterious way which he is unable to define. His explanation, however, takes the form of a baffling and unsatisfactory metaphor. This is especially strange, because Plotinus is usually quite aware of the unsatisfactoriness of metaphors as a final form of philosophical exposition, and criticizes his own acutely.

We can, of course, bring forward general considerations which make the difficulty less formidable. We can say that this confusion of thought was the price which had to be paid to maintain the organic unity of the cosmos, an indispensable postulate alike of magic, Greek religion, and Greek philosophy. We can agree with Arnou that every term in Plotinus' philosophical vocabulary brings a little piece of its parent system with it, that his tradition was too complex for him to master completely. That this is true can be seen clearly throughout the *Enneads*. It would, however, be satisfactory if we could make some approach to a more detailed solution. This it seems possible to do by investigating the past history of the conception of emanation, even if at first sight such an investigation only seems to make confusion worse confounded.

The first appearance of anything that can be called a theory of emanation in the Greek philosophical tradition is to be found in that later Stoicism which goes under the name of Posidonius. It appears in the account of the history of the soul. The modifications which the divine substance endures in the cosmologies of the older Stoicism have disappeared. We find a genuine emanation of the *hegemonikon* (ruling principle) from the sun, combined with the distinctive theory of "undiminished giving" of light which is the basis of Plotinus' light metaphor. The important thing to notice for the present purpose is that the theory is completely materialistic. What comes from the visible sun and returns to it again is a fiery breath. Given Stoic physics and Stoic materialism this idea of a material outflowing of the material *hegemonikon* is perfectly natural and in place; but it is by no means in place in an account of the relations between spiritual beings in the system of a thinker like Plotinus, who is very clear about the distinction between material and spiritual. Further, Plotinus is extremely conscious that materialism is the supreme defect of Stoic thought, and criticizes it vigorously. The unsatisfactoriness of the concept of emanation, therefore, becomes even more marked when we realize that it involves a concealed admission of Stoic materialism into Plotinus' system.

The only investigation which seems to throw any light on how this came about is the following up of the history of a subsidiary doctrine vital to Plotinus' theory of emanation, that of the incorporeality of light. If the passages in the *Enneads* in which this doctrine occurs are considered in chronological order it becomes apparent that it underwent a certain development, or at least modification, in Plotinus' mind. In the later treatises, II. I and IV. 5, we have simply the statement that light is incorporeal though dependent on body, an *energeia* of body. In IV. 5. 6-7, this statement appears as a criticism of the Aristotelian doctrine according to which light is also incorporeal, but is simply "a phenomenon in the diaphanous," the presence in it of the luminary source. Aristotle, while maintaining that light was not technically a *soma,* regarded it simply as a physical phenomenon. Plotinus is concerned to give it a more august status. His own doctrine is doubtless dependent on the account of color as a material *aporroë* of particles given in the *Timaeus* and is deeply affected by the Posidonian theory of light. What seems to be his own is the combination of the doctrines that light is incorporeal and that it is the outflow of the luminary, and also the very close parallelism that he maintains exists between light and life, the Act or *energeia* of the soul. This last point should be noted, as it at once raises the status of light in the universe enormously. It is no longer a mere physical incident but a manifestation of the spiritual principle of reality or activity in the luminary, its *logos* or *eidos.*

In I. 6. 3 Plotinus goes even further than he does in the passages above referred to and says that light is itself *logos* and *eidos,* the principle of form in the material world. Moreover, he goes on to make the surprising statements that fire "holds the position of Form in relation to the other elements" though itself a body, and that it is near to the incorporeal inasmuch as it is the subtlest of bodies, that the others receive it into themselves but it does not receive the others. This would fit well enough in a Stoic, but it is startling to find it in Plotinus, even in an early treatise. The whole passage is on the border line between neo-Platonism and Stoicism. It combines the doctrine that there is no clear frontier between material and spiritual because the principle of reality even in material things is spiritual with the doctrine that there is no clear frontier because "spirit" is only the finest and subtlest form of matter.

This unguarded remark about the nature of fire is, I think, unparalleled in Plotinus. He is not usually in danger of lapsing into naïve confusions between matter and spirit. What is, however, clear from all the passages referred to above is that Plotinus, in asserting the incorporeality of light, does not simply mean like Aristotle to maintain that light is not a body but an incident of a body. He gives to light a very special status on the frontier of spirit and matter. This conclusion is supported by another passage in which the same type of thought takes a rather different form. The eleventh chapter of the first treatise on the Problems of the Soul begins with an exposition of the doctrine of "appropriate physical receptacles" of soul. This is a further development of the doctrine of "analogy," of the exact correspondence of the visible and intelligible universe. As applied here to the making of shrines and images it implies that some physical bodies are naturally more receptive of soul than others. Plotinus then goes on to describe the connection between the world of *Nous* and the sense-world in a way that gives a position of peculiar importance to the sun. *Nous* is described—rather casually, as a *paradeigma* for the immediate purpose—by the image so often applied to the One, as "the sun of the other world." The soul is said to be an intermediary between this sun of the other world and the visible sun. With this may be compared another passage where "the visible gods as far as the moon," i.e., the sun and stars, are said to be related to the *noētoi theoi* (intelligible gods) as its radiance is to a star. Here we find not only light, but the luminous bodies, and especially the sun, brought into especially close relation with the intelligible universe, standing on the frontiers of visible and invisible; a position which is confirmed in the case of the sun by the frequent use of the sun-metaphor for the One and, as here, for *Nous*.

This peculiar position of the sun is, of course, well known in the later developments of neo-Platonism, and is particularly characteristic of the theology of the Emperor Julian. It is, however, interesting to discover traces of the "solar theology" in the works of a writer so independent of contemporary religious ideas as Plotinus, particularly as the passages in question occur in treatises written apparently later than the penetrating criticism of this very theology of radiation contained in VI. 4 and 5. No doubt Plotinus thought that he was simply following the teaching of Plato about the Sun in *Republic* VI-VII and was influenced in the working out of his theory by Plato's emphatic assertion of the divinity of the heavenly bodies in *Timaeus* 40B and still more in the *Laws* 821B, 898D f. The passages just quoted seem however to go beyond anything in Plato and to show distinct traces of contemporary influences. Their interest is still further enhanced by comparison with a passage in the *Hermetica* which may be roughly contemporary with Plotinus. In this passage the light of the sun, source of all being and life in the visible world, is said to be the receptacle of *noētē ousia*, "but of what the substance consists or whence it flows God (or the sun) only knows." The Hermetic writer is rather clumsily trying to solve the problem created by the superimposition on the organic universe of the "Posidonian" solar theology of the Platonic intelligible universe, whose existence he rather grudgingly admits. This has points of contact with the problem which Plotinus is trying to solve by his theory of emanation. The solution, too, proposed by the Hermetist corresponds very closely with the doctrine of "appropriate physical receptacles" and the important place given to the sun in *Enneads*, IV. 3. II.

I do not wish to suggest that Plotinus was influenced by Hermetic teaching, either through that unknown and probably unknowable intermediary, the teaching of Ammonius Saccas, or in any other way. Still less do I wish to suggest that Plotinus could at any period of his life have been called a "solar theologian" or a sun worshipper. What does seem to be true is that he was familiar with a type of solar theory (perhaps partly his own invention) in which the sun's light was thought of either as the appropriate receptacle for the immaterial substance of the intelligible world, as the intermediary between material and spiritual, or as itself incorporeal, closely parallel to the life of soul, and again on the frontier of spiritual and material (this last form of the theory may be a refinement of Plotinus' own). Allied to the principle of "analogy" this theory would provide very good ground for the growth of Plotinus' theory of emanation. Given that everything in the visible cosmos is an image of something in the intelligible, and that light is itself a spiritual energy or activity, what is more natural than to represent spiritual activity and productivity in terms of light? It would be much better suited to this purpose than the original "Posidonian" theory of the emanation of the fiery soul from the sun, the materialism of which would naturally repel Plotinus, and the influence of which is more clearly apparent in neo-Platonic theories about *pneuma* and astral bodies than in the Plotinian theory of emanation itself.

The theory of emanation expressed in the metaphor of radiation belongs to a type of thought in which there is a wide and doubtful borderland between matter and spirit. What seems to lie behind it is not simply the late Stoic theory of an organic universe centering in the sun but an attempt to reconcile this theory with the Platonic conception of a hierarchy of reality, sensible and intelligible, through the mediation of a half-spiritual, half-material realm of light. This is the theory which we find in *Hermetica* XVI, and the passage which I have quoted seems to show that Plotinus knew it and found it acceptable. If this is really so, the theory of emanation by radiation would be one of the very few parts of Plotinus' philosophical and religious thought to which he is generally remarkably superior. It is, perhaps, significant that this lapse from his usual clarity into a way of thinking more characteristic of his contemporaries, with their slipshod inaccuracy and reliance on the imagination rather than the reason, occurs in an attempt to maintain unbroken the organic unity of the cosmos, a postulate indispensable to all the non-Christian thought of the epoch, the foundation both of its magic and its religion.

As a pendant to this discussion of Plotinus' theory of emanation, we must consider the nearest approach which he himself makes to a criticism of it. This is contained in the treatise VI. 4. As the theory of emanation is always expressed in metaphorical terms, so the criticism of it takes the form of a very acute analysis of the metaphor. The criticism is, however, rather implicit than explicit, and Plotinus does not seem to have been altogether conscious of the very far-reaching consequences for his system which spring from this analysis and from others of the conclusions which he draws in this treatise and that which follows it.

The passage is worth translating nearly in full. It runs: "If you take a small luminous mass as centre and surround it with a larger transparent sphere, so that the light within shows over the whole of that which surrounds it . . . shall we not say that the inner [luminous] mass is not affected in any way but remains in itself and reaches over the whole of the outer mass, and that the light which is seen in the little central body has encompassed the outer? . . . Now if one takes away the material mass and keeps the power of the light you cannot surely say that the light is anywhere any longer, but that it is equally distributed over the whole outer sphere; you can no longer determine in your mind where it was situated before; nor can you say whence it came nor how . . . but can only puzzle and wonder, perceiving the light simultaneously present throughout the sphere." Now it is clear that this elimination of the materialist element in the metaphor, the actual physical centre, has in effect destroyed the idea of emanation. The distinguishing characteristic of emanation is radiation from a centre. If the centre, as here, is removed, there can be no longer any question of emanation. What is left is simply an assertion of the omnipresence of the spiritual. In the same way his modifications of a too materialistic theory of the presence of the One-Being through its "powers," his insistence that where the power is, there the source of the power must be present in all its fullness, that it is at once totally omnipresent and totally separate, again lead to a destruction of any real idea of emanation. For it is substituted the doctrine of "reception according to the capacity of the recipient." This, in a more developed form, appears as an alternative to emanation in Plotinus' account of the relation of *Nous* to the One.

What it is important to see clearly is that if the source is present in its fullness in the emanant, and the emanant is in no way less than the source, there can really be no true emanation at all—because there can be no real difference between source and emanant; and, in the same way, the doctrine that each thing participates in the One-Being according to its capacity removes the need for or possibility of a doctrine of emanation. The hold of the metaphor on Plotinus' mind must have been extraordinarily strong (due perhaps to the unique philosophical and religious position occupied for him, as for his predecessors and contemporaries, by the sun and its light) for him to continue to use it without fully perceiving the destructive force of his own closer analysis.

PART TWO

Medieval Philosophy

V. Patristic Thought

An intense and continuous effort was made during the first twelve centuries of our era to evaluate and, wherever possible, assimilate the findings of Greek philosophy within the context of the Christian revelation. Particularly during the first half of this period, a major share of the work of combining faith with understanding was carried by the Greek Fathers and Doctors. Selections (16) and (17) are brief reminders of our enormous debt to the Christian minds in the Greek tradition.

Clement was one of the earliest masters of the Christian school at Alexandria, a major center for theological and philosophical speculation during the patristic age. As E. F. Osborn establishes in Selection (16), Clement was well aware of the complex intellectual situation confronting the Christian mind under the Roman empire. Like the first apologists, he saw the need for keeping Christian doctrine free from both the infiltration of pagan cults and the distortion of the numerous heresies already present. Yet at the same time, he realized with Philo that revealed religion cannot simply turn its back upon the sound elements in human philosophy. Hence he dedicated his mind and pen to the delicate task of showing how the purity of Christian truth can be preserved in the very process of acknowledging and appropriating the particular truths achieved by natural reason and Greek philosophy. Clement of Alexandria regarded philosophy as a divine gift and testament for the Greeks, a preparatory teaching which can dispose human reason to accept the Gospel, somewhat as the Law prepared the Jewish people. Fundamentally, this was the key conception of philosophy as the handmaid of theology which was to encourage the subsequent centuries of Christian speculative work.

St. Gregory of Nyssa was one of the three great Cappadocian theologians, along with his elder brother, St. Basil, and St. Gregory Nazianzenus. An entire theological and philosophical anthropology grew around his central conviction about man as the image of God, as presented in Selection (17). St. Gregory of Nyssa was able to reinforce the Platonic teaching that philosophy should aim at achieving an imitation of the divine life in man, by developing the Scriptural doctrine on how God created man in His own image. There was an essentially moral and religious purpose behind this creative act, since it endowed men with a sufficient likeness to God to assure them some kinship with God and a natural desire for sharing in His goodness and beauty. Gregory also made some suggestions on the problems of human mortality and evil, since these facts would seem to indicate that the imago Dei *is obliterated or completely shadowed over. His emphasis upon our freedom of choice and upon the will as a shaping principle in man provided a distinctively Christian note to the philosophical study of man. He was also aware that the Christian view of humanity overrides the division into Greek and barbarian, and that there is an ultimate depth of mystery in man as well as in God. Selection (17) is an exception, in that it does not consist of a relatively continuous text from one book, but is a tissue of excerpts from several of Gregory's writings. The full impact of his views upon such subsequent Latin Christian authors as St. Bernard (Selection 25) can only be appreciated by collecting some of the frequently quoted texts from his works.*

The importance of biographical data for understanding the history of philosophy is brought home vividly by Vernon Bourke's description of the intellectual and moral conversion of St. Augustine (Selection 18). Philosophical systems do not write themselves, but have a genesis in human lives and individual perspectives. St. Augustine is an especially personal thinker, not that his problems and evidences are of a purely private nature, but that he always approaches them in terms of his personal quest for wisdom and the happy life. This personal quality in his speculation gives it a universal appeal and a definite immediacy for our own age of individual searching on religious and philosophical issues. Bourke shows how his conversion can be regarded both as a consummation of pagan thought and as a judgment passed upon it. Augustine uses the skeptics and the neo-Platonists to break the sway of materialism and cosmic dualism. But he also owes his liberation to the sermons of St. Ambrose and the teachings of Sacred Scripture. Especially in his conviction that the happy life requires a moral reformation and the aid of divine grace, he moves beyond Plotinus into the Christian way of life.

Anton Pegis uses the crucial instance of the nature of man to determine, in Selection (19), the relation of neo-Platonic and Christian themes in Augustine. A timely warning is issued against reading into the Augustinian definition of man as a rational soul using a body, the special re-

quirements of Aristotelian definition or the medieval questions on the substantial unity of man. Such anachronisms defeat the effort to understand how the African Doctor himself treated man. His standpoint resembles that of Plotinus, insofar as the human mind is related to the procession of light from the divine mind into the world of matter. The human soul has an office to perform in regard to the body, so that the Augustinian approach to the question of human unity is primarily one of practical religious ordering. Yet a paradox develops, since the very loyalty of the soul to its divinely appointed task of caring for the body involves a certain withdrawal from oneself and God, as well as a special liability to the attraction of lower goods. In pointing out that the solution lies in cultivating the life of recollection or interiority, Pegis remarks that this does not involve either a total separation from the material world or a degradation of God to a function of our own thoughts and desires. The delicate balance of many factors and relations entering into a Christian humanism becomes apparent in this discussion.

St. Augustine's active theory of sensation establishes a correlation between the act of attention on the soul's part and certain bodily modifications, but it does not permit a genuine derivation of the intellectual factor from the sensible world. The stress upon the perceiver's activity yields a rich harvest of observations on the contribution of memory to meaning and temporality, but it also cuts short certain investigations which lead in the direction of human reception from material existents. This dual aspect is evident in the analysis of Augustine's theory of signs, made by R. A. Markus (Selection 20). The interests of our own age often lead us to inquire about new facets of thought, even in such a well-scanned author as Augustine. The present concern about language and semantics has led Markus to examine Augustine's conception of signs for its own sake. The fact that this doctrine is found embedded in a Scriptural and theological context reminds us that St. Augustine is primarily a religious thinker, not a philosopher in the present-day specialized meaning. A notable parallel is nevertheless established between him and Charles S. Peirce, concerning the triadic nature of signs. The whole situation of signification involves not only the sign itself, but also the object signified and the interpreting subject. There is a supple account of the different functions of linguistic signs, now as manifesting something about an object, now as expressing the feelings, perceptions, and judgments of the sign-maker, and now as communicating to another person. Here we can sense the importance of Augus-

tine's training in rhetoric, his profound study of Scriptural expressions, his introspective bent, his zeal for sacramental grace, and his indefatigable search after human analogies for the interpersonal life of the Trinity. Where he fails to follow through on his own leads, however, is with regard to what we today call the ground floor words or signs indicating our direct experiential knowledge of sensible things.

Boethius stands at the end of the Latin patristic age and points forward to the Schoolmen of the coming middle ages. His formulation of the problem of the universals and his scholarly labors in translating and commenting upon the Greek philosophers made a deep impress upon the subsequent line of thinkers, as Selection (23) will bring out. One area where his influence is lasting, but by no means unambiguous, is the metaphysics of infinite and finite being. He grapples with the problem of synthesizing the Greek views on participation and causality with the Christian teaching on creation and the divine infinity. In Selection (21), Charles Fay counsels against reading back into Boethius the medieval and later Scholastic meanings given to esse. *The sharp distinctions and rigid systematic implications which characterize the later treatments of form, essence, and existence, are notably absent in his treatises. That is why the Boethian axioms on being, as formulated at the beginning of the* De Hebdomadibus, *were interpreted in diverse ways and employed within conflicting metaphysical contexts during the middle ages. That the famous* Consolation of Philosophy *should be pertinent to a metaphysical inquiry into the constituents of being indicates the unity of Boethius' speculation. He sees a need to interweave the metaphysical analysis of the good with a moral search for the good. To give us reliable consolation, moral philosophy cannot be content with being a purely formal analysis or with expressing our wishes and emotions, as some of the emotive theories of ethics today maintain. It must grow out of a metaphysical study of the structure of being and the dynamism of human nature, in its tendency toward the perfect good.*

16

CLEMENT OF ALEXANDRIA ON CHRISTIAN TRUTH AND PHILOSOPHY [1]

THERE are two main tendencies in Clement of Alexandria's account of truth. The first is to call the essential elements of Christianity true and everything else false. This is the way Clement speaks when he is talking about heresy. The second tendency is to include within truth not only all valid Christian teaching, but everything that is consistent with it. This is the way Clement speaks when he is talking about philosophy.

I. PROPERTIES OF TRUTH

(1) *One and only.* Clement divides truth from error very sharply. It is distinguished from opinion and from images. The truth itself is distinct from partial truths or names, as God is distinct from the things said about God. "Guessing at truth is one thing and truth is another. Likeness is one thing and the real thing another. This one is the result of learning and practice and the other the result of power and faith." [2] To turn from truth to heresy is a tragic thing. There is only one truth, as there is only one Church. Variety, falsehood, and deceit go together and contrast with the simplicity and uniqueness of truth. Truth is to error as wheat is to tares, as real fruit is to wax imitations, as the king's highway to dangerous byroads, as plants to weeds.

(2) *Very powerful.* There is nothing greater than this truth. It is strong to deliver. "Let us bring truth down from heaven . . . and let her, making her light shine to the farthest point, send out light all around to those who are tossed about in darkness. Let her deliver men from deception, holding out her strong right hand." [3]

Truth cannot be overthrown. People who are afraid that philosophy will destroy faith are like children who are frightened of hobgoblins. If persuasive argument can dissolve their faith, they cannot believe in the truth, "for truth is unconquerable but false opinion dissolves." [4] Clement's faith in the power of truth made him ready to examine all sorts of teaching, without fear of being led into error.

[1] [From E. F. Osborn, *The Philosophy of Clement of Alexandria* (Cambridge: The University Press, 1957), pp. 113, 117-125. Reprinted by permission. There are omissions in the text and notes, and two modifications in the text.]

[2] *Stromateis*, I, 38.

[3] *Protrepticus*, 2.

[4] *Stromateis*, VI, 81.

(3) *Divine origin.* The greatness of truth is due to its divine origin or even its divine identity. Our Lord said. "I am the truth," He is the indemonstrable first principle whose authority gives us a firm basis for our demonstrations. He speaks through the prophets, Gospels, and apostles. Truth is derived from the Scriptures, which are of God and of the Lord. The Greeks claim to have truth, but admit that they have only received it from men. But

no man can speak worthily the truth about God, as the weak and perishing cannot speak about the unborn and immortal, nor the work about its maker. . . . For human speech is essentially weak and unable to declare God. . . . The only wisdom then is that taught by God and this wisdom is ours. On it depend all the sources of wisdom which aim at the truth.[5]

Our adherence to the truth is loyalty to our Lord, and to abandon the truth is a disloyalty similar to that of the soldier who deserts his post. Part of the work of the Logos was to simplify the truth. The Law was given through Moses, but eternal grace and truth came through Jesus Christ.

(4) *Tradition.* Clement connects truth very closely with "the teaching," "the canon of the Church," "the confession" and "the tradition." The teaching of which he speaks is derived from the Lord as first principle. It is one, apostolic, of the Lord, divine, and kingly. Clement regards the canon of the Church as important for the recognition of truth. Truth was in this way linked to a living tradition, delivered by our Lord and the apostles, preserved in the unity of the Church, "this unity which is not only a unity of social life but a unity of faith, unity of instruction and unity of truth, as also a unity of the means of salvation. Church and Tradition for him are blended into one unique, living, present reality." [6]

Truth can be concisely and simply expressed, though the way to it may be exacting. Deviations from truth can be readily established, and there lies a great gulf fixed between truth and heresy. If those outside the Church have any truth, it is because they have stolen it. Truth is lofty and exclusive. It is chosen by "apprehending vision" and "authoritative reasoning," and its first principle is received by faith. Yet Clement does not deny the need for reasoning, when dealing with ultimate truth. The Christian uses logical techniques to find the truth in Scripture. He connects the different elements of the truth with the first principle by means of demonstration, and the tests for truth are tests of consistency.

II. TRUTH AND PHILOSOPHY

Elsewhere Clement speaks more widely of truth, and regards it as embracing rather than excluding human opinions. This second view of truth is connected with a second attitude which Clement held toward

[5] *Ibid.,* VI, 91.
[6] Claude Mondésert, S.J., *Clément d'Alexandrie* (Paris, 1944), p. 117.

those outside the Christian Church. He was concerned in the first place to vindicate the Church as having divine truth, and to condemn the heretics as having departed from this truth. He was also concerned to show to the pagan world on the one hand that Christianity was not a narrow isolated religion which ignored culture and philosophy, and to show to Christians on the other hand that they had nothing to lose and much to gain by appropriating culture and philosophy. He maintained that Christianity included all that was good in non-Christian thought. When he speaks of the heretics, the truth is an exclusive, unique and transcendent thing. When he speaks of philosophy, the truth is an inclusive, all-embracing thing. "The way of truth is one, but into it as into an everflowing river flow rivulets from every side." [7] We find this view of truth particularly in Book I of the *Stromateis,* where Clement describes and justifies his use of philosophy.

(1) *Philosophy.* Clement's attitude to philosophy was important, because here he departed from previous Christian tradition. Religion and philosophy had gone together at various periods in the history of the Greeks, but Christians, except for Justin and Athenagoras, had little to do with philosophy. Even these two had practically nothing to contribute to the *rapprochement* of Christianity with classical philosophy.

Clement defines the philosophy which he finds acceptable. Philosophy is "an investigation concerning truth and the nature of things, and this is the truth of which the Lord himself said: 'I am the Truth'. . . . And philosophy—I do not speak of the Stoic or Platonic or Aristotelian philosophy, but whatever has been well said by each of these sects, which teaches righteousness with reverent understanding—this eclectic whole I call philosophy." [8] Philosophy must teach a Creator God, the mutability of physical elements, the good as assimilation to God, and the dispensation of the Gospel as the chief part of all training. Philosophy is from God, but was stolen from him like the fire of Prometheus. It is inferior to truth but it is not worthless. It is necessary, because we would have to use it to show that it was unnecessary. It is desirable, because a money-changer must know what false coins are like, if he would distinguish the true.

The problem for Clement lay in the fact that while philosophy was not truth it was not merely error. A similar problem faced Plato, when he was dealing with art. Art, says Plato in the *Republic,* is not truth, but it is not error. It is like philosophy for Clement, some kind of intermediate thing. Both Clement and Plato use the same argument. Philosophy or art is a preparatory education for truth. Clement compares philosophy to the Law of Moses, which St. Paul had described as a schoolmaster to the Jews to prepare them for the truth. Philosophy was a schoolmaster to the Greeks in the same way. The same idea is conveyed

[7] *Stromateis,* I, 29.
[8] *Ibid.,* I, 37.

by other similes. Philosophy is the irrigation of the land in preparation
for the truth, a stepping stone of the truth. Another justification of
philosophy complicates the explanation. The Law and philosophy not
only fulfilled the same function but were identical in content. The
Greeks stole their ideas from the Hebrews and from one another. The
subject of Greek plagiarism is discussed with masses of evidence throughout the *Stromateis.* Clement quotes Numenius: "For what is Plato but
Moses speaking Attic Greek." [9]

Among the remaining descriptions of philosophy which Clement gives,
the most important has been analyzed as follows:

The four alternatives which Clement puts forward form a climax. He begins
with the possibility that the truth contained in philosophy is to be ascribed to
an accident involved in God's providential economy. He continues with explanations attributing the element of truth in philosophy to the general revelation,
or even making the Greek philosophers prophets similar to those of the Old
Testament. And he ends by indicating that philosophy owes its existence to a
reflection of the eternal truth itself, and that the philosophers have beheld God—
an imperfect, vague, unclear, yet true vision.[10]

(2) *Truth.* We can now examine the different attitude to truth which
Clement's treatment of philosophy necessitated.

The truth being one, for falsehood has countless byroads, just as the Bacchantes
tore apart the limbs of Pentheus, so the schools of philosophy, both barbarian
and Greek, have done with truth, and each claims that the part he has obtained
is the whole truth. But all things, I consider, are illumined by the dawning light.
It may therefore be shown that all, both Greek and barbarians, who have sought
after truth, possess either no small amount or at least some part of the word of
truth. Eternity, indeed, unites in one moment present and future time, besides
the past as well. But truth is more capable than eternity of bringing together
its own seeds, though they have fallen on foreign ground. For we shall find that
many of the opinions entertained by the schools which are not utterly absurd and
are not cut off from natural connection, although they seem unlike one another,
agree in their basis and with all the truth (as a whole). For as a limb, or as a
part, or as a species, or as a genus, they come together into one; just as the lowest note is the opposite of the highest, but both are one harmony, and in numbers the even number differs from the odd, but both have their place in arithmetic. This is the case also in form, where there are the circle, the triangle, the
square, and whatever shapes differ from one another. Also in the whole cosmos,
all the parts, though they differ among themselves, preserve their relation to the
whole. Similarly, then, barbarian and Greek philosophy have torn off a piece of
the eternal truth, not from the mythology of Dionysus, but from the theology of
the Logos who eternally is. And he who brings together again the divided parts
and makes them one, mark well, shall without danger of error look upon the
perfect Logos, the truth.[11]

[9] *Ibid.,* I, 150.
[10] Einar Molland, *Clement of Alexandria on the Origin of Greek Philosophy* (Oslo,
1936), p. 71.
[11] *Stromateis,* I, 57.

This truth is a whole of many parts. The many parts when separated are not the whole truth, but are pieces of truth. Their truth in this separated condition depends on what they were originally, and will be, one complex whole. The important thing about them is not that they "seem alike," but that they "agree in their basis and with all the truth as a whole," They have the same starting point and fit together in the same whole. The different metaphors used—eternity, genus, species, part, harmony, number, figure, universe, body—indicate the kind of thing which truth is. Each example is something whose parts "preserve their relation to the whole."

Perhaps the most interesting thing is the conciliatory tone of the whole passage. The truth is, as before, divine in origin, a consistent system, powerful and one. But each of these qualities is interpreted not (as before) to exclude error, but to enable us to include the partial truth. The divine truth was contrasted with the human opinions of the heretics. Now the light of Christ shines on all. The heretics were too lazy to think consistently. Now consistency and coherence provide a means of reconciling conflicting views. The power of truth and the stability of those who follow it were contrasted with the weakness of human opinion and the insecurity of those who follow it. Now the power of truth enables it to collect the seeds which have fallen on foreign soil. The unity of truth, like the unity of the Church, was unique and separate from all else. Now the unity of truth enables it to make all things one.

Clement speaks of the truth of philosophy as partial. Truth, he says, is commonly ascribed to all things, whether perceived by intellect or sense-perceived. There is true painting in contrast to vulgar, dignified music in contrast to chaotic, true philosophy in contrast to other philosophy, and a true beauty in contrast to an artificial one. But one should be concerned with the truth itself, not just with true things or partial truths. There is a difference between seeking God and seeking things about God, as there is between substance and accidents. Christians have the substance of truth. Others have its accidents. Another description of the truth of Greek philosophy as partial says that it is revealed by the real truth in the same way as the sun shines on colors and shows what they are.

The inclusive, reconciling idea of truth never suggests that there is an equality betwen philosophy and the real truth. Philosophy, says Clement, is a joint cause in the comprehension of truth. Truth is one, while many things contribute to its investigation, and it is found through the Son. Virtue is one thing with many forms—wisdom, self-control, bravery, justice. Truth is one thing, but there is a truth of geometry in geometry, of music in music, and there is truth in the right Hellenic philosophy. "But there is only one truth, supreme and impregnable—that in which we are instructed by the Son of God." [12] The truth of Greek phi-

12 Ibid., II, 62.

losophy is distinct from our truth in the extent of the knowledge which
it gives, its demonstrative force and its divine power. We are taught by
God, learning our sacred letters by the Son of God. The saving doctrine
is complete and self-sufficient. Greek philosophy cannot make it any
stronger. It can only hedge it around. The truth of faith is as necessary to
life as bread. Philosophy is like a dessert, which is very nice but not
essential to the meal.

17

MAN AS THE IMAGE OF GOD: THE THEORY IN ST. GREGORY OF NYSSA [1]

GOD is the Maker of the nature of man, not urged to framing him
by any necessity, but in the superabundance of love working
the production of such a creature. For it was needful that neither
his light should be unseen, nor his glory without witness, nor his goodness unenjoyed, nor that any other quality observed in the divine nature
should in any case lie idle, with none to share it or enjoy it. If, therefore, man comes to his birth upon these conditions, namely, to be a
partaker of the good things in God, he is necessarily fashioned of such
a kind as to be adapted to the participation of such good. It was needful
that a certain affinity with the divine should be mingled with the nature
of man, in order that by means of this correspondence it might aim
at that which was native to it. Born for the enjoyment of divine good,
man must have something in his nature akin to that in which he is to
participate. For this purpose, he has been furnished with life, with
thought, with skill, and with all the excellences that we attribute to God,
in order that by each of them he might have his desire set upon that
which is not strange to him. Since, then, one of the excellences connected
with the divine nature is also eternal existence, it was altogether needful
that the equipment of our nature should not be without the further gift
of this attribute but should be immortal in itself, so that by its inherent
faculty it might both recognize what is above it, and be possessed with a
desire for the divine and eternal life.

In his own nature, God is everything which our mind can conceive of
good, or rather, he is transcending every good that we can conceive or
comprehend. He creates man for no reason than that he is good. Being
such, and having this as his reason for entering upon the creation of
our nature, He would not exhibit the power of his goodness in an im-

1 [Excerpts drawn from the following works of St. Gregory of Nyssa: *On the Making
of Man; On the Soul and the Resurrection; The Great Catechism*. The passages will be
found in *A Select Library of Nicene and Post-Nicene Fathers*, second series, vol. V
(Oxford: Parker, 1893), pp. 396-397, 405, 406, 436-437, 478-480, 481.]

perfect form, giving our nature some one of the things at his disposal, and grudging it a share in another. But the perfect form of goodness is here to be seen, both by his bringing man into being from nothing and by his fully supplying him with all good gifts. Yet since the list of individual good gifts is a long one, it is out of the question to apprehend it numerically. The language of Scripture therefore expresses it concisely by a comprehensive phrase, in saying that man was made "in the image of God." For this is the same as to say that he made human nature a participant in all good. If the Deity is the fullness of good, and this is his image, then the image finds its resemblance to the archetype in being filled with all good.

Thus there is in us the principle of all excellence, all virtue and wisdom, and every higher thing that we can conceive .But pre-eminent among all of them is the fact that we are free from necessity, and not in bondage to any natural power, but have decision in our own power as we please. For virtue is a voluntary thing, subject to no dominion: that which is the result of compulsion and force cannot be virtue. Moreover, man was appointed king over the earth and all things on it. He was beautiful in his form, being created an image of the archetypal beauty. He was without passion in his nature, for he was an imitation of the unimpassioned. He was full of frankness, delighting in a face-to-face manifestation of the personal Deity.

Now as the image bears in all respects the likeness of the archetypal excellence, if it had no aspect of difference, being absolutely without divergence from the divine, it would no longer be a likeness. In that case, it clearly would be absolutely identical with the prototype. What difference, then, do we discern between the divine and that which has been made like to the divine? We find it in the fact that the former is uncreated, while the latter has its being from creation. This distinction of property brings with it a train of other properties. For it is very certainly acknowledged that the uncreated nature is also immutable and always remains the same, while the created nature cannot exist without change. Its very passage from non-existence to existence is a certain motion and change of the non-existent, transmuted by the divine purpose into being.

That which is "made in the image" of the Deity necessarily possesses a likeness to its prototype in every respect. It resembles the prototype in being intellectual, immaterial, unconnected with any notion of weight, and in eluding any measurement of its dimensions. Yet as regards its own peculiar nature, it is something different from that prototype. Indeed, it would no longer be an "image," if it were altogether identical with that other being. Where we have A in that uncreated prototype, we have a in the image.

But perhaps what has been said will be contradicted by someone who looks only to the present condition of things and aims to show the untruthfulness of our statement, inasmuch as man is seen no longer under those primeval circumstances, but under almost entirely opposite ones. "Where is the divine resemblance in the soul? Where is the body's freedom from suffering? Where is the eternity of life? Man is of brief existence, subject to passions, liable to decay, and ready both in body and mind for every form of suffering." By these and the like assertions, and by directing the attack against human nature, the opponent will think that he upsets the account that has been offered respecting man.

In the case of our living bodies, composed as they are from the blending of atoms, there is no sort of agreement in substance between the simplicity and invisibility of the soul and the grossness of those bodies. Still, there is doubtless in them the soul's vivifying influence, exerted by a law which it is beyond the human understanding to comprehend. Not even when those atoms have again been dissolved into themselves [at death] has that bond of a vivifying influence vanished. While the framework of the body still holds together, each individual part is possessed of the soul which penetrates equally every component member. Yet one could not call that soul hard and resistant, even though it is blended with the solid, nor humid or cold or the reverse, even though it transmits life to all and each of such parts. Similarly, when that framework is dissolved and has returned to its kindred elements, there is nothing against the probability that that simple and incomposite essence, which has once for all by some inexplicable law grown with the growth of the bodily framework, should remain beside the atoms with which it has been blended, and should in no way be sundered from a union once formed. For it does not follow that, because the composite is dissolved, the incomposite must be dissolved with it.

God made man for the participation of his own peculiar good, and incorporated in him the instincts for all that was excellent, in order that his desire might be carried forward by a corresponding movement in each case toward its like. He would never have deprived man of that most excellent and precious of all goods: I mean the gift implied in being his own master, and having a free will. For if necessity was in any way the master of the life of man, the "image" would have been falsified in that particular part, by being estranged through this unlikeness to its archetype. How can that nature which is under a yoke and bondage to any kind of necessity be called an image of a master being? Was it not most right, then, that that which is in every detail made like the divine being should possess in its nature a self-ruling and independent principle, such as to enable the participation of good to be the reward of its virtue?

Whence comes it, then, you will ask, that he who had been distinguished throughout with the most excellent endowments exchanged these good things for the worse? The reason for this is also plain. No growth of evil had its beginning in the divine will. The evil is engendered in some way or other from within, springing up in [man's] will at that moment when there is a regression from the beautiful [being of

God]. For, as sight is an activity of nature and blindness a deprivation of that natural operation, such is the kind of opposition between virtue and vice. In fact, it is not possible to form any other notion of the origin of vice except as the absence of virtue. As long as the good is present in the nature, vice is a thing that has no inherent existence. The departure of the better state becomes the origin of its opposite. Since this is the peculiarity of the possession of a free will that it chooses as it likes the thing that pleases it, you will find that it is not God who is the author of present evils, seeing that he has ordered your nature so as to be its own master and free. The author is, rather, the recklessness that makes choice of the worse in preference to the better.

Moreover, mind is implanted alike in all men, for all have the power of understanding and deliberating, and of all else whereby the divine nature finds its image in that which was made according to it. The man that was manifested at the first creation of the world, and he that shall be after the consummation of all things, are alike. They equally bear in themselves the divine image. The whole race was spoken of as one man, for this reason, that to God's power nothing is either past or future. Even that which we expect to come is included equally with that which is at present existing, by the all-sustaining energy. Our whole nature, then, extending from the first to the last man, is (so to speak) one image of Him Who Is.

Finally since one of the attributes we contemplate in the divine nature is incomprehensibility of essence, it is clearly necessary that in this point also the image should be able to show its imitation of the archetype. For if, while the archetype transcends comprehension, the nature of the image were comprehended, the contrary character of the attributes we behold in them would prove the defect of the image. But since the nature of our mind, which is the likeness of the creator, evades our knowledge, it has an accurate resemblance to the superior nature. It figures forth by its own unknowableness the incomprehensible nature [of God].

18

THE INFLUENCE OF NEO-PLATONISM ON ST. AUGUSTINE [1]

IN THE years from 383 to 386 Augustine gradually freed himself from his Manichean philosophy of life and discovered the wisdom which was to bring him some measure of peace and happiness in later life. He had come to Rome from Carthage with his mind freshly disillusioned because of Faustus' failure to lead him to truth, by way of Manicheism.

[1] [From Vernon J. Bourke, *Augustine's Quest of Wisdom* (Milwaukee: Bruce Publishing Company, 1945), pp. 48-51, 54-58, 67-68. Reprinted by permission. Most notes are omitted.]

He had found no philosopher in Carthage to initiate him into that wisdom which he so much desired after reading the *Hortensius* of Cicero. Nor did he ever find a teacher in philosophy. This must be kept in mind in attempting to appreciate Augustine's mental struggles. He was a self-made philosopher and even, to some extent, a self-made theologian.

While recovering from his illness in Rome, Augustine had much time to think. He no longer hoped to find in Manicheism the answers to his difficulties. He now knew that its speculative structure was very weak and he bluntly told his host, the Manichee auditor, that much of the teaching of his religion was mere fiction. But for practical reasons Augustine remained a Manichee. His adherence to Manicheism was at this time much more than a nominal one, however. He still retained some of the basic concepts of that religion. Evil was an eternal, infinite, and material substance, standing in contraposition to God. Mind was a subtle body; as yet he had no concept at all of a spiritual substance. Christ was a part of the effulgent, but material, mass which was God; he did not know the Christian teaching on the Incarnation.

While in Rome, Augustine began to think that Academic skepticism was the best philosophical position. He had read Cicero's work, *On the Academics,* and had seen references to that school in Varro and other Latin authors, but all that he was interested in now was the general attitude of the Academics. They taught that man could not know anything with absolute certitude; all that was humanly possible in knowledge was a high degree of probability. Hence, according to this view, the prudent and wise man would withold his judgment on all speculative questions and proceed very carefully in all practical affairs. This skeptical attitude recommended itself to Augustine, now that the bottom had fallen out, so to speak, of his Manichean materialism.

It was in this condition of mind that he went to Milan, intellectually and morally discouraged, but still in hope of marrying a rich wife, gaining professional honors, and becoming wealthy. He was doubtful now of being able ever to attain that philosophical wisdom of which he had read in Cicero. He continued to imitate the Academics in their suspense of judgment and their refusal to assent to anything as absolutely true. It is difficult to decide whether this period of skepticism should be considered a distinct "stage" in the intellectual development of Augustine or not. His references to it are very brief and simply mention the fact that he was attracted by skepticism for a time.

The chief value of this interlude of doubt seems to have been negative. By it Augustine was enabled to cast away any last vestiges of his allegiance to Manichean thought. He decided then that it would be best for him to sever connections with this religion to which, he now felt, some types of philosophy were superior. There was one great point which held him back from devoting himself to the pursuit of philosophy; this was the lack of any mention of Christ in the books of philosophy.

This was one of the persistent relics of his early religious training. From it he had acquired a great respect for the name of Christ, and though he did not grasp the significance of the Christian dogma of the Incarnation, he half consciously judged any suggested form of wisdom by this standard. Did it speak of Christ? If so, it might be right. It may be noted in passing that Manicheism contained a perverted doctrine of the Divine Trinity and that Augustine heard much of Christ from this source.

From the sermons of Ambrose, the bishop of Milan, whom he had gone to hear because of a professional interest in the noted preacher's rhetoric and not at first from any desire of learning new doctrine, Augustine gained another valuable lesson. He found that Ambrose was a more learned man than Faustus, though not as ingratiating a speaker. More important was the discovery that the bishop was able to expound the *Old Testament* in a manner that was new to Augustine, but which seemed rather reasonable. Instead of taking all its texts merely literally (on which basis the Manichees were accustomed to ridicule the Jewish Scriptures), Ambrose explained many sections allegorically. The great Milanese churchman was fond of discovering figurative meanings in texts which, taken literally, had seemed to Augustine to be incomprehensible. Ambrose's recommendation of the exegetical rule that "The letter killeth, but the spirit giveth life" opened up for Augustine a new avenue of approach to Holy Scripture. He was now ready to return to his boyhood status as a catechumen in the Catholic Church, though he was not yet convinced that the Catholic way was that of the wisdom he was seeking. He knew that Manicheism was no good; now he saw that there might be something good in Catholicism, but he was still uncertain about its positive value. Still unable to comprehend the nature of spiritual substance, still bothered by the problem of the origin and nature of evil, still bound by the things of the flesh, he wallowed in the mire of intellectual uncertainty and moral indecision.

It was fortunate that Augustine happened at this time to read some philosophical treatises which enabled him to advance to a solution of his intellectual problems, to know the nature of spirit and of evil. These works Augustine describes as Latin translations of certain "Platonic works." Though he does not definitely name the books or the authors, it is possible to guess, with a good deal of probability, the names of the "Platonic" works. Very probably they were not works of Plato himself; Augustine plainly says that they were translated by Victorinus and his translations were from three authors, Aristotle, Plotinus, and Porphyry. Of these, it is possible to exclude Aristotle, for besides the *Categories,* which Augustine had read in Carthage, the only Aristotelian work translated by Victorinus was a short logical treatise, *On Interpretation,* which would not be calculated to produce the effect on Augustine's mind which he attributed to this reading. Hence the conclusion arises that Augustine most probably read some of the *Enneads* of Plotinus, or possibly some of the minor works of Porphyry (who was Plotinus' pupil), or both. These philosophers lived in the third century of the Christian era and are now known as neo-Platonists, but Augustine simply calls them Platonists.

In these neo-Platonic works Augustine found a type of philosophy which was in direct contradiction both to his erstwhile Manicheism and to much of the current philosophy of the period. Stoicism and Epicureanism were still quite important philosophies in the Roman world. Though somewhat opposed in their ethical teachings, these philosophies were in broad agreement regarding the nature of reality. They were both materialisms. As for the Manicheans, so also for the Stoics and Epicureans, all real things were bodies; they might speak of spirit, but by that term they meant some subtle form of matter. Again, these two late forms of Greek philosophy were agreed in their opposition to supernaturalism. For them a philosophical explanation must use only natural causes, never supernatural ones. Now Augustine met a radically different type of philosophy. It is quite possible that the reduction of the Platonic Academy to skepticism after the death of Plato led some centuries later to the first feature of neo-Platonism, its supernaturalism. When a man comes to doubt the ability of his natural powers to know the truth about things, there is but one other pathway to truth. He may endeavor to use supernatural powers. Possibly one of the finest manifestations of this tendency among pagan authors is to be found in the mysticism of Plotinus. He was a very thoughtful man, prevented from following the career of an ordinary scholar by partial blindness, and so he developed a method of meditation which resulted in a body of very striking and high-minded teachings.

It is well known that Plato distinguished two worlds, the one which is known to the senses and the other which is known to the intellect. He dared to suggest that the latter, the intelligible world, was the better and the more real. Stimulated by this doctrine, and influenced perhaps by his blindness, Plotinus reiterated this distinction and proceeded to belittle the importance and reality of the sensible world, to emphasize and magnify the reality of the things of mind. For him the chief object of knowledge became his own mind and the things which it contained. He tried, too, to go above his own soul and find the One, that great Reality upon which his mind depended for its truth, goodness, and beauty. This neo-Platonism advocated a personal excursion of the philosopher's mind to God, via his own soul. To turn away from the contemptible things of the material world, to concentrate upon the much more valuable things of one's own spirit, to strain after an ecstatic union with the Source of all wisdom, this was the method of Plotinus.

It became the method of Augustine. "Having read these books of the Platonists, and been advised therein to seek for incorporeal truth, I came to see intellectually Thy invisible things, through those things

which are made; . . ." His release from the narrow horizons of materialism is more fully described in the following passage:

And thus, gradually, [I progressed] from bodies to the soul which senses
through the body, and thence to that internal power, to which the bodily senses
bring information about external things (and brute animals can go this far); and
again from this to that reasoning power, to which everything, that is taken in by
the bodily senses, is brought for judgment. Finding this also to be changeable,
my soul ascended to its own intelligence, withdrew its attention from customary
channels, releasing itself from the tumult of disagreeing images, in order to find
by what light it was irradiated; whereupon, without any hesitation, it cried out
that the unchangeable is to be preferred to the changeable. From this it knew
the unchangeable itself, for unless it knew the unchangeable the soul would not
know that the unchangeable is preferable to the changeable. And it arrived, in
the flash of an anxious glance, at that which is. Then indeed I saw intellectually
Thy invisible things, through those things which are made, but I could not maintain my gaze. My weakness was beaten back and I returned to my ordinary
thoughts, bringing with me nothing but a loving memory of those things, which
I had, as it were, eagerly scented but which I was not yet able to eat.[2]

Thus, not suddenly but gradually, Augustine formed a concept of
spirit. Thinking of it in terms of what it did, he discovered that, though
its objects might be the likenesses of bodily things, its activity tran-
scended, to some extent, the physical limitations of space and time. He
came to conceive spirit as that aspect of man's nature by which he
thought of the images of bodies. In this he was following, as he later
acknowledges, Porphyry's theory. One meaning of spirit which Augustine
always retained is that of a certain nature in man, by which the images
of corporeal things are formed. It may represent within man the things
he is sensing without; it may enable man to remember corporeal things
which he has perceived but which are no longer present to him; it may
serve to fashion images of things which have never been sensed but
which are known to exist in reality; and it may even be used after the
fashion of a productive or creative imagination to fabricate phantasms
of things which either do not exist or which we do not know as existent.
Eventually this Porphyrian notion of spirit as reproductive imagination
and memory, was complemented by a further refinement suggested by
Augustine's reading of Scripture (particularly St. Paul), but it is well to
remember that the neo-Platonic concept of spirit performed a valuable
service in enabling Augustine to bridge the gap between Manichean materialism and the Christian understanding of a purely immaterial substance.

Now that he was on the road to a settlement of his difficulty regarding
spirit, Augustine found also that he could, with the help of neo-Platonic
concepts, advance to a solution of the problem of evil. Previously, as a
Manichee, he had thought of evil as a real substance, existing in op-

2 These two texts are from the Confessions, VII, 20, 26; VII, 17, 23.

position to the good. Such a real, positive evil would either require a real cause or it would have to be the eternal reason for its own existence. Rather than attribute the causation of a positive and absolute evil to the Good Principle, to God, the Manichees had maintained that evil itself was an eternal and self-sufficient principle. Plotinus' simple suggestion was that evil was not a substance; it was nonbeing; this lack of absolute goodness was necessarily present in an imperfect world. This suggestion was all that Augustine needed. He decided that evil, in the cosmic sense, was not a substance but the privation or corruption of what is good. God has made all things good, but not perfectly so. The imperfection of the universe, its relative goodness in comparison with the absolute Goodness of God, implies a lack of harmony in created things, which appears to man as evil.

Augustine underwent two conversions while he was resident in Milan. The one was intellectual; the other volitional. His intellect was turned toward the spiritual world, which had been hidden from him during his Manichean period. There can be little doubt that neo-Platonic philosophy was the chief natural agency in bringing about this development of his thought. It provided him with a method of thinking about immaterial being; and, if later he almost restricts his interests to this type of object, to God and his own soul, it must never be forgotten that this step in the evolution of his mind was made possible by the philosophy of the Platonists. Secondly, his will was converted from its desire of worldly honors, wealth, and sense pleasures to the love of humble Christian virtue, of chastity, comparative poverty, and detachment from the world.

It is not advisable to go to the extreme of separating entirely these two conversions. While they are distinct in time, they are interdependent in their causal relations. He could not have profited by his reading of Plotinus unless he had been willing to admit a higher form of truth than the knowledge of material things. It is perfectly clear that Augustine was never a complete sensualist, a libertine who valued only bodily pleasure. His interest in what he conceived to be the Epicurean doctrine of happiness as corporeal pleasure was but momentary. His will did not close up his mind to the infiltration of spiritual truth when he was reading Plotinus. Nor, on the other hand, was his moral reform independent of his advance in knowledge of the spirit. As his understanding grew, he grasped more and more the necessity of a good moral life to one who aimed to achieve the highest wisdom. He was not two agents, the one intellectual and the other voluntary, undergoing two distinct changes. He was one man, particularly one soul, who first came to know a world that had previously been hidden and who then came to realize that this knowledge demanded a change in his practical behavior.

19

AUGUSTINIAN MAN: BETWEEN GOD AND MATTER [1]

INTERIORISM, as Augustine slowly reveals to us, is a journey to the intelligible nature of being. It is not *within* us in the sense that it implies a flight from the world: it is rather *within* in the sense that we reach more intimately the reality and the truth of the beings around us. ✓
We must bear this point in mind, for the interiorism of modern philosophy, established by Descartes, is not at all that of Augustine. Augustine went within himself and experienced and discovered a world of truth: if his interiorism means anything, it means that he never left the world of being in going within himself. But Descartes went within himself never to return to the world. He *intended* to return, and he *tried,* which ought to mean at least that he knew he had *left* the world; but he did not succeed in building a way from his mind to the world.

But that is another story. Here let us notice only that Augustinian interiorism contains within itself a Platonic vision of the world, and a Platonic way of experiencing its truth. It is Plato who saves Augustine from the prison within which Descartes, unknowingly, locked himself; though I ought to add in all fairness that to accept Plato was not an unmixed blessing for Augustine, just as to reject him was at least a partial good. The only question is whether, in going to his solitary prison, Descartes was not being a victim rather than a liberator. But again, this, too, is another story. In any case, the Augustinian notion of man is the counterpart of Augustine's Platonic conception of the world. *Interiorism* led us to intelligibility in the world: it will lead us to *mind* as the center of man, and to *mentalism* as our focus on this center. And while such an experience with the mentalism of Augustine will illustrate how far removed we are from the closed self of Descartes, what is more immediately pertinent is that it will show us how near we are to the divine self of Plotinus. More important than this, we shall see how St. Augustine, however near he may be to Plotinus, is enormously far from him; for St. Paul stands between them.

When Augustine proved to Navigius and Evodius that they were living, thinking beings, he was implicitly proving not only the substantiality of the soul within itself, but also its transcendence over the body. Furthermore, in proving such an independence of the soul over the body, he was thereby raising a tremendous difficulty for himself. This difficulty

[1] [From Anton Pegis, "The Mind of St. Augustine," *Mediaeval Studies*, vol. 6 (1944), pp. 37-48. Reprinted by permission. Some notes are omitted.]

concerns the relations between soul and body, and it is brought out with particular gravity in the problem of sensation. We must now briefly consider this cycle of ideas.

The defeat of the skeptics occurs when the soul *knows* it is a thinking being. This is a basic experience. Whatever we may *think,* there are some things we *know.* Does the mind, for example, *think* it is made of air? Then, says St. Augustine, when the mind thinks that it is air, it *thinks* that air has understanding, but it *knows* that it itself has understanding. "It does not know itself to be air, it only thinks so. Let it remove what it *thinks* it is, and let it perceive what it *knows* it is. There will then be left to the mind what could not be doubted even by those who thought that the mind was this or that body." [2] Exactly. When the mind seeks to know itself, it is not seeking a stranger: it is there all the time, *it grasps its own reality* at the moment it hears the injunction: *know thyself.* But for the mind to grasp itself immediately is for it to know not only that it lives, but also that its life is the life of *understanding.* For it grasps its own understanding. Hence, be it noted, the same immediacy of thought to itself which refuted skepticism will now be used to discover the nature of mind. When I am *certain* of myself, it is not only a certitude I grasp: I grasp myself as the *mind* that I am, and I grasp myself with an immediacy which is as unique as I am to myself. I am as immediately aware of my *nature* as of my existence. In knowing that I know, I necessarily know that I am a knower. If I cannot doubt that I think, I cannot doubt that I am a thinking being: we are beyond not only skepticism but also materialism. We know that mind is not a body or a modification of a body, for we know that mind grasps its own thinking substance.

The significance and the decisiveness of this self-possession of the mind by itself can be felt immediately. We have thus far been speaking of *I, soul* and *mind* somewhat indiscriminately: we must now consider *man* in a more orderly way. What is man? Let us plunge into the midst of some interesting reflections for an answer. The setting of these reflections is entirely familiar: Augustine is seeking the highest good, immediately present to us, cause of our beatitude, and therefore above us in perfection. We are already veterans in going *above* ourselves. Hence, let us come to the point without comment:

> Let us therefore seek what is more perfect than man. Now it is extremely difficult to discover this unless we first examine and discuss what man is. We are agreed that man is composed of soul and body. The question is: what is man? Of these two, is he the soul alone, or the body alone? For, although soul and body are two realities, and neither one of them would be called *man* unless the other were present (the body would not be man without the soul, and the soul would not be man if the body were not animated by it), yet it is quite possible that one of them may be considered to be man, and be so called.

[2] *De Trinitate* X, 10, 13.

Well, which of them do we call man? (i) Is man soul-and-body, as in the case of a *team* of horses or a centaur? (ii) Or is man the body alone, which is in the service of the soul that rules it? An analogy would be a lantern. We call a lantern, not the flame-and-vessel together, but simply the vessel, though we mean a vessel for the purpose of carrying a flame. (iii) Or is man nothing other than what we call the *soul,* though we so call it because of the body that it rules? For example, when we speak of a *rider,* the reference is not to a man-and-a-horse together, but to the man alone, even though it is true that we call him a rider because he is suited to the task of ruling a horse.

It is difficult to come to a conclusion in the foregoing discussion. And even if the reason could settle it easily, it would involve us in a lengthy discourse. We do not here need to undertake and to undergo the delay of such a labor. For whether the pair together or the soul alone appropriates the name *man,* man's highest good is not whatever is the highest good of the body. The highest good of man is whatever is the highest good for body-and-soul together or for the soul alone.[3]

It is clear that Augustine knows the answer to these questions. He is not at all in doubt as to whether *man,* when it applies to soul and body, means the team together, or only the vessel which is the body, or even only the rider which is the soul. These questions, we might observe in passing, are not intended to argue that if we say that man is a soul *with* a body, we are implying that soul and body add up to man *plus* another reality, the body. Soul and body are together *one man.* Nor are we intending to place the whole essence of man in the soul alone. Augustine has declared caustically that "anyone who wishes to separate the body from human nature is stupid"![4] (Let us not allow thirteenth century disputes to rear their heads here. How two substances can be added together and make one substance, will always remain an extremely awkward question for St. Thomas' contemporaries and successors; and St. Thomas Aquinas will always retain on this problem a uniqueness which is as decisive as it is triumphant. In the presence of this question, however, Augustine is innocent rather than wrong: he does not even know the meaning of this thirteenth century problem.) Augustine's point refers to the center of gravity in the human composite. What interests him is the question of questions: to discover what is highest and most perfect within himself in order—can we doubt it?—to pursue the higher-highest good above him. Hence, be it noted, the Augustinian definition of man undertakes to answer the question, not *what is man?* but *how is man ordered and governed?* As we shall see, this is a decisive point, for it enables us at length to understand Augustine.

To this last question the Augustinian answers have been invariable. "*Man,* therefore, according to his own understanding of himself, is a rational soul using a mortal and earthly body." [5] During the same time

3 *De Moribus Ecclesiae* I, 4, 6; PL 32, 1313.
4 *De Anima et ejus Origine* IV, 2, 3; PL 44, 525.
5 *De Moribus Ecclesiae* I, 27, 52; PL 32, 1332.

(in 388) we hear the following: "*The soul,* as it seems to me, is a certain substance, sharing in reason and suited to the task of ruling the body." [6] Note well: the first defines *man,* the second defines the *soul.* This should not be surprising, for Augustine's point is simply that fundamentally and primarily man is what is best in himself. But we must not think that, Platonic as they are, these definitions are destined to be discarded. For their purpose is not to exclude the body from membership in the human composite; *it is to find the true and central man in the composite.* If, therefore, late in the treatise *On the Trinity,* Augustine is content to say with the tradition of the philosophers that "man is a rational, mortal animal" or that "man is a rational substance composed of soul and body," [7] he is not saying anything which he had earlier denied, nor have his interests changed. Without denying that man is the composite of soul and body, he is, as ever, seeking what is best in man—and this at the very moment when he cites these rather neutral philosophical definitions of man. He finds a trinity of mind, knowledge and love in man and he says, "these are not man; *they are what is noblest in him.*" He then finds that this trinity resides in what is best in the soul, and he adds, "therefore, it is not the soul, *but what is noblest in the soul which is called mind.*" [8] In *The City of God* Augustine even gives us the formula of such a search and discovery when, speaking of Varro, he says: "He rightly feels that there are two realities in the nature of man, namely soul and body, and he does not in the least doubt that of the two *the soul is the better and, by far, the more excellent reality. . . .*" [9]

It is in this direction that Augustine develops his conception of the relations between soul and body. For *how* the soul is related to the body is an expression of its very excellence. The soul is present to the body, not locally or spatially, but by a certain *vital attention.* That is to say, it is present in its entirety to all parts of the body: it is the whole soul which perceives an impression even in the smallest point of the body; and what is more, whatever is perceived is perceived only in that part of the body where it takes place:

> The whole soul perceives what is going on in *one* part of the body, but it does not perceive this in the *whole* body. Thus, when there is a pain in the foot, the eye sees it, the tongue reports it, and the hand reaches towards it. This would not be so unless the soul were present in these parts in the same way as it senses in the foot. . . . The soul is, therefore, at one and the same time as a whole in each part of the body, just as it senses as a whole in each part.[10]

This is really a commentary on Plotinus: we perceive *in the finger,* observes Plotinus, that we have a pain *there.*

6 *De Quantitate Animae* XIII, 22; PL 32, 1048.
7 *De Trinitate* XV, 7, 11; PL 42, 1065.
8 *Ibid.*
9 *De Civitate Dei* XIX, 3; PL 41, 625.
10 *De Immortalitate Animae* XVI, 25; PL 32, 1034.

Two problems now present themselves. One will help to explain *why* this union takes place; the other, by illustrating *how* the union between soul and body operates, will lead us to the center of the Augustinian man. These two problems are connected, for the reason why a spiritual substance goes *below itself* to do a work which its own nature does not demand is the embarrassing *why* which an embarrassed *how* is never allowed to forget. These embarrassments simply mean that we are near Plotinus once more; for it was Plotinus, as we may remember, who wondered why anyone who was made for heaven should come down and dwell in a body. If St. Augustine has here no intentions of following after Plotinus, he explains along Plotinian lines the reason why soul is joined to matter.

St. Augustine *does* say that the soul naturally desires to be joined to the body, and by this he means that "the soul is created with such a nature as to desire this, in the same way as it is natural to us to desire to live." [11] But in considering the motives in this desire, we find that the soul enters the body as a messenger of light from the divine ideas. The soul is nearer to the divine ideas than is the body; it is therefore more perfect than the body, and this priority of the soul is as it ought to be. Order and organization and life come down to the body by way of, and through the mediation of, the soul. The hierarchy of *divine ideas, soul* and *body* has as its fundamental motive the transmission of organization to matter, which can take place only this way. The soul is thus a sort of intermediate nature, with the divine ideas immediately above it and the body immediately below: "There is nothing that comes between the highest life, which is immutable Wisdom and Truth, and that which is the last reality to receive life, namely, the body, except the soul." [12] One remark will perhaps explain the meaning of this point. Augustine is conceiving the union of soul and body on the principle that *it is the body which will be benefited by it:* there is nothing in his remarks to suggest any *need* which the soul has in its very nature and which this union with the body supplies. Centuries later, St. Thomas Aquinas, speculating on these Platonic views, will hold firmly to the principle that the soul is joined to matter for its own good: the soul *needs* the body and it is incapable of doing its work as an intellectual substance unless it is joined to it. It is not the good of the body, but that of the soul, which this union has in view. Without denying the unity of man, St. Augustine is too near Plotinus and too conscious of his own tempestuous life to seek any intellectual good in the body. The ministering angel of Plotinus, however, who still lives in the Augustinian notion of soul, ceases to exist with St. Thomas Aquinas.

The first result of the superiority of the Augustinian soul over the body is that the body can never act on the soul. Whatever acts is superior

11 *De Genesi ad Litteram* VII, 27, 38; PL 34, 369.
12 *De Immortalitate Animae* XV, 24; PL 32, 1033.

to that on which it is acting; hence "we must not suppose that the body produces any effect on the soul, as though the soul, in the role of matter, is subjected to a body acting on it." [13] But to say that body never acts on soul is, perhaps, to say more than we realize. When I *see* something which I had not seen previously, does not body act on soul? Nothing of the kind. Indeed, we have scarcely observed how much the *soul itself acts* when, in sensation, we might imagine that the body acts on it. Not only does the body *not* act on the soul, but it is also true that the continued action of the soul is what makes sensation itself a *continuous* process:

Therefore, although we see a body which we had not previously seen, and its image then begins to exist in our souls (by which image we remember this body when it will no longer be present to us), nevertheless, it is not the body which impresses the image in the soul; it is the soul itself which produces it within itself with a remarkable swiftness which far outstrips the slowness of the body. Just as soon as the body appears before the eyes, its image is formed instantaneously in the soul of the one seeing it.

So too in the case of hearing. Unless the soul continued to form in itself the images of the sound perceived by the ears, and unless it retained this sound by means of memory, the second syllable [of a word] would not be known as the second syllable, since the first syllable, which had come and gone when the ear was struck, was no longer in existence. And, in general, all use of speech, all the sweetness of singing, as well as all bodily movements in our actions would be dissipated and lost, and they would have no means of maintaining themselves, if the soul did not retain through memory the already performed movements of the body, to which it would then relate the movements which take place after them. This is to say that the soul does not retain these movements unless it forms their images within itself.[14]

Two points thus appear with considerable clearness: the radical independence of soul from body, manifested particularly by the activity of the soul in the production of sensations; and the place of memory in sensation. Both of these points are vindications of the superiority of the soul over the body, but they also illustrate how the soul operates in the body. The sixth book of the treatise *On Music* has further and celebrated elaborations of these points. And while we are particularly concerned with the problem of sensation, nevertheless, the more ultimate horizons of Augustine will interest us even more.

In discussing the experience of hearing a line of verse, St. Augustine arrives finally at the difficulty we have already met. Such an experience implies that the body acts on the soul, but we know that an inferior reality cannot act on a superior one. How then are we to explain sensation? St. Augustine's solution is quite direct:

For my part, I think that this body is animated by the soul because such was the intention of God. I think, furthermore, that the soul does not suffer anything from the body, but rather acts on it and in it as on something put under

13 *De Genesi ad Litteram* XII, 16, 33; PL 34, 467.
14 *Loc. cit.*

its domination by God. At times the soul acts with ease, and at other times with difficulty; it depends on its merits whether the body is subject to it more or less. Now when any other bodies from the outside affect or disturb this body, it is not in the soul but in the body that they make an impression. This impression, in turn, either disagrees or agrees with the activity of the soul in the body.

Hence it is that when the soul opposes something harmful, and with difficulty forces the material body subject to it to the performance of its work, this difficulty makes the soul to become more attentive towards its own activity. Since this difficulty does not escape the attention of the soul, it is called sensation, the kind of sensation which is called pain or anguish.[15]

What is sensation, then? It is the special state of tension or attention of the soul in the body. The business of the soul in the body is to animate it. How could the soul do this if it did not perceive whatever went on in the body? When sound strikes the ear, is it not striking a *living member of the body*? And does not the soul continue to animate the ear during sensation? But is its movement in the ear the same now as before the sound came? How could the soul do its work in the body properly unless it modified its attention according to the modifications of the body, accepting or resisting according as they are agreeable or harmful? But if such is the case, if the very health of the body and its organs depends on this watchfulness on the part of the soul, we have found what sensation is: when the soul senses, it does not receive the affections of the body; it puts forth actions which correspond to these affections in the body; and this concentration of attention, brought about by disturbances in the body, is what we call sensation.

Sensations are thus intensified moments of action by the soul in the body. The intensification is an expression of the soul's guardianship and watchfulness over the body which it is animating. Since, therefore, sensations are actions of the soul in the body, "there is nothing absurd in believing that, when the soul senses, its own movements, or actions, or operations, or however else they may be conveniently described, do not escape its attention." Furthermore, when we say that in a sensation the soul is affected by an object, we know what we mean: we really mean, not that the soul is affected by the body, but that it is affected by its own operations in the body: "when the soul is affected in some way by its own operations, the affection comes from itself, not from the body; and this takes place when it accommodates itself to the body. *For this reason the soul is less with itself, because the body is always a lesser reality than the soul.*" [16]

This last reflection brings us back to the main Augustinian highway as well as to familiar territory. For if sensation is thus a particular manifestation of the government of the soul over the body, it is also the symptom of a grave problem for the soul. This is, in fact, the sad burden of the soul, that though it ought to be the servant of God, its very govern-

15 *De Musica* VI, 5, 9; PL 32, 1168.
16 *Op. cit.* VI, 5, 12; PL 32, 1170.

ment over the body can attract it to the point of making it the servant of the body. How well Augustine knew *this!* How well he knew that those who seek God are sometimes so lost as to plunge their search into the concupiscence of the flesh! This poor body of ours! It depends so much on the soul for protection, and that soul must be such a faithful servant of God in order to be a wise governor and protector! But the more this body of ours seeks the protection of the soul, the more the soul becomes implicated in its care; and the more the soul becomes implicated in the body, the more it stays to enjoy where it should have stayed only to rule. Had it ruled properly, had it been a perfect servant of God who is its only superior, it would have found in the body the readiest of servants. A healthy body is no problem: it is ruled with ease; but an ailing body requires considerable attention. So, too, in the present case, the more the soul needs to attend to the body, the more it reveals that it is living in stormy times: gone are the ease and the health of order. The soul now loses itself so much in the troubles of this mortal and fragile body, that it can come to love its bonds: the soul "comes to think more of the desire of the body, because the flesh yields to its attention, than of health itself for which no attention whatever is necessary"! [17]

What is extraordinary about this conclusion is that we should be so near the mentalism of Plotinus and yet so completely removed from it. We are, are we not, seeking the real man in the composite of soul and body which we are? And yet, what an arduous search this is! This is no academic question, for it is not a vague *body* that we are seeking to transcend, but living flesh: it is not Plotinus, but Paul, who expressed the search of Augustine: *Unhappy man that I am, who shall deliver me from the body of this death?* And it is with Paul's answer that Augustine continues: *The grace of God, by Jesus Christ our Lord.* The *interior man* of Augustine is not the intelligence of Plotinus, but the man of Paul, the *inward man* who *is renewed day by day.*

The search for deliverance is the secret of Augustine's disquietude. He is not seeking a definition, he is seeking liberty; he is not seeking Plotinian immaterialism, he is seeking liberation from servitude to the flesh whose care he finds so attractive and in whose attractiveness he has lost himself and God; he is not seeking to recall and to recapture the life of a Plotinian divinity, he is seeking the grace of God. Christian liberty: *this* is Augustine's ultimate search. Hence, in considering the Augustinian doctrine of sensation, of memory and of mind, we must see the goal to which they point. Are we, in our highest selves, *minds?* We are—and we have, as yet, not seen entirely how much we really are minds! But, then, our misery is that, being minds, we are so plunged in servitude to the flesh. Of what good is our release from matter, if we are not released from the flesh? The weight of our servitude hangs more

[17] *Op. cit.* VI, 5, 13-14; PL 32, 1170.

stiflingly upon us according as we probe more and more the depth of the spiritual center of our being.

And how much we do a spiritual work even in sensation! We know now that sensation is an activity of the soul. We need to know also how much this activity makes the very sensations which we think come to us from the bodies outside us. What happens when I *hear* a line of verse? We turn, at this point, to the doctrine of Augustine, already cited, that the soul *by remembering* makes sensation possible. It is clear that a line of verse, or even a word, is never spoken or heard *all at once*: it is spread out in time; so that we may say, even in the case of a syllable, that its end is never spoken at the same moment as its beginning. There is a temporal stretch between its beginning and its end: it begins at one time and ends in another. This interval in the duration of sound forces us *to perceive together elements which we do not hear together*. It is memory which makes hearing possible even as a sensation; for it is memory which gives to sensation the simultaneity that it must have and that otherwise it would not have. Sensation straddles time, and memory gives to it a continuous canvas. Truly how much our souls must remember in order to have sensation! And while we may thus marvel, as Augustine never ceases to marvel, at the great power of the memory, let us notice here how much we are liberated from materialism, how much on the spiritual life of the soul the body depends, and how much we are led to the soul even by the analysis of sensation.

Having noticed how much the soul, through its power of memory, must do for the body and its fragilities, let us now notice how much there is in the memory of the soul which has nothing to do with the images of things experienced or remembered. So far we have seen how the interior man perceives external things through the ministry of the senses of the body. "I the interior man, I, I the soul, have knowledge of those things through the senses of the body." We ought to realize, too, that because of this doctrine of the relations of soul and body, we have crossed the threshold into mind even in sensation itself. We have not met any problem of going from the sensible to the intelligible, for Augustinian sensible experience is itself mental. The whole problem of knowledge consists for Augustine in going from participated truths in things to the necessary truth which they reveal when, in the presence of intelligence, they *speak* what they are. The forms of things speak, but only to those who hear, *and to hear things is to judge of their truth*. Here is the core of the Augustinian theory of knowledge: it is nothing other and nothing less than an ascending experience of the necessity of truth revealed in reality. What is knowledge? A conversation between the soul and things in a world of truth. Here is, in fact, the real Augustinian mood on knowledge and truth:

The interior man has knowledge of these things through the ministry of the exterior man. I the interior man, I, I the soul, have knowledge of these things through the senses of my body. I have questioned the great bulk of the world concerning my God, and it has replied to me: "I am not He, but He has made me."

Is not this form of the world manifest to all whose senses are unimpaired? Animals, both small and large, see it, and yet they cannot ask questions of it. For there does not exist in them a reason which can preside as a judge over the messages of the senses. But men can ask questions of the world, so that they may understand and see the invisible things of God through the things that are made. However, through love they become the servants of these things and, having entered servitude, are unable to judge.

Nor do these things that are made reply to all who question them. *They reply only to those who judge.* They do not change their voice, that is, their form, so as to appear in one way to him who only sees, and to appear in another way to him who sees *and questions* them. Without changing its appearance, it [the form of each thing] is silent in the presence of one, whereas it speaks to another. Indeed, it speaks to all men, but they understand it who, receiving its voice outside themselves, compare it within themselves with truth. For truth says to me "Your God is not the heavens and the earth or any other body whatever." The nature of things says this. Those who understand see that the world is a body, smaller therefore in one of its parts than in the whole. O my soul, I say to you that you are clearly more perfect than a body, since you vivify the bulk of your own body by giving it life—which no body can give to another. But your God is the life even of your life.[18]

Once more, therefore, we are on the way to God, but this time we pass through the memory. It is true that we did so before, but did not know it. Now we are going upward through the grades of life which *I the soul,* as Augustine says, manifest. "I shall transcend that power of mine by which I cling to the body and fill its bodily structure with life." [19] I shall reach, but only to transcend, the power by which I give sensation to my flesh, "which my Lord has fashioned for me, commanding the eye not to hear, but to be the instrument of my seeing, and the ear not to see, but to be the instrument of hearing, and assigning, in the case of each of the other senses, their proper seats and functions. I, one soul, perform these various functions by means of the senses." [20] Above life and above sense—and behold "the plains and the broad courtyard of memory." In the vastness of the memory are the images of things I have seen, heard, smelled, tasted and touched whether in other bodies or within my own. Who will say how the memory preserves these images? I can remember colors and sounds as I please; by memory I can distinguish between the odor of lilies and that of violets; and, again by memory alone, I can distinguish the taste of honey from that of wine. All this is in my memory. And men go out of themselves to wonder at the mountains, the seas, the rivers and the stars, and they ignore the wonder of their own memory!

18 *Confessions* X, 6, 9-10; PL 32, 783.
19 *Confessions* X, 7, 11; PL 32, 784.
20 *Loc. cit.*

But the real wonders have still to come. There are in my memory realities which I know, which did not come to me by any of the senses. How did the truths of the sciences get into my memory? They are there and I was not taught them. When I hear something true, I talk like a man who already know it. I say, "that is *so,* that is *true.*" The principles and the laws of numbers are in my memory, *and* they did not come by sense. There are not images of the numbers I can think, and no image can represent the line I can think. I remember errors, and I can distinguish between truth and error. I remember that I have known these truths, and I remember that I remember them, just as in the future I shall be able to recall that I remember them.

And now an even greater wonder. All men desire to be happy. Where did we learn this? Beatitude is the joyous possession of truth, and not of any truth, but of God. Where did we learn this? That we know it means that it is in our memory; that we do not always discern it means that we are implicated in the life of the body. But that we cannot deny this search for beatitude means that somewhere in the deepest roots of our memory—and even beyond—we somehow *remember* God! Not indeed in the sense I once knew him and now *recall* what I knew! And yet there is a sense in which I cannot avoid God. Why is it that we seek so much to know ourselves? Is it ourselves we want to know—or is it our most intimate roots that we are seeking? To Augustine, self-knowledge—the return of the soul to itself as a pure mind—is not aimed at the self but at what makes the self seek. No, self-knowledge seeks its own motives, not the seeker. In brief, at the moment we discover ourselves as minds, we are freed from the life of sense, but at this moment we discover the presence of God.

Perhaps the word *memory* is here twice transformed. For this is not a memory of the past, but, as St. Augustine himself calls it, a *memory of the present.* Yet, even more, how can we really remember God without saying that He is *in* our memory? The difficulty is more apparent than real. What we are discovering is really the conclusion to which the dialogue *On Music* has already pointed, which is the constant motive of the Augustinian man, and which has been expressed by saying that it is not in ourselves but in God alone that we seek God. And there is nothing surprising in this. Do we not recognize the theme of wisdom when we hear Augustine say that a man remembers to turn to his Lord as to a light which *touched* him, even when he turned away from it? This touch of God explains why even those who are turned away can form true judgments of praise and blame in human conduct. Now the point is this: "By what rules, then, do they judge except those in which they see how each man ought to live—even if they themselves are not so living?" Truth! And *where* do they see these rules? Not in themselves, for the *mind* which sees them is mutable, and these rules are immutable. Truth *above us,* therefore! Where are these rules written?

Where therefore are they written, except in the book of that light which is called truth? From it is every just law copied and transferred to the heart of every man who does the work of justice. This transfer does not take place by moving, but by impressing itself—as the shape of a ring is impressed on wax and yet does not leave the ring.[21]

This is a conclusion which has already delighted Evodius. From the standpoint of the present problem, let us note, as Augustine explains in the same reference, God is immutably present to all beings: *We are in his sustaining power and presence, and all our experience of truth is a revelation that we are and think in his presence.*

It might easily appear that in such a conclusion we have lost our original aim. How, it may be asked, does this conclusion terminate a study of man? For it would seem that we have found God rather than man. Yet it is entirely distinctive of Augustine that this conclusion should reach God and still be a study of man. The point is worth emphasizing, and the reader of the later books of the treaties *On the Trinity* can verify for himself what it is that dominates the mind of Augustine in his study of man. He is not seeking to define an essence, and from this point of view Augustine has really never given a metaphysical interpretation of human nature. One might work such an interpretation out of his texts, but in that case the purpose would be one which Augustine never set himself. When in this work *On the Trinity* he shows how man is a mind, when he ponders on the distinction between wisdom and science, when he shows that wisdom is concerned with the contemplation of eternal truths and science with the direction of the temporal and historical life of the Christian believer in this world, he is proceeding as one who is interested in the *religious organization of life*.

The study of man in Augustine thus turns out to be a study in the ordering of the active and contemplative life. When Augustine says that just as the soul is the life of the body so God is the life of a happy soul; when he says that a soul that is not happy is dead, he points to exactly that aspect of the study of man which interests him. In this sense, the distinction between wisdom and science is not to be taken as a distinction between two bodies of abstract truths. On the contrary far from being a distinction between Plato and Aristotle, it is really a distinction between Mary and Martha. To come to this conclusion is to have defined the Augustinian man; it is also to see that at the moment of being very near to Plotinus, St. Augustine is very far from him. For this conclusion is not the discovery of an eternal Plotinian essence, since it is not the discovery of an essence at all. It is an interior search for liberty, and to give true life to the interior man within us is at one and the same time to have found man in his most intimate and ultimate nature and to have given him Christian liberty.

21 *De Trinitate* XIV, 15, 21; PL 42, 1052.

Only such a conclusion permits us to see clearly what it is that enables Augustine to be so perilously open to the influence of Plotinus and still not feel the full pressure of his ideas. The thought of Augustine centers around the ordering and the conduct of life; it is not concerned with essences and ideas in themselves. At the moment of setting out to define man, his secret ambition is to release man from the slavery of his subjection to the body, to reveal him to himself in his ultimate nature, to *reorder* him, or at least to point to the direction of this reorganization of the life of man. The Augustinian concept of man thus turns out to be a living journey in which we are more aware of a desire for beatitude and liberation than of the abstract analysis of the essence of man. Augustine does not change: Rachel is still his love. He still believes that man is where his heart is, and he still believes that man may fill his heart with a treasure of beatitude or with the confusion of misery according as he opens it to God or allows it to be tortured by the passions of the body.

Is this conclusion a definition of man? Surely not. It is a lesson on love; it is a religious psychology of interior purification to which Plotinus contributes many of the signposts but whose motives Augustine found in his own trembling heart: "You have made us for Yourself, and our heart is restless until it rests in You." [22] Peace and liberty, order and liberation from the body—such is the religious motive that urges Augustine when he seeks the inner man. As a journey in spiritual love, this search is entirely free of Plotinus, and in his deepest desires Augustine was always free of Plotinus. If the philosophical doctrines of Plotinus leave the thought of Augustine unguardedly Greek in its intellectual content, it is love which triumphs in Augustine; and his Greek reason, already illumined by wisdom and charity, is the disciple, not the teacher, of the Christian heart of Augustine. Just when the Plotinian man, that divinity from the Platonic heaven, threatens to overpower Augustine, we realize that there never was a conflict at all: Augustine looks at the Plotinian man with the troubled eyes of one who is already in pursuit of Rachel. One can scarcely doubt that to subject the Plotinian meditations to the purpose of furthering the search of the Christian soul is to realize an astonishing paradox: here is Augustine seeking heaven with all the humility of a creature—and yet so often he speaks the lines of a Plotinian god! This paradox is destined to become also a veritable conflict in the course of history; for the day will come when the Plotinian god will awake and claim all his divine privileges. In Augustine himself, however, the tongue is schooled by the heart, and the heart knows only the hand of the Christian God who stilled its turmoil and increased its peace.

[22] *Confessions* I, 1, 1; PL 32, 661.

20

ST. AUGUSTINE ON SIGNS [1]

MANY of the topics of Augustinian theology and philosophy in which the notion of "signs" is central have received a good deal of attention. This is true, above all, of Augustine's sacramental theology. His definition of *sacramentum* in terms of *signum* became classical. His definition of *signum* is rarely mentioned by later writers except in the context of sacramental theology; nevertheless, the notion plays an important part in other contexts. Chief among these is Augustine's discussion of the meanings of Scripture, but the concept enters into such diverse fields of his interest as his theory of language, his discussion of miracles, of the relation of the world to God, and of man's way of acquiring knowledge, not least knowledge of himself. Notwithstanding the focal interest of the notions of sign and of meaning in Augustine's thought, they have, so far as I know, not received treatment as such. This essay is, therefore, an attempt to disentangle what Augustine thought about signs, in particular, about words, and meaning. At the risk of ascribing to him preoccupations which he would scarcely have recognized, no attempt is made here to deal with any of the applications made by Augustine of the notion.

In Roman rhetoric and early Christian theology, the theory of signs is conceived primarily as a theory of inference. Language is hardly mentioned in this context, and when it is explicitly recognised as relevant—since words *signify* and are therefore inescapably signs—the linguistic interest is only incidental. A powerful influence which would tend to suggest a theory of language conceived in terms of a theory of signs was, in all probability, the primacy in Augustine's interests of Scriptural "signs." A theory of language as a system of signs must have been tempting, since it secured the possibility of bringing under one head, that of "signs," two enquiries, into the literal meaning and the figurative or typological sense of Scripture. At any rate, whatever the reasons, words are for Augustine, signs *par excellence,* and his theory of signs is meant to be, from the start, a theory of language as well as of the other types of sign. In this consists the originality of his reflection on meaning, and its ability to focus so many of his interests.

1. THE INTERPRETING SIGNS: THE INTERIOR TEACHER

Augustine's first *ex professo* discussion of the meaning of signs occurs in the early *De Magistro*.[2] This work, dated about 389, is a dialogue, gen-

[1] [From R. A. Markus, "St. Augustine on Signs," *Phronesis*, vol. 2 (1957), pp. 60, 64, 65-82. Reprinted by permission. Most notes and several paragraphs are omitted.]

uine and historical, as Augustine claims in the *Confessions,* between himself and his son Adeodatus.

The inquiry concerns the meaning of signs, and of spoken words in particular, which are the most common important sort of sign. Why do we use signs?—is Augustine's opening question. The purpose of all speaking, we are told, is "either to teach or to remind others or ourselves" (*De Mag.* I. 1.). Other apparent purposes, such as asking questions in order to learn, can all be brought under these two heads: for in asking questions we do no more than teach other people what we want to know. But there are more serious objections to be answered, the answers to which give some hint of how wide a range of functions will be ascribed to "reminding" and to *memoria* (which I am content, for the present purpose, to render by the word "memory"). Thus the objection has to be met that Christ taught his disciples to pray in set forms of words, whereas God can have no need of being taught or reminded of men's needs and desires. This difficulty is solved by agreeing that Christ "did not teach them words, but realities by means of words. They were to remind themselves to whom to pray and what to pray for. . . ." (I. 2). With such a broad acceptance of *memoria* nothing is in the way of establishing as a conclusion to Chapter I that "even when we merely strain our minds towards something, although we utter no sound, yet because we ponder the words themselves, we do speak within our own minds. So, too, speech is a recalling to mind, since the memory in which the words are stored, by considering them, brings to mind the realities themselves of which the words are signs" (*ibid.*). Thus speech puts before the mind what was previously either altogether absent from it, or at least not present to it in the sense of being actually thought about.

This then is the common ground from which proceeds the inquiry begun in Chapter II of what words "signify" (II.3). The first part of the argument, extending over the following five chapters and summarized in Chapter VIII, is designed to establish, first, that signs are the indispensable means of directing the mind's attention to things, and that nothing, therefore, can be learned without the use of signs (III. 6; cf. X. 29-31). The meaning of a sign, what it "signifies," can only be expounded and established by means of further signs, as it were by giving synonyms; by circumlocution; by pointing or gesture; or by pictorial representation. The only exceptions granted at this stage in the discussion are words standing for actions, the meaning of which can be illustrated by actually performing the actions named by the words, for instance by walking or by speaking when one is asked for the meaning of *ambulare* or *loqui.* But even this is taken back later on, when these results established in the first part of the dialogue are recapitulated in the course of the argument of the second part. Adeodatus there rightly points out that such direct

---

2 [See the English version of St. Augustine's treatise, *The Teacher,* translated along with his *The Greatness of the Soul* by J. M. Colleran, C.Ss.R. (Westminster, Maryland: The Newman Press, 1950). Editor's note.]

illustrative performance cannot be understood as giving the meaning of a word without any sign whatsoever: for it involves that the particular bit of walking done be performed and understood precisely as signifying any instance of walking, at any speed, by anybody, for any distance, etc. (X. 29). Even at this point, however, Adeodatus is inclined to except the case of teaching and of speaking, both of which, he thinks, can be directly exemplified; but Augustine induces him to take the final step: "We have as yet found nothing which can be shown directly by itself except speech, which also signifies itself along with other things. But since speech itself consists of signs, there is still nothing that can be taught without signs" (X. 30).

To establish this conclusion is the main burden of the first part of the work, and the rest of this part is taken up with a bewildering and often sophistical discussion of the ways in which "speech also signifies itself along with other things." To mark the end of this first part of the discussion, Augustine apologizes for all this seemingly childish playing with words, but defends it as a prelude intended "to exercise the power and keenness of our minds and so to prepare ourselves not only to be able to support, but also to love the warmth and light of the blessed life" (VIII. 21). And so we pass to the second part of the dialogue which deals with signs signifying not other signs, but things which are not themselves signs but *significabilia* as they had agreed to call them.

This part begins with the long overdue distinction between use and mention, that is to say between, for example, "man" as being a noun and man as being an animal (VIII. 24). To solve the puzzles which arise from neglecting this distinction Adeodatus points out that "the things we speak of, we signify; and what comes forth from the mouth of the speaker is not the reality signified but the sign by which it is signified" (VIII. 23). Neither of the speakers seems to be aware of the relevance of this observation to the first part of the discussion. Adeodatus goes on to deny the applicability to words of the distinction just drawn between use and mention: "the exception [to this rule] is when it is the signs themselves that are signified, a class we treated of a little while ago" (VIII. 23). These exceptions apart, then, in general we use words to talk about the things they stand for, in order to gain and to communicate knowledge about them (IX); and indeed, as the first part of the argument claims to have established already, nothing can be learned without signs, not even things which can be directly illustrated by the teacher (X. 29-31).

What happens, then, in the course of a conversation when a word or phrase crops up whose meaning is not understood by one of the parties? "Thus when I read the words *et saraballae eorum non sunt immutatae*, the word *saraballae* does not manifest to me the reality which it signifies. If it is head coverings of some sort that are called by this name, did I upon hearing this learn either what a head or what coverings are? These

I had known before; and my knowledge of them was gained, not when they were called such by others, but when they were seen by myself. The first time the two syllables *caput* struck my ears, I was just as ignorant of what they signified as when I first read *saraballae*. But when the word *caput* was repeatedly pronounced, I discovered that it was the word for a thing which was already most familiar to me from sight. Before I made that discovery, this word was a mere noise to me; but I learned that it was a sign, when I discovered what it was a sign of. And that reality I got to know, as I said, not from being signified to me, but by seeing it. Therefore, it is the sign that is learned from the thing rather than the thing from the sign given" (X. 33). Failure in communication, the argument runs, can only be remedied by an explanation of the word or sign which fails in its task of manifesting the reality it signifies; but as the example of *saraballae* shows, such explanation must ultimately reach a point at which direct acquaintance with the *significata* of primitive words is presupposed.

In the following paragraph Augustine goes on to generalize this conclusion: "What I am above all trying to convince you of, if I can, is that we do not learn anything by means of the signs we call words. For, on the contrary as I have said we learn the meaning of the word—that is to say the significance that is hidden in the sound—only after recognizing the reality which it signifies; we do not first perceive this reality by means of such signification" (X. 34). The pointing with the finger (*intentio digitis*) whereby we establish the meaning of primitive signs, he maintains, is not a sign of the reality pointed to, nor of the word which is being explained by this means, but rather of the indication (*demonstrationis*) itself. In this way it resembles the function of the adverb *ecce*. "By means of the pointing, then, I cannot get to know either the thing [the head], since I already know that, nor the sign [the word *caput*], for the finger is not pointed at that" (X. 34).

The conclusion that we cannot get to know the meaning of signs without knowing the realities they stand for appears to contradict the conclusion of the first part of the work, namely that we require signs in order that we may get to know things. But Augustine means both these positions to be taken quite seriously, and indeed reiterates the conclusions of the first part in the course of this argument. His thesis is precisely that no knowledge can either be acquired or communicated on the basis of the account so far given: in order that I may know the meaning of signs I have to know, in the last resort, the things they stand for. On the other hand, I have to rely on the words and signs of teachers to receive the direct experience of these things. "The value of words, to state the most that can be said for them, consists in that they bid us look for things. These they do not display to us for our knowledge" (XI. 36). Either, Augustine seems to be arguing, we get to know the meaning of words together with the things which exemplify that meaning, or we have a mere mass of unorganized experience on the one hand, and a mere series of meaningless noises on the other. The inquiry after the meaning of symbols is at the same time the inquiry into the reality they speak of: "If we know [the meaning of words together with the things signified] we recall rather than learn; but if we do not know, we do not even recall, though perhaps we may be prompted to inquire" (XI. 36).

Human teachers, on the one hand, can only teach us the meanings of words and signs, and experience, on the other hand, only furnishes us with brute givenness. Only the Interior Teacher, which is Christ dwelling in the mind, can teach by at once displaying to the mind the reality to be known and providing the language for its understanding. He is the source of both the objects encountered and the light which illuminates them for our understanding. This is the teacher whose activity is presupposed by all learning. The remaining three chapters are devoted to showing that this Interior Teacher is the source of all truth and knowledge; that he is the invisible light "which we confessedly consult in regard to visible things, that it may manifest them to us to the extent that we are able to perceive them" (XI. 38).

Augustine concluded from the argument of the dialogue that nothing external to the mind can, in the last resort, be regarded as the source of its knowledge. Neither the crude data of experience nor the "pointers" to it in language and gesture can give knowledge without what M. Gilson has called the mind's "irreducible spontaneity." In the *De Magistro* Augustine is content to short-circuit an examination of what this spontaneity consists in by invoking his favorite theory in one of its forms at the crucial point. A further exploration here might have brought him face to face with the inadequacy of a theory of language conceived, as it is in this work, as running parallel to the stream of experience and alongside it, so to speak, rather than within it. There is, indeed, a hint of another view of linguistic expression even in this work, the pursuit of which might have led Augustine to question the adequacy of the picture which is implicit in the rest of the dialogue. This is the suggestion he throws out that certain signs, linguistic or gestural, might be signs of indication, not of objects signified. On this suggestion, a system of signs might contain in itself the "pointing to" (*intentio*) its objects for which Augustine could find no place in language. But this hint is not developed because, as Augustine says à *propos* of this suggestion, he is not interested in it precisely for the reason, as he puts it, that this pointing is "only a sign of the indication itself rather than of any things indicated" (X. 34). The further development of such a suggestion would have broken through the barrier between signs and *significata*, the mutual externality to each other of language and experience, related only by conventional rules of "signification." But by invoking the interpretative activity of the Interior Teacher, Augustine was able to escape the difficulties of this view of language and felt absolved from subjecting it to further scrutiny, at any rate, for the present.

2. SYMPTOM AND SYMBOL

In the *De Doctrina Christiana* [*On Christian Doctrine*] a sign is said to be a "thing which, in additional to what it is perceived to be by the senses also brings something else to mind" *(De Doctr. Christ.* II. 1. 1). A sign, to paraphrase this definition in more modern language, is an element in a situation in which three terms are related. These we may call the object or *significatum* for which the sign stands, the sign itself, and the subject to whom the sign stands for the object signified.[3] It may be noted in passing that Augustine appears to be the first to have stressed this triadic nature of the relation of "signifying."

A thing is a sign, for Augustine, precisely in so far as it stands *for* some thing *to* somebody. This three-term relation is essential to any situation in order that one element in it should function as a sign. A sign-situation is simply a situation in which, among others, this relation obtains. Whatever element in such a situation functions as a sign, may also be related to other elements in the situation in a large variety of other ways. A sign-situation presupposes some of these simpler, two-term relations in which the sign-thing or sign-event must stand to other things or events in order that it may function as a sign. For instance, that smoke may be a sign of fire, its causal dependence on fire independent of any observer is presupposed. Likewise, in order that a noise made by a living organism may be a sign, it must be a product of its activity; and it has to stand in a specific relation to it if is to be a word with meaning. The triadic relation of "signifying" is built upon such dyadic relations, and different types of "signifying" may be distinguished according to what these presupposed two-term relations are in each case.

Augustine distinguishes two fundamental types of sign according to whether the relation of dependence is between the sign and the object, or between the sign and the subject. The first type he calls *signa naturalia,* and defines these as things (or events) "which from themselves make known something other than themselves without any desire on anybody's part of 'signifying'; as for instance, smoke signifies fire. For smoke is not made by someone wanting to 'signify' something, but on being apprehended and noted as a thing experienced, makes known the presence of fire. . . ." (II. 2. 2). As further examples of this class he refers to footprints left by an animal passed out of sight, to facial expressions registering emotions like pain or anger without the person's wishing to show his feelings, and their like. For convenience, and without begging any of the questions that this terminology may suggest, I shall call these

---

3 This paraphrase displays the substantial identity of Augustine's with the modern definitions. *Sign (Representamen)—Object—Subject (Interpretant)*: This is Peirce's terminology, and it coincides closely with Augustine's. Peirce's definition of "sign" is equally close to that given by Augustine: "A sign or *representamen* is something which stands to somebody for something in some respect or capacity" (Justus Buchler, *The Philosophy of Peirce,* New York: Harcourt, Brace and Company, 1940, p. 99). Modern definitions known to me are all variants of this.

types of sign "symptoms." A "symptom," on this usage, which implies a certain extension of its sense in normal usage, is anything which "goes together with" that of which it is taken to be the sign. It may be a "symptom" in the conventional sense, a "portent," or "evidence" in a more general sense; it might depend on its *significatum* as an effect on its cause, as for instance, smoke depends on fire; it might be part of a total condition as a rash is of measles; or it might give rise to its *significatum,* as a southwesterly wind may both bring and signify rain. The sign may be contemporaneous with its *significatum,* or occur before or after it, and the sign-relations may be reversible according to circumstances. But Augustine, as he says, is not concerned with this type of sign, except to distinguish it from the second type, which he calls *signa data.*

These he defines as "signs which living organisms make to each other in order to indicate, as far as they are able, what they feel or perceive or understand. The only reason we have for 'signifying,' that is, for giving signs, is to bring forth what is going on in the mind of the sign-maker and to communicate it to another's mind" (II. 2. 3.). Here the thing or event which is the sign is the product of the sign-maker's activity and owes its significance entirely to this. What it means, or more precisely, what he means by it, it means in virtue of what he is doing with it. Let us call signs of this kind "symbols." The most important class of "symbols" is, of course, that of words: not because they differ fundamentally from gesture, facial expression and other forms of expressive activity—all these are *quasi quaedam visibilia verba* (II. 3. 4)—but because words are used solely for the purpose of "signifying" (I. 2. 2). They are, so to speak, diaphanous and do not distract attention from what they are employed to mean by claiming attention to what they are in their own right. The sign-signified relation is not here reversible, as it is in the case of "symptoms," nor is there a causal relation between them on which an inference could be based of the occurrence of the one from the other. On the other hand, a "symbol" has the determinate meaning or range of meanings which the sign-maker's activity bestows on it. These ways in which "symbols" differ from "symptoms" are fundamental, and must not be allowed to be blurred by the fact that there are signs which look as if they might belong to either one or the other class.

3. EXPRESSION AND THE WORD

In the setting of Trinitarian theology, and particularly in the course of his search for created analogies in human activity and mental functioning of the ineffable Trinity, Augustine uses the notion of the "word" as a key-concept. "The word heard sounding outside is the sign of the word which is luminous within, which is more appropriately called a 'word.' For what is brought forth by the mouth of the body is the utterance of the word; and though this, too, is called a 'word,' it is so only on account of that which it is being used to manifest externally. . . . That word . . . is neither brought forth in sound, nor thought in the likeness of any sound, and need not, therefore, be of any particular language; it precedes all the signs whereby it is signified and is begotten by the knowledge which remains in the mind, when that knowledge is expressed as it is" (De Trinitate XV. 11. 20). Language like this marks a profound shift of perspective: words are not now thought of as signs of things, or as standing for things; the word which sounds outside is the sign of the word which shines within, but of this latter Augustine never speaks as a sign; and yet, this is, in his view, the "word" most properly so called.

Augustine's theory of the "word" approaches language from the side of the speaker, unlike the sign-theories of the De Magistro and the De Doctrina Christiana. The latter are theories of meaning for the spectator and the interpreter, and prima facie plausible only so long as we keep to that model. They do not describe what the speaker or thinker is doing when he is using words or engaging in any other form of symbolizing activity, however rudimentary this may be. When one is using words, images, gestures, etc. in thinking and expressing what one thinks—to oneself or to others—one is not only listening to or looking at them; one is using them precisely to focus, canalize and give form to one's thinking, often in ways quite startling to oneself. There are not two separate activities here, a process we may call "creative" and a subsequent one of "translation," but just one process which we may call "expressive." Unlike the sign-theories already discussed, Augustine's theory of the "word" recognises the "creative" aspect of symbol-making, even though it fixes a gulf between it and its concrete embodiment. The sign-theories, though not dwelt on in this context, do not appear to be superseded, because they can be invoked to account for understanding the sensuous embodiment of the symbol.

Augustine would probably not have seen in his abandoning his earlier mode of speaking a change of view. No conviction had for him a compelling force comparable to that of his vision of the truth known to him as being imparted to him by God, speaking through his Scriptures or his creatures from without, and through his own mind from within. In Augustine's contemplation of this mystery words and thoughts were bound to converge in pointing towards the one ineffable source of light: what mattered to him is what they were pointing at, even if they happened to be pointing there from many different places and directions. He is much more concerned with the Interior Teacher dwelling in the mind and teaching within, than with the external signs which he deciphers for us; and he is much more interested in his identity with the Word "whose participation is our illumination, the Word who is the life which is the light of men" (De Trin. IV. 2. 4.), than he is in the difference between the signs and words interpreted by the one and the "words" begotten in the light of the other.

21

BOETHIUS' THEORY OF GOODNESS AND BEING [1]

Anicius Manlius Torquatus Severinus Boethius was born in 480. A.D. He was appointed consul by Theodoric, the Ostrogoth ruler of Rome, in 510. After a career of public service Boethius was charged with treason, condemned, sent to prison, and finally executed. While he was in prison, he wrote the famous *Consolation of Philosophy*.

In view of his active political life, Boethius' accomplishments as a scholar are impressive. Failing to realize his initial intention to translate all the writings of Plato and Aristotle into Latin, he nevertheless composed translations and commentaries on most of Aristotle's logical works. He also produced original works on arithmetic, music, and geometry, and wrote at least four short *Theological Tractates*, in addition to the renowned *Consolation*. All of these works, especially the books in logic, exercised tremendous influence throughout the entire middle ages.

Boethius' philosophic views on goodness and being, although less commented upon, are as important as his contributions to logic. This summary interpretation of Boethius' positions regarding goodness and being, is based on Book III of the *Consolation of Philosophy*, on part of the *De Trinitate*, and on the entire *De Hebdomadibus*. These last two writings belong to his *Theological Tractates*, which deal with philosophical as well as theological issues.

1. GOD AS THE PERFECT GOOD FOR MAN

The Consolation of Philosophy is written in the form of a dialogue between Boethius and philosophy. Prose and verse alternate, and philosophy appears in the guise of a majestic woman who comes to comfort the imprisoned Boethius, thus giving the work its title. In the third book, the dialogue centers on a philosophic analysis of the end of human life.[2] In the course of the discussion, which is predominantly moral, but also metaphysical, Boethius presents his conception of God as goodness itself, together with a sort of proof of his existence. Although written after the

---

[1] [An essay written especially for this volume by Charles Fay.]

[2] All references are to the H. F. Stewart and E. K. Rand edition of Boethius, *The Theological Tractates* and *The Consolation of Philosophy*, in The Loeb Classical Library (Cambridge, Massachusetts: Harvard University Press, 1936). Cf. *The Consolation of Philosophy*, Book III, pp. 224-297.

Theological Tractates, the *Consolation* can be viewed as an introduction to the basic doctrines of the former concerning the being and goodness of God and creatures.

Boethius begins with the fact of experience that every man strives in his own way for happiness. There is some object which every man judges to be his greatest good, something which, when once attained, would satisfy his desires. This desire for what seems good is a natural tendency in man. However, error frequently deflects this innate tendency, so that it seeks that which falsely appears to be good.

But men are never entirely mistaken about the true end of human life, inasmuch as both a desire and a knowledge of this end are naturally implanted in the human mind. False conceptions of human happiness always involve an obscure awareness of the true nature of happiness. All men wish to enjoy some object or state which they believe will be perfectly satisfying. The attributes of an object or state which will truly satisfy man can be established by reflecting upon certain typical errors concerning this object. The Stoic philosopher endeavors to cultivate a state of apathy, of wanting nothing, inasmuch as he dimly perceives that happiness is a state of self-sufficiency, wherein nothing is wanted. Insofar as one possesses all that is good, he is necessarily self-sufficient. Those who incorrectly identify the highest good with fame and recognition are nevertheless correct in their view that what is best, is most intrinsically worthy of glory. It is no vile or contemptible thing which all men labor to obtain. Not even those whose burning ambition is the attainment of a position of power and influence have entirely misconstrued the goal of human life, since that good thing which is highest is necessarily more powerful than any other good. Nor does the hedonist entirely succeed in extinguishing in himself his natural knowledge of happiness; for even in the smallest matter we naturally seek delight and enjoyment. Hence joy and pleasure cannot be absent in the highest good.

Happiness consists in the enjoyment and possession of the highest good. The essential characteristics of such a state are: self-sufficiency, intrinsic glory, power, and joy. In the light of his own mature experience and learning, Boethius shows how the majority of men are mistaken in identifying such a state with the possession and enjoyment of wealth, offices, glory, and bodily pleasure. As an illustration of the way he argues, Boethius recalls the many anxieties and vexations which, in his own case, wealth failed to remove. The wealthy man does not enjoy a state of wanting nothing or self-sufficiency. Wealth tends to increase rather than to satiate the desire of a covetous man. While it relieves the basic natural desires for food, drink, and bodily comfort, it does not completely satisfy them.

The highest good is perfectly one with all its attributes; self-sufficiency, power, glory, and joy are ultimately identical with it. Self-sufficiency is not really a special portion of happiness, for happiness is a perfect unity, and consequently is entirely lacking in parts. Hence all the essential characteristics of true happiness are *indivisibly* united. Self-sufficiency is the same in substance and differs only in name from power, glory, and perfect joy.

The ultimate reason for moral failure consists in the attempt to divide that which is indivisible. The miser, due to his imperfect grasp of happiness, apprehends it only under the aspect of self-sufficiency and is blind to the other attributes which happiness essentially involves. Through the acquisition of wealth he seeks security and freedom from want. Because of his dedication, he endures indignities, withdraws from the pursuit of recognition and power, and renounces natural pleasures. He seeks a part of that which has no parts; hence he fails to receive the whole. The same applies to those who concern themselves exclusively with the attainment of pleasure or glory by temporal agencies. They seek to divide that which is simple and indivisible, and so they fail to achieve the true good which alone beatifies.

Such a good cannot be found in the temporal order. What real thing possesses all the characteristics of the highest good in an indivisible unity?

It is first of all necessary to show that such an object is extant among real objects. Boethius bases his argument upon the principle that if imperfection is found in any genus, there must also be something perfect in the same genus. For if perfection be removed, how could there be imperfection? It is impossible for something to be imperfectly white, for example, unless there be some standard in the order of whiteness with which it can be compared and judged wanting in whiteness. The same is true of the goods of our experience. We know their imperfection. But they can be imperfect only in relation to some perfect good.

This argument is reinforced by a neo-Platonic theory of the descent of forms. There must be a source for the goodness found in things. As they proceed from the source, there is a diminution in perfection corresponding to their ontological distance from their origin. The imperfection and incompleteness of goodness can be accounted for only as a result of a descent from that which is unqualifiedly and perfectly good. Hence temporal happiness, precisely because of its insecurity and imperfection, attests to the reality of some perfect happiness which can be peacefully and tranquilly possessed.

That this perfect good is God, is established by means of the principle that God is that being than which nothing more perfect can be conceived. If God were not perfectly good, there would be something better than he, having greater antiquity and eminence. Consequently, the same argument establishes the reality both of the perfect good and of God. Behind the imperfect lies the more perfect, which in turn directs our attention to the still more perfect. This regress from essence to essence must of necessity terminate in a perfect good, than which nothing higher can be conceived. The imperfect goods of our experience require such a good, since they can only be regarded as diminished versions of it. Their lack of perfection can be understood as the result of a departure from perfection. Thus reason, operating exclusively in the realm of essence, arrives at God, the perfect good, the source of the goodness imperfectly mirrored in his creation.

The perfect good is good in a unique way. God does not receive his goodness from another, inasmuch as he is the highest being. For he who gives is better than the recipient. Nor is God distinct from his goodness. To the extent that perfections and things are distinct, they are united, not of themselves but only through another, which is necessary prior to their union. But nothing is prior to God, who is the radical origin of everything. Further, if goodness were in God without being the same as God, God would differ from the highest good, and hence not be the highest good. But nothing is better than God. Hence God is indivisibly one with his goodness.

Boethius draws an important corollary. Men are made happy by possessing the highest good, namely, God. Hence men are made happy inasmuch as they *participate* in what God *is* essentially. Since the happy man obtains God, he is himself a god by participation.

We have seen that the perfect good is indivisibly one with perfect self-sufficiency, power, intrinsic glory, and the highest pleasure. However, goodness is the most proper name for God, inasmuch as it best expresses his essence. For all the other attributes are referred to goodness as particular expressions of it. Sufficiency, power, and the other aspects of perfect goodness are desired, inasmuch as they are good. The origin and cause of all that is sought after, is rightly thought to be goodness. Hence goodness is most primary and most properly defines God, the highest being. Hence the substance of God consists in nothing else but goodness.

Having concluded that God is nothing else but goodness, Boethius goes on to establish that goodness is the same as unity. In fact, this follows from an earlier insight. We have seen that sufficiency, power, fame, and pleasure are not—as separate objects of pursuit—true and perfect goods. They cause complete and unqualified goodness only when they are united into one form and causality. Insofar as they are one, they are worthy objects of pursuit. Unity and goodness are the same, because things are good insofar as they are one.

Boethius shows, next, that everything desires unity, and hence desires goodness. Everything desires unity inasmuch as it desires to remain in being. Everything acts in a way which is suitable to its nature. It has a natural and non-voluntary tendency, implanted by providence, to resist corrupting influences and to continue in its own being. But if unity is taken away, being itself cannot remain. The human body, for instance, is no longer the same being when its parts separate and its unity is lost. Hence all things desire unity. But it has already been established that unity is the same as goodness. Consequently, goodness may be defined as that which is desired by all things or as the end of all things.

The final conclusion is drawn which is necessary for the consolation of Boethius. The world, which is composed of different and contrary parts, would tend to dissolution, unless some governing force brings the parts into a unity. The natures of things, insofar as they are different, would be inclined to go their separate ways. But it is a fact of experience that nature is a stable, uniform, and harmonious whole. There must, therefore, be one who remains immutably himself, who disposes and orders this variety of motions. Thus God governs the world. Given his perfect self-sufficiency and goodness, it must follow that he disposes all things according to his goodness. And inasmuch as things themselves seek goodness as their natural end, all things are governed willingly, that is, in accord with their natural inclinations. Given the fact that God is all-powerful, it necessarily follows that evil is nothing, since God cannot do evil, yet can do anything. This is the substance of the consolation which philosophy offers to Boethius in his misfortune.

2. SIMPLE AND COMPOSITE BEING

The *Theological Tractates* give a fuller treatment of the precise relation of created and uncreated being, especially in respect to goodness, the most proper attribute of God.

In the context of the division of the sciences, in the essay *On the Trinity*,[3] Boethius outlines his theory of the metaphysical structure of created and uncreated being. The object of theology is pure form, which is being itself and that from which every other being is derived. Form and being (*esse*) are identical in artificial and natural things; for example, to be a statue is to have received a form. In general, a thing is not said to be according to its matter, but it is what it is through its form.

God and the creature are distinguished primarily by the opposition between the simple and the composite. In God, form and individual being are identical. Hence God is what he is. In the creature, there is a composition in the essential order between form and matter, with the result that form is only part of the whole, and the entire creature cannot be said to be what it is. The composite structure here established is an essential one, and it seems neither to include nor exclude actual existence.

Because God is only form, he cannot be a subject or exist in matter. Because the corporeal creature is composed of matter and form, it can receive further accidental determinations. The form of the material creature, the source of its being, comes from and imitates the primary forms existing apart from matter. Primary forms cannot exist in matter, for then they would no longer be truly original forms. Consequently, the forms in matter can only be images, that is, diminished realities, which

[3] *The Theological Tractates, De Trinitate,* ch. II, pp. 8-12.

merely imitate the original forms. There is no need to suppose that these forms exist apart from God, although Boethius in this text leaves their precise location undetermined. A true form is absolutely simple: it is what it is. It is incapable of being a subject, and hence is immutable, most beautiful, and durable. Although these are characteristics of Plato's separated forms, it is clear from the context that Boethius understands them to be divine perfections. Hence these forms are probably divine ideas, identical with the very substance of God or at least very closely associated with it.

3. CREATURELY PARTICIPATION IN GOODNESS AND BEING

The treatise entitled *In What Way are Substances Good?* is a purely philosophical work. It is devoted to this question: how can substances be good in their form and actual existence, since they are not good substantially? [4]

It is evident to well-schooled people that every being is good, inasmuch as beings tend toward the good, and everything tends toward its like. The problem dealt with in this work centers on the manner in which creatures are good, whether by participation or by substance. These two alternatives are conceived as being mutually exclusive. If a creature were good by participation, then it would be in no way good in its substance. For nothing which participates in a certain quality is constituted in its very essence by this quality. But if a thing were not good in its own substance, then presumably it would not tend toward the good, as toward the term of its natural inclination. We notice, however, that things do have a tendency toward the good, and hence there is a genuine difficulty about regarding created things as participants in goodness. On the other hand, if they were to be considered as being good in virtue of their own substance, then their very *esse* (form or essence) would be good. But in this case the creature would be identical with the first good or God.

In his solution, Boethius performs a thought experiment. Since many things can be separated by thought which cannot be actually separated, he mentally removes the first good and inquires in what way existing things are good in its absence. On such a hypothesis, it would follow that substance and goodness differ in them, because goodness must be regarded as a quality of substance. On this assumption, goodness would have the same ontological status as the roundness, heaviness, and whiteness of a thing. Now these qualities cannot be the same as substance, for then they would all be identical with each other. Thus, if goodness were the same as substance, weight also would be the same as substance. Hence the weight of a thing and its goodness would be identical. In conclusion, when the creature's goodness is considered in itself, apart from

---

[4] *The Theological Tractates, Quomodo substantiae in eo quod sint bonae sint, cum non sint substantialia bona,* pp. 38-50. In the middle ages, this work was usually cited as the *De Hebdomadibus.*

170 READINGS IN ANCIENT AND MEDIEVAL PHILOSOPHY

the first good, the only reality it can have is that of an accident. This
removes the creature's substance from the order of goodness.

This negative result leads Boethius to his central insight: because
creatures are not simple, they could not in any way exist unless that
which is solely good willed them to be. Creatures are good in their existence, inasmuch as their existence proceeds from the will of the first
good, which is good in what it is. God's goodness and causality must be
restored to our analysis of creaturely goodness.

Throughout Boethius' problem and solution, there is a basic ambiguity in regard to the meaning of being (*esse*), that is, being signifies
form, essence, and/or actual existence. However, at an especially critical
moment in his solution, his conception of being manifests its openness
to actual existence (although it is never equivalent in meaning to the
Thomistic act of being). Boethius declares that if creatures are considered apart from the first good, they cannot be good in their actual existence. But inasmuch as creatures could not actually exist unless that
which is truly good produced them, their existence is good. Yet it is not
like the substantial good from which it flows, since the latter is un-
derived. Nevertheless, although Boethius solves his problem along the
lines of actual existence, he clearly does not regard this existence as something different from essence.

In the light of Boethius' solution in the *De Hebdomadibus* and the
parallel treatment of *esse* in the *De Trinitate,* the meaning of the celebrated axioms with which the former work begins can now be stated.[5]

According to the second axiom, the entire reality of a concretely existing thing (*id quod est*) differs from its *esse* or *forma essendi,* a principle or part of the whole which indifferently signifies form and actual
existence. "Being itself never is," is a particular application of the more
general principle from the *De Trinitate:* only the composite whole exists
and not the parts taken separately. Through receiving the form of being,
the *quod est* exists; *esse,* however, is incapable of existence by itself
alone.

Axiom three: *quod est* can participate something, but *ipsum esse* can
in no way participate anything. The reason for this difference is that
participation occurs inasmuch as something already exists. But something
is, insofar as it has received *esse.* This reason limits participation to the
reception of an accident by a previously existing subject.

The fourth axiom: *id quod est* can have something other than its essence, which is only a part of its reality, but *ipsum esse* cannot be mixed
with anything other than itself. This parallels the statement of the *De
Trinitate:* form cannot be a subject or receive accidents. The purity of
ipsum esse excludes the reception of extraneous elements.

5 *Ibid.,* pp. 40-44. No comment is required here for the first axiom, which says that
" a common conception is a statement generally accepted as soon as it is made " (p. 41).
The remaining axioms are instances of statements directly intelligible to the learned
mind.

Fifth axiom: there is a difference between merely being something in a qualified way and being something in an essential way or in one's very substance. In other words, there is a distinction between the substance of a thing and the qualities which it participates. This implies for Boethius that if a thing is good by participation, then goodness does not penetrate its inmost structure. The substantial reality of a thing—its essence and existence—differs from its accidental qualities.

Axiom six: every *quod est* participates *esse* in order to exist; it participates in accidental qualities in order to be a particular something. Here, participation is used in the broad sense as equivalent to any reception, and not in the strict sense as the reception of a determination extraneous to the original form or essence of a thing.

Axiom seven: in every simple thing (only God is meant), *esse* and *id quod est* are one.

Axiom eight: in every composite (that is, in every creature), its *esse* (form and existence) is distinct from the concretely existing thing.

Composition in creatures is explained in the *De Trinitate* entirely on the plane of essence. The creature appears to be nothing other than a quidditative whole, made up of essential parts: matter, form, and various accidents. Composition in the *De Hebdomadibus* refers to an existing as well as to an essential whole. Hence there is some basis for saying that Boethius distinguishes that which is from its actual existence, or that in virtue of which it is. But there is no basis for regarding this *esse* as distinct from form.

CONCLUSION

It is well known that on the problem of the universals Boethius hesitates between Plato and Aristotle concerning the status of genus and species. This is consistent with his lack of a fully developed conception of being. There is in Boethius a fundamental ambiguity in regard to what it means to be real. Much modern scholarship has committed the serious error of seeking in Boethius a "pure position" concerning being.[6]

There are evidences of tendencies toward neo-Platonism and essentialism. In the *Consolation of Philosophy,* it is the pure unity of the highest good which establishes its goodness, and its reality is proved by an argument which moves from essence to essence and is entirely cut off from actual existence. In the *De Trinitate,* form and being are simply equated. However, Boethius' thought does not focus upon essence to the total exclusion of actual existence. Actual existence still has some philosophic relevance. Thus, in the *De Hebdomadibus,* he solves the problem of how created substances are good in their being by regarding the latter as

6 For instance, Hermann Josef Brosch, *Der Seinsbegriff bei Boethius* (Innsbruck, 1931). According to Brosch, *esse* in *The Theological Tractates* and in the *Consolation of Philosophy* is used exclusively in the sense of *esse essentiae* or quidditative being, without any reference to existence.

synonymous with actual existence. These substances are good because they are willed and produced in actual existence by the first good.

There is, then, a complex of competing positions in Boethius' metaphysics. This incompletely developed theory of being and goodness is not surprising in a thinker who hoped to reconcile Plato and Aristotle, but never found a way to do so.

VI. Christian Philosophies from St. Anselm to St. Bernard

In the eleventh century, St. Anselm of Canterbury stands at the head-waters of the intense and varied developments in medieval theology and philosophy. His type of Christian philosophy inquires in a systematic, speculative way into the reasons which can be supplied for the content of the Christian faith. In asking about the rational grounds for accepting the existence of God, he conducts his investigation within the context of his firm religious acceptance of this fundamental truth. As a confident and meditative believer in God, he nevertheless wants to find an intrinsically cogent proof of God's existence which will satisfy both his own mind and that of others, who may have reached their concept of God through natural reasoning. Father Robert Miller's essay, Selection (22), invites us to consider the so-called ontological argument initially on Anselm's own terms, before viewing it prismatically in its reformulation by Descartes and Hegel, or in its rejection by Aquinas and Kant. From the Anselmian perspective, the problem of the truth of the idea of God is the crux of the issue. That *it is necessarily true follows inexorably from the contradictory results of thinking of the most perfect being as really nonexistent. But* if *it is true, then, like every other necessarily true idea, it must be caused by the actual being of the nature expressed in the idea. Going from idea to being, the Anselmian proof rests upon a realism of universals and an essentialism of beings. In the degree that these wider premises are accepted, this proof continues to remain attractive and to find new formulations in somewhat similar philosophical traditions. And to be relevant to the case, criticism of the argument has to be directed primarily toward the theory of knowledge and being, upon which it ultimately rests.*

St. Anselm's proof and his correlative rejection of Roscelin's word-theory of universals are indicative of the broad implications of the problem of the universals for philosophy and theology. It was not just a strong appetite for logic, but also a recognition that many fundamental issues hinged upon the solution, which sustained the lively interest con-

cerning universals of thinkers in the eleventh and twelfth centuries. We are fortunate in having the main positions reported in Selection (23) by so keen-eyed a humanist as John of Salisbury, who studied under most of the men whose views he describes. He enjoyed a thorough education at Paris and Chartres, served in high ecclesiastical posts in England, was secretary to St. Thomas à Becket, witnessed his murder, and eventually became bishop of Chartres. John of Salisbury composed the Metalogicon *as a defense of the liberal trivium of logic, rhetoric, and grammar (including literature and history), against the "Cornificians" or obscurantist opponents of a liberal training in the spoken and written word and logical reasoning. Yet he was also well aware of defects in the current way of teaching logic, as well as of the danger involved in isolating logic from the other sciences and making over-extended claims for demonstrative reasoning in the region of changing natural facts. "If it is to fecundate the soul to bear the fruits of philosophy, logic must conceive from an external source," and must cultivate the technique of probability in addition to demonstration.* (Metalogicon, *pp. 100, 105.) To overcome the stalemate over universals, John of Salisbury recommended that the logical analysis be reintegrated with a theory of abstraction, but the psychological and metaphysical texts of Aristotle were not yet available for completing his program.*

Peter Abelard, whose own contribution to the discussion about universals was more intricate than a reading of John of Salisbury would suggest, also did some original work in ethics. Selection (24) presents some of his views on the morality of human acts. He agreed fully with St. Augustine that moral evil has no substantial reality of its own, no independent foothold in being, and that its presence is achieved through the deficient will of man. But he wanted to determine as closely as possible the specifying principle of the moral good or evil quality of the act proceeding from the will. It does not consist precisely in the habitual disposition of the will, whereby it is denominated virtuous or vicious, since the vicious inclination does not always beget an evil act. Nor does the deed itself determine the morality of the act, because of the frequent gap between intention and outcome. What does specify the act as morally good or bad is the intention of the agent, his aim of conforming with or contending against the will of God. Not content with stressing the importance of personal intention, however, Abelard made it the sole determinant of the moral character of the act. In doing so, he passed over the contribution of the object of the act and the circumstances.

Consequently, he found it difficult to supply a moral meaning for a good or bad deed as such, and to determine the particular way in which different acts are morally qualified.

On this score and many others, Abelard's most vigorous critic was St. Bernard of Clairvaux. Etienne Gilson shows, in Selection (25), how he treats the problem of morality within the context of a doctrine obtained from Gregory of Nyssa and Augustine concerning the image of God and freedom. For Bernard, the sinful act can be regarded radically as a darkening and disfiguring of our likeness to God, as a breakdown of some aspects of human freedom, and as an emigration from God's presence to the land of unlikeness. One can detect here a note surprisingly similar to present-day existentialist descriptions of "the underground man," alienated from God but struggling to retain his personal freedom in an impersonally determined world. Bernard will not allow that man's turning away from God is ever so complete as to obliterate the core of kinship with him which consists in our freedom from necessity. There remains something in man which can respond to grace and to the call of loving God once more. In The Mystical Theology of St. Bernard, *Gilson goes on to explore the positive side of the doctrine, which consists essentially in asking us "to put our liberty on its only true basis by assimilating it to God's. . . . In the measure in which this purification has been brought about, the soul has recovered its lost likeness." (Gilson, ibid., pp. 97, 99). The Christian interpretation of the Socratic maxim:* Know thyself, *involves a movement of recovering the likeness of God and the plenitude of freedom.*

22

ST. ANSELM ON THE EXISTENCE OF GOD [1]

S T. ANSELM'S so-called ontological argument for the existence of God may be paraphrased as follows: By faith we believe God to be a being than which none greater can be thought. Even the fool who says in his heart "there is no God," hearing what we believe God to be, understands what he hears, and what he understands at least exists in

---

[1] [From Robert Miller, C.S.B., "The Ontological Argument in St. Anselm and Descartes," *The Modern Schoolman*, vol. 32 (1954-55), pp. 342-349. Reprinted by permission. The exposition is based mainly on Anselm's *Proslogion*, chs. 2-3, and his *Dialogue on Truth*. The notes are omitted.]

his understanding. Now it is evident that "that than which a greater cannot be thought" cannot exist solely in the understanding, for existing in
reality is greater than merely in the understanding. If such a being exists
merely in the understanding, then that being than which a greater cannot be thought is that than which a greater can be thought. But this is
contradictory. Hence the being than which a greater cannot be thought
exists both in the understanding and in reality. That is the proof for
which Anselm searched so long, a proof, he tells us, needing only itself
as demonstration.

What are the factors in St. Anselm's thought which we need to grasp
to see the argument as closely as possible to the way he himself saw it?
First, the idea of God whose object is the essence of God (*id quod Deus
est*) is neither a capricious construction nor a refinement from sensible
experience. Anselm unequivocally affirms that, in the *Proslogion,* he accepts the concept of God from which his proof begins from sacred authority; that is, from faith. However, those not accepting this source for
their vague but preliminary notion of the nature of God may by natural
reasoning arrive at the same notion of God. Consequently *the source* of
the initial concept in the proof is no locale for cogent objection. In
Anselm's opinion neither of those two ways in which the idea of God is
achieved would permit it to be designated as a purely arbitrary idea.

The second factor is St. Anselm's conviction that the objects of ideas
are universal substances; that these universal substances are what we call
essences; that every universal substance is in itself a reality; that when
the essence is known, this reality, which the essence is, is in its reality in
the intellect; that this existence of the essence in thought is a true way
for the essence to be. These aspects of Anselm's thought are the bases
for the proper and accurate term "Anselmian realism."

Because, for St. Anselm, (1) the object of every true idea is a reality
and (2) when known this reality has an existence in thought, the essence
of fire or water is a reality; and when it is known *id quod* fire is or *id
quod* water is, this reality which is the essence of fire or water is in the
understanding with a true existence. Such is also the case with the idea
of God. *Id quod Deus est* or the essence of God is but vaguely, primi-
tively, and imperfectly expressed in the term "a being than which none
greater can be thought." Nevertheless, God's essence, *id quod* God is,
somehow has being in the intellect, when it is understanding that God
is "a being than which none greater can be thought." The existence in
the mind of a real essence is not nothing, nor is it the highest modality
of reality which it may exercise. The ontological argument is indeed
unintelligible apart from a knowledge of the universality of Anselm's
realism.

The question for St. Anselm obviously is, in the case of the idea of
God, can the essence of "that than which none greater can be thought"
exist only in the mind? If it existed only in the mind, Anselm is convinced that a greater could be thought of; namely, one which would also

have existence outside thought, in actual reality. Then that which existed only in the mind would not be that than which none greater can be thought. This is the third factor in St. Anselm's thought: that existence both in thought and in reality is greater than existence in thought alone.

The conclusive step of the Anselmian dialectic provides us with the fourth factor. Having been a professor of logic and considering himself an orthodox dialectician, in opposition to the heretical dialectics of the nominalist Roscelin, Anselm taught the reality of the objects of ideas— for him, a necessary alternative to the theologically impossible consequences of Roscelin's nominalism. Now the primary criterion of a true idea, for St. Anselm, was the self-evident necessity of the principle of contradiction. Anselm uses that criterion in the following way.

God is that than which nothing greater can be thought. What is thought to be both in the intellect and in actual reality is greater than what is thought to be only in the intellect. Now if that than which a greater cannot be thought exists only in the intellect, then that than which a greater cannot be thought is that than which a greater can be thought. But such a condition is impossible, because of the principle of of contradiction. It is therefore contradictory to maintain that the being than which a greater cannot be conceived exists only in the intellect. A notion of that than which a greater cannot be conceived, which being would be lacking actual existence, is for Anselm a self-contradictory notion. Such a being lacking existence is impossible to conceive; hence it is necessary to think of God as existing. And because it is necessary to think of God as actually existing, St. Anselm finds himself compelled to affirm that God does in actual fact exist.

To repeat: Because it is impossible to think of God as nonexistent, it is necessary to think of God as existent. And for St. Anselm, to demonstrate the necessity of thinking God as existing is, by that very act, to demonstrate that God exists. The necessity of God's existing follows from the necessity of our thinking that God exists.

In a penetrating analysis of St. Anselm's thought, Etienne Gilson has pointed out that, behind Anselm's position that the necessity of affirming existence guarantees the reality of the existence, there is the fundamental Anselmian position that the necessity of such an affirmation of existence presupposes the existence of the object of that affirmation. In effect, this amounts to saying that behind the dialectical structure of the Anselmian proof is an epistemological doctrine, the core of which is that the existence of a truth always presupposes the existence of its object.

The significance of this insight for an Anselmian understanding of the ontological argument may be appreciated by listing briefly four essentially related elements in Anselm's doctrine of truth. (1) Spoken, written, or sign-language propositions are true when they do what their normal function is to do; namely, to signify thought faithfully. (2) Thought is true when it does what is its normal function to do; namely, to signify things according to the way things are, for things are the causes of true thought, the rule and measure of true thought. (3) Things are true when they do what is their normal function; namely, to be exactly what their essences requires them to be—that is, to exist and operate according to their pattern, the divine ideas of God who is the cause of their truth. (4) God is supreme truth itself. Caused by nothing, supreme truth is the cause of all other truth. Truth is, therefore, improperly said of everything but God, for whatever is true is so only because of the one supreme truth.

It is eminently clear from this list of Anselmian propositions that thought in no way fabricates its own truth; its truth is *caused* by whatsoever is the object of the true thought. Reason's idea of God as existing is necessary and true. Since a true thought is *caused* by its object, the true thought presupposes the existence of its object. Consequently, once we are in possession of a true thought regarding the existence of God we not only may but must conclude to the real existence of God, unique *cause* of such a true thought. The crucial question now to be answered by St. Anselm is, When are we certain that our thought is true?

It is the position of St. Anselm that where there is a necessary thought that necessary thought is a true thought. What, then, constitutes a necessary thought for Anselm? A thought is necessary when its content—that is, the reality which is the essence—squares with the principle of contradiction. Every self-contradictory thought is an impossible thought. St. Anselm repeatedly indicates, both in the *Proslogion* and in the *Apologetic to Gaunilon,* that it is contradictory to think of "the being than which a greater cannot be thought" as nonexistent. The necessary thought, then, is that which cannot be otherwise than it is without being self-contradictory. It is necessary, for example, to think that fire is not water, because, for St. Anselm, it is contradictory and therefore impossible to think that fire is water. Similarly, the impossibility of thinking of God as nonexistent is equivalent to the necessity of thinking of God as existent.

The core problem, quite evidently, is whether there is an objective root for that necessity of thought and, if so, what is it. Within St. Anselm's realism there is such an objective root; and it is the stable reality which is, in effect, the essence, which inflexible essence is the content of thought. Not constructed by the mind, the essences are received by each mind which does what it is made to do; when the understanding works normally it simply receives, for example, *id quod* fire is, *id quod* water is, *id quod* God is. And no one understanding the reality or essence which fire is and the essence water is can think that fire is water. In exactly the same way, no one understanding the nature of God (*id quod Deus est*) can think of God as nonexistent.

Although St. Anselm considers that the content of thought is the immutable, intrinsic necessity of an essence, he is by no means explicit in explaining *how* thought receives or acquires that essence, except in referring to the relation of the understanding and the senses as somehow involved, along with the illumination of the soul by God, in knowing the intrinsic necessity of the real essence. *How it occurs, however, is not a matter of importance in* the adequate discussion of our problem. What is of importance is to realize that, for St. Anselm, our mind is submitted to, ruled and measured by, the internal, immutable necessity of the essence. We must recognize that in such cases, when thought expresses or signifies the necessity of the essence, it is signifying that what is is. For to be is to be an immutable essence; and for thought to express what is or essence, is for thought to be true.

Thus we see that, in St. Anselm's position, the intrinsic necessity of the real essence is the objective foundation of the necessity of thought not being otherwise than it is without being self-contradictory. A "non-existing being than whom no greater can be conceived" is a self-contradictory thought. Its contrary is a necessary thought. And because, in a necessary thought, thought is doing what it is made to do—namely, submitting to the necessity of an essence, being ruled and measured by it and therefore expressing what is—each necessary thought is a true thought.

And each true thought presupposes the reality of its object as *cause* of the truth of that thought. No exception is made for that necessary and therefore true thought which must think of "the being than which none greater can be thought" as existent. Its *cause* can be nothing less than its object; that is, the real and necessary existence of God. In other words, it could never be necessary, and therefore true, to think of God as existing unless God were in actual fact existing. Hence, as soon as St. Anselm demonstrates the necessity of affirming the existence of God, he is certain he has demonstrated the real existence of God.

Only God's essence is so immutable that existence is an intrinsic necessity of it. St. Anselm is clearly in the Platonic and Augustinian tradition in which being consists in immutability of essence, in which the degree of immutability constitutes the degree of being. God alone is absolutely immutable, always entirely what he is, always the same, having no aspect of otherness or nonbeing; and hence he alone is being properly and absolutely. And because being is the immutability of essence, God as most properly and absolutely being is most properly called essence. According to St. Anselm, such a being, than whom none greater can be conceived—that is, being in its proper and absolutely limitless significance—cannot be thought as nonexistent. In fact, the analysis of God's essence implies the necessity of his existence.

Anselm's position is what is known today as an essentialism; that is, a doctrine which commences with an assumed true and adequate knowledge of essence and derives from this essence, if possible, even the knowledge of existence. If to be is to be an essence, then all knowledge of existence must be derived from an analysis of the essence. If it belongs to the essence of an absolute being "than whom none greater can be conceived" to exist then he exists. For St. Anselm, that essence which is properly and absolutely being is being under amplification to the infinite, being extended without any limitations. Being "than which none greater can be conceived," when understood as essence, contains all that can be predicated of that essence; that is, there is no more in such a being than can be fully achieved by the simple understanding of the essence. In effect, existence is already contained in being amplified to the infinite; hence existence is grasped in the same intellectual act of understanding by which the essence (*id quod Deus est*) of God is grasped.

The submission of the known essence of God, being in its absolute and proper fullness, to the principle of contradiction is Anselm's way of demonstrating that such an essence must necessarily be conceived as existent and hence must necessarily exist. In fine, in the simple act of understanding absolutely limitless and supreme being or essence, Anselm discovers necessary existence as a property peculiar to such an unlimited absolute essence or being. Because existence is a property of absolute essence or being, existence is attained when absolute essence is understood. In this sense St. Anselm would readily agree that he remains at all times on the essential level because, for him, existence is but a necessary property of being extended to its absolutely highest degree or modality. Such being is *essentia;* that is, God.

23

THE TWELFTH-CENTURY CONFLICT ON UNIVERSALS: A REPORT BY JOHN OF SALISBURY[1]

1. THE PERNICIOUS MANNER OF TEACHING LOGIC

To show off their knowledge, our contemporaries dispense their instruction in such a way that their listeners are at a loss to understand them. They seem to have the impression that every letter of the alphabet is pregnant with the secrets of Minerva. They analyze and press upon tender ears everything that anyone has ever said or done. Falling into the error condemned by Cicero, they frequently come to be unintelligible to their hearers more because of the multiplicity than the profundity of their statements. "It is indeed useful and advantageous for disputants," as Aristotle observes, "to take cognizance of several opinions on a topic." From the mutual disagreement thus brought into relief, what is seen to be poorly stated may be disproved or modified. Instruc-

---

[1] [From *The Metalogicon of John of Salisbury,* translated by D. D. McGarry (Berkeley and Los Angeles: University of California Press, 1955), pp. 111-116, 118-121. Reprinted by permission. Headings are inserted, and notes are omitted.]

tion in elementary logic does not, however, constitute the proper occasion for such procedure. Simplicity, brevity, and easy subject matter are, so far as is possible, appropriate in introductory studies. This is so true that it is permissible to expound many difficult points in a simpler way than their nature strictly requires. Thus, much that we have learned in our youth must later be amended in more advanced philosophical studies.

2. OPINIONS ABOUT THE UNIVERSALS

Nevertheless, at present, all are here [in introductory logical studies] declaiming on the nature of universals, and attempting to explain, contrary to the intention of the author [Aristotle], what is really a most profound question, and a matter [that should be reserved] for more advanced studies. One holds that universals are merely word sounds, although this opinion, along with its author *Roscelin,* has already almost completely passed into oblivion. Another maintains that universals are word concepts, and twists to support his thesis everything that he can remember to have ever been written on the subject. Our *Peripatetic of Pallet, Abelard,* was ensnared in this opinion. He left many, and still has, to this day, some followers and proponents of his doctrine. They are friends of mine, although they often so torture the helpless letter that even the hardest heart is filled with compassion for the latter. They hold that it is preposterous to predicate a thing concerning a thing, although Aristotle is author of this monstrosity. For Aristotle frequently asserts that a thing is predicated concerning a thing, as is evident to anyone who is really familiar with his teaching. Another is wrapped up in a consideration of acts of the [intuitive] understanding, and says that genera and species are nothing more than the latter. Proponents of this view take their cue from Cicero and Boethius, who cite Aristotle as saying that universals should be regarded as and called "notions." "A notion," they tell us, "is the cognition of something, derived from its previously perceived form, and in need of unravelment." Or again [they say]: "A notion is an act of the [intuitive] understanding, a simple mental comprehension." They accordingly distort everything written, with an eye to making acts of [intuitive] understanding or "notions" include the universality of universals.

Those who adhere to the view that universals are things, have various and sundry opinions. One, reasoning from the fact that everything which exists is singular in number, concludes that either the universal is numerically one, or it is non-existent. But since it is impossible for things that are substantial to be nonexistent, if those things for which they are substantial exist, they further conclude that universals must be essentially one with particular things. Accordingly, following *Walter of Mortagne,* they distinguish [various] states [of existence], and say that Plato is an individual in so far as he is Plato; a species in so far as he is a man; a genus of a subaltern [subordinate] kind in so far as he is an animal; and a most general genus in so far as he is a substance. Although this opinion formerly had some proponents, it has been a long time since anyone has asserted it.

Walter now upholds [the doctrine of] ideas, emulating Plato and imitating *Bernard of Chartres*, and maintains that genus and species are nothing more nor less than these, namely, ideas. "An idea," according to Seneca's definition, "is an eternal exemplar of those things which come to be as a result of nature." And since universals are not subject to corruption, and are not altered by the changes that transform particular things and cause them to come and go, succeeding one another almost momentarily, ideas are properly and correctly called "universals." Indeed, particular things are deemed incapable of supporting the substantive verb, [i.e., of being said "to be"], since they are not at all stable, and disappear without even waiting to receive names. For they vary so much in their qualities, time, location, and numerous different properties, that their whole existence seems to be more a mutable transition than a stable status. In contrast, Boethius declares: "We say that things 'are' when they may neither be increased nor diminished, but always continue as they are, firmly sustained by the foundations of their own nature." These [foundations] include their quantities, qualities, relations, places, times, conditions, and whatever is found in a way united with bodies. Although these adjuncts of bodies may seem to be changed, they remain immutable in their own nature. In like manner, although individuals [of species] may change, species remain the same. The waves of a stream wash on, yet the same flow of water continues, and we refer to the stream as the same river. Whence the statement of Seneca, which, in fact, he has borrowed from another: "In one sense it is true that we may descend twice into the same river, although in another sense this is not so." These "ideas," or "exemplary forms," are the original plans of all things. They may neither be decreased nor augmented; and they are so permanent and perpetual, that even if the whole world were to come to an end, they could not perish. They include all things, and, as Augustine seems to maintain in his book *On Free Will*, their number neither increases nor diminishes, because the ideas always continue, even when it happens that [particular] temporal things cease to exist.

What these men promise is wonderful, and familiar to philosophers who rise to the contemplation of higher things. But, as Boethius and numerous other authors testify, it is utterly foreign to the mind of Aristotle. For Aristotle very frequently opposes this view, as is clear from his books. Bernard of Chartres and his followers labored strenuously to compose the differences between Aristotle and Plato. But I opine that they arrived on the scene too late, so that their efforts to reconcile two dead men, who disagreed as long as they were alive and could do so, were in vain.

Still another, in his endeavor to explain Aristotle, places universality in "native forms," as does *Gilbert, Bishop of Poitiers,* who labors to prove that "native forms" and universals are identical. A "native form" is an example of an original [exemplar]. It [the native form, unlike the original] inheres in created things, instead of subsisting in the divine mind. In Greek it is called the *idos,* since it stands in relation to the idea as the example does to its exemplar. The native form is sensible in things that are perceptible by the senses; but insensible as conceived in the mind. It is singular in individuals, but universal in all [of a kind]. Another, with *Joscelin, Bishop of Soissons,* attributes universality to collections of things, while denying it to things as individuals. When Joscelin tries to explain the authorities, he has his troubles and is hard put, for in many places he cannot bear the gaping astonishment of the indignant letter.

Still another takes refuge in a new tongue, since he does not have sufficient command of Latin. When he hears the words "genus" and "species," at one time he says they should be understood as universals, and at another that they refer to the *maneries* of things. I know not in which of the authors he has found this term or this distinction, unless perhaps he has dug it out of lists of abstruse and obsolete words, or it is an item of jargon [in the baggage] of present-day doctors. I am further at a loss to see what it can mean here, unless it refers to collections of things, which would be the same as Joscelin's view, or to a universal thing, which, however, could hardly be called a *maneries.* For a *maneries* may be interpreted as referring to both [collections and universals], since a number of things, or the status in which a thing of such and such a type continues to exist may be called a *maneries.* Finally, there are some who fix their attention on the status of things, and say that genera and species consist in the latter.

3. THE POSITION OF JOHN OF SALISBURY

Aristotle stated that genera and species do not exist [as such], but are only understood. What is the point, then, in inquiring as to what genus is, when Aristotle has definitely asserted that it does not exist? Is it not inane to try to determine the nature, quantity, and quality of something that has no existence? If substance be lacking, then none of these other attributes can be present. If Aristotle, who says that genera and species do not exist [as such], is right, then the labors of the foregoing inquiry as to their substance, quantity, quality, or origin, are futile. We cannot describe the quality or quantity of something that lacks substance. Neither can we give the reason why something that does not exist is one thing or another, and of this or that size or kind. Wherefore, unless one wants to break with Aristotle, by granting that universals exist, he must reject opinions which would identify universals with word sounds, word concepts, sensible things, ideas, native forms, or collections. For all of the latter doubtless exist. In short, one who maintains that universals exist, contradicts Aristotle.

We should not, however, fear that our understanding is empty when it perceives universals as abstracted from particular things, although the former have no [actual] existence apart from the latter. Our understanding [has two different modes of operation:] at times [it] looks directly at the simple essence of things, apart from composition, as when it conceives of "man" *per se,* or "stone" *per se,* in which operation it is simple. But at times it proceeds gradually, step by step, as when it considers a man as white, or a horse as running, in which case its operation is composite. A simple act of the understanding at times considers a thing as it is, as when it considers Plato; but at other times it conceives of a thing as otherwise. Sometimes it combines things that are [in actual life] uncombined, at other times it separates things that cannot [in reality] be dissociated. One who imagines a goat-stag or a centaur, conceives of a combination of man and beast that is alien to nature, or a combination of two species of animals. On the other hand, one who considers line or surface apart from a given mass, dissociates form from matter by the keen blade of his contemplative insight, although, actually, it is impossible for them to exist apart from each other. However, the abstracting intellect does not in this case conceive of form as existing apart from matter. If it did, its operation would be composite. Rather, it simply contemplates the form, without considering the matter, even though in fact the former cannot exist apart from the latter. Such an operation agrees with the intellect's simplicity, which comes into sharper relief in proportion as it considers simpler things in themselves, namely, apart from composition with other things. Nor is this procedure contrary to the order of nature, which has bestowed on the [human] intellect this faculty of distinguishing things that are combined, and putting together things that exist separately, in order to facilitate its investigation of nature itself.

The combining process of the intellect, whereby things that are not united are copulated, lacks objectivity; but its abstracting process is both accurate and true to reality. The latter constitutes, as it were, the common factory of all the arts. While things possess but one manner of existence which they have received from nature, they may nevertheless be understood or signified in more than one way. Although a man who is not a specific man cannot exist, "man" may still be conceived mentally and represented in such a way that no given individual man is thought of or denoted. Therefore genera and species may be conceived by the abstracting intellect, in order to signify things [as considered] apart from composition. But if one were, ever so diligently, to search for the latter in nature, dissociated from sensible things, he would be wasting his time, and laboring in vain, as nature does not count anything of the sort among her brood.

Reason, on considering the substantial mutual resemblances of certain individual things, has discerned genera and species. Thus it has, as Boethius tells us, defined the general concept: "Rational mortal animal," which it has, on reflection, concluded from the mutual conformity existing among men, even though such a "rational mortal animal" [actually] exists only in individual cases. Consequently, genera and species are not things that are really and by their nature unrelated to individual things. Rather, they are mental representations of actual, natural things, intellectual images of the mutual likenesses of real things, reflected, as it were, in the mirror of the soul's native purity. These concepts the Greek call *ennoyas* or *yconoyfanas*, that is to say images of things clearly discernible by the mind.

For the soul, as it were by the reflected ray of its own contemplation, finds in itself what it defines. The exemplar of what is defined exists in the mind, while the example exists among actual things. A similar condition maintains when we say in grammar: "Names which have such and such an ending are feminine or neuter." A general rule is laid down, which provides, so to speak, an exemplar for many declinable words. The examples, in turn, are to be found in all the words with a given termination. In like manner, certain exemplars are mentally conceived after their examples have been formed and presented to the senses by nature. According to Aristotle, these exemplars are conceptual, and are, as it were, images and shadows of things that really exist. But if one attempts to lay hold of them, supposing them to have an existence of their own, apart from particular things, they vanish [into thin air] as do dreams. "For they are representations," apparent only to the intellect.

24

ABELARD ON CONSENT, INTENTION, AND MORAL ACTION [1]

1. THE DEFECT OF MIND BEARING UPON CONDUCT

CERTAIN defects or merits of mind have no connection with morals. They do not make human life a matter of praise or blame. Such are dull wits or quick insight; a good or a bad memory; ignorance or knowledge. Each of these features is found in good and bad alike. They have nothing to do with the system of morals, nor with making life base or honourable. To exclude these, we must safeguard the

[1] [From *Abailard's Ethics*, translated by J. R. McCallum (Oxford: Basil Blackwell, 1935), pp. 11, 12, 17-21, 46-48. Reprinted by permission. This is a translation of Abelard's *Know Thyself*.]

phrase "defects of mind" by adding "which dispose to bad actions," that is, those defects which incline the will to what least of all either should be done or should be left undone.

2. HOW DOES SIN DIFFER FROM A DISPOSITION TO EVIL?

Defect of this mental kind is not the same thing as sin. Sin, too, is not the same as a bad action. For example, to be irascible, that is, prone or easily roused to the agitation of anger is a defect and moves the mind to unpleasantly impetuous and irrational action. This defect, however, is in the mind so that the mind is liable to wrath, even when it is not actually roused to it. Similarly, lameness, by reason of which a man is said to be lame, is in the man himself even when he does not walk and reveal his lameness. For the defect is there, though action be lacking. So, also, their nature or constitution renders many people liable to luxury. Yet they do not sin because they are like this, but from this very fact they have the material of a struggle whereby they may, in the virtue of temperance, triumph over themselves and win the crown. As Solomon says: "The patient man is better than the valiant: and he that ruleth his spirit, then he that taketh cities" (*Prov.* xvi, 32). For religion does not think it degrading to be beaten by man; but it is degrading to be beaten by one's lower self. The former defeat has been the fate of good men. But in the latter we fall below ourselves. The Apostle commends victory of this sort: "For he also that striveth for the mastery, is not crowned, except he strive lawfully" (2 *Tim.* ii, 5).

This striving, I repeat, means standing less against men than against myself, so that defects may not lure me into base consent. Though men cease to oppose us, our defects do not cease. The fight with them is the more dangerous because of its repetition. And as it is the more difficult, so victory is the more glorious. Men, however much they prevail over us, do not force baseness upon us, unless by their practice of vice they turn us also to it and overcome us through our own wretched consent. They may dominate our body; but while our mind is free, there is no danger to true freedom. We run no risk of base servitude. Subservience to vice, not to man, is degradation. It is the overlordship of defects and not physical serfdom which debases the soul.

3. DEFINITION OF "DEFECTS" AND OF SIN

Defect, then, is that whereby we are disposed to sin. We are, that is, inclined to consent to what we ought not to do, or to leave undone what we ought to do. Consent of this kind we rightly call sin. Here is the reproach of the soul meriting damnation or being declared guilty by ＿d. What is that consent but to despise God and to violate his laws? ＿ cannot be set at enmity by injury, but by contempt. He is the high ＿ ＿er, and is not diminished by any injury, but he avenges contempt of himself. Our sin, therefore, is contempt of the Creator. To sin is to despise the Creator; that is, not to do for him what we believe we should do for him, or, not to renounce what we think should be renounced on his behalf. We have defined sin negatively, by saying that it means not doing or not renouncing what we ought to do or renounce. Clearly, then, we have shown that sin has no reality. It exists rather in *not being* than in *being*. Similarly we could define shadows by saying: The absence of light where light usually is

Perhaps you object that sin is the desire or will to do an evil deed, and that this will or desire condemns us before God in the same way as the will to do a good deed justifies us. There is as much quality, you suggest, in the good will as there is sin in the evil will; and it is no less "in being" in the latter than in the former. By willing to do what we believe to be pleasing to God we please him. Equally, by willing to do what we believe to be displeasing to God, we displease him and seem either to violate or despise his nature.

But diligent attention will show that we think far otherwise of this point. We frequently err; and from no evil will at all. Indeed, the evil will itself, when restrained, though it may not be quenched, procures the palm-wreath for those who resist it. It provides, not merely the materials for combat, but also the crown of glory. It should be spoken of rather as a certain inevitable weakness than as sin. Take, for example, the case of an innocent servant whose harsh master is moved with fury against him. He pursues the servant, drawing his sword with intent to kill him. For a while the servant flies and avoids death as best he can. At last, forced all unwillingly to it, he kills his master so as not to be killed by him. Let anyone say what sort of evil will there was in this deed. His will was only to flee from death and preserve his own life. Was this an evil will? You reply: "I do not think this was an evil will. But the will that he had to kill the master who was pursuing him was evil." Your answer would be admirable and acute, if you could show that the servant really willed what you say that he did. But, as I insisted, he was unwillingly forced to his deed. He protracted his master's life as long as he could, knowing that danger also threatened his own life from such a crime. How, then, was a deed done voluntarily by which he incurred danger to his own life?

Your reply may be that the action was voluntary because the man's will was to escape death, even though it may not have been to kill his master. This charge might easily be preferred against him. I do not rebut it. Nevertheless, as has been said, that will by which he sought to evade death, as you urge, and not to kill his master, cannot at all be condemned as bad. He did, however, fail by consenting, though driven to it through fear of death, to an unjust murder which he ought rather to have endured than committed. Of his own will, I mean, he took the sword. It was not handed to him by authority. The Truth saith: "All that take the sword shall perish with the sword" (*Mt.* xxvi, 52). By his rashness, he risked the death and damnation of his soul. The servant's wish, then, was not to kill his master, but to avoid death. Because he *consented,* however, as he should not have done, to murder, this wrongful consent preceding the crime was sin.

Someone may interpose: "But you cannot conclude that he wished to kill his master because, in order to escape death, he was willing to kill his master. I might say to a man: I am willing for you to have my cape, so that you may give me five shillings. Or, I am glad for you to have it at this price. But I do not hand it over because I desire you to have possession of it." No, and if a man in prison desired under duress, to put his son there in his place, so that he might secure his own ransom, should we therefore admit that he wished to send his son to prison?

It was only with many a tear and groan that he consented to such a course.

The fact is that this kind of will, existing with much internal regret, is not, if I may so say, *will,* but a passive submission of mind. It is so because the man wills one thing, on account of another. He puts up with *this* because he really desires *that.* A patient is said to submit to cautery or lancet, so that he may obtain health. Martyrs endured so that they might come to Christ; and Christ, too, so that we may be saved by his passion.

4. THE GOOD ACTION SPRINGS FROM THE GOOD INTENTION

We call the intention good which is right in itself, but the action is good, not because it contains within it some good, but because it issues from a good intention. The same act may be done by the same man at different times. According to the diversity of his intention, however, this act may be at one time good, at another bad. So goodness and badness vary. Compare the proposition: "Socrates sits." One conceives this statement either truly or falsely according as Socrates actually does sit, or stands. This alteration in truth and falsity, Aristotle affirms, comes about not from any change in the circumstances which compose the true or false situation, but because the subject-matter of the statement (that is, Socrates) moves in itself, I mean changes from sitting to standing or vice versa.

5. WHAT ARE THE GROUNDS OF GOOD INTENTION?

Good or right intention is held by some to be when anyone believes that he acts well, and that what he does pleases God. An example is supplied by those who persecuted the martyrs. About them the Gospel 'th says: "The hour cometh, that whosoever killeth you, will think doth a service to God." (*John* xvi, 2). In sympathy with the igno- such the Apostle exclaims: "I bear them witness, that they have 'od, but not according to knowledge" (*Rom.* x, 2). That is to say, they are fervently eager to do what they believe pleases God. Since, however, in this desire or keenness of mind they are deceived, their intention is a mistake. The eye of the heart is not so simple as to be capable of seeing clearly and to guard itself from error. For this reason the Lord, when he distinguished works according to right and wrong intention, spoke of the eye of the mind, that is the intention, as either *single*, pure, as it were, from spot, so that it could see clearly, or, on the contrary, as *clouded*. "If thy eye be single, thy whole body shall be lightsome." (*Mt.* vi, 22). This means that, provided the intention was right, all the acts proceeding from the intention which can possibly be forseen in the manner of mortal affairs, will be worthy of the light; that is to say, good. And, contrarily, from wrong intention arise dark deeds.

The intention, therefore, must not be called good, merely because it seems good, but over and above this, because it is such as it is estimated to be. I mean that, if it thinks to please God in what it aims at, its aim therein should not be mistaken. Otherwise the heathen, just like us, could count their good works, since they no less than we believe themselves either to be saved or to please God by their deeds.

25

ST. BERNARD ON THE LAND OF UNLIKENESS [1]

ST. BERNARD never ceases to insist on the inevitable distress to which we condemn ourselves when we walk in the ways of cupidity. Whoever gives himself up to that enters upon what St. Bernard, in another of these Scriptural metaphors which for him have an almost technical significance, calls "the circle of the impious." For they revolve in a vicious circle. Continually urged on by desire, they naturally go in search of all that may serve to slake it, but always they pursue it by running endlessly round and round the same circle, instead of breaking out of it once and for all, and entering the straight way that would bring them nearer to their end. No longer now to one of these false ends where we consume and are consumed, but to the end where we are consummated: *fini dico non consumptioni sed consummationi.* What we have to do, instead of running about the world and trying first one thing and then another, is rather to seek to attain to the Lord of the world. A man perhaps might begin to think of that when he had satisfied his desire for the whole earth, and come to be possessed at last of all things—of all things, that is, save the Source of all. Then, by the very law of his own

1 [From Etienne Gilson, *The Mystical Theology of Saint Bernard* (New York: Sheed and Ward, 1940), pp. 44-54. Reprinted by permission. Most notes and some paragraphs from the main text are omitted.]

cupidity, whereby he always wearies of what he has and hungers for what
he has not, he might perhaps at last despise all earthly goods and cling to
the one thing that would now be lacking: God. But the world is great,
and life is short. Why follow a road so hard and circuitous? The sole
remedy for the evil is to allow reason to take charge of sense, instead of
trailing miserably after it. For what in fact does reason teach? That the
very impotence of our desire to achieve satisfaction must needs have a
positive significance.

This strange restlessness that moves a man to abandon the good he
possesses in order eternally to go in search of another he lacks—this, besides being a fact, is it not also a question? Undoubtedly; and here is the
answer—we are attracted by the Good. The restlessness, the instability of
desire, are nothing but the excess of a love too great for the thing that
it loves, because mistaken in its object. How can it halt at any finite
good, this love that can be satisfied by nothing short of an infinite good?
Created by God and for God, our human love may refuse with good
reason to break off its unfinished quest until at last it shall have found
the sole Object that can finally set it at rest. Here, then, we hold the
key to the mystery; all that remains is to see why it arises. Whence this
madness? Why this stubborn will of the impious man to turn for ever
in the "circuit" where his strength is spent, desiring without knowing,
and nevertheless rejecting, the thing that would bring him to his end?
Cupidity is but a love of God become unaware of itself. But why, then,
is man in this state?

The reason is, to adopt a comparison more than once employed by
St. Bernard, that man is an exile. He no longer inhabits the land of his
birth. We might say, in terms but slightly different, that he lives in a
climate that is not his. As God made him, he was a noble creature—
nobilis creatura—and he was so because God created him to his own
image. Disfigured by original sin, man has in fact exiled himself from
the Land of Likeness to enter into the Land of Unlikeness: *Regio dissimilitudinis*. There we have the first inversion of order, from which all
the evil has arisen. Conversion reversed, conversion forever "execrable,"
by which man exchanged the glory of the Divine image for the shame of
the earthly image, peace with God and with himself for war against God
and against himself, liberty under the law of charity for slavery under
the law of his own self-will. We might go still further and say that man,
by that conversion, has exchanged heaven for hell; a word in which all
the foregoing is summed up, for hell is at once self-will, and its consequence, unlikeness to God, and war set up between creature and Creator. Now this evil that Adam brought into the world is hereditary, and
the proper object of the Christian life is to wage war on its effects. We
are born corrupt: "Engendered in sin, we engender sinners; born debtors, we give birth to debtors; corrupted, to the corrupt; in slavery, to
slaves. . . . We are crippled souls from the moment when we enter into
this world, and as long as we live there, and we shall still be so when

we leave it; from the sole of our foot to the crown of our head there is no health in us." [2] If cupidity draws us on endlessly and inevitably from finite goods to finite, this is because man's nature is no longer in the state in which it ought to be; each man born henceforth is born deformed.

At once the question rises in the mind—is the evil irremediable? No reply is possible, except by way of a closer analysis of the nature of the Divine likeness, also of the ravages left there by sin. As soon as we follow St. Bernard into this field, we come at once face to face with a doctrine in which the combined influences of St. Augustine and St. Anselm are easily recognizable, while its profoundly original character is none the less evident. He borrows; but all that he borrows is ordered in such a way as to prepare the solution of his own particular problem, namely: to give a coherent doctrinal interpretation and a complete theological justification of the Cistercian life, so that the doctrine, born of and nurtured on this life, may nurture and give it life in its turn.

In full accord with St. Augustine, St. Bernard places the image of God in the mind of man: *mens*. But while Augustine seeks it for preference in intellectual cognition, where the Divine illumination attests the continuous presence of the Creator to the creature, St. Bernard puts it rather in the will, and very especially in freedom. However, here again we have to distinguish. Scripture says that God made man "to his image and likeness" (*Gen.*, I, 26). Each of these words has a weight of its own and they have to be separately defined.

God created man that he might associate him with his own beatitude; all our history begins with this free decision. Now to be happy we have to enjoy; in order to enjoy we require a will; this will enjoys only by laying hold of its object by an act of consent; and to consent is to be free. That is why, creating man in order to associate him with his own beatitude, God created him with the gift of free will (*liberum arbitrium*), and it is chiefly on account of his freedom that man is this "noble" creature, made to the image of God, and capable of entering into society with God.

This gift of liberty made by the Creator to his creature is, furthermore, complex, for it implies three liberties, one of them being immutable, inalienable, and the other two not. Consider free will in itself. It may be resolved into two elements, namely voluntary consent and a power of moral decision. The liberty of free will is to be identified in the first place with the power of consenting or refusing consent, a power inseparable from the will as such. A voluntary agent is able to accept such and such a thing or to refuse it, to say yes or no, and this in virtue

2 *De Diversis*, Sermo XLII, 2; Migne, P.L. 183, 662. The expression "regio dissimilitudinis" is taken from St. Augustine, *Confessions*, VII, 10, 16. The "regio dissimilitudinis" of the *Confessions* is essentially the Platonic region of becoming, hovering between the nonbeing of mere nought and the immutable being of God. That of St. Bernard is essentially the region of sin and the deformity of the lost likeness.

of the sole fact that he is gifted with a will. It is this natural liberty, inherent in the very essence of volition, that is called "freedom from necessity"—*libertas a necessitate*. The expression therefore signifies above all that the idea of the voluntary is radically incompatible with that of constraint, and that is why it is also sometimes called "freedom from constraint"—*libertas a coactione*. For whatever the external circumstances may be which contribute to bring a decision to maturity, when nevertheless the decision is taken it is very certainly the will that consents, and it is strictly contradictory to suppose that anyone can "consent in spite of himself."

So utterly inalienable is this privilege of freedom from every voluntary agent that it can in no wise be less in us than it is in God himself: "Freedom from necessity belongs to all reasonable creatures, whether good or bad, equally and indifferently with God. Nor is this freedom lost or diminished either by sin or by misery, nor is it greater in the righteous than in the unrighteous, or more complete in the angels than in men. For just as the consent of the human will, when grace turns it towards the good, becomes thereby freely good, and makes the man free in doing good, that is to say leads him to will it and does not force him to it in spite of himself—so also the consent of the will, when spontaneously turned aside to evil, no less makes a man as free and spontaneous in evil doing, since he is brought to it by his will and not made evil by any coercion. And as the angels in heaven, and indeed God himself, remain good freely, that is to say of their own will and by no extrinsic necessity, so in just the same way the devil fell headlong into evil and there remains freely, that is to say in virtue of a voluntary movement and not of any external compulsion. Freedom of will subsists therefore even where thought is enslaved, and as fully in the wicked as in the good, although in the latter in a better ordered state; it remains also as complete after its own mode, in the creature as in the Creator, though in him it is more powerful." [3]

We see then well enough how radically St. Bernard is opposed to any doctrine of a slave-will. If, in his affirmation of freedom, he goes so far as to maintain its existence even in the damned, that is because it is indestructible by any wickedness whatsoever. And if it be objected that this henceforth inefficacious free will is now only a word void of meaning, we are confronted with this further fundamental thesis which makes of the free will of man, even after sin, even in damnation, an analogue of the free will of the blessed in heaven, of the angels, and of God himself. It is a point on which we cannot sufficiently insist: this freedom from necessity, whatever may now be its miserable condition among us, amounts to no less in the human act than it does in the act of the angel. Taken in itself, independently of the conditions that qualify it, the will of the just who adhere to good, of the sinner who consents to evil, or of

[3] *De Gratia et Libero Arbitrio*, IV, 9; Migne, P.L. 182, 1006-1007. It is of interest to compare this text with those of Descartes on liberty.

the damned who confirms himself in it for ever, lays hold of its object no less efficaciously than does the will by which God eternally wills his own perfection and his own beatitude.

That is why this freedom from necessity, which is altogether one with the faculty of consent, and consequently with the will, far from being, or being able to become, a negligible factor in our constitution, is on the contrary a rightful title of honour, of which no reasonable creature, in whatsoever state he may be, can ever be deprived. The creature may so act as to degrade it, but can never lose it without thereby also ceasing to exist. And that also is why this freedom, inalienable, indestructible, is that whereby we are chiefly made in the image of God. This image also therefore is inalienable, indestructible, like the freedom from contraint and the will itself: "Hence it is, perhaps, that free will alone suffers no defect or diminution of itself, because it is in this free will above all else that there seems to be impressed a kind of substantial image of the eternal and unchangeable God-head. For it had indeed a beginning, but it will know no destruction; neither will it be in any way increased by righteousness or glory, nor suffer diminution from sin or from misery. What, save Eternity itself, could bear a greater likeness to eternity?" [4]

Up to this point all is clear. We have only to add this inevitable complication, that if all we have just been describing in free will is inalienable, there is nothing else in us that is. Now there are other things in us. Suppress freedom from necessity and you suppress the will, you suppress therefore the man himself. But although we cannot imagine a man incapable of willing, we can very well imagine one incapable of willing the good. Let us suppose him in fact incapable of willing the good, that does not prove that he now lacks free will, but something else that remains to be defined. Suppose even that he is capable of willing, and of willing the good, but incapable of doing the good that he wills—in that case too he still retains his free will, but now a third thing is wanting. What then is the missing element?

To settle that point let us resume and complete our analysis of free will (*liberum arbitrium*). It is in the first place, as we have said, a freedom coessential with the will itself, a freedom to consent or not consent; and this is what is expressed in the word *liberum*. But next, it is a power to bring a judgment to bear upon our consent, that is, on our will itself, and to declare it good if it be good, evil if evil; and this is what is expressed in the word *arbitrium*. In a sense we might say that it is the will that judges itself, nor would this be at all incorrect, since the will is a will only in virtue of its close association with the reason; otherwise it would be no longer a will, but an appetite. It remains true, none the less, that strictly speaking it is the *liberum* that consents and the *arbitrium* that decides. Now to decide (*arbitrer*) is to judge, and just as every man, as man, is always capable of willing, so is he always capable

4 *Ibid.*, IX, 28; Migne, P.L. 182, 1016.

of bringing a judgment to bear upon his voluntary decisions. St. Bernard, who here undoubtedly has St. Paul's *ut sint inexcusabiles* in mind, shows himself extremely firm on this point: that what we should nowadays call the voice of conscience is never extinguished in man. Always capable of distinguishing good from evil, we are always capable of judging our own decisions, and we have therefore always with us our free *arbitrium*.

Only, to consent and to judge the consent is not yet all. We can will evil and know it to be evil, and choose nevertheless to do it. To the "judgment" there is therefore added a "choice," and this act of choosing (*eligere*) is itself the upshot of a deliberation (*consilium*). Now, as a result of original sin, we are not of necessity always capable of choosing the good or of avoiding evil, even when reason has judged them as such. We must therefore say that, if the *liberum arbitrium* is never lacking, we can nevertheless, and without ceasing to be men, lack the *liberum consilium*. And supposing further that knowing what is good we choose to do it, we can still want strength to carry it out. If this strength fails us we shall indeed retain the *liberum arbitrium* and the *liberum consilium*, but, along with the *posse* it is the *liberum complacitum* which will have disappeared.

There then we have man, a complex structure, and one in which all the component elements are far from being equally indestructible. The central point in St. Bernard's doctrine is that the Image of God in us can never be lost, and that is why man remains man, after transgression as before: *ipse liber sui propter voluntatem, ipse judex sui propter rationem.* But the likeness to God in us can be lost, and that is why, when he lost the virtues bestowed on him by God in order that his deliberations, his choices, and his actions might follow the judgment of reason, man lost also his divine likeness. Always gifted with free will, he has no longer either the liberty of choosing which would set him free from sin, or that of acting in accordance with his choice which would set him free from the misery of an impotent will. In short, the *libertas a necessitate* remains to us, but we have lost the *libertas a peccato* and the *libertas a miseria*. By abusing the first, man has lost the other two; he has preserved the image, and the two likenesses have disappeared. Why? Because, unlike the former, the two latter kinds of freedom are susceptible of degrees.

One word may serve to designate the likenesses: man's "rectitude"— erection, uprightness. The soul is "great" inasmuch as it is capable of participation in the Divine life, but it is "upright" inasmuch as it desires to participate in this life. The soul's uprightness, like its greatness, is distinct from the soul, but uprightness and greatness are furthermore distinct from each other, and the proof of this is that although the soul's greatness is inseparably bound up with the soul, its uprightness is not so. Incapable of ceasing to be great and to be God's image, under pain of ceasing to exist, it can nevertheless cease to be upright and to be his likeness, without being destroyed. To cease to be that, it has only to lose its virtues, that is to say to lose its love for eternal things and to begin to prefer earthly, temporal, perishable things. Now what is eternal is God's portion, remaining essentially his, even when offered to us: what is temporal, earthly, is man's share, remaining man's even when God invites him to a higher heritage. Rejecting the divine for the sake of the earthly, man accordingly demands his own portion in preference to God's, and, in so doing, loses his upright stature, stoops, bends down, turns away from heaven to which God had erected him, to bow himself down to earth to which his animal nature attracts him.

VII. Arabian and Jewish Philosophies

The outburst of speculative activity in the thirteenth century was due not only to the recovery of Aristotle's writings but also to the translation of numerous commentaries and independent treatises of the Arabian and Jewish philosophers. This influx produced a theological and philosophical crisis, the acuteness of which can be sampled from some of the issues treated in the present Section: the freedom of the creative act, personal immortality, a universal matter, and the attribution of perfections to God. On these and other questions, the thirteenth-century Schoolmen were faced with a grave challenge and the need to evaluate the new sources. It is not altogether accidental, therefore, that our readings concerning Avicenna and Avicebron should be taken from comparative studies on St. Thomas Aquinas, or that the problems discussed by Averroes and Maimonides should also be central to the Thomistic intellectual reconstruction.

There is no surer way of access to the heart of Avicenna's emanationist theory of finite things than through the teaching on the possibles, as explained by Father Gerard Smith in Selection (26). The Avicennian God is properly named necesse-esse, *the unconditionally necessary being. By comparison with this being, all other things are only possibles, since they require a cause and do not exist by the power of their own essence. Existence is a perfection supervening upon the finite essence as its concomitant, and in this sense existence is accidental in every finite thing. Avicenna is not merely teaching a real distinction between essence and existence. For he adds that the possibles have some shadowy but real being of their own, apart from divine knowledge and volition, and that the divine creative act wells over necessarily to endow the possibles with existential act. Hence there is an existential necessity about finite beings in respect to their first cause, even though intrinsically considered their structure does not include existence. Smith notes how the Thomistic critique consists basically in removing any autonomous status from the possibles and substituting the free creative act for a necessary emanation from God. Averroes' opposition to Avicenna is based on more rigorously necessitarian grounds and will be considered in its restatement by Siger of Brabant.*

Selection (27) cautions us that there may be discrepancies between the Arabic text of Averroes and the Latin translation upon which most comment is based, and also that even the translation is usually interpreted in the light of special preoccupations of the Christian mind. As a case in point, Beatrice Zedler criticizes the traditional ascription of monopsychism and nonpersonal immortality to Averroes. These doctrines were developed by some of his Latin followers, and were the object of both philosophical criticism and official censure. Holding that philosophical truth is divinely embodied in Aristotle, Averroes himself tries to remain as faithful as possible to the doctrine of the De Anima, although his interpretation of it is not unaffected by the intervening centuries of Greek and Arabian speculation. His own theory is a one-intellect view, rather than a one-soul view. But from the Christian perspective of the soul and its powers, the theory of a separated and impersonally one intellect implies that there is no basis in man for personal immortality. In Averroes' remarks on the human cogitative power and its contact with the separated intellect, Zedler finds some ground in him for the personal survival of the human soul, along with the negative testimony that he does not outrightly deny the possibility of personal immortality. It should be added, however, that the subsequent Renaissance work of Pomponazzi on this issue denies that a functional contact with the separated intellect is sufficient to ascribe subsistent being to the human soul. Unless the immaterial intellectual operations belong to a power of the human soul itself, the subsistent being and hence the immortality of the latter cannot be philosophically established.

Avicebron was an eleventh-century Spanish Jew, whom the Latins thought to be a Moslem or even a Christian, because of many congenial notions found in him. The basis for John Riedl's analysis, Selection (28), is Avicebron's chief work, the Source of Life. His general standpoint is that of theistic creationism. God is the sole creator, is totally transcendent of the universe, and produces it through his will and not through an emanation of his nature. Yet in safeguarding the divine transcendence and the creative act, Avicebron courts the danger of cutting off our mind and will from any communion with God. As a guarantee of some pathway to God, he proposes the doctrine of a universal composition of matter-and-forms which holds continuously for all creatures, and thus enables the attentive mind to ascend to God. A dual systematic purpose is served by this doctrine: it provides an unequivocal way of distinguishing the entire universe from God, and it provides a foundation for human knowledge and love of God. These advantages appealed strongly to the Franciscan school, as did Avicebron's notion of a plurality of forms in man, whose soul is thereby kept from being compromised in its union with matter. St. Thomas, on the other hand, rejected the theory of universal matter as being a univocal view of the potential subject, and kept the essence of angels free from even a tenuous, spiritual matter.

Selection (29) is drawn from The Guide for the Perplexed, *composed toward the end of the twelfth century by the greatest medieval Jewish thinker, Moses Maimonides. His intention was to aid those faithful Jewish students who were finding it difficult to reconcile the philosophical conceptions of God or the first cause with the expressions used about God in the Old Testament, the Talmud, and the Midrash. He was dissatisfied with the too facile method of the Moslem theology of the Kalam, which treated as demonstrative any philosophical argument strengthening its position, which deprived finite agents of causal power, and which multiplied attributes in God without reconciling them with his simplicity. Maimonides made a twofold proposal: to accept the philosophy of Aristotle, insofar as it does furnish demonstrative proofs, and to analyze carefully the terms and figures employed in Scripture concerning God. Yet he found it difficult to admit the presence of any positive or essential attributes in God, given Avicenna's meaning for existence as a supervening accident or attribute of the essence. To say that God has attributes in this sense, is to import composition, potency, and the need for causal influx into his being. Rather than admit this, Maimonides held that the positive attributes have only a community of name as applied to God and creature. He did permit the negative and operational attributes, but only on condition that they merely designate what God is opposed to and how his actions are expressed in effects, without telling us anything about the divine being in itself. Reflecting on his formula that God exists without having the attribute of existence, Maimonides found confirmation for the absolute identity of essence and existence in God in the famous passage in* Exodus *which also attracted Augustine and Aquinas. The Thomistic doctrine on analogical predication of perfections to God seeks to avoid the Maimonidean alternatives of nominal likeness and extrinsic likeness, without destroying the transcendence of the divine existential act.*

26

AVICENNA AND THE POSSIBLES [1]

ONE may get at St. Thomas' notion of created being by contrasting his with the notion which "essentialist" philosophers propose. As a sophisticated essentialist, Avicenna will do excellently. It is in his doctrine on the possibles that Avicenna seems best to reveal his notion of created being. A possible being, according to Avicenna, is one of the two classes of being.

Necessary being is being which, if it be posited not to be, involves a contradiction. Possible being, on the other hand, is that which, whether it be posited to be or not to be, is not on that score a source of contradiction. Necessary being is that whose being is necessary. But possible being is that which comports no necessity on any score, that is, neither in its being nor in its nonbeing, and this is what we understand here by possible being. . . .

There is more in this than meets the eye. The divisions of being, familar to Christian philosophers, are 1) being *a se,* God, and 2) being *ab alio,* creatures. These last are divided again into a) possible being, which can, but does not, exist, and b) actual being, which does and can exist. Whence, the question arises, Why does Avicenna lump together a) possible and b) actual being *ab alio?* Or, conversely, Why do Christians divide being *ab alio* into a) possible and b) actual being? The reason, as we shall see, is because for Avicenna possible being sooner or later will be; whence, the member, actual being, is superfluous. Whereas for Christians, not only might actual being *ab alio* (b) possibly not exist at all; possible being itself (a) would not even be possible unless it were *ab alio.*

To return to Avicenna and his point that the dividing members of being are the necessary and the possible.

Next, necessary being can be necessary of itself (*per se*), and it can be necessary, but not of itself. Now, what is necessary of itself is that which, if posited not to be, is contradictory; not, of course, because of something other than itself, whatsoever that other being may be, but [contradictory] by reason of its own very essence. But being which is necessary but not of itself, is that which, when some other being, not the one in question (*quod non sit ipsum*), is posited, the one in question becomes necessary. . . . One and the same thing cannot be at

¹ [From Gerard Smith, S.J., "Avicenna and the Possibles," *The New Scholasticism,* vol. 17 (1943), pp. 340-349, 357. Reprinted by permission. Most notes are omitted. All quotations from Avicenna in the main text are taken either from his *Metaphysices Compendium* or from his *Philosophia Prima.*]

the same time necessary of itself and necessary through another. For, once that other is removed, or once its being is not considered, it cannot but be that the necessity of this thing's being either remain in its disposition—and then the necessity of its being will not be through another; or that the necessity of its being do not remain, but vanish—and then the necessity of its being will not at all be through itself. Now, whatsoever is necessary through another is precisely the possible in itself.

Clearly, Avicenna means by his possible being: one which must exist, not, so to say, under its own steam, but rather through the causality of another; a sort of adamantine atom to which existence will inevitably accrue. In short, Avicenna's possible being is *both* possible, that is, it is of itself able to be, and necessary, through God.

Those two points need emphasis. First, possible being is possible in itself.

Whatsoever is necessary through another, the very necessity of its being is of course consequent upon a sort of connection (*habitudo*) or relation. However, the consideration of the connection or relation is different from the consideration of the very essence of the thing itself which has that connection or relation. Whence, since the necessity of being [of that which exists through another] is not fixed unless that connection be considered, it then becomes necessary that the consideration of only the essence of the thing demands either the necessity or the possibility or the impossibility of its being. Now, it cannot be admitted that the essence, considered in itself, demands the impossibility of its being: for, nothing whose being is in itself impossible will ever be, not even through another. Nor can it be admitted that it demands the necessity of its being: for we have already said that it is contradictory for a thing whose being is necessary of itself to be necessary through another. It remains therefore that that thing, considered according to its essence, is possible; but considered according to the actuation of its relation to that other, it is necessary; and considered as having that connection with the other removed, it is impossible. But when one considers the essence of the thing itself, quite apart from any condition, the thing itself is possible of itself.

Not only is possible being, when considered quite apart from any extrinsic condition, possible in itself, it is also such that in relation to its cause it must exist.

It has, therefore, been now clearly shown that every being which is necessary through another not itself is possible in itself. The proposition is thus converted: everything possible in itself is, when its being is educed into act, forthwith necessary through another. For, it cannot but be that actual existence either be or not be its true predicate. But it is contradictory that actual existence be not its true predicate, else it would be impossible. It remains, therefore, that actual existence is its true predicate. But then, either its being is necessary or not necessary. If its being is not necessary—the while, nevertheless, that whose being is not necessary is still possible, then there would be no difference discernible between its being and nonbeing, and there would be no distinction given between the disposition which it now has [when existent] and its former disposition. The reason is, before its actual existence it was already possible, and it now remains in that, its disposition, just as it was before. If, therefore, a new disposition be posited to accrue to it, then the question will come up about this new disposition, whether, namely, it also be possible or necessary. If it be posited as possible—since this same disposition was already in its possibility beforehand, it follows that no new disposition has accrued to it. But if that newly accruing disposition be posited as necessary and as itself necessitating prior existence, then there should necessarily have been present in that prior existence a sort of disposition which cannot be anything else except its passage to act. It follows, therefore, that its passage to act is necessary.

In sum, a possible being, considered apart from the cause which makes it to exist, either can be or cannot be. Now, one may not say that a possible being so considered cannot be, else it would be impossible. And if one says, as one must, that a possible being can be, then the predicate *exists* must either be true or not true of it. But one cannot say that the predicate *exists* is not true of it, else it would be impossible. In what sense, then, is actual existence true of possible being? Certainly, *exists* is not true of possible being by reason of a necessity which is the possible being's own. That would erase the distinction between possible and necessary being. Whence, the predicate *exists* is true of possible being as being necessary *per aliud*.

So far it is clear that the Avicennian possible must exist, even though it be only possible in itself—*necesse-esse per aliud est quidem possible in se*. Would St. Thomas agree? He would agree thus far: "everything which had its being from another is not of itself necessary, as Avicenna proves, and so possibility involves dependence upon that from which it has being."[2] But St. Thomas means thereby that a possible depends upon the necessary for its existence if it is to exist; whereas Avicenna means that since a possible depends upon the necessary, therefore it must exist, though possible withal. As is clear, both men make possible being depend upon necessary being for existence. The only area left in which they might disagree lies, therefore, in their answers to this question, What is the relation of the possible before it exists to the cause of its existence?

For Avicenna that relation is not exactly that of something unknown or unwilled by God, the cause of a possible's existence. Obviously God knows and wills the possible: "the fact that he [God] understands his essence is the cause of his understanding that which comes after his essence." That God wills the possible is also patent: a possible is *necesse-esse per aliud* (necessary through God). Avicenna's point, however, is this: a possible being, that is, a non-existent, able to exist, must be possible apart from any relation of dependence upon God's will and knowledge in order that it may be possible, because if it were not so possible, it would be impossible. Now, a cause cannot effect the impossible. Whence, possibles are such, not because God knows and wills them to be such, though he does that, but because such they are in themselves.

2 St. Thomas Aquinas, *In II Sent.*, D. 8, q. 3, a. 2.

In what sense are possibles such as they are in themselves, apart from God's causality? Possibles are of two sorts, possible immaterial and possible material substances. First, the material possibles: they are such as they are in themselves apart from God's causality in the same sense that a material subject of substantial change is presupposed to the action of a cause of that change: that is, possible material beings begin to be from a material subject.

Now, the possibility of being [of a generable substance] is not in this, namely, that an agent can effect it or that there be an agent having power over it. In fact, an agent has no power at all over it if this thing itself had not been possible in itself. . . . For if the possibility in itself of the being of anything whatsoever were the same as the power of effecting it, then this would be tantamount to saying that to be able to be something is nothing else but to have power over that over which power is given; and [it is tantamount to saying that] there is no power given over the impossible because power over it is not given. And then we should not know at all, by considering the thing itself, whether or no it were "possibled," that is, whether anything had power over the thing itself; but [we should know] by considering the disposition of the active power of the agent, whether or not, namely, it had power over the thing. But if we should have some doubt left as to whether power were given or not given over that thing, this we shall in no wise be able to know. . . . . It is therefore quite clear that a thing's possibility in itself means something different from there being a power over the thing, though both are of themselves the same. That a thing be possible in itself is [known] by considering its essence; but that there be a power over it, that is [known] through the consideration of its relation to the one who gives to it being. Accordingly, now that these things have been solidly established, we say: whatsoever begins anew to be, before its inception it was either in itself possible for it to be, or impossible for it to be. Now, what is repugnant to being will never be. And what is possible that it be, surely the possibility of its being preceded it. . . . Now, possibility (capacity) for being, that we call the power of being, and that which sustains the power of being, in which this power of being lies, we call a subject, *hylen*, and matter. There has therefore already preceded everything which begins to be, matter.

As to the relation of possible immaterial substances to the cause of their being, that should cause no difficulty. Quite simply, they do not begin to be. Of course if one wishes to expand the meaning of "beginning to be" so as to signify by it a posteriority, not of time, but of essence, then all things whose possibility of being is logically, not really, anterior to their being may be said to begin to be, even though there never was a time in which they were not. Hence, the possibility of immaterial beings is a logical, not a real, possibility: their essence is logically without act, even though it never was without act.

The point Avicenna is making needs insistence. Stiff and spiky with reality, the possible is set over against God. He eyes it with the same constraint with which we should eye it. We, if we wish to make something, must have something to go on, something to start with. Even should we wish no more than to be up and doing, our doing must follow a groove whose possibility it did not create. Our doing follows those skids of action whose possibility follows the laws of being. We cannot make a silk purse out of a sow's ear. That is impossible, precisely because the possible is a datum given to, but not by, us. We are bound by laws of possibility which do not depend upon us. Just so with Avicenna's God. Possibles are his data, given to, not by, him. He eyes these data, and what he sees does not depend for its being, such as it is, upon his seeing. Nor is God's willing of the possible to exist anything more than just that, viz., a willing of the possible to exist; it is not a willing of the possible to be able to exist. Thus, God's willing the possible into existence is a consent to a pre-established state of affairs by which his consent is bound. One may say that God's consent is an acquiescence to the possible's existence; it is neither a willing of the possible to be possible (*that* the possible is in itself), nor is it a free willing of the possible to exist. God wills the possible to exist necessarily though cheerfully.

We may summarize Avicenna's doctrine in the transcription of it which Algazel made. Let us refer to the state of a possible being which is not but can be, as its nonbeing. Now, this nonbeing of a possible does not have any relation whatsoever to the one who can make a possible thing to be.

Let us, therefore, consider that since a thing made depends upon its maker, it must either depend upon him for its being, which now is, or for its nonbeing which preceded . . .; now, it is false that it depends for its nonbeing, because the nonbeing which preceded had no relation or connection whatsoever with its maker, since the maker acted on it in no wise whatsoever. . . . Since, after it is made, it is clear that a thing made does not depend upon its maker for its nonbeing, and yet it must depend upon its maker; obviously, the only dependence left is for its being. Its dependence, therefore, upon its maker is for its being, not for its nonbeing.[3]

In other words, the non-existent possible depends upon God only for its existence, which is inevitable, but it does not depend upon God for its possibility. A possible is possible in itself alone, and necessary in its cause.

In what exactly lies St. Thomas' disagreement with Avicenna? Avicenna maintains 1) that the possibles in themselves are possible, independently of God's power, and 2) that they are necessarily willed into existence by God. St. Thomas denies, in the first point, the exclusion of God's power, and maintains that the possibles are willed into existence by God freely.

Let us make St. Thomas' position clearer by the following picture. Let there be God and creatures. Rub out creatures. There are left in Avicenna's Platonic world, between God and the now non-existent creatures,

[3] *Algazel's Metaphysics,* edited by J. T. Muckle, C.S.B. (Toronto: St. Michael's College, 1933), p. 49, 1. 5 ff.

the Avicennian possibles dangling in a metaphysical void. Once you delete creatures, in St. Thomas' world, there is nothing left except God.

From the very fact that to-be is attributed to quiddity [this is possible being], not only the to-be but even the quiddity itself is said to be created, because, before it had to-be, it was nothing, unless perchance in the intellect of the Creator where there is no creature, but only creative essence.[4]

It is thus that St. Thomas answers the objection, since quiddity is outside of or beyond the to-be, therefore quiddity is not created. The answer, quite simply, is that quiddity *is* created. A possible, before creation, so far forth as it has any existential status at all, is God himself. Now, God is not created, but possibles are created.

To conclude, both Avicenna and St. Thomas agree that creatures depend upon God for their existence. Avicenna maintains that creatures do not depend upon God for their possibility. St. Thomas maintains that they do: they depend for their possibility upon God's knowing and willing them to be possible. The necessarily possible, God knows and wills to be necessarily possible; the contingently possible, God knows and wills to be contingently possible. To Avicenna's creatures God gives their to-be, not their to-be-able-to-be. God gives to St. Thomas's creatures both their to-be and their to-be-able-to-be: their to-be, God gives freely; their to-be-able-to-be God gives necessarily. If one fails to see how Avicenna's God can give existence to that to which he has not given the capacity for existence, one has quite seen the point: Avicenna's God cannot create. St. Thomas's God creates: he makes that to exist which can exist because he can make it to exist.

4 St. Thomas Aquinas, *De Potentia*, q. 3, a. 5, ad 2.

27

AVERROES AND IMMORTALITY [1]

IN THE story of medieval Christian thought, Averroes usually appears in the role of the adversary. Though honored as the Commentator of Aristotle, he was also feared as an impious blasphemer, an enemy of the truths of religion. Did he not assert, among other dangerous doctrines, that there is one agent and possible intellect for all men? And did he not thereby deny the personal immortality of each human soul? It is no wonder that some have called him "the accursèd Averroes."

1 [From Beatrice Zedler, "Averroes and Immortality," *The New Scholasticism*, vol. 28 (1954), pp. 436-453. Reprinted by permission. The notes are omitted. All quotations from Averroes in the main text are either from his commentary on Aristotle's *De Anima* or from his *Destructio Destructionum Philosophiae Algazelis*.]

That Averroes *did* deny the immortality of each human soul, is the common teaching of historians of medieval Christian thought, for it is the common teaching of the medieval Christians themselves. Yet there might be a reason for asking whether that common teaching clearly reflects the doctrine of Averroes himself. Can we see in the text of Averroes an explicit and definite denial of personal immorality? Or do some texts suggest a view that is more complex than we usually think?

For the real Averroes—the Moor, Ibn Rochd—to be more complex than his Christian opponents suspected, would not be surprising since he was known through Latin translations of varying degrees of fidelity. But our question relates primarily to the Moor-in-Latin-translation, to Averroes as knowable to medieval Christians. Does the *Latin* text of Averroes contain a denial of personal immortality? Or does it reveal a view that is less simple and direct than that? There are some texts that seem to suggest another view than the one usually attributed to Averroes. But before turning to them, we might note one reason why a denial of personal immortality has so often been associated with the name of Averroes.

1. MONOPSYCHISM?

No historian of medieval thought has cited any text in which Averroes says: "I deny that there is personal immorality for man." But historians *have* cited texts in which Averroes asserts that there is one intellect for all men and that this intellect, a separated substance, is incorruptible, spiritual, and eternal. Now if all men share in one intellect, it would seem that all men share in one soul. If then there be *any* immortality for man, it would perhaps be secured by immersion in the impersonal and eternal separated substance that is common to the whole human race. A medieval soldier put the point well when he said: "If the soul of blessed Peter is saved, I shall be too. Having the same intellect, we shall have the same destiny." Even if explicit denials of personal immortality be lacking, therefore, it might seem that the clear assertion of the unity of the possible intellect for all men is equivalent to such a denial. A philosophy of monopsychism automatically rules out any personal survival.

The logic of this interpretation is sound, but one of the facts is open to question. For a Christian, what is said of the intellect can also be said of the human soul of which it is a characteristic power. The spirituality of the soul, for example, is proved by establishing the spirituality of the intellect. A divorce between the intellect and the soul would be so destructive to man's unity as to be almost unthinkable. Man's intellect *is* a power of his soul. Confronted, therefore, with a doctrine of the unity of the intellect, a Christian is very likely to think of it as a doctrine of the unity of the soul, i.e., as a monopsychism.

Now there is no doubt that Averroes asserts the unity of the intellect, but is it equally certain that he professes the unity of the soul? Can we properly describe this cardinal tenet of his philosophy as monopsychist? Averroes himself is quite clear on this question. Far from asserting that unity of intellect necessarily involves unity of soul, he criticizes those philosophers who make that identification. Because of the unity of knowledge, he finds it reasonable to hold that intellect is not divided nor divisible among individuals. But the same cannot be said of soul. Too many "inconveniences" follow, if we assert that soul is one in number and identical with intellect. It would mean, for example, that Socrates' life is numerically the same as Plato's life. It would mean, too, that when Socrates knows something, Plato also would know it; and when Plato is ignorant of it, Socrates also would be ignorant of it. Besides, it would mean that there would be no difference between the apprehension of intellect and the apprehension of sense.

Intellect and soul are not identical nor is intellect a power of man's soul. The "judging powers of the soul" are individual and mixed and capable of judging only particular or finite intentions; the possible (or material) intellect is "not mixed" and can judge infinite things. The soul is individuated, but intellect is not. The soul is the first act of a physical organic body, but the nature of intellect is superior to the nature of the soul. Intellect is neither soul nor a part of the soul. This view is not, therefore, a monopsychism. There is one intellect for all men, but each man has his own individual soul.

But if intellect and soul are distinct for Averroes, the doctrine of the intellect's unity does not in itself exclude the chance of a personal survival for men. There is not only one question of immortality here; there are two. First, is the impersonal separated intellect immortal? Second, is each individual human soul immortal? To answer the first is not automatically to have answered the second. The first is easily answered. The impersonal separated intellect *is* immortal; it is not only immortal, but even eternal. Though men may come and men may go, the spiritual intellect always endures in its constant impersonal existence. But it is Averroes' handling of the second question on immortality with which we are especially concerned, i.e., is each individual human soul immortal? His comments on the nature and the powers of the soul give the setting for his answer.

2. NATURE AND POWERS OF THE SOUL

Soul is not itself body, nor an accident of body, Averroes thinks. The soul is a substance, and substance is more noble than accidents; the more noble does not exist by the less noble.

In what sense, then, is soul a substance? Following Aristotle, Averroes holds that soul is a substance by which the body lives. It is substance in the sense of a form that gives life to potentially alive elements. It is the entelechy or perfection of an organized body having life in potency, and it exists in the body as its subject. It is the first act of a physical organic body.

Soul as first act gives life to the body, but it is also the source of further acts that a living being has. Among the powers possessed by the human soul, Averroes includes motive, sensitive, imaginative, memorative, and cogitative powers. By the motive power, man is impelled towards what should be pursued and from what should be avoided; from this arise the emotions or affections of the soul. By the sensitive power, the sense objects of the five senses are apprehended. In the imaginative power, though, we encounter a special perfection of sensitive life. Imagination conserves impressions of things sensed, even after the act of sensation has ceased; it combines one with another and separates one from another, as in dreams. Memory, too, can present the image of an absent thing.

Imagination and memory work together with an important power that is found only in man: the cogitative power. This should not be confused with the estimative power of animals: the power, that is, by which an animal knows what is helpful or harmful for the needs of its animal nature. The cogitative power has the following functions: it can make an absent object appear as though present; it can compare and distinguish the re-presented objects with each other; it can judge whether a given re-presented object bears a relation to a directly presented sense intention. Although this work of comparison and judgment is individual and not universal, it is a work that must be done to clear the way for the action of the separated intellect. So important is the cogitative power in this preparatory work, that it, too, together with its aide—the imagination, is sometimes honored with the name of intellect: *possible* intellect, to designate its material and hence generable and corruptible nature. For possible intellect is a particular material power. Once the cogitative power has done its work of preparation, the agent intellect (or intellect in its active aspect) actuates the potentially intelligible content of possible intellect, the phantasms, so that the actuated intelligible forms may be received by the material intellect (intellect in its receptive aspect). When the material intellect has been actuated by the agent intellect through use of the disposition in us, that material intellect-in-act is then called the *intellectus adeptus*. Though from the *Commentary on III de Anima* it appears that man's function is to furnish the phantasms for the knowledge of a separated intellect, Averroes would have us believe that man shares a little in the intellectual knowledge he thus helps to secure for the impersonal intellect.

If man has no intellect of his own, it might seem that there is nothing to distinguish him from the animal. Yet Averroes finds an important point of distinction in man's possession of the cogitative power or possible intellect and in the consequent conclusion that man, alone among animals, has the distinction of being able to serve the separated intellect and by that service to be momentarily united with it in knowledge.

3. THE HUMAN SOUL AND IMMORTALITY

Nothing so far in Averroes' account of the individual soul and its powers would seem to insure its personal immortality. The soul is the form of the body; it possesses as its most remarkable faculty the cogitative power, but this has a generable and corruptible nature. Is it therefore possible for the human soul to exist after death? Strangely enough, Averroes suggests that the answer is: *yes*.

In the *Destructio Destructionum* Averroes approaches this question by saying: "As form is not taken away in the destruction of a part or parts of a subject, so it is not taken away in the destruction of the whole." That is: in the partial or total destruction of a subject, the form is not destroyed, but only the subject that it informs. He then continues: "The taking away of the action of form on account of a subject is like the taking away of the action of a worker on account of the instrument." What Averroes seems to suggest is that to deprive a worker of a tool is to deprive him of the operation accomplished through the tool, but it is not to deprive him of the power of accomplishing it, nor of his own existence. So to deprive form of its subject (body) is to deprive form of the action accomplished through the subject, but it is not to deprive form of its power nor of its existence.

To elaborate on his meaning, Averroes here cites Aristotle's example that poor eyesight on the part of an old man is not due to any weakening of the *power* of sight, but to the weakness of the instrument. The same principle holds when the apprehensions of the senses are destroyed by the destruction of an instrument or of most of its parts in sleep, in a stroke, in drunkenness, or in illness. "For there is no doubt," Averroes says, "but that the powers are not destroyed during those times." That is, the parts of an instrument or the instrument itself can be injured or destroyed without destroying the powers. This is seen even in those animals which can be cut in two parts and still live!

Though recognizing that the discussion concerning the human soul is on a deeper level, Averooes suggests that the same principle holds, namely, that the destruction of the instrument does not necessarily involve the destruction of the power or the form. He argues, in particular, from the likeness between sleep and death:

The likeness of death to sleep is evident proof of the permanence of the soul. Since the operation of the soul is destroyed in sleep from the destruction of its instruments, and it itself is not destroyed, therefore its disposition in death must be like its disposition in sleep. For the judgment of the parts is the same, and the proof is common to all, suitable to the vulgar for believing truth, and it arouses wise men to the way in which they may know the immortality of the soul.

That is to say: sleep prevents the soul from engaging in its usual activity because it cannot use its customary instruments; yet the soul itself is not thereby destroyed. So also in death: though the soul will be unable to operate through its usual instruments (since they will be destroyed), it does not follow that soul itself will cease to exist. The analogy in itself is not a formal demonstration, but it is a "persuasive proof" for the common man, and it can suggest to "wise men" the distinction of the soul from its "instruments."

Averroes has led up to this analogical reasoning by proposing a principle: that a form is not necessarily destroyed with the destruction of its instruments. He has seemed to hint that form may have an existence that is independent of that which it informs. Is this equivalent to saying that form, or the human soul in particular, is a substance in the sense of a *per se* existent? He does not go so far as to make such an assertion. The most he has said is that soul is not body, not an accident of a body, but substance in the sense of a form which makes a potentially alive body to be a living body.

If the human soul is by nature a subsistent form, then its acts should reveal an independence of matter; but do they? Averroes distinguishes two main levels of cognitive activity: (a) the knowledge of the separated intellect which is essentially eternal; (b) the sense knowledge of animals which is subject to corruption, and here we must note that Averroes grants no individual immortality to them, but only the immortality of the species. But within the genus of sense powers there is a unique faculty which seems almost to give rise to a third level of cognitive activity. Between the extremes of corruption and eternity is cogitation, which distinguishes man from animals. Unlike the knowledge of the separated intellect it has an essential dependence on imagination and memory. Unlike ordinary sense knowledge, it involves an apprehension which surpasses the functions of the estimative power, as was noted above. It is the cogitative power which enables man to achieve union with the separated intellect. It cannot be expected to have the independence of matter, the spirituality and eternity of intellect itself, since it is a sense faculty; but bcause of its unique function as the power linking man to a separated spiritual substance, its soul perhaps may subsist. Though it is not by nature a subsistent form, its corruption may not be inevitable. The cogitative power is different from intellect, but it also is different from the sense powers of animals. But to what exent does it differ from them? In kind or only in degree? On the basis of Averroes' own comments, it is difficult to see how cogitation is specifically or essentially different from other sense knowledge, since it too proceeds from a sense power. What gives it its dignity and entitles it to be called the "possible intellect" is not its lowly origin but the service that it renders to intellect. In terms of its purpose, it is more akin to intellect than to sense. The soul that it characterizes may therefore not necessarily have to die with the death of the body.

This can scarcely be called a demonstration of the soul's immortality. Averroes is aware that he has given no such demonstration. In the context of his psychology he cannot grant to the human soul a purely spiritual activity. He can give no good philosophical reason why the soul *must* exist after death, but only an indication of why it *may* exist after death. He can provide no guarantee of its natural immortality, but only a "persuasive proof" which suggests that the soul *could* be maintained in existence. The stress on the stability of form and the corruptibility of matter and on the superiority of soul to body point to the intrinsic possibility of the soul's immortality, though they do not establish it by means of a demonstration. That was as far as Averroes could go.

But the lack of a true demonstration does not keep him from apparently assenting to the doctrine. In another text, he accepts the resurrection of the body: a doctrine that would have no meaning apart from the acceptance of an after-life for the individual soul. Averroes does not, it is true, agree with the view that many of his fellow Moslems have of the doctrine. But he never takes issue with the doctrine itself; he rejects only the interpretation that some have given to it. He holds, for example, that the doctrine cannot mean that the same particles of flesh are restored, since he says they corrupt. The body that will be resurrected, then, will be not numerically but specifically the same as the body we now have. But that there *is* a resurrection he clearly asserts.

Many problems remain in Averroes' treatment of the soul's immortality. He himself recognized the inadequacy and incompleteness of his remarks on the soul, but he pleads the difficulty of the subject matter. "Sermo . . . de anima est nimis profundus," he says. Yet however inadequate his discussion may be, what he teaches is this: Each man will live after death.

4. AVERROES' MEANING?

A question might well occur to the student of medieval thought at this point. Even if Averroes did teach as possibility or as fact a doctrine of personal immortality, nevertheless—how do we know that he meant what he said? Must not his comments on immortality be seen in the larger context of his stand on the question of faith and reason? Some say Averroes was a fideist or anti-rationalist and then he might well have accepted individual immortality even though it disagreed with his view of the teaching of Aristotle. The more prevalent view is that he was rather a rationalist. In this case, one could rule out whatever he says of individual immortality and the resurrection of the body as being wholly insincere and intentionally deceptive, for the sake of avoiding persecution in the fanatical Moslem community in which he lived. Still others hold that Averroes was a rationalist with respect to the approach that a philosopher should have, but an anti-rationalist with respect to the approach that the "vulgar" should have. In this case, the philosopher would accept by reason a doctrine of impersonal immortality, whereas the common man, who is unable to grasp a philosophic demonstration, would accept on faith a doctrine of personal immortality. The philosopher would have attained to the fullness of truth; the believer—to an allegorical or symbolic representation of the full truth, which would serve as well in the practical conduct of his life as the truth of the philosopher.

Of these interpretations the first two seem inapplicable to the texts on the soul. The Commentary on the *De Anima* and the praise for Aristotle do not sound like the work of a fideist, but of a commentator and philosopher who is struggling with difficult problems. Nor does Averroes sound like a rationalist who is deliberately trying, in the *Destructio Destructionum,* to deceive his readers by his comments on immortality and the resurrection. We cannot, of course, read a man's heart. We cannot know whether in fact he is speaking in all sincerity. But if he meant to deceive, it seems unlikely that he would have warned his readers that his arguments in that work were not demonstrations.

His position might be the third: he might be a rationalist in philosophy and a fideist in religion. He might be saying: the philosopher knows that the only immortality is the impersonal immortality of the separated intellect, but a belief in personal immortality is the best way in which the common people can reach an approximation of the full truth. But this would not explain Averroes' own apparent acceptance of the resurrection of the body, nor would it explain why he makes a special point of stressing the perfect agreement of philosophy and religion on the question of immortality. He does not say this of all beliefs but only of a chosen few.

Perhaps a fourth alternative represents his position. Averroes does seem to hold that philosophy leads man to the truth by means of demonstrative arguments; and religion sometimes does give a symbolic or allegorical representation of the truth. But on the question of immortality perhaps the positions of both philosophy and religion are true. There may be a "double immortality": that of the intellect and that of the individual soul. Philosophical demonstration has established that the separated intellect is immortal; that is certainly true. Philosophy leaves open the question of the immortality of the individual soul. In the context of Averroes' thought, this is not a demonstrable doctrine; but it *may* be true.

After seven centuries of comments on the Commentator there is still no universal agreement on exactly what his position was on the question of faith and reason; but on the question of immortality, at least this negative conclusion emerges: he does not explicitly deny that the individual soul can exist after death.

Why, then, did Christians fail to see this? A part of the answer has already been given. First, their identification of intellect with soul—the result of looking at Averroes' view through their own convictions—would have kept them from seeing it. The Averroistic doctrine of one intellect for all men meant to them a doctrine of one *soul* for all men, and therefore ruled out even the possibility of personal immortality. Then, too, they did not see the *Destructio Destructionum* in Latin until the fourteenth century; but by that era the "accursèd Averroes" legend was well established. And we might add that even if they had seen the passages on immortality and the resurrection, their opinion of Averroes might not have been changed, except perhaps for the worse. Having attributed to him a monopsychist view, they would have had to think him deliberately insincere in these passages—in brief, a liar as well as an enemy of religion.

Medieval Christians have attributed to Averroes a position that he *should* perhaps have had. They have done him the honor of assuming that his thought was fully coherent, consistent, and well-integrated. Logically, they thought, he should have denied the doctrine of personal immortality. Such a denial might well have been more consistent with his total position than an acceptance of the possibility of the doctrine. But Averroes may not have been the logical, well-integrated thinker he was believed to have been. Whether he was mainly impelled by a fear of persecution, by a desire to leave philosophy open to faith, or by a glimpse of the truth that his own philosophy could not fully account for, we cannot say with certainty. What we can say is that the real scandal for Christians in Averroes' view of immortality was not so much what he actually said, but rather what they *thought* he had said.

But shall we continue to say, without qualification, that Averroes denied that the individual soul can exist after death? To do so would seem to ignore the very real complexity in Averroes' position. On the question of personal immortality Averroes may have been inadequate and unclear, but there seems little point in perpetuating the legend of the "accursèd Averroes."

28

AVICEBRON ON UNIVERSAL MATTER AND FORM [1]

AVICEBRON believed, contrary to the opinions of both Plato and Aristotle, that all separate substances under God, are composed of matter and form. He was mistaken in two respects, says St. Thomas. (1) In the first place, he thought that there must be a real composition in things themselves to correspond to the composition in the order of intelligibility which is found in things according to their kinds, as for example a species is composed of genus and difference. Thus in

---

[1] [From John Riedl, "The Nature of the Angels," in *Essays in Thomism*, edited by R. E. Brennan, O.P. (New York: Sheed and Ward, 1942), pp. 123-124. Reprinted by permission. The notes are omitted. The exposition is based on Avicebron's *Fons Vitae*.]

the case of a thing belonging to a genus, the genus would be its matter, and the difference its form. (2) In the second place, he believed that the expressions: "to be in potency," "to be a substrate" or "to be a recipient" are used always with the same signification. With these two principles as starting points he investigated the composition of things, even of intellectual substance.

First he noted that in artificial objects the natural substance of which they are made, e.g., wood or iron, is the matter which is related to the artificial form as potency to act. Then he noted that natural substance is composed of the four elements, which are the matter of the natural forms. Then he noted that the elements are all bodies and that body is the matter of the contrary qualities of the elements (dry and moist, hot and cold). But the body of the heavens is not receptive of contrary qualities. Now body, whether of the heavens or not, always signifies substance having length and breadth and thickness, and these three dimensions are as the form to the substance which is the material substrate. But besides substance which has quantity there is also substance which does not have it, and this kind is called separate substance.

If we reverse the process to see how the universe of Avicebron is built up, we find that at its core is a neutral stuff called substance. Substance can be given the form of quantity or the form of opposition to quantity. If it is given the form of opposition to quantity, it is immediately in the class of separate substances. If it is given the form of quantity it is immediately in the class of the visible world of dimension. Granted that it is quantitative, it can be given either any one of the four forms of the contrary qualities or the form of opposition to the contrary qualities. If it is given the form of opposition to the contrary qualities, it is immediately in the class of the heavenly bodies. If it is given any one of the four forms of the contrary qualities, it becomes that element. Granted that it is an element, it can be given the form of any one of many natural bodies, e.g., iron or wood. Granted that it is wood, it can be given any one of several artificial forms, e.g., mallet, Indian, etc. If it actually becomes a wooden Indian, its nature as such would be essentially the primary substance with a series of forms attached to it as accidents in a substrate.

On the basis of a universe such as this, Avicebron gave the following five arguments in support of his opinion that separate substances are constituted of matter and form.

(1) Unless they are so constituted, there can be no diversity among them, for they would then have to be either matter alone or form alone. If they are matter alone, then there would be no diversity, because matter of itself is one and the same, and is diversified through forms. If they are form alone, then there would be no diversity except according as they were the subject of perfection or imperfection. But to be a subject is proper to the notion of matter, but not to the notion of form.

(2) The notion of spirituality is distinct from that of corporeity. Thus

corporeal substance and spiritual substance have something in which they differ, and something in which they agree, since both are substances. Thus substance functions as the matter, supporting on the one hand corporeity and on the other spirituality. And these spiritual substances are higher and lower in proportion as their matter participates more or less in the form of spirituality.

(3) Being is found alike in both corporeal and spiritual substances. Therefore that which is consequent upon being in corporeal substances will also be consequent upon being in spiritual substances. But in corporeal substances there is a kind of body which has density, that is, the body of the elements, and a kind of body which is the body of the heavens, and besides, body is constituted of matter and form. Now, we find also in spiritual substance a lower kind which is united to a body, and a higher kind which is not united to a body. Therefore, on grounds of the analogy, there must also be matter and form of which spiritual substance is composed.

(4) Every created substance must be distinguished from the creator. But the creator is pure unity. Therefore no created substance can be pure unity but must be composed of two parts, and one of these must be form and the other matter because nothing can be made either out of two matters or out of two forms.

(5) Every spiritual created substance is finite. But a thing is not finite except through its form, because a thing which does not have a form through which it is made an individual is infinite. Therefore every created spiritual substance is composed of matter and form.

29

THE ATTRIBUTES OF GOD ACCORDING TO MAIMONIDES [1]

1. GOD'S ESSENTIAL ATTRIBUTES

THOSE who believe in the presence of essential attributes in God, viz., Existence, Life, Power, Wisdom, and Will, should know that these attributes, when applied to God, have not the same meaning as when applied to us, and that the difference does not only consist in magnitude, or in the degree of perfection, stability, and durability. It cannot be said, as they practically believe,[2] that his existence is only

1 [From Moses Maimonides, *The Guide for the Perplexed*, translated by M. Friedländer (second edition; London: Routledge and Kegan Paul Ltd., 1928), pp. 79-83, 94-95, with omissions. Reprinted by permission.]

2 [The "they" in question are referred to in a general way by Maimonides as "The Attributists." This group would include the Moslem theologians (the Mutakallemim)

more stable, his life more permanent, his power greater, his wisdom more perfect, and his will more general than ours, and that the same definition applies to both. This is in no way admissible, for the expression "more than" is used in comparing two things as regards a certain attribute predicated of both of them in exactly the same sense, and consequently implies similarity [between God and his creatures]. When they ascribe to God essential attributes, these so-called essential attributes should not have any similarity to the attributes of other things, and should according to their own opinion not be included in one and the same definition, just as there is no similarity between the essence of God and that of other beings. They do not follow this principle, for they hold that one definition may include them, and that, nevertheless, there is no similarity between them.

Those who are familiar with the meaning of similarity will certainly understand that the *term* existence, when applied to God and to other beings, is perfectly homonymous. In like manner, the terms Wisdom, Power, Will, and Life are applied to God and to other beings by way of perfect homonymity, admitting of no comparison whatever. Nor must you think that these attributes are employed as hybrid terms; for hybrid terms are such as are applied to two things which have a similarity to each other in respect to a certain property which is in both of them an accident, not an essential, constituent element. The attributes of God, however, are not considered as accidental by any intelligent person, while all attributes applied to man are accidents, according to the Mutakallemim. I am therefore at a loss to see how they can find any similarity [between the attributes of God and those of man]; how their definitions can be identical, and their significations the same! This is a decisive proof that there is, in no way or sense, anything common to the attributes predicated of God, and those used in reference to ourselves; they have only the same names, and nothing else is common to them. Such being the case, it is not proper to believe, on account of the use of the same attributes, that there is in God something additional to his essence, in the same way as attributes are joined to our essence. This is most important for those who understand it. Keep it in memory, and study it thoroughly, in order to be well prepared for that which I am going to explain to you.

2. ESSENCE, EXISTENCE, AND UNITY OF GOD

It is known that existence is an accident appertaining to all things, and therefore an element superadded to their essence. This must evidently be the case as regards everything the existence of which is due to some cause; its existence is an element superadded to its essence. But as

---

and philosophers, as well as the Jewish thinkers, who uphold the presence of essential attributes in God.]

regards a being whose existence is not due to any cause—God alone is that being, for his existence, as we have said, is absolute—existence and essence are perfectly identical; he is not a substance to which existence is joined as an accident, as an additional element. His existence is always absolute, and there has never been a new element or an accident in him. Consequently God exists without possessing the attribute of existence. Similarly he lives, without possessing the attribute of life; knows, without possessing the attribute of knowledge; is omnipotent without possessing the attribute of omnipotence; is wise, without possessing the attribute of wisdom; all this reduces itself to one and the same entity; there is no plurality in him. It is further necessary to consider that unity and plurality are accidents supervening to an object, according as it consists of many elements or of one. This is fully explained in the book [by Aristotle] called *Metaphysics*. In the same way as number is not the substance of the things numbered, so is unity not the substance of the thing which has the attribute of unity, for unity and plurality are accidents belonging to the category of discrete quantity, and supervening to such objects as are capable of receiving them.

To that being, however, which has truly simple, absolute existence, and in which composition is inconceivable, the accident of unity is as inadmissible as the accident of plurality; that is to say, God's unity is not an element superadded, but he is one without possessing the attribute of unity. The investigation of this subject, which is almost too subtle for our understanding, must not be based on current expressions employed in describing it, for these are the great source of error. It would be extremely difficult for us to find, in any language whatsoever, words adequate to this subject, and we can only employ inadequate language. In our endeavour to show that God does not include a plurality, we can only say "he is one," although "one" and "many" are both terms which serve to distinguish quantity. We therefore make the subject clearer, and show to the understanding the way of truth by saying he is one but does not possess the attribute of unity. We use "one" in reference to God, to express that there is nothing similar to him, but we do not mean to say that an attribute of unity is added to his essence.

3. THE NEGATIVE MEANING OF DIVINE ATTRIBUTES

Know that the negative attributes of God are the true attributes: they do not include any incorrect notions or any deficiency whatever in reference to God, while positive attributes imply polytheism, and are inadequate, as we have already shown. It is now necessary to explain how negative expressions can in a certain sense be employed as attributes, and how they are distinguished from positive attributes. Then I shall show that we cannot describe the Creator by any means except by negative attributes.

An attribute does not exclusively belong to the object to which it is related; while qualifying one thing, it can also be employed to qualify other things, and is in that case not peculiar to that one thing. E.g., if you see an object from a distance, and on enquiring what it is, are told that it is a living being, you have certainly learned an attribute of the object seen, and although that attribute does not exclusively belong to the object perceived, it expresses that the object is not a plant or a mineral. Again, if a man is in a certain house, and you know that something is in the house, but not exactly what, you ask what is in that house, and you are told, not a plant nor a mineral. You have thereby obtained some special knowledge of the thing; you have learned that it is a living being, although you do not yet know what kind of living being it is. The negative attributes have this in common with the positive, that they necessarily circumscribe the object to some extent, although such circumscription consists only in the exclusion of what otherwise would not be excluded. In the following point however, the negative attributes are distinguished from the positive. The positive attributes, although not peculiar to one thing, describe a portion of what we desire to know, either some part of its essence or some of its accidents; the negative attributes, on the other hand, do not, as regards the essence of the thing which we desire to know, in any way tell us what it is, except it be indirectly, as has been shown in the instance given by us.

After this introduction, I would observe that God's existence is absolute, that it includes no composition, and that we comprehend only the fact that he exists, not his essence. Consequently it is a false assumption to hold that he has any positive attribute; for he does not possess existence in addition to his essence. It therefore cannot be said that the one may be described as an attribute [of the other]. Much less has he [in addition to his existence] a compound essence, consisting of two constituent elements to which the attribute could refer; still less has he accidents, which could be described by an attribute. Hence it is clear that he has no positive attribute whatever.

The negative attributes, however, are those which are necessary to direct the mind to the truths which we must believe concerning God. For, on the one hand, they do not imply any plurality, and, on the other, they convey to man the highest possible knowledge of God. Thus it has been established by proof that some being must exist besides those things which can be perceived by the senses, or apprehended by the mind; when we say of this being, that it exists, we mean that its non-existence is impossible. We then perceive that such a being is not, for instance, like the four elements, which are inanimate, and we therefore say that it is living, expressing thereby that it is not dead. We call such a being incorporeal, because we notice that it is unlike the heavens, which are living, but material. Seeing that it is also different from the intellect, which, though incorporeal and living, owes its existence to some cause, we say it is the first, expressing thereby that its existence is not due to any cause.

We further notice, that the existence, that is the essence, of this being is not limited to its own existence. Many existences emanate from it, and its influence is not like that of the fire in producing heat, or that of the sun in sending forth light, but consists in constantly giving them stability and order by well-established rule. We say, on that account, it has power, wisdom, and will, i.e., it is not feeble or ignorant, or hasty, and does not abandon its creatures. When we say that it is not feeble, we mean that its existence is capable of producing the existence of many other things; by saying that it is not ignorant, we mean "it perceives" or "it lives,"—for everything that perceives is living; by saying "it is not hasty, and does not abandon its creatures," we mean that all these creatures preserve a certain order and arrangement. They are not left to themselves; they are not produced aimlessly, but whatever condition they receive from that being is given with design and intention. We thus learn that there is no other being like unto God, and we say that he is one, i.e., there are not more Gods than one.

It has thus been shown that every attribute predicated of God either denotes the quality of an action, or—when the attribute is intended to convey some idea of the Divine Being itself, and not of his actions—the negation of the opposite.

4. GOD THE EXISTING BEING

When God appeared to our Teacher Moses, and commanded him to address the people and to bring them the message, Moses replied that he might first be asked to prove the existence of God in the Universe, and that only after doing so, he would be able to announce to them that God sent him. For all men, with few exceptions, were ignorant of the existence of God; their highest thoughts did not extend beyond the heavenly sphere, its forms or its influences. They could not yet emancipate themselves from sensation, and had not yet attained to any intellectual perfection. Then God taught Moses how to teach them, and how to establish amongst them the belief in the existence of himself, namely, by saying *Ehyeh asher Ehyeh* [*Exodus,* 3, 14: "I am that I am."], a name derived from the verb *hayah* in the sense of "existing," for the verb *hayah* denotes "to be," and in Hebrew no difference is made between the verbs "to be" and "to exist."

The principal point in this phrase is that the same word which denotes "existence," is repeated as an attribute. The word *asher,* "that," corresponds to the Arabic *illadi* and *illati,* and is an incomplete noun that must be completed by another noun; it may be considered as the subject of the predicate which follows. The first noun which is to be described is *ehyeh;* the second, by which the first is described, is likewise *ehyeh,* the identical word, as if to show that the object which is to be described and the attribute by which it is described are in this case necessarily identical. This is, therefore, the expression of the idea that

God exists, but not in the ordinary sense of the term; or, in other words, He is "the existing Being which is the existing Being," that is to say, the being whose existence is absolute. The proof which he [Moses] was to give consisted in demonstrating that there is a Being of absolute existence, that has never been and never will be without existence. Absolute existence includes the idea of eternity, i.e., the necessity of existence.

VIII. Thirteenth-Century Masters: Grosseteste to Aquinas

There was a rich profusion and variety of philosophical viewpoints in the writings of the thirteenth-century theologians, many of whom were teachers at the new universities and members of the newly founded religious orders. The following two Sections furnish a sampling of the work done in the philosophy of science, philosophy of man, metaphysics, and the general synthesis of Christian wisdom. There was independent thinking in all these areas and a constant interchange of critical estimates. The individual thinkers represented here were influential, but their teachings were also subjected to severe examination by other minds.

The history of medieval science and scientific theory is still in a nascent condition, but it is fairly clear that there was constant development both at the technical level and in the order of method and theory. In the latter order, a major role must be assigned to the Oxford School and especially to Robert Grosseteste, professor and chancellor at Oxford and Bishop of Lincoln. In Selection (30), A.C. Crombie summarizes the various facets of his scientific contribution. Along with a considerable amount of translating and commenting, Grosseteste made an original combination of the neo-Platonic metaphysics of light, popular within the Augustinian tradition, with an advanced mathematical theory of optics. He looked upon light as a universal form of energy and continuity in things. Hence the geometrical basis of optics can also serve as a general principle of explanation for all natural things. There is here, in germ, the idea of a universal mathematico-physical method for dealing with all problems in our visible world, at least from the standpoint of a precise description of events and functions. Grosseteste's more particular investigations into fire, tides, and the rainbow continued to mix geometrical and experimental explanations with a good deal of qualitative description and deduction from the general principles of light. But there was also a definite awareness that scientific knowledge, constructed by way of mathematical theories and experimental testing for probability, is distinct in kind from either purely mathematical proof or the demonstrations in Aristotelian natural philosophy.

Roger Bacon had a turbulent career as a Franciscan friar, developer of the scientific doctrines of Grosseteste and Adam of March, and ardent reformer of the advanced curriculum. He dreamed of strengthening theology with all the resources of linguistic studies, mathematics, experimental science, the technological control of nature, metaphysics, and canon law. At the invitation of Pope Clement IV whom he had known in Paris, Bacon drew up a sketch of his program for the revision and improvement of Christian training in the religious houses and universities. His most extensive plan was set forth in the Opus Majus *or* Longer Work, *from which Selection (31) is taken. Both Grosseteste and Bacon acknowledged their general debt to the* Posterior Analytics *of Aristotle for a conception of scientific method, but they also stressed the distinctive mathematical and experimental procedures being used in the sciences. Among the scientific authorities cited to strengthen his case for a concentrated training in that field, Bacon included not only Boethius, the Greeks, and the Arabs, but also his own contemporaries, because of an explicit recognition of the progressive as well as the traditional factor in the sciences. His plea contained some far fetched and fantastic arguments, but also expressed the common Oxford view about the certitude and universal applicability of mathematics, the method of resolution and composition, and the need for experimental testing of all proposed theories about physical phenomena. The roots of Galileo reach back to the medieval schools at Oxford, Paris, and Padua, even though there had to be a new development of basic mathematics and experimental techniques before the modern physical methods could fully emerge.*

The central mission for the Dominican, St. Albert the Great, was to assimilate the philosophical and scientific learning of the Greeks and Arabs, and then to attempt to incorporate it within a more adequate Christian synthesis. This work led him to make vast summaries of the leading views, which he presented along with his own positions. His method of treating philosophical issues can be seen from Anton Pegis' report, Selection (32), on his treatment of the problem of the soul. It was characteristic of Albert's twofold respect for revelation and for human learning that he should report both on what the saints or Church Fathers say about the essence of the soul and on what the chief philosophers say. It was also wholly natural that he should allow his own stand-

point to come forth only gradually and in function of a careful analysis of the work of his predecessors. Pegis notes his dependence upon Avicenna for a way of harmonizing the Platonic definition of the soul as an incorporeal substance (expressive of the soul's essence) and the Aristotelian definition of it as the primary act and mover of the body (expressive of the soul's functional relation to something else).

Throughout his account of the soul in general, St. Albert bore in mind the special character of the human soul as an immaterial substance. Like Roger Bacon, he was more readily satisfied on this score with the mediating solution proposed by Avicenna than was St. Thomas. The latter was developing a distinctive theory of act and potency, which led him to regard the human soul as the substantial form and first act of matter, to which it is essentially united. But to Albert, this theory would endanger the human soul's substantiality and immateriality, so that he regarded its union with the body as a relational function lying beyond the essential constitution of the soul. The Albertine soul is substance above all else, even though as a consequence its union with the body is something less than essential, and its intrinsic way of being is only functionally different from that of an angel. A somewhat unexpected application of this doctrine to the problem of God will be found in the Meister Eckhart Selection (43).

In the case of the medieval thinkers as well as those of every other age, we must inquire about their relevance for our own generation. It is this question that prevents the history of philosophy from becoming merely an antiquarian occupation or an act of pious recall. It is primarily a means of gaining access to the living thought of minds of another day, in order to share their insight and bring it to bear, in varying degrees of relevance and inclusiveness, upon the problems which we face. One fruitful way of posing this question in respect to St. Thomas Aquinas is outlined by Jacques Maritain in Selection (33). He suggests that the postmodern intellectual and social order will be both humanistic and oriented toward God, or rather, will be humanistic precisely in its ordination to God and to those human values which come most clearly into view when man's relation to God is borne steadily in mind. That this does not involve any mechanical reading-off of human properties from an exemplar idea of man (as the contemporary existentialist, Jean-Paul Sartre, claims in his charge of anti-humanism against every theistic philosophy) is evident from the order of exposition followed by Maritain. In the speculative philosophical sphere, the Thomistic inquiry begins in the only region where experiential conditions permit us to begin: the sensibly existent world and our human operations of perceiving and judging about that world in its existential being. St. Thomas is confident that when human intelligence accepts this experiential starting point, it can attain to some certain knowledge about both the human person and the transcendent, personal existence of God.

What revelation and philosophical study tell us about the bond of existence and personal action uniting the individual man with God and with his fellow men, is not merely speculative in its import, but has an intensely practical significance. Maritain calls this practical aspect of Christian humanism a rehabilitation of human life in God, a renewal which encourages the development of better forms of temporal society. And against Dewey's instrumentalist interpretation of the Christian mind, he observes that the primacy of contemplation over technique is not necessarily bound up with a dualism of the elite against the masses. Christian humanism undercuts this dualism by emphasizing the personal love of God and of other men. Since this love is open to us all, it overcomes the tendency to carry specialization into the region of our final end, and since it is a personal act, it requires a community of persons and not an impersonal mass for its effective presence among us.

30

ROBERT GROSSETESTE ON THE LOGIC OF SCIENCE [1]

ROBERT GROSSETESTE belonged to a generation of Western philosophers for whom the Latin translations of Greek and Arabic scientific and philosophical writings had been in circulation long enough for them to become the starting point for original work. Grosseteste's basic contributions to the logic of scientific inquiry and to the conception of scientific explanation took their point of departure from Aristotle's *Posterior Analytics* and *Physics* and Euclid's *Elements*.[2]

[1] [From A. C. Crombie, "Robert Grosseteste on the Logic of the Sciences," in *Proceedings of the XIth International Congress of Philosophy* (14 vols.; Amsterdam: North-Holland Publishing Company, 1953), vol. 12, pp. 171-173. Reprinted by permission.]

[2] Full documentation of the statements made in this summary will be found in my *Robert Grosseteste and the Origins of Experimental Science* (Oxford: Clarendon Press, 1953). See also my essay in *Robert Grosseteste, Scholar and Bishop. Essays in Com-*

The common Greek conception, clearly expressed by Aristotle, was that the aim of a scientific inquiry was to find premises from which something already known as a fact could be deduced. This gave the investigator knowledge not only of "the fact" (*to hoti*), but also of "the reason for the fact" (*to dihoti*). These two kinds of knowledge were distinguished in medieval Latin by the terms, respectively, *demonstratio quia* and *demonstratio propter quid* (or *quare*). An observed phenomenon was held to be explained when it had been deduced from a set of premisses, forming a theory, which related the phenomenon to other similar phenomena. Accepting this conception of deductive explanation, Grosseteste's contributions were to the problems, first, of constructing and testing theories, and secondly, of the use of mathematical theories to explain the physical world.

Taking up a discussion in the first chapter of Aristotle's *Physics*, Grosseteste said, in his commentary on that work, that the phenomena perceived through the senses were composite. The first stage of an inquiry was to break up the composite phenomenon into the principles or elements by which it was formed. This process he called *resolutio*, a translation of *analysis*. Having isolated the separate principles involved, the next stage was, by recombining them, to reconstruct the phenomenon theoretically. This he called *compositio* (*synthesis*). The truth of the principles was tested by comparing the composite of theory, deduced from them, with the composite of observation. In his commentary on the *Posterior Analytics* Grosseteste gave examples of this resolutive compositive method of finding the conditions necessary and sufficient to produce a phenomenon, examining the power of scammony to cure fever and the connection between the possession of horns, upper teeth, and more than one stomach in certain mammals. Some of his followers, notably Roger Bacon, Witelo, Theodoric of Freiberg, and Themon Judaei used the same method to find an explanation of the rainbow.

An important point made by Grosseteste about explanatory theories in physics was that they were suggested by, rather than strictly inferred from, the ordering of the facts made by *resolutio*. They were invented, or grasped, by an act of what might be called in English "intellectual intuition" (*virtus intellectiva, nous*). Since they might be false, they had to be tested by examining their consequences experimentally. Theories "falsified" (to use Grosseteste's own term) by experiment were discarded, the form of argument used being the *modus tollens*. He gave several examples of this method of elimination in his treatises on special physical problems, notably *On the Generation of the Stars, On the Heat of the Sun,* and *On the Rainbow.* The argument was based on two metaphysical assumptions: first, the principle of the uniformity of nature; and secondly, the principle of the economy of nature, which provided an

memoration of the Seventh Centenary of His Death, ed. D. A. Callus (Oxford: Clarendon Press, 1955), pp. 98-120.

additional criterion for choosing between experimentally verified theories. Grosseteste also used the principle of economy pragmatically, saying, in his commentary on the *Posterior Analytics,* that the better of two "demonstrations" is that with "a smaller number of suppositions and premisses, . . . because it makes us know more quickly."

Of the means whereby "demonstrated knowledge" could be obtained of the physical world, Grosseteste gave unique importance to mathematics. He had two reasons for this, one methodological, the other metaphysical.

The method by which he used mathematics to provide explanations of phenomena was Aristotle's method of "subordination." For example, the physical sciences of optics and astronomy are logically subordinate to geometry, in the sense that the relations between the phenomena they describe can be deduced from the geometry of the straight line and the circle. Grosseteste maintained that mathematics could provide the formal cause of physical phenomena, but was explicitly an abstraction from the efficient and material causes.

The metaphysical reason for the unique importance of mathematics in explaining the physical world derived from Grosseteste's conception of the fundamental physical substance. In his short treatise, *On Light,* he described how in the beginning of time God created unformed matter and a point of light, which, propagating itself in a sphere, produced the dimensions of space, and subsequently, by a complicated process, generated the whole physical universe, including plants and animals. Because of this theory, Grosseteste held that optics was the fundamental physical science; mathematics was necessary for the study of optics and therefore for the whole of physics. His main optical treatises are *On Lines, Angles, and Figures* and *On the Nature of Places.*

Grosseteste's ideas on scientific method established a tradition of scientific thought and experiment which flourished in Oxford for about a century after his death and included such names as Roger Bacon, John Pecham, Duns Scotus, William of Ockham, and Thomas Bradwardine. On the Continent his ideas were take up by Albertus Magnus and passed on to Theodoric of Freiberg, Themon Judaei and other in the 14th century. They reappeared in 15th- and 16th-century Italy, and became part of the revival of science in 16th-century England. Galileo and Newton used the terms *resolutio* and *compositio* in describing the logic of experimental inquiry.[3]

3 For a history of the experimental method down to Newton see my *Robert Grosseteste;* see also my *Augustine to Galileo. The History of Science A.D. 400-1650* (London: Falcon Press, 1952). [There is now a revised two-volume paperback edition of the latter work: *Medieval and Early Modern Science* (2 vols.; New York: Doubleday Anchor Books, 1959). See also Marshall Clagett, *The Science of Mechanics in the Middle Ages* (Madison: University of Wisconsin Press, 1959), which concludes that "the medieval mechanics occupied an important middle position between the terms of Aristotelian and Newtonian mechanics" (p. 670). This holds specially for the work done at Oxford, Paris, and Padua between 1350 and 1600.]

Speaking in his commentary on the *Posterior Analytics* of the "demonstrations" provided by natural science, Grosseteste said they were "probable rather than strictly scientific. . . . Only in pure mathematics is there science and demonstration in the strictest sense." He distinguished natural science also from metaphysics, which was concerned with the real causes of phenomena. Natural science, he said in effect, was a structure of theories designed only to "save the phenomena." The full significance of this view of the nature of scientific theories, grasped only after much more experience of them had been obtained than was available for Grosseteste, was shown by another British empirical philosopher, George Berkeley. In his admirable treatise, *On Motion*, Berkeley based his critique of current theories of motion, and especially of Newton's conception of absolute motion, on the rule: "to distinguish mathematical hypotheses from the natures of things" (§ 66). The achievements of modern physics have depended to a large extent on freedom to make this distinction.

31

ROGER BACON'S PLEA FOR MATHEMATICS AND EXPERIMENTAL SCIENCE [1]

O F THE basic sciences the gate and key is mathematics, which the saints discovered at the beginning of the world, as I shall show, and which has always been used by all the saints and sages more than all other sciences. Neglect of this branch now for thirty or forty years has destroyed the whole system of study of the Latins. For he who is ignorant of this cannot know the other sciences nor the affairs of this world, as I shall prove. And what is worse, men ignorant of this do not perceive their own ignorance, and therefore do not seek a remedy. And on the contrary, the knowledge of this science prepares the mind and elevates it to a certain knowledge of all things, so that if one learns the roots of knowledge placed about it and rightly applies them to the knowledge of the other sciences and matters, he will then be able to know all that follows without error and doubt, easily and effectually. For without these, neither what precedes nor what follows can be known; whence they perfect what precedes and regulate it, even as the end perfects those things pertaining to it, and they arrange and open the

1 [From *The Opus Majus of Roger Bacon*, translated by R. B. Burke (2 vols.; Philadelphia: University of Pennsylvania Press, 1928), vol. 1, pp. 116-126; vol. 2, pp. 583-588, 615-616, 627. Reprinted by permission. There are omissions from the text, and the translation is slightly modified.]

way to what follows.[2] This I now intend to intimate through authority and reason.

1. PROOF FROM AUTHORITY THAT EVERY SCIENCE REQUIRES MATHEMATICS

As regards authority I so proceed. Boethius says in the second prologue to his *Arithmetic,* "If an inquirer lacks the four parts of mathematics, he has very little ability to discover truth." And again, "Without this theory no one can have a correct insight into truth." And he says also, "I warn the man who spurns these paths of knowledge that he cannot philosophize correctly." And again, "It is clear that whosoever passes these by, has lost the knowledge of all learning." He confirms this by the opinion of all men of weight saying, "Among all the men of influence in the past, who have flourished under the leadership of Pythagoras with a finer mental grasp, it is an evident fact that no one reaches the summit of perfection in philosophical studies, unless he examines the noble quality of such wisdom with the help of the so-called quadrivium."

And in particular Ptolemy and Boethius himself are illustrations of this fact. For since there are three essential parts of philosophy, as Aristotle says in the sixth book of the *Metaphysics,* mathematical, natural, and divine, the mathematical is of no small importance in grasping the knowledge of the other two parts, as Ptolemy teaches in the first chapter of the *Almagest,* which statement he also explains further in that place. And the divine part is twofold, as is clear from the first book of the *Metaphysics,* namely, the first philosophy, which shows that God exists, whose exalted properties it investigates, and civil science, which determines divine worship, and explains many matters concerning God as far as man can receive them. Ptolemy likewise asserts and declares that mathematics is potent in regard to both of these branches. Hence Boethius asserts at the end of his *Arithmetic* that the mathematical means are discovered in civil polity. For he says that an arithmetical mean is comparable to a state that is ruled by a few, for this reason, that in its lesser terms is the greater proportion; but he states that there is a harmonic mean in an aristocratic state, for the reason that in the greater terms the greater proportionality is found. The geometrical mean is comparable to a democratic state equalized in some manner; for whether in their lesser or greater terms, they are composed of an equal proportion of all. For there is among all a certain parity of mean preserving a law of equality in their relations. Aristotle and his expositors teach in the *Ethics,* in many places, that a state cannot be ruled without these means. Concerning these means an exposition will be given, with an application to divine truths. Since all the essential parts of philosophy, which are

2 [Mathematics perfects and regulates philosophy of nature and the natural sciences. In turn, mathematics prepares the mind for metaphysics and ethics.]

more than forty sciences distinct in their turn, may be reduced to these three, it suffices now that the value of mathematics has been established by the authorities mentioned.

A knowledge of logic depends on mathematics because of its middle and heart, which is the book of *Posterior Analytics,* for that book teaches the art of demonstration. But neither can the fundamental principles of demonstration, nor conclusions, nor the subject as a whole be learned or made clear except in the realm of mathematics, because there alone is there true and forceful demonstration, as all know and as we shall explain later. Therefore, of necessity, logic depends on mathematics.

What has been said is applicable likewise because of its beginning, and not only because of its middle and end. For the book of *Categories* is the first book of logic according to Aristotle. But it is clear that the category of quantity cannot be known without mathematics. For the knowledge of quantity belongs to mathematics alone. Connected with quantity are the categories of when and where. For when has to do with time, and where arises from place. The category of habit cannot be known without the category of place, as Averroes teaches in the fifth book of the *Metaphysics.* But the greater part of the category of quality contains the attributes and properties of quantities, because all things that are in the fourth class of quality are called qualities in quantities. And all the attributes of these which are absolutely essential to them are qualities, with which a large part of geometry and arithmetic is concerned, such as straight and curved and other essential qualities of the line, and triangularity and other figures belonging to surface or to a solid body; and the prime and non-factorable in numbers, as Aristotle teaches in the fifth book of the *Metaphysics,* as well as other essential attributes of numbers.

Moreover, whatever is worthy of consideration in the category of relation is the property of quantity, such as proportions and proportionalities, and geometrical, arithmetical, and harmonic means, and the kinds of greater and lesser inequality. Moreover, spiritual substances are known by philosophy only through the medium of the corporeal, and especially the heavenly bodies, as Aristotle teaches in the eleventh book of the *Metaphysics.* Nor are inferior things known except through superior ones, because the heavenly bodies are the causes of things that are lower. But the heavenly bodies are known only through quantity, as is clear from astronomy. Therefore all the categories depend on a knowledge of quantity, of which mathematics treats, and therefore the whole excellence of logic depends on mathematics.

2. PROOF FROM REASON THAT EVERY SCIENCE
REQUIRES MATHEMATICS

What has been shown as regards mathematics as a whole through authority, can now be shown likewise by reason. And I make this statement in the first place, because other sciences use mathematical examples, but examples are given to make clear the subjects treated by the sciences. Wherefore, ignorance of the examples involves an ignorance of the subjects, for the understanding of which the examples are adduced. Thus change in natural objects is not found without some augmentation and diminution, nor do these latter take place without change. Hence Aristotle was not able to make clear, without complications, the difference between augmentation and change by any natural example, because augmentation and diminution go together always with change in some way. Wherefore, he gave the mathematical example of the rectangle which, augmented by a gnomon, increases in magnitude and is not altered in shape. This example cannot be understood before the twenty-second proposition of the sixth book of the *Elements* [of Euclid]. For in that proposition of the sixth book, it is proved that a smaller rectangle is similar in every particular to a larger one and therefore a smaller one is not altered in shape, although it becomes larger by the addition of the gnomon.

Secondly, because comprehension of mathematical truths is innate, as it were, in us. For a small boy, as Cicero states in the first book of the *Tusculan Disputations,* when questioned by Socrates on geometrical truths, replied as though he had learned geometry. And this experiment has been tried in many cases, and does not hold in other sciences, as will appear more clearly from what follows. Wherefore, since this knowledge is almost innate, and as it were precedes discovery and learning, or at least is less in need of them than other sciences, it will be first among sciences and will precede others, disposing us toward them. What is innate or almost so disposes toward what is acquired.

Thirdly, because this science, of all the parts of philosophy, was the earliest discovered. For this was first discovered at the beginning of the human race, since it was discovered before the flood and then later by the sons of Adam, and by Noah and his sons, as is clear from the prologue to the *Construction of the Astrolabe* according to Ptolemy, and from Albumazar in the *Larger Introduction to Astronomy,* and from the first book of the *Antiquities,* and this is true as regards all its parts, geometry, arithmetic, music, astronomy. But this would not have been the case except for the fact that this science is earlier than the others and naturally precedes them. Hence it is clear that it should be studied first, that through it we may advance to all the later sciences.

Fourthly, because the natural road for us is from what is easy to that which is more difficult. But this science is the easiest. This is clearly proved by the fact that mathematics is not beyond the intellectual grasp of anyone. For the people at large and those wholly illiterate know how to draw figures and compute and sing, all of which are mathematical operations. But we must begin first with what is common to the laity and to the educated; and it is not only hurtful to the clergy, but disgraceful and abominable that they are ignorant of what the laity knows well and profitably. Fifthly, we see that the clergy, even the most ignorant, are able to grasp mathematical truths, although they are unable to attain to the other sciences. Besides, a man by listening once or twice can learn more about this science with certainty and reality without error, than he can by listening ten times about the other parts of philosophy, as is clear to one making the experiment.

Sixthly, since the natural road for us is to begin with things which befit the state and nature of childhood, because children begin with facts that are better known by us and that must be acquired first. But of this sort is mathematics, since children are first taught to sing, and in the same way they can learn the method of making figures and of counting. It would be far easier and more necessary for them to know about numbers before singing, because in the relations of numbers in music the whole theory of numbers is set forth by example, just as the authors on music teach, both in ecclesiastical music and in philosophy. But the theory of numbers depends on figures, since numbers relating to lines, surfaces, solids, squares, cubes, pentagons, hexagons, and other figures, are known from lines, figures, and angles. For it has been found that children learn mathematical truths better and more quickly, as is clear in singing, and we also know by experience that children learn and acquire mathematical truths better than the other parts of philosophy. For Aristotle says in the sixth book of the *Ethics* that youths are able to grasp mathematical truths quickly, but not matters pertaining to nature, metaphysics, and morals. Wherefore the mind must be trained first through the former, rather than through these latter sciences.

Seventhly, where the same things are not known to us and to nature, there the natural road for us is from the things better known to us to those better known to nature, or known more simply. More easily do we grasp what is better known to ourselves, and with great difficulty we arrive at a knowledge of those things which are better known to nature. And the things known to nature are erroneously and imperfectly known by us, because our intellect bears the same relation to what is so clear to nature, as the eye of the bat to the light of the sun, as Aristotle maintains in the second book of the *Metaphysics*. Such, for example, are especially God and the angels, and future life and heavenly things, and creatures nobler than others, because the nobler they are the less known are they to us. And these are called things known to nature and known simply. Therefore, on the contrary, where the same things are known both to us and to nature, we make much progress in regard to what is known to nature and in regard to all that is there included, and we are able to attain a perfect knowledge of them. But in mathematics only, as Averroes says in the first book of the *Physics* and in the seventh of the *Metaphysics* and in his commentary on the third book of *On the Heavens and the World,* are the same things known to us and to nature or simply. Therefore, as in mathematics we touch upon what is known fully to us, so also do we touch upon what is known to nature and known simply. Therefore we are able to reach directly an intimate knowledge of that science. Since, therefore, we have not this ability in other sciences, clearly mathematics is better known. Therefore the acquisition of this subject is the beginning of our knowledge.

Likewise, eighthly, because every doubt gives place to certainty and every error is cleared away by unshaken truth. But in mathematics we are able to arrive at the full truth without error, and at a certainty of all points involved without doubt, since in this subject, demonstration by means of a proper and necessary cause can be given. Demonstration causes the truth to be known. And likewise in this subject, it is possible to have for all things an example that may be perceived by the senses, and a test perceptible to the senses in drawing figures and in counting, so that all may be clear to the sense. For this reason there can be no doubt in this science. But in other sciences, the assistance of mathematics being excluded, there are so many doubts, so many opinions, so many errors on the part of man, that these sciences cannot be unfolded. For demonstration by means of a proper and necessary cause does not exist in them from their own nature, because in natural phenomena, owing to the genesis and destruction of their proper causes as well as of the effects, there is no such thing as necessity. In metaphysics there can be no demonstration except through effect, since spiritual facts are discovered through corporeal effects, and the creator through the creature, as is clear in that science. In morals there cannot be demonstrations from proper causes, as Aristotle teaches. And likewise neither in matters pertaining to logic nor in grammar, as is clear, can there be very convincing demonstrations, because of the weak nature of the material concerning which those sciences treat. And therefore in mathematics alone are there demonstrations of the most convincing kind through a necessary cause. And therefore here alone can a man arrive at the truth from the nature of this science. Likewise in the other sciences there are doubts and opinions and contradictions on our part, so that we scarcely agree on the most trifling question or in a single sophism. For, from the nature of these sciences, there are no processes of drawing figures and of reckonings, by which all things must be proved true. And therefore in mathematics alone is there certainty without doubt.

Moreover, full confirmation can be drawn from the experience of men of science. For all scientists in ancient times labored in mathematics, in order that they might know all things, just as we have seen in the case of men of our own times, and have heard in the case of others who by means of mathematics, of which they had an excellent knowledge, have learned all science. For very illustrious men have been found, like Bishop Robert [Grosseteste] of Lincoln and Friar Adam of Marsh, and many others, who by the power of mathematics have learned to explain the causes of all things, and expound adequately things human and divine. Moreover, the sure proof of this matter is found in the writings of those men, as, for example, on impressions such as the rainbow, comets, generation of heat, investigation of localities on the earth and other matters, of which both theology and philosophy make use. Wherefore it is clear that mathematics is absolutely necessary and useful to other sciences.

3. THE NEED FOR EXPERIMENTAL SCIENCE

I now wish to unfold the principles of experimental science, since without experience nothing can be sufficiently known. For there are two modes of acquiring knowledge, namely, by reasoning and experience. Reasoning draws a conclusion and makes us grant the conclusion. But it does not make the conclusion certain, nor does it remove doubt so that the mind may rest on the intuition of truth, unless the mind discovers it by the path of experience. Many people have the arguments relating to what can be known, but because they lack experience they neglect the arguments, and neither avoid what is harmful nor follow what is good. For if a man who has never seen fire should prove by adequate reasoning that fire burns and injures things and destroys them, his mind would not be satisfied thereby, nor would he avoid fire, until he placed his hand or some combustible substance in the fire, so that he might prove by experience that which reasoning taught. But when he has had actual experience of combustion, his mind is made certain and rests in the full light of truth. Therefore reasoning does not suffice, but experience does.

This is also evident in mathematics, where proof is most convincing. But the mind of one who has the most convincing proof in regard to the equilateral triangle will never cleave to the conclusion, without experience. Nor will he heed it, but will disregard it, until experience is offered him by the intersection of two circles, from either intersection of which two lines may be drawn to the extremities of the given line. But then the man accepts the conclusion without any question. Aristotle's statement, then, that proof is reasoning that causes us to know is to be understood with the proviso that the proof is accompanied by its appropriate experience, and is not to be understood of the bare proof. His statement also in the first book of the *Metaphysics* that those who understand the reason and the cause are wiser than those who have empirical knowledge of a fact, is spoken about such men as know only the bare truth [of fact] without the cause. But I am here speaking of the man who knows the reason and the cause through experience.

Experience is of two kinds [through sense perception and through interior illumination]. One kind is gained through our external senses, and in this way we gain our experience of those things that are in the heavens by instruments made for this purpose, and of those things here below by means attested by our vision. Things that do not belong in our part of the world we know through other scientists, who have had experience of them. For example, Aristotle on the authority of Alexander sent two thousand men through different parts of the world to gain experimental knowledge of all things that are on the surface of the earth, as Pliny bears witness in his *Natural History*. This experience is both human and philosophical, as far as man can act in accordance with the grace given him. But this experience does not suffice him, because it does not give full attestation in regard to things corporeal, owing to its difficulty, and does not touch at all on things spiritual. It is necessary, therefore, that the intellect of man should be otherwise aided. For this reason, the holy patriarchs and prophets, who first gave sciences to the world, received illumination within and were not dependent on sense alone. The same is true of many believers since the time of Christ.

Experimental science has three leading characteristics, with respect to other sciences. The first is that it investigates by experiment the notable conclusions of all those sciences. For the other sciences know how to discover their principles by experiments, but their conclusions are reached by reasoning drawn from the principles discovered. But if they want to gain a particular and complete experience of their own conclusions, they must gain it with the aid of this noble science. For it is true that mathematics has general experiments as regards its conclusions in its figures and calculations, which also are applied to all sciences and to this kind of experiment, because no science can be known without mathematics. But if we give our attention to particular and complete experiments and such as are attested wholly by the proper method [in each special science], we must employ the principles of this science which is called experimental. I give as an example the rainbow and phenomena connected with it, such as the circle [corona] around the sun and the stars. The natural philosopher discusses these phenomena, and the researcher on perspective has much to add pertaining to the mode of vision that is necessary in this case. But neither Aristotle nor Avicenna in their Natural Histories has given us a knowledge of phenomena of this kind, nor has Seneca, who composed a special book on them. But experimental science attests them.

Secondly, this mistress of the speculative sciences alone is able to give us important truths within the confines of the other sciences, which those sciences can learn in no other way. Hence these truths are not connected with the discussion of principles but are wholly outside of them, although they are within the confines of these sciences, since they are neither conclusions nor principles. The man without experience must not seek a reason in order that he may first understand, for he will never have this reason except after experiment. Hence in the first place, there should be a readiness to believe, until in the second place experiment follows, so that in the third place reasoning may function. Thus if a man is without experience that a magnet attracts iron, and has not heard from others that it attracts, he will never discover this fact before experiment. Therefore, in the beginning he must believe those who have made the experiment, or who have reliable information from experimenters. Nor should he reject the truth, simply because he is ignorant of it, and because he does not arrive at it by reasoning [alone].

But there is a third dignity of this science. It arises from those properties through which it has no connection with the other sciences, but by its own power investigates the secrets of nature. This consists in two things, namely, in the knowledge of the future, the past, and the present, and in wonderful works by which it excels in the power of forming judgments the ordinary astronomy which deals with judgments.

32

ST. ALBERT'S DEFINITION OF THE SOUL [1]

BY APPEALING to Avicenna and to the *saints,* St. Albert the Great defends the substantiality of the soul through denying that it is an accident of the body, which is exactly the procedure of Avicenna, and then through saying that it is a substance using a body, thus defending its superiority over the body. Briefly, the conclusion which can be drawn from the *saints* assisted by Avicenna is that since the soul is not an accident, it is a substance.

Under the title *On the philosophers' definitions of the essence of the soul,* St. Albert considers first the definition of Plato that *"the soul is an incorporeal substance moving a body."* The article which follows this new question is quite naturally entitled, *"How does the soul move the body?"* What exactly is this motion which Plato attributes to the soul? When the soul moves the body, is it itself moved or unmoved? The [objector's] first argument proves that Plato held that the soul was itself moved in moving the body; while the next four arguments show that this conclusion has to follow as a necessary consequence, partly on the ground that the soul has to have motion in order to communicate it, and partly because, as a matter of experience, we see that the soul does change, as in sorrow, joy and hope, or in the reception of sensations and intelligible species. But these theses—that the soul moves itself and that sensation is a motion in it—St. Albert rejects. In his defense he invokes the names of Aristotle, Avicenna, Averroes, Costa-ben Luca, Alfarabi, John of Spain, "et multi alii naturales." The soul moves the body and remains itself unmoved, except *per accidens,* when the body is moved. Indeed, according to St. Augustine, the soul is in the body as God is in the world. That is, just as God is in the world and moves all things

1 [From Anton Pegis, *St. Thomas and the Problem of the Soul in the Thirteenth Century* (Toronto: St. Michael's College, 1934), pp. 90-96. Reprinted by permission. The notes are omitted. The exposition is based upon the *Summa De Creaturis* of St. Albert the Great.]

without being moved essentially or accidentally, so does the soul move the body, remaining itself unmoved, but not accidentally, because its power of motion falls short of that of God.

Having rejected the idea that the soul is essentially moved in moving the body, St. Albert turns to Aristotle's criticism of Plato. To say that the soul becomes angry or is afraid, is the same as saying that the soul weaves or builds. It would be better to say, Aristotle observes, that *man* does these things because of the soul. This is not to be taken as meaning that motion is in the soul, but that at times motion comes as far as the soul, at times proceeds from it. The first is illustrated by sensation, while for the latter Aristotle uses memory. Age would be an example of the change or motion of the soul, but Aristotle remarks that if you give an old man the eye of a young man he would see as a young man. And if the soul is not moved, much less will it move itself. Thus far, then, the soul is found to be unmoved in its relation to the body. This last point has been gained chiefly through the criticism of Aristotle. Now the question which becomes interesting at this stage of St. Albert's development is to know how he would interpret Aristotle's definition of the soul. This is the subject of the next inquiry: *On the definitions of the soul according to Aristotle.*[2]

Is the soul the *actus* of the body? Now Avicenna calls the soul the *perfectio* of the body. Apparently, then, according to the first objector, *perfectio* and *actus* ought to mean the same thing. But if the soul is a perfection, the objector continues, it is in a subject perfected and has existence only in that subject; which would mean that the soul is a purely material form. The objector, therefore, does not like the word *perfectio* because, thus explained, it is not applicable to a rational soul.

Here is the solution of St. Albert. The substantial difference between an angel and the soul is that the soul is inclined towards the body as its *actus,* while the angel is not. Now we may consider the soul from two points of view. We may consider it in itself, and then it would not be defined with reference to the body, but according as it has existence in itself. Or, we may define it by considering it in relation to the body, and not according to the existence which it has in itself, and this would give us a definition of the soul in relation to the body. Accordingly, we have two definitions of the soul, one of the soul in itself, the other, in relation to the body. The reason for this, says St. Albert, is that some souls can be considered to exist without bodies. That is why, he continues, and here follows a reflection worth noting, Avicenna could say that the name *soul* is not a name indicating the essence of the thing to which it is referred. For this reason the definition of Aristotle does not look to the *esse* or nature of the thing defined, except in so far as it is the source

2 [St. Albert is concerned mainly with the two well-known statements in Aristotle's *De Anima,* 412a: "The soul must be a substance in the sense of the form of a natural body having life potentially within it. . . . The soul is the first grade of actuality of a natural body having life potentially in it." (J. A. Smith translation.)]

of certain affections or activities. In other words, the definition of Aristotle does not consider the essence of the soul, but certain activities which are accidental to its nature, though necessary indications of the essence in itself.

Avicenna goes on to give an example which St. Albert takes over from him. If we say that what moves has a mover, we do not, therefore, know in this way what the essence of the mover is in itself. Avicenna means to say, observes St. Albert, acting as interpreter, that just as the mover has a twofold definition, that is, with respect to that *proprietas,* which makes it a mover, and, secondly, with respect to its own essence, in the same way the soul has a twofold definition: it may be considered in so far as it is a soul, that is, the *actus* of the body and its *motor,* or, again, in so far as it is a substance contained, according to its nature, in the category of substance.

Thus, Avicenna is St. Albert's master in the definition of the soul. According to this interpretation, we must distinguish two aspects of the soul. In itself it is a substance. But it also has certain powers which enable it to act as the *motor* of the body. In this way, by means of Avicenna, St. Albert is enabled to interpret Aristotle's definition in such a way that it gives a valid but, for all that, not essential definition of the soul. We can make this point a little more precise by looking at the sixth objection and its answer. Referring to the text of the *De Anima,* the objector wants to know why Aristotle, if he calls the soul a *forma,* does not define the soul as the *forma prima* rather than as the *actus primus* of the body. St. Albert replies that there are two reasons why the soul is better called an *actus* than a *forma.* The first is that the *forma,* according to natural philosophy, refers to that which has its existence in this determinate matter and cannot exist without it; but a *perfectio* can exist according to its substantiality without the being it perfects, as a sailor can exist without a ship: *sicut nauta sine navi.* Since, therefore, a particular kind of soul can exist separately, the soul is better called a *perfectio* or *actus* than a *forma.* The second reason is that, unlike *forma,* which refers to what is remotest from its complement, namely, the potency of matter, *perfectio* refers to, and implies a comparison with, a being that is perfect not only in its matter, but also in all aspects necessary to the perfection of that being. That is, whereas *matter* would be the subject of form, *body* is the subject of the soul as *actus* or *perfectio.*

33

THE HUMANISM OF ST. THOMAS AQUINAS[1]

I

I AM convinced that St. Thomas is, if we may use a word in favor today, the most *existential* of the philosophers. It is because he is par excellence a philosopher of existence that St. Thomas (St. Thomas, the "Angelic Doctor") is an incomparably human thinker, and that he is par excellence the philosopher of Christian humanism. What is human is, in fact, rooted in existence. The Middle Ages understood more and more clearly that man is not an idea—man is not an idea but a person. Man subsists in the universe and before God; man is at the very heart of existence, and it is there that he is struck by all the darts of good and evil, and that action, the incomprehensible action of the Primal Being and other beings, reaches and upholds him, or else wounds him, and it is there that he himself, within time, pursues the tenacious career of a creature raised out of nothingness and created for happiness. The metaphysical principle of medieval humanism could be formulated as follows: only he who himself made existence can know *what there is within man*. Only thought centered on existence can in any way approach the inner recesses of the human heart, man's original grandeur and also his obscure depths, and attune itself to the aspirations of that strange image of God. "God is called zealous," said the pseudo-Dionysius, "because of his great love for everything that exists." St. Thomas often repeats that saying. It is because he himself has the zeal for existence that he has that faculty of reassuring, appeasing and strengthening with supreme serenity all that is truly human in us.

The great philosophical doctrines can be summarily divided into two groups. In the first group could be classed those philosophers who venerate the intellect and philosophy, but who limit themselves to considering essences, possibles and intelligibles, contemplated in the heavens of abstraction and cut off from effective existence. Those philosophers, Descartes, Malebranche, Leibniz, Spinoza, and Hegel, are all more or less enchanted by the magic flute of Plato. They have a knowledge, not of the universe, but of a picture book. They leaf through the pages of that lovely book and think that they are touching reality. What an illusion!

[1] [From Jacques Maritain, "The Humanism of St. Thomas Aquinas," in *Twentieth Century Philosophy*, edited by D. D. Runes (New York: Philosophical Library, 1943), pp. 295-310. Reprinted by permission.]

Reality, human life, the inner depths of man, these can be reached only by breaking through the book.

Annoyed by such impotence, the philosophers of the other group, the anti-Platonists, the great pessimists of the human will, or of the elemental life, Schopenhauer, Nietzsche, shatter at the same time as the picture book, philosophy and reason itself. But idealism torn to shreds is not realism, and it is not by ruining reason that one discovers human life and the inner depths of man—these are merely disfigured and mutilated. At the lowest point a Klages is heard savagely proclaiming war between life and the spirit, and finally there will be the declarations of unfortunate youths perverted by the new barbarism. I quote the young author, Ernst Jünger: "The best answer to the betrayal of life by the spirit is the betrayal of the spirit by the spirit. And one of the greatest and cruellest pleasures of our time is to participate in this work of destruction."

I honestly believe that between these two groups of philosophers there is only St. Thomas who truly respects human life and the inner depths of man and reaches *existence* itself through the *intellect* itself. He has a highly classical conception of science; he is scrupulously attentive to the slightest demands, the finest rules and norms of logic, of reason and of the art of formulating ideas. And what he knows is not a picture book: it is that Heaven and Earth which contain more things than are dreamed of by builders of systems—it is that existing universe, resting on first data which must be acknowledged, not deduced, that universe swept by all the being-producing currents which vitalize and unify it.

II

I should like, in the three parts of this essay, to consider briefly certain typical examples of this *existentialism* and humanism of St. Thomas, first in the order of speculative knowledge, then in the order of practical knowledge, and finally in the order of the spiritual life.

In the order of speculative knowledge, the first typical characteristic, which is immediately apparent from this vantage point, is the *realism* of St. Thomas.

Veritas sequitur esse rerum, he constantly affirms. Truth follows the existence of things, and is the adequation of the actual immanence of our thought with what exists outside our thought. A spiritual superexistence by which, in a supreme vital act, I become the other, in so far as it is other, a superexistence which corresponds to the existence exercised or enjoyed by that other in the field of reality which properly belongs to it—this is in what true knowledge consists.

This knowledge is bathed in existence. Existence—the existence of things—is first given to us through the senses. The senses reach the object as actually existing, in so far as it exerts a real and existing action on our sensory organs. And that is why the paradigm of all true knowledge is the intuition of the thing which I see and which radiates toward me. The senses actually reach existence, without knowing that it is existence. They give it to the intellect as an intelligible treasure, which they themselves do not know as intelligible, but which the intellect does know and calls by its name—Being.

And the intellect, seizing upon the intelligibilities which it extracts by its own strength from sensory experience, reaches, at the core of its own internal vitality, those natures or real essences which it has disengaged by abstraction from their material existence at a given point in space and time—but for what purpose? Solely to contemplate in its ideas the scheme of the essences? Surely not! But to restore them to existence through the act in which intellection is completed and consummated—that is to say, through judgment, which declares *ita est,* it is so. For example, when I say, "The sum of the angles of every Euclidian triangle is two right angles," or, "The earth revolves around the sun," what I am in fact saying is, "Every Euclidian triangle *exists* in mathematical existence as having the property in question. The earth *exists* in physical existence as having the motion in question." The function of judgment is an existential one.

The intelligibility on which judgment bears is more mysterious than that which is given us by ideas or notions; it is not expressed in a concept, but in the very act of affirming or denying—it is, if I may term it so, the superintelligibility of the very act of existing, either possibly or actually. And it is to this superintelligibility of existence that St. Thomas attaches the whole life of the intellect.

That is why he places at the root of metaphysical knowledge the intellectual intuition of that hidden reality which is concealed in the most common everyday word of our language, the word *to be,* and which reveals itself to us as an incomprehensible glory, when we are lucky enough one day to perceive in the mose humble thing that act of existing which it exercises, that victorious thrust by which it triumphs over nothingness. For the realism of St. Thomas, the act of existing, whether considered in some wretched blade of grass, or in some weak flutter of hearts, is already the action and perfection of all form. Is it surprising that at the transcendental summit of all things, beyond the whole realm of beings, he beholds God as the infinite ocean of the act of being, subsisting through himself, and for that very reason resplendent with all perfections?

Descartes and the whole of the rationalist philosophy which stems from the Cartesian revolution have posited an insurmountable enmity between the intellect and mystery. And there you have the deepest origin of the fundamental inhumanity of a civilization based on rationalism. At the heart of being, at the heart of existence, St. Thomas reconciles the intellect and mystery; and by so doing he frees our intellect, he restores it to its nature by restoring it to its object. But, at the same time, by so doing he apears as the most fundamentally human, the most truly humanistic of thinkers. He gives us the strength and the courage to accomplish our human task in the midst of strange nature and our own strangeness. By making peace between our minds and the mysterious universe, he also establishes peace between our minds and the mysterious Creator. Instead of separating philosophy from theology, as Descartes was to do, he places philosophy in continuity with theology, and rationally shapes the eminence of theological wisdom, which is, as he put it, the participation within us of the knowledge of those spirits who see God.

I shall mention briefly another typical characteristic of the speculative thought of St. Thomas, one that is narrowly linked to that realism of which I have just spoken, from the very fact that this thought is centered not on essences, but on existence, on that mysterious welling forth of the act of existing in which, according to the analogical diversity of the degrees of Being, are actualized and formed all the qualities and all the natures which refract and multiply the transcendent unity of the actual subsistent Being in his created participations. From the very beginning, the thought of St. Thomas grasps being as superabounding. Everywhere being superabounds, it gives forth, and this is the *action* by which, here below, all beings are in intercommunication. In this we have one of the fundamental features of the Thomistic synthesis. Above time, in the primary and transcendent Source, it is the superabundance of the divine existence, a superabundance in pure act, which, as Revelation teaches us, is manifested in God Himself by the plurality of the divine Persons, and, as reason itself is quite apt to know, by the fact that the very existence of God is Intelligence, is Love, and that it is freely creative. Nor does that divine Fullness merely give: It actually gives Itself, and it is for the purpose of giving Itself to spirits capable of receiving It that, in the final analysis, It created the world. "It is not for himself but for us," says St. Thomas, "the God created all things for his glory."

If then being is superabundant and self-communicating, if it gives itself, then love is justified—and with it that urge and that aspiration (to get out of one's self in order to live the very life of the loved one) which are consubstantial with the human being, and which scandalize all the philosophers of pure essences. For a Spinoza, the peak of wisdom and of human perfection is to love God intellectually, in other words, to consent as a mere disinterested spectator to the universal order of things, without asking to be loved in return, because the God of Spinoza is not a creative Person capable of loving freely and of giving himself freely; he is naught but a subsisting essence, and all things are the expression and, as it were, the unfolding of the attributes and modes of this essence. But for St. Thomas Aquinas, the peak of wisdom and of human perfection is to love God *lovingly* in a communion of love, in other words, freely to lay oneself open to the fullness of love of the living God descending into us, and overflowing from us to make us continue his work in time, and communicate his goodness.

The rationalist philosophers all inevitably posit a fatal divorce between knowledge and love. Thomistic existentialism brings them into agreement and unity, bases love upon intelligence, and strengthens intelligence by love—at the same time showing us that love can be a beneficent and pacifying stream only if it passes through the lake of the Word. And by this trait Thomistic thought again appears as a thought profoundly human and truly humanistic, which not only emancipates the intellect, but reconciles it with the heart and reconciles us with ourselves.

Once we have understood this primacy of *existence* in the thought of St. Thomas, we can also understand the power of synthesis it manifests to such a high degree towards the whole inheritance of human and divine wisdom, as well as its capacity for welcoming all truths, the humblest and the greatest, which the searchings and systems of men so often hold prisoners of error, and which must be brought home to their native habitat. Such a power of synthesis and of welcome requires a very high degree of originality and an exceptional poetic energy. It is this intuition of being, the very simple and infinitely fertile apperception of existence—perfection of perfections and unification of what is multiple in all the degrees of its analogical values—which is the secret of St. Thomas, and which gave to the great mute ox of Sicily the strength to integrate all the truths uttered by pagan philosophers, by Aristotle and his dazzling clique of Jews and Arabs, as well as by the Church Fathers, and by St. Augustine with his Platonism transfigured by the wisdom of grace, to blend all those precious voices under the one Word, superior to all philosophy and to all theology, which is transmitted to us by the Gospel. And here again is the lesson in humanism that we owe to St. Thomas. He venerated antiquity so intelligently that, at every step, he opened up new vistas, brought everywhere the freshness of the childlike spirit, and was, without meaning to be, the greatest instigator of newness ever known to the medieval schools.

But the power of synthesis I have just mentioned must be thought of in a much deeper sense. It is in Man that the spirit and doctrine of St. Thomas tend to create unity, and always by virtue of the same secret, which consists in understanding everything in the light and generosity of existence. Nature and grace, faith and reason, supernatural virtues and natural ones, science and wisdom, speculative energies and practical ones, the world of metaphysics and that of ethics, the world of knowledge and that of art: to every constellation of our human sky St. Thomas diligently assigns its proper domain and its particular rights, but he does not separate them; he distinguishes between them in order to unite them, and makes all our forces converge into a synergy which saves and stimulates our being.

The principles of St. Thomas particularly make it possible to understand how, at the immaterial focus of the soul's energies, mystical wisdom and theological wisdom vitalize and strengthen metaphysical wisdom, just as metaphysical wisdom vitalizes and strengthens the philosophical activities of lesser rank. Here arises the question of Christian philosophy. I shall not take it up in this paper. I shall merely note that St. Thomas, without explicitly treating this question, held a very clear position on the subject. He affirmed this position not only by his principles, but by his action—by strife and suffering. For his struggle consisted wholly in bringing about the recognition of Aristotle and the overthrow of Averroes; in other words, this meant bringing about, at the same time, the recognition of the autonomy of philosophy, like that of natural law and of the temporal community, and the subordination of philosophy to faith, and of natural law and the temporal community to the law of grace and the kingdom of God. If today there are Thomistic philosophers who can be scandalized by the idea of a Christian philosophy, it simply proves that one can quote a master's formulae without knowing of what spirit one is, and that Thomism like any great doctrine can be dissected like a cadaver by teachers of anatomy, instead of being taught by philosophers. Many attempts at humanism, generous in themselves, even at Christian humanism, like the attempt of Erasmus and his friends, failed because they did not take their origin high enough. For we believe that only one form of humanism can descend deep enough into the inner recesses of the human being, the humanism which stems from the wisdom of the saints while ensuring and integrally respecting the order and dignity of nature. It is here that resides, to my mind, the privileged position of St. Thomas: in his theology, in his epistemology, and in his ethics.

III

And so I come to the second part of this paper, that which concerns practical knowledge. In the realm of practical knowledge and moral life, what I should like to recall first of all is the classic doctrine of St. Thomas on the perfection of human life and on charity. He teaches that it is in the love of charity that perfection consists, and that everyone is expected to strive for the perfection of love according to his ability and his particular condition of life. This is not a counsel; it is a precept. The existentialism I have pointed out is found here in a really typical form; for love, as St. Thomas says, does not go out to possibilities or to pure essences: it goes out to existing realities. It is because God is the supreme and superabundant act of existing, that the perfect love of God is the supreme perfection of our being.

To say that the perfection of human life consists in love is to say that this perfection consists in a relationship among persons and primarily between the person of man and that of God. Henceforth this is essential —the ever-increasing fullness and sensitiveness of union among persons, until that transfiguration is reached which, as St. John of the Cross says, makes of man a God by participation. Thus, when the ramifications of Thomistic philosophy are followed in the behavior of the great mystics, it appears that the perfection of human life is a perfection of the art of loving, and not of the art of perfecting ourselves and of being sufficient unto ourselves in our intelligence, our strength or our virtue. When we consider the practical attitude of the men of the Middle Ages in the spiritual domain, we see that for them the perfection of the Gospel was not the perfection of a spiritual athlete, by which a man would make himself spotless, but the perfection of love, of that love for Another Whom the soul loves more than itself, and Whom it is essential for the soul to love still more and to rejoin, even if it is carrying imperfections and failings—which he takes upon himself to remove. Who can fail to see the profound humanity of such superhuman detachment from perfection within perfection itself?

Such then is St. Thomas' conception of the "meaning of human life." We are here at the very heart of his humanism, and we see how this humanism is an integral whole, and at the same time how, in a very particular way, it answers an urgent need of our times. For the typical significance of Thomism, from the point of view of the philosophy of culture, is that it shows the inherent consistency, value and dignity of nature—subject to grace "of which a single benefit outweighs all the benefits of the universe," and proceeding from the holy superabundance of the subsistent Being himself. Let us say that the significance of Thomism is that it *dignifies* and rehabilitates the creature in God and for God; and that dignifying and theocentric rehabilitation of the creature, and particularly of the human being, is, I am sure, precisely what our civilization requires if it is to be restored. The human person and human life should be truly and deeply respected *in* their affinity with God, and *because* they derive from him; created things, and the efforts and labor of the secular community, should not be despised—nor again worshipped, or ruined by the enslaving mania for domination of man over man. This *rehabilitation of human life in God* appears to me characteristic of a new era of Christianity, and of a new humanism essentially different from the humanism of the Renaissance, or from that of the classical period. It is theocentric humanism, rooted where man has roots, a humanism which might be called the humanism of the Incarnation and of which St. Thomas Aquinas appears to me to be the propounder. "To be human," he said, "is to have for man a feeling of love and pity" (*Summa Theologiae*, II-II, 80, 1, ad 2).

To gain a fuller idea of the humanism of St. Thomas Aquinas, it would be necessary to mention many more significant points in his doctrine: he not only teaches that grace does not destroy nature, but perfects it, he teaches also that every being—including inanimate objects, with their ontological aspiration—loves God above all. He teaches that in order to kill egotistical self-love, the root of all evil, we must love ourselves, our body and our soul with the love of charity. He also teaches that without charity there is no perfect virtue, and that nevertheless the virtues of the heathens, described by the Jansenists as resplendent vices, are real though imperfect virtues of a natural order, and that supernatural virtues do not replace natural virtues, but strengthen and superelevate them. He teaches that what matters most in the New Law—which is not a written law, but mainly one infused into the heart—is the grace of the Holy Spirit, given by living faith. That is in what *the whole power* of the New Law consists; without that, it has no efficacy, it is but an empty image. This is equivalent to saying that authentic Christianity is an *existential* Christianity, in which evangelical love and the interior grace of the Holy Spirit are most important.

The humanism of St. Thomas rehabilitates the life of the secular community, the social and political order, and progress. To avoid further elaboration, I shall merely make the following remarks: St. Thomas believed that our nature is wounded, that the world will never become the kingdom of God; but he also believed that the goal of temporal society is a good and upright earthly life of the community, and that throughout all the vicissitudes of history and the failures of men we must strive for a temporal regime worthy of human dignity. Moreover, he taught that, while social and political realities of themselves belong to the natural order, they concern nevertheless the moral more than the physical realm; they can reach their fulfillment only if they are helped and superelevated within their own order by the energies of grace, so that a temporal civilization (I do not mean one without fault or blemish, but one really worthy of man) must be called by its real name—a Christendom.

Thus the position of St. Thomas is just as far removed from the pessimism of Hobbes as from the optimism of Rousseau. His is an integralist and progressive position. Obviously, the social problems we deal with today did not exist in his own day. But he has established principles showing plainly the direction of his thought. He teaches that a minimum amount of security is needed for man to cultivate virtue so that the question of public morality is primarily a question of work and of bread. He teaches that the ownership of goods and of means of production must be private as to management but common as to "use." He insists on the dignity of the human person, the image of God, and sees in the common good of a civil society an essentially human good. He characterizes political leaders of any regime as trustees of an authority, the source of which is God, and at the same time as vicars of the multitude. He affirms that the consent of the people is requisite to the legitimacy of a regime, whether of the monarchic type or of any type. This consent is an integral part of the dynamism of political life; and a government truly political, in contrast with a despotic government, is a government of free men treated not as children, but as adults. In general, we can say that St. Thomas Aquinas draws a broad outline of a true social and political humanism, the application of which depends upon the particular circumstances of each historic era.

IV

At last I come to the third part of this paper, in which I would like to show the humanism of St. Thomas as it appears in the actual realm of spiritual life. Frankly, when one considers all the endeavors outside the Judaeo-Christian tradition, this realm appears also as one of the great failures and one of the supreme antinomies of our being. The great civilizations of antiquity, that of Greece and above all that of India, contended that contemplative life is superior to active life. But, because they conceived of supreme contemplation as a benefit to be acquired by the highest straining of man's energies, and because they placed everything in the intellect, this contemplation was limited to a small number of privileged beings in whom alone and for whom alone the human race existed, and for whom the enslaved multitudes had to toil. The modern world has proclaimed the emancipation of those multitudes and their right to a share of the goods by which human life is rendered perfect; and in doing so the modern world is right. But it scarcely knows where those goods lie; it ignores as though by principle the whole realm of supreme, immanent and contemplative activities by which, at the summit of the intellect and of the will, human life bears its fruit. In brief, it prefers technique to wisdom, and seeks blessedness in science and work— and we are beginning to perceive today how disappointing this is. This reminds me of Montaigne's thought: "Although we may be learned with the learning of others," he used to say, "at least we can only be wise with our own wisdom."

The solution offered by St. Thomas Aquinas is a typically Christian solution and can be briefly summarized as follows. Yes, Aristotle and old wisdom were right in declaring that contemplative life is superior to active life: it alone throws open to man the portals of divine life. But when they spoke thus, the wise men of antiquity, like certain prophets and poets, spoke better than they thought and did not know what they were saying. The Gospels give true meaning to the formulae of Aristotle. The contemplation of the philosophers stops in the intellect and is achieved by the sole effort of the highest energies of man. The contemplation of the saints does not stop in the intellect, but passes on into the heart. It is achieved not by the supreme straining of the natural energies of man, but by the love of charity, making us one spirit with God and becoming, under the superior inspiration of his gifts, the means of a supreme experiential knowledge. This knowledge does not aim at the personal welfare of the wise man or at his perfect self-sufficiency, but at the love of him Who is contemplated, at the communication of love and the cooperation of love with God Whose beatitude, beauty and work of goodness and salvation are more important than the personal perfection and personal work of the sage.

Such is, within the Thomistic perspective, the end to which spiritual life tends here below. It shows that this spiritual life and the fruits of human perfection are not reserved for an aristocracy of privileged beings.

The tremendous revolution thus accomplished by Christianity, in so far as Christianity summons all men to perfection, was essentially and above all a spiritual revolution effected by the grace of God. We must say that this spiritual revolution yielded also great truths in the natural order; it was also to effect, gradually and indirectly, great changes in the temporal order. It was, namely, to eliminate first from conscience and then from existence the necessity for slavery; to bring about the recognition of the fundamental equality of all men in their dignity, as rational creatures endowed with the same primary rights; and to promote a proportionately increasing equality in the common enjoyment of the benefits accruing to each human person from the treasury of the community. "All men born of Adam," writes St. Thomas, "can be considered as one single man, in so far as they share in one single nature received from their first father" (Summa Theologiae, I-II, 81, 1). The great revelation of the Gospel taught humankind the fact that there are not two kinds of men, those made for labor, and those made for wisdom, but that every man is both homo faber and homo sapiens, and that he is homo faber in order to be homo sapiens, a man made for labor in order to be a man made for wisdom, a man made for labor so as to find happiness and the meaning of his life not in labor, but in wisdom and in the freedom of expansion to which his spiritual nature aspires.

And here we come once more to the integral humanism of St. Thomas. The antinomy pointed out earlier in connection with man's aspirations to spiritual life is surmounted, if it is true that, as St. Thomas teaches, contemplation (contemplation by union of love) is superior to action though required to superabound in action; it is no longer reserved to a class of specialists and privileged beings, but is available to all men without exception who hear the call of God. And this is true not only on the superior plane of spiritual life in its supreme achievement, which is closely linked with grace and the kingdom of God; it is true also on the plane of temporal life and of the worldly civilization. The humanism of which we are speaking holds as an essential truth the fact that the purpose of man's labor is to give him access to the interior benefits of the soul, that is, to activities of leisure or rest. If it is true that some day— at least when a great moral transformation, beginning perhaps today in horror and in blood, will have taught us to make use of technical advances for the good of man, and not for a bestial regression to the worst forms of domination—if some day technical progress will permit the masses to earn through daily labor of relatively short duration the material goods they need, then, to quote Mr. Bergson, the mechanical will summon up the mystical, and it will become obvious that labor, which produces economic values, is by nature directed toward the activities of free development and of fruition.

It can be readily seen also that the common good of a temporal community is valuable chiefly for the access it gives human beings to the inner riches and freedom which dignify them. It is evident also that the common work of a temporal community does not have as its main object some material and outward activity, whether it tend to control nature through industrial power, or to control other nations through political power, but aims at those immaterial activities of which I have just spoken, and which are primarily translated in the social domain by an heroic effort towards the creation of a regime of justice and civil amity, of freedom and brotherly cooperation.

These implications and requirements of an integral humanism descending from the spiritual plane to the social-temporal plane, find their rational justification in the doctrine of St. Thomas Aquinas. At the same time St. Thomas' conception of human nature leaves no illusions as to what such an ideal requires in terms of progressive energy and patience over a long period of generations. In terms of St. Thomas' humanism, it may seem that we are still in the first stages of Christianity from the point of view of social-temporal accomplishments.

I shall close by pointing out that, after the example of his Master, St. Thomas Aquinas received a visible homage of men only on a brief Palm Sunday. He wielded hardly any influence on the temporal structures of his age. However great his glory, however strong his influence in the Church, his work did not *succeed* at his time in affecting the course of history. He showed to his period a supra-temporal pattern which the Middle Ages did not know how to use; he lived at a critical time, when the high culture of the Middle Ages was casting its last rays. When he passed away, the radiant dissolution of medieval civilization was already in progress. His theocentric humanism was too much for his time. But it is permissible to think of St. Thomas as a prophetic saint, reserved for the future; in fact, it is up to men of today to avail themselves of his wisdom for the aims of culture and of his humanism for the aims of community life.

IX. Thirteenth-Century Masters: Giles of Rome to Dante

Revision of accepted estimates of thinkers is constantly going on in the history of philosophy. The data and problems in this field are so closely knit that advances made in the understanding of one philosopher are bound to have repercussions elsewhere and to entail fresh interpretations of other men. Thus it was held for a long while that Giles of Rome was a faithful disciple of St. Thomas, albeit an overzealous one lacking in nuance and systematic balance. One indirect effect of the twentieth-century research into the Thomistic metaphysics of act and potency, essence and existence, however, is to accentuate the differences between these two minds and hence to require a new consideration of the proper originality of Giles and the import of his criticism of St. Thomas.

Father Peter Nash centers his comparison between the two authors, in Selection (34), around their respective doctrines on finite esse, its relation with essence, and its function in the individual composite. Giles is shown to be much closer to Avicenna than to Aquinas, when he defends the metaphysical primacy of essence and the accidental nature of esse. But his presence in the Thomistic milieu reveals itself in his special concern about the problem of the unity of the individual. Since he does not view esse as the ultimate actuality and perfection, he does not arrive at anything more than a unity of aggregation in the individual. This comparative study provides a particular case history of how the medieval thinkers employed their "authorities." Nash points out that the lavish appeal to previous authors does not mean that these men were uncritical toward the speculation of the past. Similarly, their use of a fairly uniform terminology and procedure should not deceive the reader into thinking that the medieval theologians and philosophers formed a united front and were in studied agreement with each other. Giles deals quite independently with Boethius, for instance, quoting only those portions of a text which can support his own view and interpreting the passage from his own systematic viewpoint. And although he follows much the same order as Aquinas in commenting on Peter Lombard's Sentences, *his thought is regulated by a distinctive metaphysical principle and remains open to self-correction throughout his writing career.*

Siger of Brabant was a leading representative of the Arts faculty at Paris. He was a philosopher in the tradition of Aristotle and Averroes, rather than a theologian employing philosophical arguments. Although his position included elements taken from Proclus and Avicenna, he stood with Averroes on many crucial points, including the separation between philosophy and theology. Yet he did not share the Moslem thinker's disdain for theology or his refusal to accord anything except material truth to religious faith. Siger maintained that philosophy can make a necessary rational demonstration of conclusions which contradict the deliverances of faith, yet he did not add that the necessarily demonstrated conclusions of philosophy are true ones. Instead, he assigned the truth to revealed faith, wherever such conflict developed, but it was a truth lacking in any rational foundation and even opposing the natural reasoning of our mind. His standpoint was regarded by opponents as a theory of two truths, but it would be more precise to call it a theory of the systematic separation between truth and philosophical demonstration.

The arguments whereby Siger defended the necessity of creation, the eternity of the world, and a cyclism of finite species, are set forth by Lottie Kendzierski in Selection (35). When these positions are taken in conjunction with his restrictions upon divine knowledge and providence, his separation of the knowing intellect from man, his notion of natural beatitude here on earth, and his doctrine against human freedom and personal immortality, they constitute a major internal threat to the Christian faith. At least, they are such a threat to anyone who accepts the fundamental harmony between faith and reason, and hence who cannot agree with Siger's position on their relation. All these theses were included in the two condemnations issued by Bishop Tempier of Paris in 1270 and 1277. Thereafter, Christian thinkers were much less confident about the desirability of assimilating the Greek outlook and the possibility of purging it of a necessitarian and eternalist presupposition. Where issues involving the teachings of the Christian faith were at stake, "Latin Averroism" came to be regarded as a pure position which had to be avoided.

The mind of Dante is not simply a reflection of the several facets of medieval culture, and certainly not a mere literary receptacle for some-

one's Summa. *Along with mastering the speculative, historical, and literary materials then available, he transfuses them through his poetic sensibility and also through his own intellectual principles.* Dante's high esteem for Siger of Brabant and, simultaneously, his reverence for St. Thomas and knowledge of his writings have always puzzled the commentators upon the Divine Comedy. *Etienne Gilson's purpose in Selection (36) is to suggest a relatively comprehensive framework within which to study Dante's attitude toward these two men and his specific references to the relations among other authorities. Orientation can be gained by noticing a common pattern of thought which runs through the* Banquet *and the* Monarchy, *as well as the* Divine Comedy. *There are three main orders of human instruction and authority: philosophy or human wisdom, the Empire, and theology or the Church. They are directed, respectively, toward three distinct types of beatitude: the temporal happiness of the individual, the temporal happiness of mankind, and the eternal salvation of men. Within its own order, each authority has sole competence and its representatives give true guidance. Dante accepts neither the Thomistic ordination of one authority to another nor the Sigerian divorce between demonstration and truth. Each order furnishes its own truths and maintains its own autonomy, and through the divine providence there is concord precisely when we respect their separate jurisdictions. One tendency in later medieval political philosophy followed this general view of a separate yet concordant relationship between the authorities in theoretical and practical life.*

34

GILES OF ROME: A PUPIL BUT NOT A DISCIPLE OF THOMAS AQUINAS[1]

WHEN Giles of Rome first listened to St. Thomas Aquinas at the University of Paris in 1269, he was twenty-one and his master forty-five. Giles had already been in the Order of the Hermits of St. Augustine for seven years, and a master of arts for three. It was while preparing for his licentiate in theology that Giles sat under St. Thomas during those great years of the *Summa Theologiae* and the

[1] [An essay written especially for this volume by Peter Nash, S.J. Based mainly upon Peter Nash, S.J., "Giles of Rome, Auditor and Critic of St. Thomas," *The Modern Schoolman,* vol. 28 (1950-1951), pp. 1-20.]

Quaestiones Disputatae, 1269-1272. It was only in 1275, several years after St. Thomas' final departure for Rome, that Giles became a Baccalareus Sententiarius and began his own commentary on the first book of Peter Lombard's *Sentences.* About the time he finished this commentary (1277), Giles ran into trouble at the University of Paris, partly for having defended the uniqueness of substantial forms, but mainly for having held certain Aristotelian propositions similar to those condemned by Bishop Tempier. As he would not retract he had to leave Paris, but was reinstated at the intervention of Pope Honorius IV in 1285. He became the first Master of Theology in his Order. Though his election as General in 1292 put an end to his teaching career, it did not stop his writing: his commentary on the second book of the *Sentences* was finally completed in 1302, while that on the third book was unfinished at the time of his death in 1316.

From the only two writings of his which have been critically edited, the *Errores Philosophorum* (written around 1270), and the *Theoremata de Esse et Essentia,* written during his enforced absence from the University of Paris (1277-1285), one might be led to suppose that Giles was an ardent, if somewhat exaggerated, disciple of St. Thomas. In the *Theoremata,* for instance, the "real distinction" is upheld. If Giles seems to reify essence and the act of existence, one could put this down to imagination doing duty for insight. On the basis of this work alone, one would not be justified in attributing to him a radical doctrinal opposition to St. Thomas. Add to this Giles' earlier defence of the unpopular doctrine of uniqueness of substantial form, and it is not entirely surprising that in a later century he came to be looked on as an authentic disciple of St. Thomas. Yet in his own day, Giles was considered an independent thinker.

The contemporary judgment is correct. It can be substantiated by the many trenchant criticisms Giles made of St. Thomas, criticisms given not merely in the spirit of a bright student flexing his intellectual muscles by the satisfying sport of tripping up his teacher, but rather in the spirit of an opposing metaphysical outlook. This shows, for example, in his failure to grasp the peculiarly Thomist notion of entitative act and potency.

It is from Giles' *Commentary on the First Book of the Sentences,* written shortly after St. Thomas' death and with at least three of St. Thomas' works open before him (the *In I Sent., De Potentia,* and *Summa Theologiae,* Pars la), that we can begin to judge how deeply ran Giles' opposition to his master. Giles opens the commentary, as St. Thomas did, with a neat scriptural "summary" of the subject matter of all four books of the *Sentences.* He then sets out to discuss theology according to the four causes. In treating its material cause Giles states what he takes to be the subject of theology: it is God considered under the special aspect of restorer and glorifier. He rejects positions that assign either too wide a formal object or the wrong one. St. Thomas comes under censure for assigning a wrong object, not entirely wrong, since he does make God the subject of theology, but partly so. According to Giles, the error of his former teacher is that he fails to assign that special aspect according to which theology must treat of God (as our redeemer), if it is to be a science distinct from the knowledge which God has of himself. St. Thomas comes in for further criticisms for failing to assign the correct final cause of theology. Giles, the professed Augustinian, must teach the Dominican that the end of theology is love, and not contemplation. Theology is primarily affective, not speculative.

It would take us too far afield to pursue the ultimate reasons for this opposition on the nature of theology: Giles was to fight about it with Henry of Ghent and Godfrey of Fontaines for the rest of his life. It would also take too long to go into all the criticisms of St. Thomas in the works of Giles. We shall, therefore, concentrate on a basic philosophical problem, the role *esse* plays in the constitution of created being. His differences with St. Thomas on this point are the quickest way to see how little Giles understood him.

Anyone commenting on the first book of the *Sentences* was bound, when he came to the 8th distinction, to run into the problem of God's simplicity and the creature's lack of it. He would have to "interpret" the many passages of St. Augustine cited by Peter Lombard. But, in accord with current practice, he would interpret his "author" in the light of his own metaphysics.

Giles' metaphysics includes the Augustinian view that immutability and simplicity of essence are proper to God alone, and the Boethian notion that the creature is necessarily composite. Along with most of his contemporaries, Giles sees the human soul as composite, though its "matter" for him is simply its potentiality for composition with the body. He also discovers this same composition in that *esse* which Boethius had distinguished from *quod est*. Giles, of course, takes *esse* to mean that complement of actuality which gives essence existence. Since this act is created, it too must be composite, at least with a *compositio huic*: it cannot be simple, because it is not pure act but an act within which is a potentiality.

Giles' metaphysics also included the Avicennian accidentality of *esse*, understood again as act of existence. He denies that *esse* is a predicamental accident, though, as we shall see, he makes it resemble it in a way St. Thomas never could.

Finally, Giles brought to his commenting an enthusiasm for Proclus. He accepted the notion that the world proceeds from its source (the One) in the way numbers do from unity. Only the One is strict and simple unity without parts (*totum ante partes*). Everything else recedes from unity and is, like any number other than unity, made up of parts (*totum ex partibus*). The further the recession the more the parts, the less the unity. Hence the individual is less of a unity than the species. All this can be accommodated to an Augustinian-Boethian scheme, in which the creature is distinguished from the Creator by not being simple.

There is, however, one element in Proclus that causes trouble: the first creature is *esse*. This follows from the doctrine of Plotinus that the One immediately produces only one thing, while all the rest become distinct and many through a descending hierarchy of intermediaries. Giles accepts the "authority," but takes Proclus' characterization of *esse* as a *totum in parte* to mean a logical whole, whose "parts" are all the individual acts of *esse*. It is really through Proclus that Giles achieves his own synthesis of all the various "authors." But what is surprising is that he criticizes St. Thomas for appealing to the *Liber de Causis,* as though St. Thomas had not been aware of the original Platonic intent of the passage. Aquinas had already explicitly remarked that "the *Liber de Causis* . . . originates from a book of Proclus, who was a disciple of Plato." Perhaps Giles had not known at this time of St. Thomas' commentary on the *Liber de Causis* and the correct assignment therein of its origin and character.

With these attitudes to St. Augustine, Boethius, Avicenna and Proclus, it will not surprise us to find Giles openly criticizing St. Thomas on the nature of God and creatures. Let us turn to the eighth distinction of the first book of the *Sentences.*

In speaking of God, Giles notes that unity, simplicity and immutability are convertible:

The more simple a thing is the more it is one, because the more indivisible and in need of nothing, because a composite thing needs its components. As Proclus says, the number One is one and simple and in need of no other. So too, the more immutable a thing, the more simple it is. As Augustine says: nothing simple is mutable.

Having equated the One of Proclus with the God of Augustine, and having laid it down that simplicity and unity are the contraries of composition and multiplicity, Giles, in a subsequent question, affirms that the human soul cannot be simple, because the less a thing is in act the more composite it is. This is true also of participated *esse*. The reason is that:

the further a thing recedes from divine simplicity and actuality, the more it approaches composition, although some say the opposite (*quamvis conversum quidam dicunt*). So too, the further a thing recedes from the divine goodness the closer it gets to evil, because, as Aristotle says, it happens that everything, except one, participates in evil.

If we compare this with the parallel passage in St. Thomas, then the identity of the "some" who "say the opposite" will be obvious. Here is St. Thomas:

Everything that proceeds from God in diversity of essence falls off from his simplicity. But by the fact that it falls off from simplicity, it is not necessary that it fall into composition; just as from the fact that anything falls off from the divine goodness, it is not necessary that some evil fall into it.

St. Thomas sees no contradiction between a thing not being composite and yet being less than God's simplicity.

For St. Thomas there can be two ways of falling off or receding from God's simplicity. A thing may be divisible, potentially or accidentally, like prime matter or form or the universal. Or it may be capable of being composed with another, a possibility foreign to God's simplicity. Giles will not admit that this being *componible alteri* (St. Thomas' phrase) is compatible with simplicity. This is because he is convinced that for a thing to have the status of being created, whether that thing be a supposit or principle thereof, it must be composed. Otherwise it is not distinct from God, who alone is one, simple, immutable. In paradoxical fashion, Giles concludes from his premises that *esse* is more composite than the supposit of which it is a part! Created *esse* (*totum in parte*) exists more divided up than the supposit itself (*totum ex partibus*). Hence *esse* is less actual, more potential, and therefore, in a way, more composed than the supposit to which it belongs.

An important corollary of the composition of the created supposit is that it is not an *unum per se*. The unity of the genus is divided by the addition of differences. What finally constitutes a specific essence as an individual is also what gives it actual existence, namely, the *esse existentiae*. When this last is added to the *esse essentiae* (St. Thomas never used this terminology), the resulting supposit has the unity of a sum, *unum unitate addita*. The individual is an aggregate: *substantia prima in istis inferioribus est individuum aggregatum*. This has to be if God alone is a simple essence, and if any essence below God has to participate in something else in order to be an individual. To Giles, the problem of the appearance of numerically distinct creatures is one of the division of an essence which has all the priority of an Avicennian quiddity.

This constitutive role which *esse actuale* plays in the individual led Giles, in the 36th distinction, to oppose St. Thomas on God's knowledge of singulars. He agrees, first, that God does know them. Then, after giving St. Thomas' reason for this, namely that God knows what he produces, and he produces both form and the principle of individuation, which is matter, he says this is not the essential reason. "For particulars are not known as particulars, except in so far as they are determined by actual *esse*." As Giles views the problem, therefore, St. Thomas has a God who either knows things only universally or increases his knowledge every time there is a new *esse*.

This dilemma is a real one only on the supposition that *esse* is the determinant of particularity. Given that it is, Giles' way out of the dilemma is to say that our minds, not being pure acts identical with *Ipsum Esse*, cannot possibly have within them every facet of being (*ratio essendi*). Hence our minds need a further determination in order to know things according to their actual *esse*. God's understanding, being identical with his *esse*, is pure act with no potentiality in need of determination. He contains every *ratio essendi*. Therefore any new *esse* on the part of creatures is not new to him. His knowledge does not increase with every new particular that comes into being. What is behind this opposition to St. Thomas?

If we keep in mind that, at least in the commentary on the first book of the *Sentences*, Giles approaches the problem of creatures as one of the diversification of essences, we will see that essence has for Giles a metaphysical priority. That which brings a specific essence down to be an individual, which can only be an existent individual, must add to essence something not in the line of essence, something not *per se* part of the essence, something accidental to essence, namely *esse*. It is *esse* which he interprets to be the accident in the dictum from Boethius' *De Trinitate* that "variety of accidents makes numerical difference." [2]

This equivalence leads Giles to a surprising suppression of part of the Boethian text, simply because it does not fit his interpretation. I underline what Giles omits:

Thus genera and species subsist only: *for neither do accidents happen to species and genera*. But individuals do not only subsist, they also substand, *for neither do they need accidents in order to be (ut sint)*.

In Boethius, the "ut sint" means, according to modern scholars, "in order to be natures or forms." There is a contradiction in Boethius only if, as Giles takes it, "ut sint" is existential. As Giles simply cannot accept his "authority" here, he saves him by omission.

Later on, as is clear from the commentary on the second book of the *Sentences*, Giles abandoned the view that *esse* is the determinant of particularity. He came to admit that the accident making for numerical difference is quantity. But he seems never to have given up his position on the aggregated unity of the individual, and he certainly never forsook his insistence that *esse* "borders on the accidental." What does he mean by this accidentality?

It comes out in his commentary on the third book of the *Sentences*, in two criticisms of St. Thomas. He opposes St. Thomas on the meaning of the phrase "vergit in accidens," when said of the humanity of Christ, and also on the application of the Averroistic distinction between predication *de genere* and predication *de accidente*. Let us look at this second attack.

For St. Thomas, that *esse* which is predicated accidentally of anything is intentional *esse*, the to-be-known. For Giles, Averroes' question *de accidente*, when concerning being, always bears on *esse actuale*. The descent of being into the genera is a *per se* descent, that is by the addition not of true differences but of modes of being, which are not accidental

---

2 [For this quotation and the next one, see Boethius, *The Theological Tractates*, E. K. Rand edition in The Loeb Classical Library, pp. 6, 88.]

differences. But actual *esse* is added accidentally to essence. That is why Averroes' question *de accidente* concerns the truth of propositions only because truth is in function of existence. Giles' metaphysics here seems governed according to the relations between logical entities. It is to be expected that he would see in *esse* a closer resemblance to predicamental accident than St. Thomas did.

For St. Thomas, the only resemblance *esse* has to an accident is that it is not necessary to essence, even though essence cannot prescind from it. For Giles, it is outside of essence, not necessary to it, and so much so that the one can prescind from the other. St. Thomas holds that *esse* is act without qualification. Giles maintains that *esse* is second act, and the first act is form. This does not mean that essence has an inchoative existence. Giles insists that neither essence nor *esse* can exist by themselves. But, metaphysically speaking, essence has the priority. Giles, apparently, never understood the absolute priority which St. Thomas gave *esse* as entitative act.

The few criticisms which we have examined are enough to show Giles' independence of thought. They also throw light on the intellectual ferment of the thirteenth century, which was faced with the task of sifting and evaluating and assimilating the wealth of new sources. The effort to digest the Platonic and Aristotelian streams was at once a cooperative effort and highly individualistic. What may fool one is the similarity of formulae. Actually the thirteenth century was anything but an era of rigid conformism: it was not extraordinary that a pupil of St. Thomas should radically disagree with him.

35

ETERNAL MATTER AND FORM IN SIGER OF BRABANT [1]

FOR Siger of Brabant, Aristotle is The Philosopher, and he prefers the solutions of Aristotle to those of any other. Siger considers his writings to be a restoration of Aristotelianism; and since he used Averroes' commentaries on Aristotle, his own interpretation of Aristotle is colored with Averroes' commentaries. Thus Aristotle and Averroes are the outstanding influences on Siger, but his doctrine also contains principles derived from the philosophy of Avicenna and Proclus.

The principal works of Siger of Brabant are *De Anima Intellectiva, De Necessitate et Contingentia Causarum, Quaestio utrum Haec Sit Vera: Homo Est Animal Nullo Homine Existente, In Libros Tres de*

[1] [From Lottie Kendzierski, "Eternal Matter and Form in Siger of Brabant," *The Modern Schoolman*, vol. 32 (1954-55), pp. 223-241. Reprinted by permission. Most of the notes are omitted, and the author's footnote translations of Latin passages are here inserted in the main text.]

Anima, In de Generatione et Corruptione, Impossibilia, De Aeternitate Mundi, and commentaries on Aristotle's *Physics* and *Metaphysics.*

Siger follows Avicenna in holding the eternity of all intelligible realities. The First Cause produces immediately and necessarily a first intelligence which is coeternal with it. This is the only immediate effect of the First Cause. The First Cause is the cause of many effects only according to a certain order; the only immediate effect of the First Cause is an effect which is itself necessary and yet a unity. The immediate effect of God must be a perfect creature; therefore, matter or that which is made from nothing cannot be produced immediately by the First Being. So, too, the human species which is made by God through generation cannot directly proceed from him.

The creation of all beings other than the immediate effect of the First Cause is by way of intermediaries which, though not immediate, are nevertheless eternal effects of the First Cause. Between the First Cause and the world there is an infinite number of intellignces which are necessary and eternal by their nature, but their capacity to be is derived from the First Cause; therefore, they do not exist as self-produced. Each intelligence is a movent of a celestial sphere and is unique in species, since multiplicity within a species would require matter. Each of these is in its very being separate from matter, and therefore is not multiplied according to the multiplication of matter.

The celestial spheres, in turn, exercise by their movement a permanent and essential influence on the infralunary world; they conserve terrestrial bodies and assure the perpetuity of species and generation. Thus, matter and all things subject to generation proceed from the First Being through the intermediary of the celestial spheres.

Since matter is the immediate effect of the celestial spheres and since the spheres are eternal, matter too is eternal. Matter is not engendered, since generation presupposes matter; but it is created by the intermediary of the celestial spheres. Matter is the permanent subject of generation, and the form alone is acquired by generation; the composite is engendered in virtue of its form. There is no possible production outside of generation; the world cannot be engendered from pre-existing matter, for matter cannot exist without form and nothing material pre-exists before the world. Matter alone is formally in potency to the form of engendered being; therefore, the subject of generation can be or not be. It is being by the matter which is in it, and nonbeing by the privation of the form engendered. Thus the engendered being is produced from being in potency, "from nonbeing simply, not from being in act, but from being in potency." [2] Thus the essence of matter is not its potentiality but rather its potentiality to all forms. Matter, therefore, never exists without form; and forms, in turn, have their whole existence as actualizations of the potency of matter. In itself, matter has neither diversity nor unity,

THIRTEENTH-CENTURY MASTERS: GILES OF ROME TO DANTE 259

but is one of several powers. It can be a principle of infinite quantity and can receive an infinite number of successive forms, which are not specifically distinct, for the number of species is finite.

Having established the eternity of movement in this world upon the eternity of the Prime Mover and the intermediate movers, Siger argues that the eternity of time follows the eternity of movement, for time is the measure of movement. Time is composed of things finite in quantity which are infinite in number. Though every second is finite, in time there is a then before the then to infinity, for what is composed of things finite in quantity yet infinite in number has to be something infinite. Siger is aware that the eternity of movement and time raises a difficulty with regard to faith and concludes that it is necessary to hold that motion is not eternal; but this cannot be proved by demonstration. In fact, Siger even insists that Aristotle proves that motion is eternal.

Aristotle, however, as is clear, proves motion to be eternal; this is clear from the reasons which he gives. Some, however, who wish to bring Aristotle's intention in accord with the faith say that Aristotle did not think because of these reasons that the world was eternal, and that he did not hold these demonstrative conclusions to be true of necessity but advanced these reasons only because of doubt, and no other reason. But this is clearly false, since then it would follow that Aristotle was in doubt in the greater part of his philosophy, and more so where he speaks of separate substances: for from the eternity of motion he proves that there are separate substances. . . . Wherefore, it must be said that in the opinion of Aristotle the world was eternal, so that it never began nor will it ever end. This is what the Peripatetics who are of his sect posit with many proofs. One of which is that, One in so far as it is One can only produce one; and even if it does produce heat in something, this is not *per se* but *per accidens*.[3]

No doubt Siger is thinking of St. Thomas in the texts just cited. St. Thomas is convinced that Aristotle's arguments from motion are not demonstrations in proving the eternity of the world, for Aristotle himself says that there are certain dialectical problems which reason cannot prove, as whether the world is eternal or not. St. Thomas states that Aristotle did not intend to prove the eternity of the world and that all he proves is that all motion requires a movable subject—which is not contrary to faith. Aristotle's arguments, therefore, are valid against those who admitted the existence of eternally movable things but denied the eternity of motion; namely, Anaxagoras and Empedocles. St. Thomas concludes that Aristotle's arguments on the eternity of movement and time are not contrary to the creation of the world but are directed against his predecessors, who said that motion had a beginning. All that Aristotle is saying, therefore, is that if the world comes by generation, there is no first motion and that motion is, therefore, without beginning. So, too, Aristotle proves that matter is unbegotten because it has not a subject from which it derives its existence; and the heavens are unbegot-

3 *In Phys.*, VIII, 6, ed. Delhaye, p. 199.

ten since they have no contrary from which to be generated. St. Thomas argues that no conclusion follows either way, except that matter and the heavens did not begin by generation.

St. Thomas raises the question whether an eternal creation is possible and concludes that it is. There is no need that the cause which is the agent—namely, God—precede in duration what he causes, had he himself wished. St. Thomas sees no contradiction in saying that something is made by God and was never nonexistent: "Sic ergo patet quod in hoc quod dicitur aliquid factum esse a Deo et nunquam non fuisse, non est intellectam aliqua repugnantia." [4]

In saying that an eternal creation is philosophically admissible, St. Thomas does not mean that coeternal creation is possible, for the creature cannot be coeternal with God. Even if the world had always existed, it would not be coeternal with God because its duration would not be wholly simultaneous, which is essential to eternity.

To establish and confirm the eternity of all things, Siger discusses, in the third part of his treatise *De Aeternitate Mundi,* the principles of potency and act and their priority in relation to one another. First, act is prior to potency in thought, though potency is prior to act in things which proceed from potency to act.

Although act precedes potency in thought—for potentiality is defined through act, as the builder is able to build—potency nevertheless is prior to act in substance and in perfection in a thing which proceeds from potency to act. The things which are later in generation are prior in substance and perfection, since generation proceeds from the imperfect to the perfect and from potentiality to act. [5]

Act is also prior to potency in substance and perfection.

Act is also before potentiality in substance and perfection, in the respect that potentiality and act are looked upon in different ways; because eternal things are prior to corruptible things in substance and perfection. But nothing eternal, in the respect that it is such a thing, is in potentiality; in corruptible beings, however, there is an admixture of potency. [6]

Though act is prior to potency in thought, perfection, and substance, there is no priority of act to potency in time, since both are eternal.

Act does not precede potentiality in time, because in eternal beings one is not before the other in time. But when the act of a certain species and the potentiality to that act are looked upon according to the species, they are both eternal. Man is always in act and is always able to be man. Thus, with things proceeding from potentiality to act, with regard to which one is to come from the other in a cycle to infinity, there is none which is first in time. The seed is from the man and the man from the seed to infinity. Therefore in such things one does not precede the other in time. Thus, from the seed from which a man

[4] *De Aet. Mundi,* ed. Mandonnet, p. 25.
[5] *De Aet. Mundi,* III, ed. Dwyer, p. 39.
[6] *Ibid.*

is generated there is another generating man previously existing; and so also previous to that generating man, since he himself was generated, there must have been a seed from which he was generated.[7]

In the order of generation, Siger continues, there is a sense in which potentiality precedes act in time.

In the order of generation potentiality is prior to act, since generation proceeds from potentiality to act; and thus it is prior in the order of time. There is no reason why act should precede potentiality in time, except that, by a power, a being is made in act through some agent of its own kind existing in act. But although from this it follows that the act of the agent precedes in time the act and perfection of the generated thing by that agent, nevertheless, it does not seem to happen that the act of the one generating precedes in time that which is in potentiality to the act of generation. Just as being in potentiality comes into actuality through something of its own species in act, so also the thing existing in act in that species is generated from something existing in potentiality to the act of that species. For just as that which is in potentiality— namely, a man—is brought into act by a man in act, so also the man generating is generated from a previous seed and from a man in potency; and so the hen has preceded the egg in time and the egg the hen, as people argue.[8]

Siger argues that if the whole universe of caused beings were at some time nonbeing, then potentiality would precede act absolutely. Further, if some entire species of being would begin to exist when it had never existed before, the potentiality of that species would precede absolutely the act, each of which is impossible.

If the whole universe of beings at some time had been in potentiality, so that none of the beings would be totally in act, then the beings and the world would not now be except in potentiality, and matter of itself would come into act, which is impossible. For things to be at rest in an infinite time and afterwards to be in motion, is the same as for matter to be self-moving.[9]

Siger states that, according to Aristotle, no species can begin anew; the species or that which is in act is always generated from a previous species in act and so on to infinity:

Since the prime mover and agent is always in act and something in potency is not prior to something in act, it follows that it always moves and acts and makes anything or does anything without an intermediate movement. From the fact that it is always moving and so acting, however, it follows that no species of being proceeds to actuality, but that it has preceded before, so that the same species which were return in a cycle. The same holds also for opinions and laws and religions and all other things, so that lower things circle around from the circling of the higher, although because of their antiquity there is no memory of the cycle of these. We say these things as the opinion of the Philosopher, although not asserting them as true.[10]

7 *Ibid.*, pp. 39-40.
8 *Ibid.*, p. 40.
9 *De Aet. Mundi*, ed. Dwyer, III, p. 42.
10 *Ibid.*

Siger continues this argument and states that in things which are generated from eternity, neither potency nor act precedes one another in time, but one comes before the other to infinity:

When potency-to-an-act and the act-educing-that-potency are of the same kind in the generator and thing generated, it is not said, in so taking them, that act precedes potentiality absolutely, nor potentiality act, unless the act is taken according to the species, and the proper potentiality is taken according to the individual. For a man in act, and a certain man in act, inasmuch as he is generating, precedes in time that which is being in potency; namely, man generated. But because in this order, just as being in potency proceeds into act through something existing in act, and so act precedes any given potentiality, so also everything existing in act in this species precedes any given act. Therefore neither simply precedes the other in time, but one comes before the other to infinity.[11]

Further, Siger concludes that there is no priority in time in things which are generated, for things which are in act and things which are in potency are both eternal:

Act precedes potentiality in the sense that the first mover leads into act all being in potentiality; but the being in act does not precede in time the being in potentiality, since being in potentiality is regarded as prime matter. Just as God always exists . . . so also does the potential man, since he is regarded as in prime matter. It is never true to say, according to Aristotle, that God existed unless potential man existed or had existed in the seed.[12]

In concluding his discussion of the relation of potency and act and their priority to one another, Siger shows a further priority of act to potency, and here his argument deals with movements which are eternally in act:

Act also simply precedes potentiality in time, because in any being in potentiality, as given in proper matter, the act of that potentiality having to educe the potency to act precedes in time. It is not thus with any given being in act that the potentiality to that act precedes it in time, as is evident in prime movers educing to actuality all beings in potentiality. Thus we utilize, as does Aristotle, prime movers as species of things which are educed from potentiality to actuality by them. And unless they were beings of a certain kind in act which do not proceed from potentiality to actuality, the act would not simply precede the potentiality in time, as Aristotle has said in the ninth book of the *Metaphysics*, saying that act precedes potentiality in time, adding the reason, because one act is always taken as before another up to the one which is always the prime mover.[13]

Having established the eternity of matter and the eternity of material species and their eternal relation to one another, Siger applies these principles to the human species; the eternity of species will be his most force-

11 *Ibid.*, p. 43.
12 *Ibid.*
13 *Ibid.*, p. 44.

ful argument for proving an eternal world. Since the being of all things is in matter, which is in potency to forms, the human species cannot be immediately produced but must be made through a generation which is either essential or accidental. The human species—and in general all things which are in matter—is not generated essentially but accidentally, since it is made through generation. Forms and species are not generated essentially because individuated matter pertains to the consideration of neither of the things from which generation essentially comes; that is, through the transmutation of the thing from nonbeing to being or from privation to form. The human species, though not generated essentially, is nevertheless generated accidentally, because just as man has been abstracted in thought from individual matter and from the individual, so might he be abstracted in existence. Man is therefore generated through the generation of any individual, and not only of one determined individual.

The human species is eternal and caused because in the individuals of the human species one is generated before the other eternally, and the species has to be and to be caused through an individual's existing and being caused. Man begins to be through the generation of a Socrates, let us say, who is generated; he exists, nevertheless, through the existence of a Plato of the previous generation. So, too, the fact that, when Socrates is generated, man begins to be does not mean that man begins to be in such a way that he had not in any way previously existed. Any individual of this kind began to be when he did not previously exist, because even though it be true that no individual man began to be after not yet existing, no individual of this kind begins to be unless another one had previously existed.

The human species comes, and came, into being accidentally by the generation of individual before individual to infinity. This is not to say, however, that the human species comes into existence only in some determined individual and when it had not existed before. Whence we should wonder about those who argue that the human species had begun through its being made and that it was not made essentially but rather by the making of the individual. To show their intention they ought to show that individual has not been generated before individual to infinity. This, however, is not shown by those who hold that there is a beginning in species; but they propose one false theory, that the human species is not able to have been made eternal by God, unless it had been created in some determined and eternal individual, just as the species of heaven was made eternal; and when they find no eternal being among human individuals, they think that they have demonstrated that the whole species began to exist when it had not been at all before.

Thus, according to Siger, the human species could not begin to be, because it would have no reason for being unless it always existed. The human species eternally exists in individuals; and the world of individuals must be eternal, since the species always exists in some individuals. For species, essence, forms of material things to exist at all, they must realize themselves in some matter; otherwise, they would not be species of material things. Species of this kind could not be except in individuals; their realization in individuals must always go on; and in this way the individuals eternally perpetuate the species through generation. The problem "whether it is true that man is an animal when no man exists" presupposes an impossible conclusion because there are always men and humanity; and in this sense the species is eternal and constantly actualized in a certain number of individuals.

In the second part of the *De Aeternitate Mundi*, Siger discusses universals and refutes Platonic idealism, which holds that the universals preexist the individuals. The universal, because it is a universal, is not a substance and is different from any singular. If, therefore, the universal, in that it is universal, would be a substance, then it would be differing in substance from any of the singulars; and each singular would be a substance in act, both singular and universal. Thus universals would be distinct substances and separated from particulars; and it amounts to saying the same thing, according to Aristotle, that universals are substances and that they are separated from particulars. If, therefore, "man" and "stone" are universals, they are universals only in the sense that they are known universally and abstractly from individual matter. These things do not exist thus in the nature of things, because if understood, those things, "man" and "stone" do not have existence except in the mind. For the abstract comprehension of those things because they are universals is in the mind.

Siger also refutes Albert the Great according to whom there is a certain priority in nature of the universal in relation to its presence in intelligence, since the universal has a causal role in the actuation of thought. Siger responds that this causality is superfluous and that the operation of intelligence is sufficiently explained by the agent intellect and the phantasms.

Siger's conclusion is that since prime matter is permanent and eternal, and since the species are successive, generative, and eternal, the world also must be eternal. For Siger, creation is eternal in all its degrees; the immediate effect of God is necessarily one and eternal, and corruptible beings depend on God through the intermediary of incorruptibles. Siger does not seem to have conceived of the idea of a truly free Creator; the effects of God must be necessary and eternal to insure the divine immutability. So, too, with species and the human species in particular. As an effect of God through intermediary causality, it is necessary that the human species be eternal and that it be eternally realized in a plurality of individuals which are perpetual and infinite in number, which individuals, in turn, account for the perpetual generation of species.

36

PHILOSOPHY IN DANTE'S *BANQUET* [1]

THE general position taken up by Dante in the *Banquet* is composed of multiple elements, all of them traditional, though he has modified and improved them with the object of balancing them in a manner that is his alone.

That is why all efforts to classify his doctrine by identifying it with any one of the attitudes already known to and described by historians were destined inevitably to end in failure. Scholars have referred to the "rationalism" of Dante in the *Banquet,* but, as Signor Michele Barbi has justly pointed out, this is a label whose exact signification can never be known. Thus, reference is made to the "Christian rationalism" of St. Anselm, but it is equally easy to demonstrate that, if his rationalism is Christian, it is not a form of rationalism, or that, if it really is a form of rationalism, it cannot be Christian. It has also been said that Dante, reversing the Anselmian formula *credo ut intelligam* ("I believe that I may understand"), had replaced it with *intelligo ut credam* ("I understand that I may believe"). We should thus have an Anselmian Beatrice and a rationalist *donna gentile.* This is a picturesque contrast; but is it a historical fact? Not only—and none disputes the fact—has Dante never referred to a formula *intelligo ut credam,* but he has definitely affirmed that, if he believes, he does so precisely where he does not quite succeed in understanding. It is not because he perceives the immortality of the soul perfectly clearly that be believes in it; he believes in it, on the contrary, because he does not perceive it perfectly clearly.

Let us, for example, refer to the famous passage in the *Banquet,* Treatise IV, 21, where Dante confronts himself with the intricate problem of the origin of the soul—a problem to which St. Augustine, who never ceased to ponder it all his life, finally confessed that he did not know the solution: *Nec tunc sciebam, nec adhuc scio* ("I did not know then, nor do I know even yet"). What does Dante think: He too thinks that he knows nothing. That is precisely the reason why we find him announcing that he will first proceed *per modo naturale, e poi per modo teologico, cioè divino e spirituale.* Taking the first point of view, that of natural knowledge, we discover a variety of opinions regarding the origin of the soul; probably they are reconcilable; but why give oneself the trouble of reconciling them, since we have only to follow Aristotle? So

[1] [From Etienne Gilson, *Dante the Philosopher* (New York: Sheed and Ward, 1949), pp. 151-161. Reprinted by permission. The notes are omitted.]

here we have him following Aristotle, that is to say what he takes to be
Aristotle's doctrine, after which he observes: "Let no man be astonished
if the manner in which I speak seems hard to understand; for I myself
think it astonishing that one should be able to see and to infer the existence of a creation of this kind through the intellect. . . ." Whereupon,
passing a little farther along the theological road, Dante confines himself
strictly to considerations of a supernatural order, none of which,
whether viewed closely or from a distance, could be justified by the resources of reason. Dante's attitude in the *Banquet* is therefore not a form
of rationalism which, supposing that the formula has a meaning, bases
faith on reason; not only does he admit that reason has its limits, but he
distinguishes them never more clearly than when dealing with the numerous questions in the case of which they are shown to him by the
Christian Revelation. In order to find room for reason in a ready-made
classification we must therefore turn elsewhere.

Why should we not try to identify his position with that of Thomism?
Certain scholars have not failed to do so, but the point is not an easy
one to make. The distinction between the two forms of beatitude understood according to the explanation of Dante himself absolutely forbids
such an identification. Nothing, I think, could be clearer than this point
as stated in the *Monarchy,* but it is already sufficiently so in the *Banquet.*
If we consider only the hierarchy of dignity which Dante accepts as existing among the three forms of beatitude—active life, contemplative life,
beatific vision—his accord with St. Thomas is virtually perfect; but in
St. Thomas, a hierarchy of dignity is at the same time invariably a
hierarchy of jurisdiction, whereas, except when God is involved, Dante
never regards a hierarchy of dignity as a hierarchy of jurisdiction. Thus,
to him, philosophic certainty is assuredly less complete than that of
theology, but these are kinds of certainty existing in different spheres
and prescribed for different ends. This is why Dante subjects philosophy
to the authority of Aristotle without accepting any limit to that authority. If he makes use of St. Thomas so readily, even in matters of philosophy, it is because he is absolutely convinced that in matters of philosophy St. Thomas, like himself, is just a perfect and always submissive
disciple of Aristotle. Where, on the contrary, he catches St. Thomas in
the act of contradicting Aristotle *in matters of philosophy,* Dante gives
him the slip and follows Aristotle faithfully.

That is precisely what he does as regards the different forms of beatitude. In Dante's eyes, the human felicity which man may obtain in this
life through the exercise of the political virtues is an end in itself, completely distinct from that higher end which is heavenly beatitude and
which is accessible through means completely distinct from those which
may lead to the felicity of the next world. Completely distinct from each
other, these two categories are therefore no less completely independent.
In short, Dante's ethic has in view an end as distinct from that of the
supernatural ethic, and pursues it by means as completely alien from

those of the Christian religion as are the end and the means of Aristotle's ethic from those of the Gospel. Moreover, this fundamental opposition between Dante and St. Thomas paves the way for their no less fundamental opposition with regard to the relations between Church and Empire. Hence, according as we probe into one or the other of these two doctrines, we enter two different worlds, not that the elements of which they are made up are not the same, but because, according as they go to the making of one or the other of these two worlds, they do not obey the same laws.

Such, moreover, is the fundamental reason why it will always be fruitless to classify Dante not merely in terms of some previously defined idea, but even in terms of the authorities which he invokes, cites and follows. Distinction between the orders is indeed carried so far in his work that, from the fact that he regards an author as the authority *par excellence* as regards a certain order, we may conclude with certainty that he will not be so as regards the remainder as well. If it is a question of classifying the heavens, the problem is one of astronomy; Dante will therefore follow Ptolemy, who is the competent authority in the matter; but the authority of Ptolemy becomes invalid in the Crystalline, where astronomy ends and theology begins. Consequently, having reached this point we shall have to describe the supernatural heaven *secondo che la Santa Chiesa vuole, che non può dire menzogna* (II, 3), for if the question is one of the supernatural, it is no longer science that is competent to discuss it, but Revelation.

More than this, Dante does not like to contradict Aristotle in the matter of philosophy and I know of no instance in which he has done so with full knowledge of the case, but he has no scruples at all about contradicting him in the matter of astronomy, because if Aristotle is the Philosopher, the Astronomer is Ptolemy. Moreover, that is what Aristotle himself did, for he recognized, in Book XII of his *Metaphysics,* "that he had simply followed the opinion of another where he had to speak of astronomy" (II, 3). If, on the contrary, it is a question of the number of the independent Intelligences, philosophers and theologians are not in agreement, but it is certainly the theologians who are right, because in these matters the philosophers are no more than partially competent. The Ancients erred on this point, with which natural reason declares itself incapable of dealing, *per difetto d'ammaestramento*—for want of instruction by the proper authority. The Jewish people were better informed in the matter. Because Angels were involved, and because on that subject their Prophets were capable of enlightening them at least in part, Israel was *in parte da li suoi profeti ammaestrato.* As for us, as Christians we are in this matter the pupils of Christ, sons of the Emperor of the world, Who is God: *Noi semo di ciò ammaestrati da colui che venne da quello, da colui che le fece, da colui che le conserva, cioè de lo Imperadore de l'Universo, che è Cristo* (II, 5). He Who created the Angels and preserves them probably knows how many of them there are.

Now it is he Who instructs us as to their number; consequently, we are completely enlightened on this subject.

This constant need of an *ammaestramento* received each time from the most competent authority is one of the most characteristic traits of Dante's thought. It is this same trait which will later imbue him wih the desire to provide himself with guides and will advise him in the remarkably judicious choice of them that he will make: Virgil as far as the Earthly Paradise, then Beatrice, finally St. Bernard of Clairvaux. For each separate order, a separate competency; for each separate competency, a separate authority. In Limbo the philosophers spontaneously group themselves around Aristotle even as the poets do honour to Virgil; St. Thomas Aquinas presides over speculative theology as St. Bonaventure does over affective theology, each in his turn speaking as a master where he really is the master and exercising authority where he really has authority. And where, it will be said, are those who wish to exercise it where they do not have it? They are in Hell. And it may indeed be said that they alone have put themselves there by their violation of the holy law of divine Justice which is not only the supreme creator of the constitutive orders of nature and supernature, but also the inexorable protector of the authorities which it has wisely placed at their head.

There is no greater crime than to betray the divine order, and it is betraying it to refuse to follow Aristotle in the matter of philosophy, because philosophy is the daughter of God and it was God himself Who desired that it should be taught to us by Aristotle. But it is no less a crime for a Franciscan to betray St. Francis, for a Dominican to betray St. Dominic, for a subject to betray the Emperor, for a Christian to betray the Gospel. And the worst crime of all, the one which in this world gives rise to disorders, abuses, wars and miseries without number, is to betray all forms of authority at once through a desire to install one of them, which is competent in its sphere, in the place of those which are equally so in theirs, for each form of authority is master in its own house and even the humblest of all is directly responsible to God alone.

Hence the indignation that we witness when Dante comes to define *gentilezza,* that is to say, practically, personal nobility. For this is a philosophical question, and yet here we have Frederick of Swabia taking a hand in its solution. The Emperor wishes to legislate in matters of philosophy! An extremely grave difficulty, and the very prototype of what may be called the *Aporia Dantesca,* because it expresses a conflict between different forms of jurisdiction and authority. Here, the whole question turns upon this point: *l'autoritade de la diffinizione de lo imperadore* (IV, 3). Once the question has been propounded, Dante cannot but settle it completely: origin of human society, its nature, its aim; origin of the Empire, nature of the Empire, aim of the Empire—until at last the conclusion leaps to the eye: the philosophical authority of the Emperor, *qua* Emperor, is nonexistent. Aristotle is the Emperor in matters of philosophy, and if the masters of this world submitted as completely as they should to his authority, their government of the Empire would only be the better for it! "It is therefore manifest that to define *gentilezza* is not a function of the art of governing the Empire; if that is not one of its functions, we are not subject to the Emperor when we discuss this question; if we are not subject to him, we do not owe him any consideration in the matter. This is what I intended to prove." Whereupon Dante declares war on the Emperor: "That is why henceforth we must, with a complete lack of inhibition and complete mental freedom, fly in the face of the accepted opinions, casting this one aside, in order that, thanks to my victory, the rightful opinion may prevail in the minds of those in whom this light shines with some strength" (IV, 9).

If we re-read the *Banquet* from beginning to end, we shall have many an opportunity to notice this attitude and, so far as I know at any rate, we shall find nothing which contradicts it. Here, then, is the necessary starting-point for a correct appreciation of Dante's position with regard to these questions. Is it an Averroistic position? Not if by Averroism we mean the position of Averroes himself, who regards philosophical learning as the prototype of perfect knowledge, to which faith only bears a useful but crude resemblance. Nothing was likely to be more repugnant to Dante's mind than such a confusion of forms of jurisdiction, which would make Beatrice his guide through Hell and the Earthly Paradise, where she would be relieved by Aristotle, relieved in his turn by the Prophet on the summit of Paradise. Not only did Dante never claim that theology is subordinate to philosophy, but we may say that such a thesis is the negation of his whole doctrine, or that his whole doctrine is the radical negation of such a thesis, as we prefer.

If the author of the *Banquet* is not an Averroist after the fashion of Averroes, is he one after the fashion of the Latin disciples of Averroes—Siger of Brabant and Boethius of Dacia, for instance? To give weight to such a theory, we should have to be able to cite one or more cases in which Dante has maintained in opposition two contradictory theses, the one propounded as being necessary for the satisfaction of reason, the other as being consonant with the demands of faith. So far as I know, the *Banquet* does not furnish a single case of this kind, and I do not believe that he who looks for one there has the slightest chance of finding it. But he will find many an example of the contrary case, in which Dante expresses his joy at establishing a perfect accord between philosophy and theology, between reason and faith. For example, the envoy of the *Canzone Terza* which precedes the Fourth Treatise of the *Banquet* begins with the line *Contra-li-erranti mia, tu te n'andrai*, which it would not be wholly inaccurate to translate: "Go, my *Contra Gentiles*." As Dante himself says in his commentary on this line, "this *Contra-li-erranti* forms but a single word, and it is the name of this *Canzone*—a name suggested by the example of the good friar Thomas Aquinas, who bestowed on the book he wrote in order to confound all who deviate from faith the title of *Contra li Gentile.*" Why this title? Dante then asks himself. Because, he answers, just when the good workman is on the point of taking leave of his work he touches it up and embellishes it to the best of his powers in order that it may leave his hands more glorious and more precious. *Contra-li-erranti,* like *Contra li Gentili,* is the most beautiful title that Dante could find. The man who wrote those lines certainly never admitted the existence of any cleavage between his reason and his faith.

We should be reduced by this to accepting the hypothesis of a Thomistic Dante if the philosophical doctrines expounded in the *Banquet,* which are certainly reconcilable with those of St. Thomas Aquinas, did not so often testify to the presence of other influences, like, for example, that of the *De Intellectu* of Albertus Magnus (III, 7), and above all if, even where he is in complete accord with him, Dante did not differ from St. Thomas by virtue of a most important peculiarity. We have solid reasons for believing that after the death of Beatrice the author of the *Banquet* went through a crisis of philosophism. It may therefore be asked if he was still involved in that crisis at the period at which he wrote the *Banquet,* or if he had emerged from it without preserving the marks of it, or—a third hypothesis—if he had emerged from it, but in such a way that the *Banquet* retained visible traces of it. To the first of these questions we may reply with certainty that if Dante really experienced a crisis of pure philosophism, that crisis was over when he wrote the *Banquet.* Theology pervades this work, like an Empyrean that envelops the world and, if it does not move it, nevertheless sheds its supernatural light over it. The *Banquet* is hallowed from its outset by the memory of a heavenly Beatrice who, although she is not yet what she will become in the *Divine Comedy,* is none the less already one of the blessed and, to Dante himself, a summons from the next world.

To the second of these questions the reply should likewise be in the negative, for if Dante has recovered a sense of theological and supernatural exigencies, he seems in the *Banquet* to profess not a philosophical rationalism directed against theology, but a doctrine of the autonomy and the adequacy of the aims of philosophy viewed in its proper setting—a doctrine which, if he really did pass through a crisis of philosophism, may be regarded as the lasting imprint with which this crisis marked his thought. If it is true that, while affirming the transcendency of theology, while allowing himself to be deeply imbued with the Christian spirit and even while stressing time and again the perfect accord between his philosophy and his faith, Dante carried the Thomistic distinction between theology and philosophy to the point of separation in order to pave the way for a second distinction—between the Priesthood and the Empire——it becomes extremely difficult to qualify his position with the epithet "Thomistic." Clearly, in this field Dante is engaged in a wholly personal enterprise, and there is nothing in the word of St. Thomas that can have suggested it to him. We may even wonder if Dante's readiness to concede to the theologians the whole essence of their theology and to leave them in peace with the philosophy which they claimed to be the true one does not betray the secret hope that, once assured of possessing what they had set their hearts on, theologians and philosophers would more readily consent to withdraw to their respective domains. When one has all that one wished to have, what more can one desire?

It will perhaps be objected that it was quite futile to claim for philosophy an independence of which it was to make no use. But that is equivalent to returning once more to the position of a professional theologian or philosopher. When an Averroist proclaims the independence of philosophy, he does so in order to protect his own against a theology with which he knows it to be at variance. When a theologian declares that theology "treats the other sciences as inferiors and servants," the truth is that he is according theology the right to control the other sciences and to regard as false everything about them that contradicts it. Having asserted once and for all that philosophy and theology are in harmony, Dante has neither a personal philosophy to protect nor a personal theology to defend, but he needs to ensure the independence of philosophy if he is to ensure that of the Empire. Now Dante clearly saw —and we may say that the certainty of the fact never ceased to haunt him —that these forms of independence are inextricably linked and that the existence of each is bound up with that one of the other two. The purity of each of the orders involved is therefore the necessary condition both of their common independence and of their individual adequacy.

His personal discovery of the merciful *donna gentile* and the profound sense of gratitude which he harbors towards her for having saved him from despair certainly lie at the root of the *Banquet,* but if he is there defending a personal thesis, it is that of the adequacy of philosophy to confer beatitude on men. The temporal happiness of the individual through human wisdom—this, then, is the lesson that the *Banquet* teaches. The temporal salvation of humanity through the Empire—such will be the conclusion of the *Monarchy.* The eternal salvation of men through the Church—this will be the ultimate teaching of the *Divine Comedy.* But since this threefold work is knit together in all its parts, Dante was never able to uphold one of these theses without preparing, formulating or even defending the other two. That is why, just as we have seen him vindicate the claims of the Empire and maintain the transcendency of theology in the *Banquet,* we can also see him affirm the autonomy of philosophy and that of theology in the *Monarchy,* pending the supreme appeal to the *Veltro* [greyhound of justice] launched in the *Divine Comedy* and the solemn beatification of the pure philosopher in the person of Siger of Brabant.

X. The Franciscan School

There is an unavoidable overlap between Sections VIII and IX and Section X, as the example of St. Bonaventure shows. Because of his considerable intellectual and spiritual influence upon most of the later Franciscan thinkers, he can be grouped along with Scotus and Ockham in a presentation of the Franciscan school, even though his standpoint is that of the mid-thirteenth century. His personal contribution is to restate and develop the basic Augustinian themes concerning knowledge, man, and God. Although the language and some of the concepts employed by Bonaventure are Aristotelian, they are made to serve an illuminationist view of the divine ideas as principles of our intellectual knowledge. There is a prominent religious emphasis upon God's presence in the soul, together with the need for an affective and practical ordering of mind and heart toward God. The centrality of Christ for the entire Bonaventurian conception of nature and human choice is underlined by Etienne Gilson in Selection (37). He points up the sharp contrast between this outlook and a purely naturalistic notion of philosophy, which remains open in no way to the transcendent being of God or to the influence of revealed data. For our interior journey toward God, St. Bonaventure wants to equip us with all the guidance obtainable from meditative reason, faith, and the actual experience of a contact with God.

His doctrine eminently typifies the note of practicality, which Father Philotheus Boehner specifies as one of the four characteristic traits of the Franciscan school ("The Spirit of Franciscan Philosophy," Franciscan Studies, vol. 2 [1942], pp. 217-237). The other three traits are its critical, scientific, and assimilative character. For these latter features, we must look to the writings of Duns Scotus and William of Ockham. They make a sharper distinction than does Bonaventure between philosophical and theological issues, and are more concerned about a rigorous method of analysis and proof, in accord with the Aristotelian canons of scientific reasoning.

The theory of distinctions outlined by Father Allan Wolter, Selec-

tion (38), was a principle tool employed by John Duns Scotus in his investigations. The epistemological need to have an objective basis for those proper concepts which represent neither different beings nor purely logical differences, led him to affirm the presence of formalities or real formal entities within the unity of the actual being. A formal distinction obtains between these formalities and thus provides an objective guarantee for our distinct proper concepts, as well as for the inferences based upon them. This distinction was fundamental for Scotus' doctrine on the common nature present in finite things, and also for his treatment of the divine intellect and will. By applying the formal distinction to these divine attributes, he sought to avoid the necessitarian consequences which followed for Avicenna upon the admission of the common nature and the basically essential structure of finite beings. The formally distinct divine will assures the freedom of the creative act and the contingency of the existence of creatures. The modal distinction also plays a major role in Scotistic philosophy, since it permits the human mind to form a concept of being which is real and univocally common to all beings, even though it is imperfect for expressing the perfection of infinite being. This concept is constitutive of metaphysics and enables us to ascertain the existence of the infinitely perfect being, without confusing his perfection with that of finite things.

How the common nature of the concept of being is made available to us, serves as a basis for the concept of the infinite being, and allows us to obtain some knowledge of this being, is the theme of Selection (39), taken from Duns Scotus' Oxford commentary on the Sentences of Peter Lombard. It is a good instance of the medieval Question, the chief technical means for philosophical and theological inquiry. The form of the Question underwent steady development from the time of Abelard onwards, and there are noticeable differences between its structure in Aquinas and in Scotus. In the latter, the body of the Question is considerably expanded to include more reporting and discussion of contrary views. This particular Question on our knowledge of God also exhibits some basic doctrinal disagreements between Aquinas and Scotus. For Scotus, knowledge of God hinges around an analysis of our concepts of necessity, producibility, being, and the infinite mode of being, rather than around judgments concerning contingent, sensible existents and their actual causes. Hence Scotus is impatient of the Thomistic distinction between showing God's existence and showing the truth of our proposition about his existence. But the main opponent is Henry of

Ghent, who taught theology at Paris during the last quarter of the thirteenth century. He helped to form Scotus' own mind through his use of the concepts of being and infinity as routes to God, but Henry stopped short of framing a univocal concept of being which is applicable to God and finite things. To stop short here is equivalent, in Scotus' eyes, to destroying the basis of strict proof and opening the gate for either a claim of intuitive vision of God or outright skepticism. Hence from our concepts of finite things, he proposed a way of forming a proper quidditative notion of the infinite being which yields some imperfect knowledge of God.

To William of Ockham, the Scotistic theory of common natures and essences permits too solid a ground of resistance to divine power to remain at the finite level. In Selection (40), Father Armand Maurer traces out Ockham's critique of his predecessor on these points, with the attendant denial that universals signify anything but the singular thing as such. If there is no formal distinction of a common nature from the individual circumstances, there is no extramental foundation for the universal concept. The latter is only the singular notion of the mind which is somehow fitted to signify many individual things. Yet it is difficult for Ockham to explain what there is about certain individual things that permits them to be more appropriately signified together by one mental act. Because the reason for the similarity of signification remains elusive to both the sense and intellectual intuition of singulars and the subsequent abstractive inferences, the latter fall short in philosophy of being strict demonstrations, whenever existential relations are involved. In Ockham's wake, the area of probability and dialectical reasoning is constantly enlarged, including within its scope the problems of the one existent God and the immortal human soul.

The history of medieval logic is still being explored, but Father Philotheus Boehner has charted some of its developments between 1250 and 1400. The topics chosen here for Selection (41) have a special interest for modern readers, because of the comparison they afford with work being done in contemporary logic. Boehner stresses this point by symbolizing some medieval results in contemporary logical form. In both the theory of supposition and that of consequences, Ockham especially made some significant findings. Particularly in the case of his teaching on supposition, the connection can be seen between his logical work and his other philosophical standpoints. Within the context of the proposition, he finds no difficulty in material supposition for the term itself as a spoken or written word. But in the case of simple suppo-

*sition for the universal concept, he must insist that the substitution is
solely for the concept itself as a singular notion of the mind, without
any reference signifying a real universal formality of the Scotistic sort.
The only instance where there can be genuine signification is in personal
supposition, but Ockham interprets this in such a way that the term
supposits only for some singular thing as such, be it a word, a concept, or
an extramental individual. Thus he provides a theory of supposition
which harmonizes with his view of the universal and the common nature.
The same careful consistency marks his treatment of consequences, although the problem becomes increasingly complicated as inferences and
truth-values are introduced.*

37

THE SPIRIT OF ST. BONAVENTURE [1]

B ECAUSE of a deep-lying analogy—above all, because of the Augustinian element so strongly active in both of them—St. Bonaventure's method is closely related to Pascal's. Often it may happen
that they explain the same thing following a different order, and each of
these orders is legitimate because in each the mind is moving about a
centre whose position grows ever more precise as the movements of
thought that bear upon it are more numerous and more diverse in their
starting points.

"Order," as Pascal was to say, "consists principally in digressions upon
each point to relate it to the end and keep the end always in sight."

This "order of the heart," with all the totally unforeseeable conclusions it involves, is St. Bonaventure's as well as Pascal's. It is possible,
by abstraction and to meet the exigencies of doctrinal exposition, to
draw out a regular line of questions; but to consider any point in this
line as separable *de facto* or *de jure* from all or any of the others, would
be to conceive an utterly false idea of his thought. *Each* of the ideas
which we have set out with a prior idea before it and a subsequent idea
following, did in reality contain *within its own compass* all that went
before it and all that was to come after it, and could not rightly be considered save in strictest connection with its past and its future. This is
true of all his ideas save one—the idea of the centre by relation to which
all the others find their place and their definition.

1 [From Etienne Gilson, *The Philosophy of St. Bonaventure* (London: Sheed and
Ward, 1938), pp. 470-479, 485-486, 490-495. Reprinted by permission. The notes are
omitted.]

To express the spirit of St. Bonaventure in isolation from the doctrine in which it finds expression cannot, therefore, consist in summarizing that spirit in a formula, or in fixing a definite road for the march of his ideas for his thought traverses innumerable roads, and consequently cannot be bound within a formula. We can express the spirit of St. Bonaventure only by showing the end towards which all digressions tended and in view of which alone they come to unity.

But even to show this end is still not enough. It would be a betrayal of St. Bonaventure if we left in any mind the impression that the abstract and so to speak geometrical determination of that central point enables us to know it as it requires to be known. Philosophy has not for its end to teach us to determine the centre of things, as we determine the centre of a circle by showing the lines which must pass through it; its end is rather to assure us the possession of this centre by conferring upon us the habit of mind whereby we turn towards it inevitably, no matter what the point at which we find ourselves, and the aptitude to relate any other point to the centre once we have established our mind in it.

Wisdom, in its highest acceptation, is the inexpugnable occupation of the centre of things by the purified soul; but philosophy, in its legitimate acceptation, is the science of the roads which lead to Wisdom, and the formation which enables the soul to traverse those roads. It is more true of this philosophy than of any other that its spirit needs not only to be described, but still more to be accepted, willed and obeyed, before it can be truly known. To know how the summit of Alvernia is reached, it is not enough to be able to rattle off a description of all the roads that lead to the summit; rather we must choose one of these roads and set our foot upon it with the firm resolution to travel it to the end. The closer we approach the interior dispositions that St. Bonaventure demands of his reader, the better we shall understand the sense of the formulas he employs and the root reason of the ways he chooses.

It may be added that, for the man who is able to bring these dispositions to life in himself in their perfect form, the universe and the soul are immediately ordered into a totally unified system.

Let us begin with the centre, which is Christ; we shall immediately find that we can enter into the right relation with everything, starting from him; and, likewise, if we start from any other thing we shall be brought back to him. Being can be conceived only as either absolute or contingent; contingent being implies the existence of absolute being; and absolute being—since it contains by definition all the conditions required in order to be—must necessarily be of itself, conformed to itself and for itself; in other words, absolute being cannot be sufficient unto itself without at the same time being its own original cause, its own exemplar cause, and its own final cause.

Now, it is clear that within such a substance the origin holds the place of principle; the exemplar, of means; the final cause, as its name indi-

278 READINGS IN ANCIENT AND MEDIEVAL PHILOSOPHY

cates, of end; and as it likewise appears that the Father is the Principle and the Holy Spirit the End, it follows of necessity that the Son is the Means. Thus the Father is the original foundation, the Holy Spirit the completion, and the Son the mental word; and it is because he is the eternal truth, at once principle of being and of knowing, that we, in our turn, find ourselves faced with an intelligible to be known and an immutable rule whereby to judge it. The measure of God himself, the measure of things, the measure of knowledge, the Word, is the central point at which the metaphysician must take his stand, and if we have placed exemplarism at the centre of metaphysics, the reason is that the Exemplar himself is, as it were, at the centre of God.

Let us now put ourselves in the position of the physicist who defines the principles of nature rather than the rules in virtue of which we judge it. As the heart is the centre of the microcosm, the source from which the vital spirits spread outwards into the body through the arteries, and the animal spirits through the veins; as the sun is the centre of the macrocosm, the source of heat and of all the kinds of generation that take place in the world, so the Word became the centre of the universe by being made flesh and dwelling among us. We know that he is also the means whereby the soul is united with God in ecstasy during this life, and the theologian can very readily show that he is also the means of eternal beatification: *Agnus in medio aquarum est Filius Dei, Filius dico, qui est media persona a qua omnis beatitudo.* To have chosen, once for all, such a centre of reference, and never to admit any other centre—this cannot fail to have a profound influence not only upon the general economy of such a doctrine, but also upon its smallest details; to forget this central fact is to lose comprehension of the whole system.

In relation to such a centre man can see both his origin and his goal, and so arrives at the recognition that he has a history. He sees his life as a passage between a beginning and a conclusion; and this certitude is capital—its effect upon his other certitudes is such that it completely transforms them. Not only has the life of man a history; the universe as a whole has a history; and in this case, too, the man who grasps the truth realizes that he can never again think as if he knew it not. You cannot reason about a universe whose astral revolutions are counted, are, each one of them, events willed by God and chosen by Providence, as you would about a universe whose essential facts would be exactly what they are even if it had existed from all eternity. And to make it more impossible still to forget this truth the history of the universe is seen by us as a drama in which we have a part, a drama whose conclusion, after all digressions and divagations, must be our beatitude or misery for all eternity.

Once the soul has come to awareness of this terrifying truth, it can never again forget it; nor can the soul ever again think of anything at all save as this truth bears upon it. All that it knows, all that it feels, all that it wills, lies under the illumination of this tragic certitude. Where the Aristotelian merely saw the satisfying of curiosity, the Christian sees the deciding of a destiny. St. Bonaventure is profoundly penetrated with this sense of high tragedy: it is this that confers upon his doctrine its character of tension, and upon the expressions he uses the poignancy we feel in them. He thinks, precisely because it is for him a problem of eternal life or death to know what one *must* think; he trembles at the mere imagined possibility that he might, in a moment of distraction, lose sight of it. It is his agony to see that practically no one is thinking about it, and that man made by a God, remade by the blood of a God, is ever busy at his own unmaking—as if all that can choose between nothingness and being did, in blind folly, choose nothingness. The intellect must be an instrument of salvation and nothing beside. In so far as it puts Christ at the centre of our history, as he is at the centre of universal history, it must ever remember that on nothing whatsoever can a Christian think as he would if he were not a Christian.

Let us consider the very idea of philosophy. It cannot begin without Christ, for he is its object, and it cannot attain completion without Christ, for he is its end. Thus, it has a choice between systematically condemning itself to error, or taking count of facts which henceforth totally inform it. The Christian philosopher knows, to begin with, that his faculties of knowing have not a coefficient of value of their own; as a consequence he knows that the evidences of things will be more or less easily accessible to him according to the point of perfection at which he himself is. The intellect, in short, thinks more or less well according as the soul is more or less completely purified of its stains; and one could not treat an argument, such as St. Anselm's proof of the existence of God from the idea of the perfect, as if its acceptance depended solely upon the definition of the terms which compose it, or upon their comprehension by any intelligence at all. Man only understands what he deserves to understand, and the same argument which seems a sophism to a materialist intellect may seem evident to that same intellect once it has been stripped clean, purified, and turned towards God.

For a reason of the same sort the Christian philosopher will realize that the expression of natural phenomena—and particularly of their metaphysical conditions—cannot be the same in his eyes as they would be if he left God out. Of two possible conclusions, of which one attributes more to nature or free will and less to God, while the other attributes more to God at the expense of nature or free will, he will always choose the second provided only that it does not contradict either free will or nature. He would rather find himself in error through humility than risk a sin of pride; for there is no great harm in underrating one's self, whereas it is a crime to underrate God.

The repercussions of such a principle in such a system as St. Bonaventure's are of necessity multiplied so that no part of his system is unaffected by them. *It is dangerous to attribute to the creature that which*

underrate oneself

belongs to God. If one reflects upon it, that is why the world could not be eternal, why the angelic substances could not be devoid of matter, why form could not be drawn from matter without pre-existent seminal reasons, why human knowledge could not find any absolute foundation without that illumination which is the source of necessity and certitude, why philosophy could not succeed without the help of grace, why nature must remain incomplete without the immediate and special concurrence of God. The doctrinal conservatism of St. Bonaventure and his anxiety in face of the danger to faith from innovators in philosophy or religion are but the most general manifestation of this fundamental tendency: one cannot place God in the centre of thought without taking account of his presence every time one thinks, and the Christian soul judges of things only in relation to God.

Let us now see what is the condition of such a soul when it has achieved completely what is thus proper to it. Filled with a sense of the intellectual and moral wretchedness in which it is, it comes to understand the true cause of its state when it finds in Scripture the story of man's fall. From that moment it knows that there is nothing healthy in itself, that the task of its whole life must necessarily be to find healing from its sickness and cleansing from the stain which infects it, and by infecting it contaminates the whole universe.

From this comes that atoning discipline of the Christian life in its most perfect form—Franciscan poverty giving life to the intellect, with the eradication of the passions, interior unification, and ecstasy for its crown.

The flaw is not annulled, but a watchful discipline, progressively stabilizing the human soul in its regained perfection, maintains in it and in things the divine order which has now been restored by the concurrence of grace and freedom.

The wayfaring man thus finds himself separated from God who is to be his reward; his intellect, even made perfect, cannot attain the face-to-face vision which would fix it once for all upon its object. This is the secret of that incessant movement which draws the mind from one object to another without any object ever being able, or even seriously looking as though it would be able, to hold the mind finally. But an intellect, even condemned to move, can at least regulate its movement and settle, once for all, the objects upon which it may rightly look. This, in one word, is the Christian soul in its state of perfection.

Hierarchically arranged, reaching out to God and rightly ordered to him, it moves back and forth according to its own individual, personal rhythm, between the ecstatic contact with God by love and the intellectual contemplation of God in the exterior or interior mirrors which reflect him. Too rarely for its liking, and for a few too short moments, it is in immediate contact with its Good; but even when that direct contact is broken the soul is charged with new desires and new energies driving it to seek, again and again, the contact it has lost.

St. Bonaventure sees the soul illumined by grace turning majestically, like a sun which can never fix its light in one single point nor cease its revolving, but which yet follows an ordered course as if the twelve houses of the heaven it traverses were the only places worthy of its passage.

An intellect ill-disciplined lets itself be drawn in unrelated directions by a movement leading it nowhere; the hierarchized intellect, on the other hand, turns about God; it has fixed for ever the spiritual constellations which make its zodiac and, having fixed them, it passes ceaselessly from one of its houses to another without ever leaving the luminous orbit which they constitute. What are these signs? We know them already, for they are necessarily the same objects upon which along with St. Bonaventure we have concentrated the effort of our philosophic reflection, plus certain others upon which rational reflection can take no hold, but which the soul illumined by grace can contemplate to its own advantage: the consideration of corporeal beings, then of spiritual substances; the consideration of the ways of knowledge conceived by the mind; of the moral virtues, then of the laws instituted by God; of the divine graces which give the soul its hierarchy, of the unsearchable judgments of God, of his mercies likewise which are as incomprehensible; of the merits which will be rewarded, and of their rewards; of the sequence of times revealed by Scripture and the order that the soul finds in them; of the eternal reasons, finally, which bring this contemplation to its term in God and unite it with the first sign of the mental zodiac—the beings of which these exemplars are the models. Thus, ever moving on the orbit proper to it, the contemplative soul ever finds itself in one or other of these signs, yet never stays in any.

Now, it follows of necessity that such a transformation of the intellect involves a correlative transformation of the universe. Natural science claims to give the universe its true meaning by multiplying to infinity individual phenomena and the theories which account for them; Christian philosophy, on the other hand, gives the universe its true meaning by subordinating it to its true end, which is to show forth God to man, and to lead man to God. For one who never loses sight of the goal of beatitude, this world can have no other *raison d'être* than to give us a foretaste of what is to come. Ceaselessly St. Bonaventure expressed this thought in every possible form; but the expression which is most striking in its Franciscan homeliness, he found when he defined man's task as the organization of our earthly exile into a sort of suburb of the heavenly Kingdom, in such wise that every day we might savor in advance something of the eternal beatitude: *Si haec caelestia gaudia jugiter in mente teneres, de hoc exilio quoddam suburbiam caelestis regni construeres, in quo illam aeternam dulcedinem quotidie spiritualiter praelibando degustares.*

If we give this formula its fullest meaning, and if further we suppose an intellect infinitely subtle and flexible given wholly to its realization, we shall see how naturally it implies the analogical universe of St. Bonaventure with its correspondences and its proportions founded in the very essence of things, penetrated through and through, and strengthened by the influx of light—that noblest analogy of the spirit in the world of bodies. Whether they concern the soul or things, all the doctrines that we have in turn examined are seen to issue from one sole and single fundamental preoccupation; creatures are what they ought to be in themselves in the exact measure in which they are what they ought to be for God.

The argument usually used to thrust St. Bonaventure outside the frontiers of the history of philosophy consists simply in dubbing him a mystic; and it is precisely to this argument that we appeal to bring him once more within that history. St. Bonaventure is essentially a mystic; but he is at the same time a philosopher, because he conceived the project of systematizing knowledge and being in terms of mysticism; indeed he is a great philosopher because, like all great philosophers, he followed out his idea to its conclusion in a real synthesis. If the mystical feeling is to be considered as an integral part of human nature, the content of the philosophy of mysticism may very well evolve because our representation of the universe evolves; but never will any doctrine do more complete justice to the experiences which are the eternal source of mysticism, nor be more comprehensive or more systematically organized than St. Bonaventure's; and if, as is still more evident, mysticism forms an integral part of the Christian life, no doctrinal synthesis will ever be found in which the aspirations of Christian mysticism receive a more abundant satisfaction. You might complain that there is too much mysticism in Bonaventure's doctrine; you can never say that there is not enough, for mysticism permeates the whole. But in permeating the whole it systematizes the whole, and it is this which confers upon this doctrine such richness in such unity.

The philosophy of St. Bonaventure is in this sense final: the profound and characteristic tendency of mediaeval Augustinianism was to place the mystical element of the doctrine in the foreground, subordinating all the rest; and with St. Bonaventure this tendency for the first time achieved full expression. The desire for ecstasy and the knowledge of things were two elements sustaining and enriching each other: and in Bonaventure they are finally developed in a vast structure into which is built the totality of human experience as it had been inherited by philosophy—a doctrine of knowledge, a theory of the metaphysical principles of nature, above all, a rule of action, and all this penetrated, sustained, held in unity by an inspiration so perfectly one that the mind rises from the humblest operations upon material objects to the highest inpourings of grace without the faintest breach in the continuity of its movement.

This undoubtedly is its gravest fault in the eyes of many of our contemporaries. Philosophy must treat of nature; mysticism can treat only of grace, and is, therefore, the business of none but the theologian. But we should be clear, to begin with, as to the meaning of the word "nature." We can, of course, use this word to mean the collection of facts given to us through the senses, with an *a priori* supposition that they contain within themselves the sufficient reason of their being and their own interpretation. In this sense the notion of the transcendent or the supernatural is evidently meaningless: but we may well ask whether the notion of philosophy itself is not equally meaningless. All that is, is in nature, and is therefore natural—but only if the idea of the supernatural, the desire and the need for the supernatural, are not an integral part of nature: only if the exigency of the thing excluded is not engraved in the very substance of that from which it is excluded; only if we ignore, and indeed specially train ourselves to ignore, those questions which are ever springing up in the depths of the human heart, questions which we repress in the name of that very nature which asks them so insistently. All is as if man and things contained virtually in themselves the sufficient reason of what they are; a being can always be explained by another being, and the totality of being would be self-explanatory if only the totality were given to us. The eternal silence of the infinite spaces no longer terrifies us; we are grown deaf to the appeals which still spring up when we least expect them from the depths of the human soul. Nothing remains but physics and in consequence all that is belongs to science alone; the radical elimination of the transcendent is the elimination of all metaphysics and hence of all knowledge that philosophy can call its own.

But there is another point of view. According to it Nature is to be defined as the totality of what is given to the mind, without any *a priori* exclusion of the conditions it requires in order to be understood. This is the true beginning of metaphysics and thus the only order of speculation in which it is possible to assign a specific content to philosophy; it is the science of the conditions required by, but not contained within, the totality of that which is given. But this inevitably implies the transcendent, and this as inevitably the supernatural. This transcendent—which the formula of pure naturalism excludes by definition—is no longer held to be a thing whose whole essence consists in its inability to form part of any experience: and its opposition to nature is no longer that of a term to its contradictory; the supernatural thus becomes an experience that we have not yet had, temporarily in eclipse, because nature itself is in darkness. It is not yet a datum but it will be one. It may even be said in a certain sense that if it is not yet a datum, at any rate its place is marked by signs so clear that an integral empiricism has no right to ignore it.

But from this point also the supernatural may be presented to philosophic reflection in a twofold aspect. Either it may be supposed that its latent presence acts only to conserve and move beings in their proper nature in such a way that it remains possible to make a separate description of their nature as science knows it, omitting the economy of the divine influences sustaining it and making its existence possible; this is St. Thomas' method. Or, on the other hand, it may be supposed that the supernatural perfects beings in their own nature so that it perpetually completes them and reveals them to themselves, and that it is impossible to describe them in themselves without recourse to it; and this is the method of St. Bonaventure. This is why for all that his doctrine remains a philosophy, it yet has the special quality we feel in it, and differs from other metaphysical systems by what is deepest in it.

If, in fact, it is the transcendent and the supernatural which constitute the very heart of the real, and if the real cries out this truth to us unceasingly by its manifold insufficiencies, the highest task of metaphysics must be the reintegration in the economy of nature of all the supernatural that it requires to become intelligible to us. Like all true philosophies St. Bonaventure's starts from experience; it thrusts its roots down to the furthest depths of our insufficiency and the insufficiency of things; but it sees this insufficiency only to see beyond it: for the evil presupposes that there is a remedy unless we are to grant that the universe is meaningless and evil incurable. Thus philosophy may either despair of things and of itself, or seek the explanation of the universe where it is to be found; but it cannot choose this latter part unless it sees, as the essential object of its effort, the discovery and the elaboration of that element of the divine implied by nature.

This is precisely the work St. Bonaventure set himself to accomplish. With a delicate logic which in the extent of its exigencies will never be surpassed, he develops the complete philosophy of that supernatural apart from which nature and man would remain insoluble enigmas. This is the glory that shall not be taken from him. In his powerful, complex philosophy knowledge enlightens charity and is fed by it. Paris does not destroy Assisi, and Assisi does not reject Paris. But if the sombre plaint of Jacopone da Todi here loses its point, it is because the doctor comes down from his professorial chair and goes to meditate upon Alvernia. Upon the summit of Alvernia and not on the slopes of the hill of St. Genevieve, he sought to fly in the track of the seraph with the six wings; and if he owed his knowledge to the University of Paris, it was in the soul of St. Francis that he found his inspiration.

Hence St. Bonaventure's doctrine marks for us the culminating point of Christian mysticism and constitutes the completest synthesis it has ever achieved. Thus it must be clear that it can never be properly comparable in any point with the doctrine of St. Thomas Aquinas. Obviously it would be absurd to deny their fundamental agreement. They are both Christian philosophies and every threat to the faith finds them united against it. As against pantheism, both of them teach creation from nothing and maintain that the gulf is infinite between absolute

Being and contingent. As against ontologism, both deny explicitly that God can be seen at all by the human mind in this life, and *a fortiori* they deny that habitual knowledge of God which ontologism attributes to us. As against fideism, they both set the most thorough effort of the intellect to prove the existence of God and interpret the data of faith. As against rationalism, both coordinate the effort of the intellect with the act of faith and maintain the beneficent influence of the habit of faith upon the operations of the intellect.

The agreement between them is deep-lying, indestructibly proclaimed by tradition, which has submitted it to the test of the centuries: an agreement such that no one even in the time of the worst doctrinal conflicts has called it in question. But if these two philosophies are equally Christian, in that they equally satisfy the requirements of revealed doctrine, they remain none the less two philosophies. That is why, in 1588 Sixtus V proclaimed, and in 1879 Leo XIII repeated, that both men were involved in the construction of the Scholastic synthesis of the Middle Ages and that today both men must be seen as representing it: *duae olivae et duo candelabra in domo Dei lucentia.*

The attempts sometimes made by their interpreters to transform their fundamental agreement into an identity of content are from the start futile and doomed to fail. For it is clear that since the two doctrines are ordered from different starting points, they will never envisage the same problems in the same aspect, and therefore one will never answer the precise question that the other asks. The philosophy of St. Thomas and the philosophy of St. Bonaventure are complementary, as the two most comprehensive interpretations of the universe as seen by Christians, and it is because they are complementary that they never either conflict or coincide.

38

FORMAL AND MODAL DISTINCTIONS IN DUNS SCOTUS [1]

I. THE FORMAL DISTINCTION

THIS approach to the formal distinction indicates that one of its greatest attractions for Scotus lay in the fact that it provided an objective basis for our real concepts. And the concepts he had in mind were not merely those of genus and specific difference, but what is of particular interest for us, the concepts of being and its attri-

[1] [From Allan Wolter, O.F.M., *The Transcendentals and Their Function in the Metaphysics of Duns Scotus* (St. Bonaventure, N. Y.: The Franciscan Institute, 1946), pp. 21-30, with omission of the notes. Reprinted by permission.]

butes as well as those relative attributes in God and creatures which play such an important part in metaphysics as a theologic. "It seems necessary to posit this distinction in other things, for example, in being and its attributes, in the relation and its foundation in God and creatures."

This formal distinction is something less than a real physical distinction *(realis simpliciter)* which exists between two or more physical entities *(inter rem et rem)*. At the same time it is not a mere distinction created by the mind *(distinctio rationis)*. It is real in the sense that the mind discovers it but does not project it into reality *(realis secundum quid)*. It exists between *rationes reales* or *formalitates,* and not between *res et res.*

The properties of these *formalitates* might be summed up as follows:

1. The formality is not a distinct physical thing, but a positive something that is somehow less than a thing. It is the *ratio objectiva* of a distinct formal concept.

2. Each formality has its own proper quiddity or entity. Though the simplicity of the formality may forbid a strict metaphysical definition, if formalities could be defined, their definitions would not be simply synonymous but would differ essentially.

3. Since these formalities do not have a distinct existence, but rather exist by the existence of the thing, they are inseparable even by the power of God. Thus, while God could annihilate the rational soul, or could create an irrational soul, he could not separate "sensitivity" or "rationality" from the human soul. The formality consequently is not the product of a distinct physical causality over and above the causality which brings the thing as a whole into existence. For these perfections of formalities are *unitive contentae,* in the sense that they constitute one indivisible *res.*

4. Just as we may speak of a real distinction between the whole and its parts, so we may speak of a formal distinction between the thing as a whole and the single formalities. Such a distinction is called inadequate. Such an inadequate formal distinction exists, for instance, between "animality" and "sensitivity", for the former includes the latter.

II. THE MODAL DISTINCTION

Besides the strict formal distinction existing between two or more formalities, Scotus introduces a similar distinction between a formality and its intrinsic mode. Such, for instance, is the distinction between intelligence and the modality of finiteness in man, or between any divine perfection, like wisdom and its mode of infinity. Scotists dispute whether this so-called *distinctio formalis modalis* is really a distinction *a parte rei* or merely a virtual or mental distinction, with an extrinsic foundation in things. While reasons for both interpretations may be found, the author is inclined to believe that Scotus regarded it as a distinction *a parte rei* but less than the strict formal distinction. Even within the limits of the strict formal distinction, Scotus admits of various gradations. The line between the least of the formal distinctions and this "modal" distinction is easily crossed, if such a line exists at all.

The modal distinction seems to be *a parte rei,* for Scotus refers to it as a *distinctio in re* and regards it as the foundation for those real, though imperfect, concepts which are predicable univocally of God and creatures. The assertion that such notions as being, wisdom, free will, are real concepts predicable of God gives rise to the same problem as did the genus and specific difference. "How can the concept which is common to God and creatures be considered real unless it be abstracted from some reality of the same kind?" The perfection and its intrinsic mode, Scotus answers, are not so identical that we cannot conceive the perfection without the mode. In other words, the perfection and its mode are not perfectly identical—not indeed in the sense that there is any possibility of separating the two (real distinction), nor even in the sense that both the perfection and the mode are each capable of terminating a distinct and proper concept (strict formal distinction), but only to the extent that the objective reality signified by a concept which includes the mode is not precisely the same as that which is signified by a concept which does not include the mode. Such a distinction in the thing suffices to safeguard the reality of those imperfect and common concepts predicable of God and creatures.

This is not yet a strict formal distinction because an intrinsic mode is not a formality in its own right. Such a mode is essentially a qualification. It includes both in thought and in definition the notion of the subject of which it is the mode, even though the subject enters the definition *ek prostheseōs,* as Aristotle put it. The mode consequently is incapable of terminating a distinct and proper concept. With the perfection which it modifies, the case is slightly different. It can be conceived without including the modality at all. But such a concept is imperfect. It does not give the full perfection of the formality in question. For instance, when we conceive God as a being, or as wise, we are using notions that are common to creatures. Yet these perfections as they actually exist in God are formally infinite. So much so that if we were gifted with the intuitive knowledge of the blessed in heaven, we should not perceive the perfection of wisdom, for instance, and the modality of infinity as two distinct formal objects but only as one.

When the perfection is conceived together with its mode, the concept is said to be proper; conceived without its mode, the concept is imperfect and common. Where the strict formal distinction obtains, two distinct formal objects are to be had. Each is capable of terminating a proper concept. Thus God's will is not proper to his intellect, nor vice versa in the sense that the modality of infinity is proper to his intellect or to his will. Even the intuitive knowledge of the blessed will not erase the formal difference of the two.

III. THE "NATURA COMMUNIS"

Scotus posits some kind of formal, or at least modal, distinction *a parte rei* between being and its transcendentals, between the various metaphysical grades of being, between the metaphysical essence and its properties, and in the realm of psychology between the faculties of the soul and the soul itself, besides the theological applications—which in Scotus' eyes—are its primary justification.

Over and above these instances, Scotus makes a very important application of the formal distinction in his theory of the *natura communis.* It is this same tendency to find an objective basis for our concepts that prompted Scotus to postulate as formally distinct from the individuating difference or *haecceitas,* a common nature *(natura communis)* which serves as the *fundamentum in re* for the universal concept. In this sense there is a definite connection between the doctrine of the formal distinction and the *natura communis.*

Scotus could not accept without reservation the Aristotelian dictum, *Intellectus est universalium, sensus singularium.* As a Christian metaphysician, looking forward someday to the beatific vision, he had to qualify it substantially. Granting that singularity *qua* singularity is not intelligible to our intellect in its present state, it is intelligible as such, and will be known one day by our intellect. Even in this life we know singular natures and know that they are singular. We do not perceive the precise formal reason why they are singulars.

For this reason all our clear and distinct concepts, in terms of which we formulate our definitions of the nature and essence of things, are only partial conceptions. They give us not the concrete individual in its full intelligibility, but only the common elements—those *rationes* which it has in common or could have in common with other individuals. And to safeguard the objectivity of these notions upon which all scientific knowledge is based, Scotus postulated the *natura communis.* Formally distinct from its principle of individuation, endowed with its own proper unity which is somehow less than numerical unity, this *natura communis,* as actualized in concrete individual things, forms the immediate and proper object of the *conceptus realis.*

Applying these distinctions to the transcendentals, it can be said that, according to Scotus, corresponding to each distinct transcendental notion is some real perfection or mode. While such realities or perfections cannot be separated physically from one another but are separable only in thought, it must be admitted that, prior to any operation of the mind, that phase of reality which a mind could grasp by real though partial knowledge is not formally identical *a parte rei* with the remaining reality which it fails to grasp. Such a distinction can be called real only *secundum quid.* As such, it does not imply any imperfection or composition, yet it suffices to guarantee the reality of the metaphysical order.

The formal and modal distinction is not easy to grasp. It raises many difficulties which neither Scotus nor his followers fully solved. Perhaps the most intelligible and still fairly accurate notion of a "formality" is to consider it as the objective basis of a concept which, though real, does not represent the whole intelligible content of the physical entity, but a part only.

While it is possible to form distinct real concepts only where some sort of formal non-identity exists *a parte rei,* Scotus nowhere implies that the mind cannot grasp many such "formalities" in one and the same simple concept. Certainly this is possible for God and also for a creature gifted with intuitive vision. But even with such knowledge, the human intellect would recognize, for instance, that God's intelligence is not formally identical with his free will, or that the intelligibility of the divine essence is not formally identical with its appetibility, and so on. In a word, the mind would recognize that a distinct real concept of one such perfection without the other is possible.

The formal distinction, in short, is not due solely to the imperfection of our knowledge, though the possibility of separating in thought such non-identical perfections *a parte rei* instead of grasping them *in uno actu,* as God does, is due to the imperfection of our created minds.

39

SCOTUS ON THE NATURE OF MAN'S KNOWLEDGE OF GOD [1]

A. TRANSLATOR'S INTRODUCTION

THOUGH taken from Scotus' greatest theological work, the *Oxford Commentary on the Sentences of Peter Lombard,* or as it was called in the Middle Ages, the *Ordinatio Scoti,* the present question is a purely philosophical discussion. Can the human mind by its natural powers, unaided by any revelation, form an idea of God? And if it can, what is the nature of this knowledge?

As to its form, the question is developed in typical scholastic fashion. It opens with a *Pro et Contra,* which is followed by the *corpus* or body of the discussion and concludes with a solution of the arguments in the

---

[1] [From John Duns Scotus, "On the Nature of Man's Knowledge of God," *The Review of Metaphysics,* vol. 1 (1947-48), pp. 4-34, with omission of notes. Translated with an Introduction by Allan Wolter, O.F.M., from Scotus' *Opus Oxoniense,* I, d. 3, q. 1. Reprinted by permission.]

Pro et Contra. In the late thirteenth and fourteenth centuries this form underwent certain modifications. For one thing, the *corpus* was greatly enlarged to include a critical exposition of current solutions other than the author's own. In the present Question of Scotus only one such solution is advanced, that of the great secular master at the University of Paris, Henry of Ghent. Another common practice, particularly with Scotus, is to group several related questions about a common *corpus*. The solutions to the arguments of the *Pro et Contra* of the respective questions are then bunched together at the end or, again, they may be inserted in the *corpus* immediately after the discussion of some point pertinent to that particular question. At times a very complicated form results. The present Question, for instance, is joined to a second Question occasioned by the position of Henry:—Is God the primary object known in this life by natural means? Only those sections pertaining to the first Question, however, have been translated and are presented as a whole.

Scanning the contents briefly, we note that Scotus in his preliminary remarks rejects a number of distinctions of pre-scholastic and Scholastic origin that were customarily introduced into a discussion on the nature of our knowledge of God. One, for instance, is the oft-quoted saying of Pseudo-Dionysius that we do not know what God is; we know only what he is not. This *docta ignorantia* was exaggerated by many. Scotus Erigena, for instance suggests that perhaps it might be more correct to say that God is not good, true, just and so on, since any term or concept we might derive from the universe of creatures is so radically inadequate to express what he is, that it could more truly be denied of God than affirmed of Him. Duns Scotus reminds us that this way of speaking cannot be taken too seriously. If our knowledge is purely negative, it is no knowledge of God at all. Similarly other distinctions are rejected, either because they are not to the point or because they will not stand up beneath the rigor of logical analysis. Such are, for instance, the assertion that we can know that God exists without knowing what he is, or that we know that the proposition, "God exists," is true, but we know nothing of God himself or of his existence as such.

Scotus develops his positive doctrine from an Aristotelian viewpoint, in the form of five propositions or statements. The tenets of Henry of Ghent, still fresh in the minds of Parisian students, provide the Augustinian background of contrast.

Scotus, in his *first proposition,* declares that God is not merely conceived as an hypostatized attribute such as "the Wise," "the Good," "the Just," and so on, as the Ghentian master suggests. Our concepts tell us something of what he is. Or to put it in the language of grammar, we describe God not merely with adjectives but also with nouns. Before we can refer to God as "wise," we must know him as "something" or "someone," as a "being," a "thing," etc. Just as an adjective modifies a noun, so must an attribute or property be conceived as a modification of some subject. And consequently we must have a previous knowledge of the subject itself. Such a concept will be a quidditative notion, since it represents an answer to the question: What is God? (*Quid est*), and not merely, What *kind* of being is he? (*Quale est*).

Due to his theory of the analogy of being, Henry made complicated distinctions which, to Scotus, were equivalent to denying the possibility of any true quidditative knowledge of God from the starting point of creatures. It is this theory of "pure" analogy, which Scotus attacks in his *second proposition*. Though in deference to the weight of authority against him Scotus presents his theory as merely probable, we can hardly doubt that he was convinced of its basic correctness. Apparently he was one of the first, if not the first, to realize what implications an Aristotelian theory of knowledge might have upon the Platonic theory of the analogy of being. To deny the possibility of abstracting a positive notion from creatures that applies univocally to God leaves but two alternatives. Either accept agnosticism or postulate some distinct source of our proper concepts of God such as the innatism of Descartes or the illuminationism of Augustine.

In his *third proposition* Scotus denies that any direct or intuitive knowledge of God's essence is natural to man. His reason is this. God is not a natural object of intuition for any created intellect. Under this aspect, he is a purely voluntary object. He does not elaborate on this argument, though he does develop it elsewhere. This argument has several interesting aspects. Not only does it represent an attempt to destroy ontologism as its very root, but it reveals an interesting characteristic of Scotus' whole philosophy of the creature-God relation. Creatures are radically contingent; God is the only necessary being. Between a necessary and contingent being no truly "natural" relationship can arise, that is, one which follows necessarily from the nature of the two related beings. All such relations, being outside and distinct from God, are as radically contingent as created intellect itself. Hence all such relations depend ultimately on the will of a God who creates contingently. For this reason, even granting that God has created a being with intellectual powers, no direct or natural causal relation between his essence as an object of intuition and the created intellect can arise. A voluntary decree on his part is required. For this reason, the "beatific vision" essentially exceeds the powers of any natural causes.

Scotus' *fourth and fifth propositions* deal with the nature of our proper concepts of God. Proper concepts are those which apply exclusively to God, such as "infinite being," "highest goodness," and the like. In the first of the two, Scotus emphasizes that "infinite" is not a specific difference or an attribute in any true sense of the term. Rather it is an intrinsic mode, expressing something that pertains to the formal character of being as found in God. For "being," "truth," "goodness," and the like, are formally and intrinsically infinite. In creatures, however, such perfections are finite. Yet this radical difference between God and creatures does not prevent us from abstracting a common, *imperfect,* concept which prescinds from the intrinsic modes of both God and creature and which is univocally predicable of both. Because "infinity" is intrinsic to all of God's perfections, our concept "infinite being" is simpler than the concept "good being," since, according to Scotus, goodness and being are not formally identical.

His fifth proposition explains how proper notions of God are formed. Presupposing a theory of univocation, Scotus indicates how such univocal elements as "cause," "being," "good," "act," and so on, can be used as so many *tesserae* to form a mosaic picture of God. The imperfections of creatures may also be negated, and thus we can form a concept of a being that is not finite (infinite being). This notion of "infinite" is not the positive notion of Descartes, Bonaventure, and the Augustinian illuminationists in general. These men could admit such a positive notion of infinity, since they had a distinct source of this knowledge. With Scotus, however, all knowledge must be abstracted through the senses, and this theory of knowledge automatically commits him to accept a negative concept of God's most positive perfection.

B. THE TEXT OF DUNS SCOTUS' QUESTION

Can God Be Known in This Life Through Natural Means?

I argue that he cannot:

Arg. I "Sense images are related to the intellect in the same way that sense objects are related to the senses." Consequntly, the intellect is unable to grasp anything whose sense image cannot be known by the senses. But of God there is no sense image; therefore, God cannot be known by natural means.

Arg. II "As the eyes of bats are to the blaze of day, so is the reason in our soul to the things which are by nature most evident of all." But if it is impossible to know such things, it is impossible to know God.

Arg. III "The infinite as infinite is unknowable." "It is not possible to know things that are infinite [in number]." Therefore, neither can the "Infinite Being" be known, since an infinite number and an Infinite Being would seem to be equally disproportionate to our intellect; for an Infinite Being exceeds the powers of our intellect in the same measure, or certainly to no less a degree, than does the infinite in number, because "infinity" is in both "Infinite Being" and "infinite in number."

Arg. IV "No matter how far our mind may have progressed in the contemplation of God, it does not attain to what he is, but to what is beneath him."

To the contrary:

Arg. I "Metaphysics is a theology of God," therefore, etc.

Arg. II Moreover, Aristotle places the happiness of man in the actual possession of such knowledge, that is to say, in the actual speculation about the separate substances.[2]

Preliminary Observations

In this first question there is no need to make the distinction that we cannot know what God is; we can know only what he is not. For every denial is intelligible only in terms of some affirmation. It is also clear that we can know negations of God only by means of affirmations; for if we deny anything of God, it is because we wish to do away with something inconsistent with what we have already affirmed. Thus, we deny composition of God only because we have attributed simplicity or something else to him.

Neither are pure negations the object of our greatest love.

Furthermore, if something is negated, either the negation is considered simply in itself or as predicated of something. If a negation, such as "not stone," is considered simply in itself, it is as characteristic of "nothing" as it is of God, for a pure negation is predicated of both "being" and "nonbeing." Consequently, what we know through such a negation is no more God than it is a chimera or nothing at all. If "not stone" is understood as modifying something, then I ask whether the underlying notion of which the negation is understood to be true is an affirmative or a negative notion. If it is negative, I inquire as I did before. Either the negation is conceived simply in itself or as predicated of something. If the first be true, then the negation applies to "nothing" as well as to God. If it is conceived as predicated of something, then I argue as before. And no matter how far we proceed with negations, either what we know is no more God than "nothing" is, or we will arrive at some affirmative concept which is the first concept of all.

Neither is there any need to distinguish between a knowledge of his existence and a knowledge of his essence, for I intend to seek a simple concept of which existence may be affirmed or denied by a judgment of the intellect. For I never know anything to exist, unless I first have some concept of that of which existence is affirmed. And this is what we seek here.

There is no need to distinguish in regard to his existence between the question of the truth of the proposition and the question of the existence of God. For, before there can be any question of the truth of a proposition wherein existence is predicated of a subject, it is necessary first of all to conceive the terms of this proposition. Now the question is this, Is it possible to have a concept of the subject [of this proposition "God exists"] by natural means?

---

2 [The sentences quoted in these arguments are taken from Aristotle, except for Argument IV, which is drawn from St. Gregory the Great.]

Neither is there any point in distinguishing between a natural and a supernatural concept, because we are interested here only in the former.

And speaking of the natural, there is no need to distinguish between "nature, absolutely speaking" and "nature, in our present state," for we are interested only in the latter.

Neither is there any point in distinguishing between knowing God in himself and knowing God in a creature. For if our knowledge comes through a creature, in the sense that the reasoning process begins with what can be known from a creature, then I ask, What do we know at the conclusion of this process? If it is God himself, then I have what I seek, for I am looking for a concept of God himself. If it is not God, but a creature, then the beginning and conclusion of the reasoning process are identical, and therefore I have no knowledge of God at all.

The meaning of the question then is this: Is it possible by natural means for someone in this present life to have a concept wherein God is conceived?

The Opinion of Henry of Ghent

A certain teacher answers the question in this way. From the standpoint of the object known, we can distinguish: *a*) a knowledge of a thing through the thing itself, *b*) a knowledge of the thing through something incidental to it, *c*) a knowledge of the thing in particular, and *d*) a knowledge of the thing in general.

1. In reality, there is no knowledge of God *through something incidental to him,* for whatever is known of God, is God himself. Nevertheless, we do know what God is in a *quasi-incidental* manner, when we know some one of his attributes. Hence Damascene says that the attributes "do not bespeak the nature of God, but something about the nature."

2. God is also known *in a general way,* that is, through some universal attribute. Not indeed that any attribute, universal by way of predication, is affirmed of him in whom nothing is universal, for his essence is singular of its very nature. He is known, however, in a "universal" that is analogically common to himself and to a creature. This universal is conceived by us as though it were one notion, because of the close resemblance of the concepts it contains, although the latter in reality are diverse.

3. God is not known *in particular* from creatures, because a creature bears only a foreign likeness to him, since it resembles him only in those attributes which do not constitute him as this particular nature. Now since one thing can be known through another only by reason of the similarity existing between the two, it follows that God is not known in particular through creatures.

Furthermore, there are three ways in which we may have a *general knowledge* of God: *a*) in a *most general way,* *b*) in a *less general way,* and *c*) in the *least general manner.*

a) The *most general* knowledge we have of God comprises three stages: (1) to know any being as "this being" is already to conceive God in a very indistinct way; for "being" is included, as it were, as part of the concept. This is the first step. (2) The second step consists in removing the "this" and conceiving simply "being." For "being," in so far as it is a concept and not simply a part of a concept, is already conceived as analogically common to God and creature. (3) We are in the third stage, if the concept of being which pertains to God is distinguished from the concept of being which pertains analogically to creatures; for instance, if God is conceived as a being that is *negatively* undetermined, that is, incapable of being determined, while a creature is conceived as a being that is *privatively* undetermined. In the first instance, "undetermined" is conceived abstractly as something self-subsistent and incapable of being participated, like a form that lacks all matter. In the second, "undetermined" is a universal abstracted from particulars and not actually shared by them.

b) In addition to these three stages of most general knowledge, God is grasped in a *less general* and more specific way, when any given attribute is conceived not in an unqualified manner as before, but as existing in the highest degree of perfection possible to such an attribute.

c) God is known in *the least general manner,* however, when the mind, on the basis of God's simplicity, identifies any of his other attributes with his primary attribute, namely, *Being* itself [*eius esse*].

Since nothing is simpler than God, he is known through a species, not in the proper sense of the term, but in a manner reminiscent of the operation of the estimative power. For just as in brutes, the estimative power, burrowing beneath the data of the senses, knows something not given by the senses, for instance, what is harmful and what is useful, so also the intellect by its acumen digs beneath the intellectual image of a creature, which represents nothing beyond the creature itself, and thus discovers by a species other than that derived from creatures, those things which pertain to and are predicated of God. And this procedure occurs in all three of the aforementioned ways of knowing God.

The Opinion of Duns Scotus

My answer to the first question is different. It will contradict on certain points the position mentioned above, for the reasons advanced in support of my position will establish the very opposite of the other.

First Statement

In the first place, I say that it is naturally possible to have not merely a concept in which God is known incidentally, as it were—for instance, under the aspect of some attribute—but also one in which he is conceived *essentially* and *quidditatively* [*per se et quidditative*].

This I prove as follows. According to him [Henry of Ghent], by conceiving "wise" we grasp a property or quasi-property which perfects the nature after the manner of a secondary act. In order to conceive "wise," therefore, it is necessary to have a conception of some prior quasi-subject, in which this quasi-property is understood to exist. And so we must look beyond all our ideas of attributes or quasi-attributes, in order to find some quidditative concept to which the former may be attributed. This other concept will be a quidditative notion of God [*conceptus quidditativus de Deo*], for our quest for a quasi-subject will not cease with any other kind of concept.

Second Statement

Though we do not advance this as a positive declaration, since it is not in accord with the common opinion, it can be said, secondly, that God is conceived not only in a concept analogous to the concept of a creature, i.e., one which is wholly other than that which is predicated of creatures, but even in some concept univocal to himself and to a creature.

And lest there be a dispute about the name "univocation," I designate that concept univocal which possesses sufficient unity in itself so that to affirm and deny it of one and the same thing would be a contradiction. It also has sufficient unity to serve as the middle term of a syllogism, so that wherever two extremes are united by a middle term that is one in this way, we may conclude to the union of the two extremes between themselves.

Univocation in this sense I establish by three arguments:

Argument I

The first is this: Every intellect that is certain about one concept but is dubious about others, has besides the concepts about which it is in doubt, another concept of which it is certain. (The subject includes the predicate.) Now in this life already, a man can be certain in his mind that something is a being, and still be in doubt whether it is a finite or an infinite being, a created or uncreated being. Consequently, in addition to these latter concepts of the thing, there is a concept of being, which as such is neither the one [e.g., finite being] nor the other [e.g., infinite being], but is included in both of them and therefore is univocal.

Proof of the major: One and the same concept cannot be both certain and dubious. Therefore, either there is another concept (which is our contention) or there is no concept at all, and consequently, no certitude about any concept.

I prove the minor: Every philosopher was certain that what he had posited as a first principle was a being; for instance, one was certain that fire was a being, another that water was a being. Yet he was not certain that it was a created or uncreated being, that it was first or not first. He could not be certain that it was the first being, for then he would have been certain about something false, and what is false is not strictly knowable. Neither was he certain that it was not first; for then he would not have claimed the opposite.

This reason is confirmed as follows: someone perceiving the disagreement among philosophers can still be certain that any of the things that they have claimed as the first principle is a being. Nevertheless, in view of the contrariety of opinions, he could be in doubt whether this or that being is primary. Now if we could demonstrate for such an individual the truth or falsity of one of these alternatives, for example, that fire is not the first being, but is posterior to the first being, we would not destroy his first certain notion of it as a being, but this notion would survive in the particular conception which we had proven. And this also proves the proposition stated as the final conclusion of the argument, namely, that this certain concept, since as such it is neither of the doubtful notions, is preserved in both of them.

Should you not care for this argument based on the diversity of opinion among philosophers, you might say perhaps that each has in his mind two concepts closely resembling each other. Yet, because of the very closeness of the analogy, they seem to be one concept. The following consideration, however, might be urged against this. By such an evasion, all possibility of proving the unity of any univocal concept would be destroyed. For if you say that "man" is one concept applicable to both Socrates and Plato, someone will deny it, asserting that there are two concepts, but they seem to be one because of their great similarity.

Argument II

My second principal argument is this. In the present life, no concept representing reality is formed naturally in the mind except by reason of those factors which naturally motivate the intellect. Now these factors are the agent intellect and the sense image or the object revealed in the sense image. No simple concept, then, is produced naturally in our mind except that which can arise in virtue of these factors. Now, as I shall prove, no concept could arise in virtue of the agent intellect and the sense image that is not univocal but only analogous with or wholly other than what is revealed in the sense image. In the present life, since no other such analogous concept could arise in the intellect naturally, it would be simply impossible to have any natural concept of God whatsoever. But this is false.

Proof of the assumption: With the cooperation of the agent and possible intellect, any object revealed in the phantasm or existing as an intelligible species can produce (at the very most) in the intellect as its adequate effect: *a*) a proper concept of itself, and *b*) a concept of all that is essentially or virtually included in it. Now this concept which they posit as analogous is neither a proper concept of the object in the sense image nor is it a proper concept of anything virtually or essentially included in it. Consequently, it cannot arise by any such moving factor.

And this argument is confirmed; for except by way of a reasoning process the mind can know nothing from this object besides the proper and adequate concept of the object itself, and whatever is included therein in one of the two aforementioned ways. But such a reasoning process presupposes a knowledge of the simple thing to which one reasons.

Consequently, the argument may be formulated briefly as follows: No object will produce a simple and proper concept of itself and a simple and proper concept of another object, unless it contain this second object essentially or virtually, No created object, however, contains the "Uncreated" essentially or virtually; therefore, etc.

We prove the second part of the minor, which is that no created object contains the "Uncreated" virtually—at least in the way that the two are actually related, namely, as what is by nature secondary is related to what is by nature prior. For it is contrary to the very notion of what is essentially secondary to include virtually what is prior to it.

It is also obvious that the created does not contain as part of its essence something that is not merely common, but is exclusively proper to the "Uncreated." Therefore, it produces no simple and proper concept of the "Uncreated" at all.

Argument III

The third proof is this: Every metaphysical inquiry about God proceeds as follows. The formal notion of something is considered; the imperfection associated with this notion in creatures is removed; the highest of all perfection is then ascribed to this formal notion, and as such it is attributed to God. Take, for example, the formal notion of "wisdom" or "intellect" or "will." Such a notion is considered first of all simply in itself and absolutely. Because this notion includes formally no imperfection nor limitation, the imperfections associated with it in creatures are removed. Retaining this same notion of "wisdom" and "will," we attribute these to God—but in a most perfect degree. Consequently, every inquiry regarding God is based upon the supposition that the intellect has the same univocal concept, which it obtained from creatures.

If you maintain that this is not true, but that the formal concept of what pertains to God is another notion, a disconcerting consequence ensues; namely, that from the proper notion of anything found in creatures nothing at all can be inferred about God, for the notion of what is in each is wholly different. We would have no more reason to conclude that God is formally wise from the wisdom we perceive in creatures than we would that he is formally a stone. For it is possible to form another notion of a stone to which the notion of a created stone bears some relation, for instance, stone as an idea in God. And so we could say formally, "God is a stone" according to this analogous concept, just as we say, "he is wise" according to another analogous concept.

What kind of univocation is ascribed to being and how far and to what it extends, will all be discussed more at length in a subsequent question on the primary object of the intellect.

Third Statement

Thirdly, I say that God is not known naturally by anyone in the present life in a *proper* and *particular manner;* that is to say, we do not know him in his essence itself precisely as *this* essence.

But the reason given for this in the preceding opinion is not conclusive. For, when he [Henry] argues that one thing can be known from another only by reason of what is similar, we can only understand this likeness to be one of univocation or of imitation. If the first is meant, then nothing is known about God, for according to this opinion there is no likeness of univocation between God and creatures whereby he might be known by us. If the second is meant, then creatures would not imitate God's essence merely under the aspect of some general attribute, but also precisely as *this essence,* as naked and as it exists in itself. By reason of this similarity, therefore, a creature according to him could be a principle of knowing the divine essence in itself and in particular.

There is, however, another reason for this conclusion that God himself as this essence is not an object of natural knowledge for us; for if he be known in this way by any intellect other than his own, it is as a voluntary and not as a natural object. Therefore he cannot be known naturally by any created intellect precisely as *this essence.* Neither is there any essence naturally knowable to us that would suffice to reveal this essence as *this essence,* whether by reason of a likeness of univocation or of imitation. For univocation obtains only where we have general notions. Imitation, too, is deficient because it is imperfect, for creatures only imperfectly imitate him.

Whether there is another reason for the impossibility of such knowledge based on the nature of the primary object of the intellect, which some claim to be the quiddity of a material thing, will be discussed in the question on the primary object of the intellect.

Fourth Statement

Fourthly, I say that we can arrive at many concepts proper to God, in the sense that they do not apply to creatures. Such are the concepts of all the pure perfections when taken in the highest degree. And the most perfect concept of all, by which we know God most perfectly, as it were, in a descriptive sort of way, is obtained by conceiving all the pure perfections and each in the highest degree. Now a less perfect but simpler concept is possible to us, namely the concept of a being that is simply infinite. For this is simpler than the concept of "good being" or "true being" or some similar concepts, since infinite is not a quasi-attribute or property of being or of that of which it is predicated. Rather it signifies an intrinsic mode of that entity, so that when I say "Infinite Being" [ens infinitum], I do not have a concept composed accidentally, as it were, of a subject and its attribute. What I do have is a concept of what is essentially one, namely of a subject with a certain grade of perfection—infinity. It is like "intense whiteness," which is not a notion that is accidentally composed such as "visible whiteness" would be, for the intenseness is an intrinsic grade of whiteness itself. Thus the simplicity of this concept, "Infinite Being," is evident.

Now the perfection of this concept is proved in more than one way. First, from the fact that this concept virtually includes more than any of the others we can conceive. As "being" virtually includes the "good" and the "true," so "Infinite Being" includes the "Infinitely Good," the "Infinitely True" and all pure perfections, under the aspect of infinity. It is also proved from this fact. With a *demonstration of the fact* [*quia*], the existence of an Infinite Being, or the fact that something has infinite being, is the last conclusion to be established. The more perfect, however, are the last to be established by a *demonstration of fact,* which begins with creatures. For their very remoteness from creatures makes knowledge of them from creatures most difficult of attainment.

But if you say that the "Highest Good" or the "Highest Being" expresses an intrinsic mode of being and includes other concepts virtually, I reply that if "highest" be taken in a comparative sense, then it includes a relation to something extrinsic to the being, whereas "infinite" is an absolute concept. But if "highest" is understood in an absolute sense, i.e., that the very nature of the thing is such that it cannot be exceeded, then this perfection is conceived even more expressly in the notion of an infinite being, because "Highest Good" does not indicate as such whether it is infinite or finite.

This obviously refutes the assertion made in the previous opinion [of Henry], namely that the most perfect knowledge we have of God is to know his attributes as identified with the divine being, in virtue of his simplicity. A knowledge of the divine being, however, as infinite is more perfect than a knowledge of him as simple, for simplicity is shared with creatures whereas infinity, as God possesses it, is not.

Fifth Statement

In the fifth place, I say that what we know of God is known through intelligible species of creatures. Whether the more universal and less universal have each their own proper intelligible species, or whether both are known through one and the same species, namely, that which is less universal, in any case this is true. Whatever can imprint or cause a species of what is less universal, can also cause any species of that which is more universal. Thus it is that creatures which impress their own proper species on the intellect can also impress the species of the transcendentals which are common to themselves and to God. In this way, the intellect in virtue of its own power can make use of many such species simultaneously, in order to conceive at one time those things of which these are the species. For instance, it can use the species of "good," the species of "highest," the species of "act" to conceive "the highest good which is pure act." This is clear from an instance of the dialectical rule *a minori*, for the imagination is able to use the species of different things perceptible to the senses and thus imagine a composite of these different elements, as is apparent, for instance, when we imagine a gold mountain.

This obviously refutes the assertion made in the previous opinion regarding the process whereby the intellect burrows beneath the concept of creatures. For by such a process, we can unearth only what lies beneath the surface. But there is nothing in the concept of a creature that would be of a totally different nature than the creature and would be proper to God, as we have proved in the second reason for the second statement. Consequently, we shall never discover such a concept by this burrowing process.

And as to the analogy of the estimative power, I would say that he [Henry of Ghent] seems to adduce one false instance to confirm another. For if a sheep were to retain its proper nature together with its natural affection towards a lamb, and yet by some miracle were to be changed accidently so as to resemble a wolf in all its sensible manifestations, for instance, in its shape, its color, its movements, its cries, and so on, a lamb would flee from such a sheep just as it would flee from a wolf. And still there is nothing in the sheep that is harmful to the lamb, but only what is beneficial. Hence the estimative power would not dig beneath the sense images to discover the friendliness, but would be moved according to the sense appetite in the very way that the sensible appearances move it.

It does not help to say that this friendliness does not propagate itself because the accidental manifestations in such a case are not in accord with it, and that this friendliness is not propagated unless the external manifestations are in accord with it. For if the lamb flees from the "wolf" only because it perceives something inimical by its estimative power, and in the present case the intention [of friendliness] is not propagated where the sensible manifestations are those [of a wolf], it follows that the lamb unearths no intention of enmity, since none exists, or if the lamb does not flee in virtue of such a burrowing process in this instance, then neither does it do so in other cases.

Solution of Arguments to the Contrary

As to the arguments at the beginning of this question:

To the first, I reply that the Philosopher's [Aristotle's] comparison applies to the initial movement of the intellect by the object, for in this case the sense images, together with the agent intellect, function in the role of primary moving object. It must not be understood, however, of all the actions which follow this initial movement. For the intellect can abstract an object which is included in that which produces the initial movement. It is able to consider the former, without considering that from which it was abstracted. Now when the intellect considers something that has been abstracted in this way, it grasps what is common to both sensible and insensible, for it is considering in a universal manner the insensible as well as the sensible. In its consideration the intellect can unite a second abstract notion with the first, so that the latter becomes proper to something else, namely, to the insensible. The sense faculty, however, is incapable of making abstractions. Therefore, in all its acts, whether they be primary or secondary, it requires some object to put it in motion first. But this is not the way that the imagination is related to the intellect.

To the second, I reply that the Commentator [Averroes] restricts this comparison of the Philosopher to what is difficult, but not impossible to know. And his reason is that otherwise, nature would have made these separate substances intelligible in vain, for no intellect would be able to know them. But this reason is invalid, first of all, because we cannot say that the sole purpose or reason for the intelligibility of these substances is that we may know them. Consequently, even if we could know nothing about them, we still could not say they are intelligible to no purpose. Secondly, it does not follow that just because these substances are unintelligible to our minds, they are unintelligible to all minds, for they are intelligible to themselves. Therefore, we have a fallacy of consequent. Wherefore I say that even though there are many ways in which this citation of the Philosopher could be explained, still the eye of the bat has only a natural and intuitive knowledge. And on the basis of these two characteristics, the Philosopher's words can be explained even in the sense of an impossibility. For just as it is impossible for the eye of the bat to consider such an object naturally and intuitively, so it is also impossible for our intellect to possess a natural and intuitive knowledge of God.

To the third I reply that the potentially infinite is unknown, because to the extent that something is in act, it is knowable. But it is not so unknown that it would be impossible for an infinite intellect to know it. Nevertheless the [potentially] infinite cannot be known by an intellect which proceeds to know it in the way that it is infinite. For it is "infinite" only in so far as the mind, in considering only one thing after another, never comes to an end. Now the mind which considers only one thing after another in this way always considers something finite and never something infinite. An infinite intellect, however, can know the whole thing at once, and not simply one part after another. And to the argument from the second book of the *Metaphysics* concerning infinite numbers and the "Infinite," I reply that there is no parity between the two, for a knowledge of an infinite number of objects would imply that the faculty of knowledge itself is infinite, since one can infer a greater power of intellect from a greater number of objects known. But a knowledge of something infinite in the order of intention does not imply that the act of knowledge itself be infinite (unless it be an act which fully comprehends the object), for it is not necessary that the act and the object have the same mode of being, since an act which by nature is finite can be related to an object which by nature is infinite. I admit, however, that we neither have, nor can have, such a comprehensive act of knowledge in regard to an infinite object.

To the fourth argument of Gregory [the Great], I reply that we should not think that contemplation terminates in some creature beneath God, for this would be to enjoy as an end what is to be used as a means. According to Augustine, this would be the greatest perversion. But the concept of God's essence under the aspect of being is more imperfect than the concept of the same essence as "this essence." Now because it is less perfect, it is inferior to, or "beneath," the knowledge of God in himself, as this singular essence.

A Reply to the Arguments of Henry

To the arguments for the first opinion:

I reply, that when he argues that God by reason of his unique singularity cannot be known through some universal, univocal concept, common to himself and creatures, the consequence is invalid. For Socrates, in so far as he is Socrates, is singular. Nevertheless several predicates can be abstracted from Socrates. Consequently, the singularity of a thing is no impediment to the abstraction of a common concept. Though in reality everything in God, since it exists of itself, is singular, so that one thing does not contract another to singularity, nevertheless one and the same thing can be conceived indistinctly or as this thing, existing in reality, and thus it can be conceived either as common or singular.

There is no need to refute what he says regarding an incidental knowledge of God, because God is known in a quasi-incidental manner in an attribute. However, this is not the sole way he can be known, as has been proved above.

40

THE PHILOSOPHY OF OCKHAM [1]

THE world of Duns Scotus is peopled not only with individual things but also with real common natures which the intellect has merely to seek out to read their intelligible messages. In such a world even the senses can perceive a reality which is in a way universal. According to Scotus, the object of sensation is not properly an individual thing as individual, but a reality common to all the sensible objects in one genus, the whiteness, for instance, of all white things. Under these circumstances there is no need of an abstractive process of the intellect, in the Thomistic sense, by which the intelligible object, bearing the stamp of singularity in a sensible image, must be rendered universal and actually intelligible in order to be known. For the object present to our cognitive faculties is a common nature in which, as a recent historian [Gilson] put it, the Agent Intellect can read, as in an open book, the intelligible object from which the concept will be born.

By his realism of common natures Duns Scotus placed himself in the long line of medieval Christian Platonists, all of whom agree that in some way there is universality or community outside the mind, corresponding to our universal concepts. Of course, historical Platonism is realized in very different forms. The rather crude realist philosophies of Boethius, John Scotus Erigena and William of Champeaux are a far cry from the refined realism of Duns Scotus; yet we can see the same Platonic inspiration behind them all. And just as early medieval Platonism aroused the unrelenting criticism of Abelard, so the Platonism of the fourteenth century found an even more formidable adversary in William of Ockham.

A student at Oxford in the first decade of the fourteenth century, William of Ockham (1290?-1349/50) became acquainted with Scotism either from the Subtle Doctor himself or, more likely, from his immediate disciples. But he was a student with an independent mind, and while listening to his teachers he formed his own philosophy in opposition to them. Ockhamism thus grew out of a criticism of contemporary doctrines, and especially of Scotism, whose founder, he says, surpassed all others in subtlety of judgment.

Duns Scotus had accepted the Avicennian metaphysics of essence, but

---

1 [From Armand Maurer, C.S.B., "Scotism and Ockhamism," in *A History of Philosophical Systems*, edited by V. Ferm (New York: Philosophical Library, 1950), pp. 216-222. Reprinted by permission. The notes are omitted.]

there was much in the Arabian's philosophy which as a Christian he rejected. For one thing, according to Avicenna God is not a free creator; all things flow from him in a definite hierarchy with all the rational necessity with which conclusions are drawn from premisses. Now, necessity enters the Avicennian world—and the world of Greek and Arabian philosophy in general—precisely because it is a rational world of intelligible essences. For even though existences or facts are contingent, essences are necessarily what they are. The problem which Scotus faced was to reconcile the freedom of God and the contingency of created things with the fact that there are intelligible essences in the universe and ideas in the divine mind. His solution was to assert the transcendence of God as infinite being above all essences, and to teach a radical voluntarism according to which all things—in a way, even the divine knowledge—are subject to God's will.

Now William of Ockham was equally certain that God is all-powerful and the free creator of the world. Like Scotus, he did not think this could be proved by natural reason; but he knew it to be true by Faith, for we say in the first article of the Creed: "I believe in God the Father Almighty." The only question for Ockham was: Can the omnipotence and liberty of God and the contingency of the world be saved in the way Scotus tried to do it? Ockham was convinced that they could not; an essential reform would have to be made in Scotism and every trace of intelligible essence removed from it, if the danger of necessitarianism was to be avoided.

At the same time, Ockham was a shrewd logician and a man who loved clarity and simplicity of thought. An explanation, to his mind, should always be in as simple terms as possible, or, to put it another way, we should not posit a plurality without necessity. This principle of thought, which has come to be called "Ockham's Razor," is not original with him. It was a common dictum of the time and is traceable to Aristotle. What is new is the devastating way Ockham used it, in accordance with his theological aims and his basic metaphysical and logical notions.

In Ockham's criticism of Scotism and other contemporary philosophies, one of his first aims is to eliminate common natures and universals from reality, and in doing so he proceeds as a logician. When terms are used in propositions, he reminds us, they serve as substitutes for things. This function of terms standing for things in propositions the Schoolmen called supposition (*suppositio*). Now, there are three ways in which a term can exercise this function. In the first place, it may stand for the word itself, as when I say "Man is a word." Here "man" stands for the word "man" taken materially. Consequently, this kind of supposition is called material supposition. Secondly, a term may stand for individual things, as in the proposition, "Man runs," for it is the individual person who is signified as running. Hence the name of this kind of supposition is personal supposition. In still a third way, a term may have a simple supposition, as when we use "man" in the proposition "Man is a species."

Now, the point which particularly interested Ockham was the meaning of simple supposition. What precisely does "man" stand for in the last proposition? Peter of Spain, whose treatise on logic served as a textbook for the Schoolmen, thought that it stood for and signified a universal thing. Obviously this is to prejudice the debate over universals in favor of realism. For if he is correct, there is a universal thing which the common term signifies and for which it can stand in a proposition. Ockham, however, had another view on the matter. For him, in simple supposition the common term simply stands for a concept in the mind and properly speaking signifies individual things. This was also giving an answer to the problem of universals, this time in favor of nominalism or conceptualism. If Ockham is right, there is nothing common or universal in reality; universality abides solely in the mind and nothing is real except individual things.

We can see how thoroughly Ockham was convinced of this by reading his treatise on universals, in his commentary on the *Sentences* of Peter Lombard. There he arranges the various realist doctrines according to the degree of reality they attribute to universals, and then proceeds to refute them one by one. The burden of his criticism is generally the same. If a universal is outside the mind and realized in things, it is either one (and then we cannot understand how it is multiplied in individuals), or it is many (and then we cannot understand how it is one). In either case we end in absurdity, and it is better to admit that universals are simply in the mind and have no reality whatsoever. They are present in things neither actually, nor virtually, nor potentially. They are strictly in no way in things.

If this is true, the comon natures so dear to Scotus lose their status as realities, and the complicated structure of being built upon them is eliminated. For one thing, there is no need of an haecceity [thisness] added to nature to account for individuality. Every individual is individual in itself and not in virtue of an added principle. Moreover, the Scotist formal distinction is banished from philosophy along with the realities which are its basis. The only kind of distinction left in reality is real distinction, in the precise Scotist sense of a distinction between individual things, one of which can exist without the other. Ockham admitted formal distinction only in theology, for instance between the three Persons and the Divine Essence, although for him this is contrary to the ordinary laws of logic. A logical distinction, such as Ockham conceived it, is simply one between concepts without any foundation in an individual thing. The distinction between the various concepts the intellect forms of a thing has thus no meaning, as far as the individual itself is concerned, for they all signify one and the same reality. That is why, for him, the concepts we form of God are all equal in signification. If we distinguish between the divine intellect and will, for example, this is purely a distinction between concepts which signify the same indistinct divine reality. We can say, then, that God knows by his will or wills by his intellect, for the two concepts have precisely the same meaning when predicated of God. The same is true of all universal concepts predicated of an individual thing. Consequently, an individual in the Ockhamist sense is absolutely impervious to distinction; it is by definition "the indistinct."

If real being is thus radically individual, what is a universal, and what relation has it to things? A universal, for Ockham, is simply a sign which stands for many things. Now signs, he tells us, are either conventional and artificial, like written or spoken words, or natural, like the noise an animal makes to signify its feelings. There are universal artificial signs outside the mind, but on analysis they are found to be simply individual things whose signification is purely conventional. Within the mind, however, we find natural signs or terms which are our universal concepts. Their signification is not conventional but natural, since they are produced in us in an obscure way by nature itself as likenesses of things. That is why the concepts of men are alike, while their languages differ. As to the exact reality of these concepts, Ockham, after some hestitation, seems to have taken the stand that they are simply our acts of understanding.

We know already that, for Ockham, concepts can have no foundation in reality save individual things. But how can the latter be a basis for *universal* concepts? If there are no common natures in reality, is not our conceptual and abstract knowledge completely out of contact with it? In the twelfth century, Abelard, faced with the same problem after his criticism of the realism of William of Champeaux, resorted to the notion that God created things with a common status or condition, which accounts for the resemblances among them. Consequently, even though things do not share a common essence, they can be designated by a common name because of their common status. Ockham adopted a similar solution, although it was more radical. It is evident, he said, that there is a greater similarity among some things than among others. Plato, for instance, is more like Socrates than he is like an animal. Accordingly the mind forms a concept of the species "man," which signifies both of these men but not the animal. Then it can form a more universal concept of the genus "animal," because of the common likeness of all three. The difficulty with this solution is that Ockham has really no intelligible explanation for the likenesses of things. They are not alike because they share in a common nature. Neither are they alike because they were created by God according to a common idea or model. Abelard had resorted to the divine ideas to explain the common status of things, but this was not acceptable to Ockham for the good reason that he did not think God's mind contained distinct ideas; the divine ideas, in his view, are simply the individual things which God creates. As a result, the likenesses of things are purely factual. They can be experienced but not rationally explained.

Once Ockham shifted the interest of philosophy from common natures to individual things, a new theory of knowledge was inevitable. The primary object of the senses and intellect can no longer be a common reality, as in Scotism, but individual things. Following the terminology of Duns Scotus, Ockham distinguished between intuitive and abstractive knowledge. Intuitive knowledge, he says, is always concerned with a singular thing as existing and present to the observer. Abstractive knowledge, on the other hand, tells us nothing about the existence or nonexistence of things, but concerns abstract ideas or representations. Now, for Ockham, all our knowledge begins with an intuition of the senses, and this is followed by an intellectual intuition. Abstractive knowledge comes afterwards and depends on them. Thus he insists as strongly on the primacy of the individual in knowledge as on its primacy in being.

Although sensible intuition is at the origin of all our knowledge, absolutely speaking it does not guarantee the existence of its object. There can be an intuition of a nonexistent thing, and even a judgment of its existence, without the actual presence of the object. This doctrine of Ockham's comes as a surprise in view of his definition of intuition; yet we can easily see what led to this conclusion. God, who is omnipotent, can always do alone what he does by secondary causes. Now, Ockham says, when we see a star, God produces our intuition of it, using the star as a secondary cause. He can, then, supernaturally conserve our sight of the star without the star. Of course, Ockham never doubted that, in the normal course of events, the object perceived is really the cause of the intuition. What is in question is simply what God is, absolutely speaking, capable of doing, not what he in fact does.

It may be objected that the Ockhamist God, for all his omnipotence, cannot do what is contradictory, and the intuition of a nonexistent thing is contrary to the very notion of intuitive knowledge. Faced with this objection, Ockham admits in one place that such a cognition would not be a true intuition, but rather an assent lacking evidence and belonging to the realm of faith, although the assent would be of the same kind as the evident judgments based on intuition. What Ockham does not explain, however, is how we could for all practical purposes distinguish between our knowledge of existing and nonexisting things, and he thus opens the way to idealism and skepticism even though he himself does not enter upon it.

We are witnessing here the final result of Ockham's attempt to rid theology and philosophy of Greco-Arabian necessitarianism. Scotus thought that he could do it, and still retain the divine ideas and common natures with the necessity which they introduce into the world, if they were subordinated to the divine will. Ockham would not concede even this much. While keeping Scotus' voluntarism, he abolished ideas from God's mind and common natures from things, with the result that he had nothing left but an omnipotent God governed by no law save that of contradiction, and a morcellated universe of individual things, no one of which has anything in common with any other. In such a universe, God can act in a very arbitrary way. He can, if he wishes, make it meritorious for us to hate him. Hatred of God, theft, adultery are bad only because of the will of God, not for any intelligible reason. So, too, God can make fire cool, just as easily as he makes it heat, for there is no necessary connection between cause and effect. The nominalist universe of Ockham is thus a world of *fact* rather than one of intelligible necessity, a world of things to be experienced rather than one of intelligible natures to be understood. Such a world, it is true, would prove interesting to the experimental sciences, which were soon to set out on their brilliant career. It was barren soil, however, for philosophy such as it was known to the Schoolmen of the thirteenth century.

41

OCKHAM AND THE MEDIEVAL LOGIC OF SUPPOSITION AND CONSEQUENCES [1]

1. THE THEORY OF SUPPOSITION

IN THE middle of the 13th century we already encounter tracts on supposition, although this doctrine was known at a much earlier date. Its origins are as yet shrouded in darkness, but we certainly have grounds for assigning an important part in its development to Abelard and the older grammarians, and, most probably, to St. Anselm.

The term "supponere" and its substantive "suppositio" have assumed various and equivocal meanings. In the English language the term "to suppose" almost exclusively conveys the meaning of the act of laying down an opinion, of assuming an hypothesis, of expecting something to be true, etc. Though the same meaning is quite often connected with the words "supponere" and "suppositio" in the language of the Scholastics, yet, in their strictly logical use, these words have a more literal meaning. For "sup-pono" etymologically means to put something under something, or to replace, or to substitute. The idea of substitution was enlarged to embrace logical substitution of a sign for that which it signifies. Thus, "to suppose" means that a term replaces or stands for that which it is intended to signify.

We are convinced that the term "suppositio," in this strictly logical meaning was used already by logicians of the 12th century, since we encounter it in various forms in the works of theologians at the beginning of the 13th century.

1 [From Philotheus Boehner, O.F.M., *Medieval Logic: An Outline of Its Development from 1250 to c. 1400* (Chicago: University of Chicago Press, 1952), pp. 27-31, 37-40, 52-58, 82-83. Reprinted by permission. The notes and some sentences in the main text are omitted.]

In any case, highly developed tracts on supposition are to be found at the middle of the 13th century in the works of William Shyreswood, Lambert of Auxerre and Peter of Spain. Since that time, such tracts simply belong to the deposit of medieval logic, though they are not usually found in the commentaries on the writings of Aristotle. Even theologians began to make increasing use of supposition, as is evidenced in the works of St. Bonaventure and St. Thomas. Indeed, it was an indispensable tool for ascertaining the exact logical functions of categorematic terms in propositions. The Aristotelian logical works were not much help in this regard, since the Stagirite showed little interest in the semantic problems, and had centred his logic primarily around the analysis of a logic of classes. The doctrine of supposition, however, had to take into account a theory of signification (Semantics), and was forced by its very subject matter to break away from a logic of classes in the direction of a logic of predicates.

Since supposition is principally, though not exclusively, concerned with the quantity of terms, it deals for the most part with the extension or range of predicates in reference to individuals. On this point the theory of supposition is, to a very large extent, one with the modern theory of quantification. While the theory of signification studies merely the sign-relation of terms in general, the theory of supposition studies the signs or terms as predicates in relation to their subject or subjects. The universal or universalized terms are not so much considered as classes, the members of which are characterized by a predicate, but, rather, as predicates, which, by various linguistic or logical devices, have a definite relation to the subject or subjects of which they are predicated.

Though we are convinced that the theory of supposition at root is comparable to the modern theory of supposition or with the functional calculus of the first order, actual comparison is made difficult, in view of the fact that modern logic uses an artificial language, whereas the Scholastics applied their analysis to a "natural" and a spoken language. Medieval logicians were satisfied with a painstaking and sometimes cumbersome clarification and determination of the structures of the Latin language. In particular, they busied themselves with ascertaining the meaning and function of those syncategoremata which regulate the range of predication for categorematic terms.

Modern logic, however, has made a decided step forward in assuming only a few constants, which serve the purpose of bringing about an extremely simplified language. With these constants, their definitions and the rules governing their use, the Scholastic theory of supposition has disappeared. It has vanished, however, at the cost of creating a new terminology foreign to that of any ordinary language. Though the language of logic has gained in clarity and precision, it has not been without a price. Keeping this important difference between the two logics in mind, we shall not be so prone to overlook the basic similarity masked beneath the apparent diversity.

An indication of this similarity is found in the fact that it is sometimes a simple matter to express Scholastic rules of suppositions in modern theorems of the functional calculus. We select but two instances. The one fits perfectly into the pattern of the modern theory of predicates; the other shows divergent interpretations.

A particular, affirmative, categorical proposition about a state of affairs (*propositio categorica affirmativa particularis de inesse*) is interpreted by the Scholastics in exactly the same manner as by modern logicians. Let us consider the following proposition: Some man is mortal. According to the Scholastics, this proposition has determinate personal supposition, which means that the proposition is true, if there is at least one subject (or individual), about which it is true to say: This is a man and this man is mortal. Though there may be more, one subject alone suffices to verify the proposition. Hence, the Scholastics state that such a particular proposition is equivalent to a disjunction, each member of which consists of a singular proposition containing the subject of its singularized form. Therefore, we obtain the equivalence: "Some man is mortal" is equivalent to "this man is mortal, or that man is mortal, or that man is mortal," and so forth for any individual. Modern logic expresses the same relation in the following equivalence:

$$\exists\, (x)\, [\mathrm{Man}(x) \cdot \mathrm{Mortal}(x)] \equiv \langle [\mathrm{Man}(x_1) \cdot \mathrm{Mortal}(x_1)]\mathrm{v}$$
$$[\mathrm{Man}(x_2) \cdot \mathrm{Mortal}(x_2)]\mathrm{v} \ldots x_n\rangle$$

It is quite a different matter, however, if we try to compare the Scholastic universal affirmative categorical proposition about a fact with that of modern logic. Let us take, for instance, the proposition: Every man is mortal. Modern logic interprets this sentence by transforming it into a conditional hypothetical proposition or its equivalents in the following symbolization: $(x)\, [\mathrm{Man}(x) \supset \mathrm{Mortal}(x)]$. We believe that the scholastics knew of this possibility. However, they were aware that this interpretation changes the categorical proposition into an hypothetical one. Furthermore, they admitted the inference "Some man is mortal" from the proposition "Every man is mortal," which inference cannot be made as such from the conditional formulation. The Scholastics, then, insisted on the existential import of a categorical, non-modal affirmative, universal proposition about the present. This could be interpreted to mean that they tacitly admitted an axiom to the effect that there is at least one subject (x_1) which satisfies the predicates. This tacitly admitted axiom proved troublesome to at least one later Scholastic logician, who made a notable start towards the modern interpretation without, however, completely attaining it. In any case, the insistence on the categorical to the exclusion of the hypothetical nature of such propositions had hindered the development towards the modern interpretation, with the result that a complicated interpretation of these universal propositions developed.

In spite of this difference, there is a parallel interpretation as regards the subject of such universal propositions. For the equivalence established by Scholastic logicians that "Every man is mortal" is equivalent to "This man is mortal, and that man is mortal, and that man is mortal," and so forth for every man, finds its corresponding counterpart in modern logic in simply singularizing the individual variable. However, we are at a loss in attempting a comparison of the supposition of the predicate with anything modern logic has to offer. For the (later) Scholastics would say that the following equivalence holds: "Every man is mortal; therefore, every man is this mortal or that mortal or that mortal" and so forth for every mortal being. In our opinion, this interpretation shows that these Scholastics who adopted it did not understand the universal, affirmative proposition in the modern sense; it likewise shows that the idea of classes was not altogether alien to their theory of supposition.

2. OCKHAM ON SUPPOSITION

According to Ockham, supposition is a property of a term, but only when it is used in a proposition. The natural supposition of the older logicians is no longer mentioned by Ockham. Since, according to him, supposition is a function of a term which is either the subject or the predicate in a proposition, he can characterize supposition by the subject or predicate function of the terms. If the suppositing term is the subject, the proposition denotes that the predicate is predicated about this term or about the demonstrative pronoun indicating the same object represented by the subject-term. For instance, let us consider the proposition: Man is an animal. This proposition denotes that at least one man is an animal; for instance, Socrates. Hence, the proposition "Socrates is an animal" is true, so that by pointing at Socrates it is true to say "This is an animal." On this account it is said that "man" in the proposition "Man is an animal" has supposition, for in the proposition it is denoted that the predicate is truly predicated about the subject or its pronoun. The case of the following proposition is somewhat different, although it ultimately comes down to the same thing: "Man" is noun. Here, too, "man" has supposition since it is denoted that "noun" is truly predicated about the word "man," and we may even point to this written noun ("man") and say, "This is a noun."

If, however, the suppositing term is the predicate, the proposition denotes that the predicate-term, or a substituting pronoun, is truly subjected in regard to the subject. For by this proposition: Socrates is white, it is denoted that Socrates is this white thing or simply, while pointing to the white thing, that Socrates is this.

It immediately becomes clear from what we have discussed that signification and supposition are not the same. We meet this distinction in the following division of supposition according to Ockham:

(A) Improper supposition. This type occurs when a term is used in its

improper meaning. Every term has a certain meaning or a certain signification stemming from its original coinage. This is considered to be
its proper meaning and the term so used is said to be taken "in virtue
of expression" (*de virtute sermonis*). When, however, a term is not used
in its proper meaning but is employed in a metaphorical sense or in
some other figure of speech, it is taken in its improper meaning and has
improper supposition. The logician should avoid this supposition, and
we should be acutely aware in discussions, especially in those involving
the quoting of authorities, of the danger which lies in metaphorical expression. We should always try to ascertain the intention of the author
of such an expression since, while metaphorical expression may be false
"in virtue of expression," it may be true according to the intention of
the author.

(B) Proper supposition. This type is divided into personal, simple and
material supposition. In order to understand this division, we must keep
in mind that Ockham, along with Boethius, distinguishes three modes
of existence of a term. First, the term may exist as a mental entity which
is a concept or a mental term. This is a natural sign which, without any
interference of the will, represents or makes known that which it signifies. Second, it may exist as a spoken term which is a vocal sound arbi-
trarily instituted to signify the same thing that the mental term signifies. Such an artificial (spoken) term is associated with the mental term
by imposition, and, in virtue of this association, a word is said to have
secondary signification, since it represents or calls to our minds the associated concept. Its primary signification, however, is the same object
which is signified by the mental sign. Third, a term may exist as a written term which is similar to the spoken term, except that it is written
rather than spoken.

While personal supposition is had only when the term, mental, spoken
or written, stands for the significates directly signified by it, simple and
material supposition is given then, and only then, when a term does not
exercise its significative function, or when it does not directly signify its
significates.

1) For *simple* supposition two things are required. First, the term in
question, be it mental, spoken or written, must not exercise signification
or its significative function. In addition, it must stand for or represent
the mental term as such. For instance, in the proposition "Man is a
species," "man" does not have a significative function, for the significates
of "man" are individual men, but it cannot be said of any individual
man, "This man is a species." Hence "man," either as a mental term or
as a spoken or written term, has no primary significative function. It
"simply" represents the concept "man," which indeed is a species, since
it is predicable of many individuals. In the case of the spoken or written
term, "man" has only secondary representation, since it calls to mind the
associated concept. It is to be noted that Ockham's conceptualism does
not admit of any "nature" which is intermediary between the indi-

viduals and the common concept. For the Realist logicians, it was this "nature" which constituted the significate of a concept in simple supposition.

(2) For *material* supposition three conditions must be verified. First, the term must not have a significative function. Secondly, it must not represent or signify indirectly and secondarily the mental term or concept. In addition, it must represent the material sound or written word. Instances of this material supposition would be: "man" is a word, "man" is composed of three letters.

(3) *Personal* supposition is distinct from the others in this: that a term, suppositing personally, exercises its significative function and stands for the significates which it primarily signifies. Every categorematic term is capable of such personal supposition. Ockham adds the cautious remark that it suffices to say that the term occurring in a proposition is denoted to exercise its significative function, though it may happen, as is the case in false or negative propositions, that a term may have no object or significate for which it supposits.

3. THE THEORY OF CONSEQUENCES

In our consideration of the theory of consequences, we approach that field in which we discover some of the finest achievements of Scholastic logic. It is in the logic of consequences that the Scholastics have reached a high degree of formality, which, in the Aristotelian tradition at least, connotes a high degree of perfection. However, we cannot ascribe complete originality in these matters to Scholastic logicians, although we can credit them with the discovery, or perhaps the rediscovery, of many theorems which hold places of honor even in modern logic.

Just as we are in the dark about the origin of the other new elements of Scholastic logic, so, too, we lack definite information as to the beginnings of the tract on consequences. To be sure, consequences, or consequential rules, were already known to the Scholastics and even to the theologians of the 13th century. Very few of the most basic rules are to be found in the works of Aristotle, and we do not find a theory of consequences of any mentionable size in the *Organon*. Nor can Boethius' work on hypothetical syllogisms be considered as a major source for this tract.

It seems that the theory of consequences developed gradually as the outcome of discussions on the systematizations of the *Topics* of Aristotle: Boethius' *On Hypothetical Syllogisms* may have given an additional impetus. The topical rules are presented by Aristotle in the form of enthymemata, i.e., the inference from one proposition to another. However, as true enthymemata, they tacitly presupposed a third proposition which transformed them into correct syllogisms. As we shall soon see, this particular viewpoint of enthymemata served as a basis for the division of the consequences, viz., they are divided according as they require a third proposition or not. This fact lends itself to the reasonable assumption that the topical rules are the historical starting points of the consequential rules. This is confirmed by another historical fact, namely, the inclusion of non-enthymematic consequences in the discussions which are concerned with or equivalent to Aristotle's *Topics*.

Hence, we believe that the occasional remarks of Aristotle in other works cannot be considered the historical starting point of consequential rules, since these remarks have led only to a clearer understanding of topical rules and of the division of conditional inferences into those that are enthymemata and those that are not. Thus, out of the *Topics*, with its numerous dialectical rules, considered useful for debates in matters which did not lend themselves to strict demonstrations, certain rules were singled out and refined, and to these others were added. These latter additions were considered to be of such great importance that a special tract was set apart for them. This tract was called the tract on consequences for which definitions, divisions and a large number of rules were formulated, and which finally developed into the most basic part of Scholastic logic. For the logic of the 14th century can aptly be characterized as a logic of consequences, since the rules of consequence pervade every tract, even to such an extent that syllogistics almost disappear.

Important though they are, the modal consequences do not enter our discussion. Bocheński rightly maintains that modal consequences, as developed by Aristotle in his *Perihermenias*, had inspired the Scholastics in the development of their theory of consequences. Modal consequences, however, are connected with that large and relatively unexplored field of modal logic which requires much more detailed discussion than we can accord it here. Despite this necessary restriction, we shall, nevertheless, not confine ourselves to conditional propositions, but shall take into account the conjunctive and disjunctive propositions as well.

4. OCKHAM ON CONSEQUENCES

At about 1300, the theory of consequences had already developed a certain definite pattern. Our example is Ockham's theory, which serves as a practical starting point.

We do not find a special tract on consequences in Ockham's *Summa Logicae*, unless we consider the third main division of the third part of this work to consitute this tract. Indeed, Ockham deals with most of the consequences, their definition and division, in this part. However, most of this part is taken up with a treatment of the topical rules. As we have already mentioned, the consequences had started their struggle for independence from their union with dialectical syllogisms, or enthymematic inferences, or that part of medieval logic which corresponds to Aristotle's *Topics*. Ockham is certainly a witness and a contemporary of this origin of consequences. Our task, therefore, will be that of sifting out a theory of consequences which is embodied in this part of Ockham's

Summa Logicae. This is not a very difficult task, since the general theory and the general rules enjoy a certain independence and distinctness from the other matter contained in this part.

According to Ockham, a consequence is an hypothetical, conditional proposition. That means that a consequence is composed of at least two categorical propositions which are joined by the syncategorematic terms "if-then" or their equivalents. In order that such a conditional proposition or consequence be true, it is not necessary that the antecedent, which precedes logically or factually, be true, nor is it necessary for the truth of the conditional proposition or consequence that the consequent, which follows from the antecedent, be true; both parts may even be impossible. Ockham, however, adds a positive condition, namely, that we speak of a true consequence or conditional proposition only then when the antecedent infers the consequent. Since at this point he does not offer any further information about the meaning of "inference," we shall determine its proper sense in the discussion about the divisions of consequences.

We find Ockham's division of consequences at the beginning of his tract on topical rules. He there explains various divisions, which, however, are not necessarily subordinated. We shall simply follow Ockham's loose arrangement and shall not supply a systematic order, which he wisely omitted.

First distinction: Consequences may be either factual or absolute. A factual consequence (*consequentia ut nunc*) is valid at one time and may be invalid at another. Thus the consequence, "Every animal is running, therefore Socrates is running," is valid only if Socrates exists, and, therefore, only for the time of Socrates' existence. If Socrates does not exist, the consequent would be false, while the antecedent, according to the hypothesis, could be true.

An absolute consequence (*consequentia simplex*), on the other hand, is always valid, regardless of the time element. Consequently, this type of consequence is had when the antecedent can at no time be true without the consequent being true. The following is this type of consequence: "No animal is running, therefore no man is running." If this proposition is formulated, it is impossible that the antecedent be true and the consequent be false.

Second distinction: A consequence may be valid in virtue of an intrinsic means or in virtue of an extrinsic means. The term "means" (*medium*) is equivocal, as our explanation will show. A consequence which is valid in virtue of an intrinsic means (*consequentia tenens per medium intrinsecum*) is in reality an enthymema. For the addition of another proposition to the antecedent transforms this consequence into a syllogism. Consequently, intrinsic means could aptly be translated as "premiss." Hence, Ockham expressly states that syllogisms are valid in virtue of such "means." For instance: The consequence, "Socrates is not running, therefore a man is not running," is valid in virtue of the proposition, "Socrates is a man," which transforms the consequence into the syllogism: "Socrates is not running, Socrates is a man, therefore, a man is not running."

A consequent follows in virtue of an extrinsic means when it is valid in virtue of a general rule, which does not concern the terms as such but which applies only to the structure of the proposition, in which case the terms become irrelevant. Consequently, the consequence will be valid regardless of the categorematic terms. Means in this case is equivalent to a logical rule. Such a consequence is represented by the following instance: Only man is a donkey, therefore, every donkey is a man. The consequence is valid not because of the terms (the variables), nor because of the truth of an additional proposition formed with the two terms, "man" and "donkey," but simply in virtue of the general rule governing the conversion of exclusive universal and affirmative propositions.

It is interesting to note that Ockham realized that even consequences, which are valid in virtue of an intrinsic rule, are ultimately though insufficiently based on an extrinsic rule or a general rule. The instance that we previously used, namely, "Socrates is not running, therefore, a man is not running," requires not only the additional premiss, Socrates is a man, but also the general rule that the consequence from a singular proposition to an indefinite proposition is valid. However, as is obvious in our case, this general rule alone is not sufficient to justify the consequence, since the additional premiss: "Socrates is a man," is absolutely required.

The third distinction: A consequence may be formal or material. This is the most important of the divisions introduced by Ockham. Let us first discuss the *formal* consequence. "Formal" is understood by Ockham in the sense of belonging to the very structure of a logical discourse. Hence, a consequence which is labelled as formal must be immediately or mediately governed by a logical rule which is not concerned with the content or the terms, but with the very structure of the propositions. Thus formal consequence comprehends both those consequences which hold in virtue of an extrinsic means as well as those which hold in virtue of an intrinsic means. The latter are mediately valid in virtue of an extrinsic means, and they are a formal consequence only in so far as they are thus mediately valid. As regards formal consequence, then, it does not matter whether the respective propositions are true or false, whether they are necessary or impossible; the only matter of concern is that the formal structure guarantee the inference, at least ultimately.

Material consequence, then, is characterized by the fact that it is not valid because of a general rule, of which it is an instance, but precisely because of the terms which enter the consequence. Since a formal consequence holds regardless of the truth or falsity of the proposition that entered the consequence, and since the truth and falsity of a proposition is determined by the terms which enter these propositions, a material consequence is only characterized by the truth or falsity of the elementary propositions. Therefore it would seem justifiable that we credit Ockham with the knowledge of material implication, in the modern sense. His definition, literally translated, is as follows: "A material consequence exists when it holds precisely because of the terms, and not because of some extrinsic means that precisely regards the general conditions of propositions. Such are the following: If a man is running, then God exists; Man is a donkey, therefore God does not exist." As the instances show, we have here a true material implication, for we can characterize a material implication by saying that it is then given, when we admit that any true proposition is inferred by any proposition, be it true or false. In symbolization:

$$p \supset (q \supset p).$$

And it is also characterized by the other relation that a false proposition infers any proposition. In symbolization:

$$\bar{p} \supset (p \supset q).$$

The two instances of Ockham satisfy these formulae, for, if the proposition "God exists" is true—which is the fact, since it is even necessarily true—then any proposition, whether true or false, infers this true proposition. We may take any proposition at random. In the second case, Ockham takes two propositions which will always be false.

Ockman's logic has certain advantages over the system presented by Peter of Spain. For the first time, as far as we know, the tracts on supposition in general find their natural place at the end of the tracts on terms and before the tracts on propositions, and they are no longer considered as an annex to the traditional Aristotelian logic. Furthermore, the central position of syllogistics in genuine Aristotelian logic is emphasized not only by the place assigned it, but also by the lengthy treatment accorded it, as well as by Ockham's tendency to reduce all inferences to the syllogism, although he is not completely successful in this regard.

The most serious shortcoming in Ockham's systematization of the parts of logic concerns the place assigned to the Consequences. This tract represents the medieval form of the propositional calculus of modern logic, and as such it has its natural place before syllogistics. To be sure, Ockham had realized syllogistics' dependence on consequences, for in his *Syllogistics* he makes use of consequences and proves certain syllogistic forms with them. At the end of the tract on propositions, he also deals with a few theorems of the theory of propositions. The fact remains, however, that the place assigned to consequences in his logic is among the topical rules, after syllogistics. The only excuse that might be raised for Ockham is that he did not intend a logical system but a "natural" system, suggested by the chance arrangement of Aristotelian and other tracts.

XI. Later Medieval Philosophies

Nicholas of Autrecourt is often cited as a precursor of empiricism and Hume. There are some definite anticipations in his restriction of natural certitude to a few immediately known facts of sense experience and introspection, his wholly immanent view of causality, and his appeal to sense appearances as a way of undermining the philosophical knowledge of substance and God. Yet more is learned historically about Nicholas by examining his thought in its own milieu than by straining this comparison with later empiricism. It is the medieval perspective which governs Father J. R. O'Donnell's study of his critical mentality in Selection (42). Nicholas accepted the Catholic faith as a norm of certitude, but he also pushed Ockham's teaching on the individual to the point where scientific generalization and demonstrative inference about existent things became impossible. Hence he regarded the demonstrative claims of Aristotelian and Averroistic philosophies as being speculatively unfounded and morally disastrous to the individual mind. His method of opposing an eternalism of individuals and atoms to an eternalism of the species (whose individual members come to be and pass away) had the purpose of setting one probable theory against another, so that there could be no valid ground for claiming demonstrative certitude for the Averroistic doctrine of the eternal world of species. In order to insure his case, however, Nicholas reduced to the status of probable dialectics all philosophical speculation which attempted to go beyond a descriptive report of the immediately known facts. This was the dead end for the "new way" of later medieval conceptualism.

Another line of philosophical descent is operative in the thought of Eckhart and Cusanus, who continued the effort to reconstruct philosohpy on a foundation of Christian Platonism. Through his spiritual treatises and sermons, Master John Eckhart of the Dominican order became a leader in the early fourteenth-century spiritual movement in Germany, which soon burgeoned forth in the mystical writings of Tauler, Suso, and Ruysbroeck. In his effort to provide a speculative basis for the immediate presence of God to creatures and of creatures to God, he developed some philosophical ideas which were condemned in 1329 for compromising the distinction between God and finite things.

In studying the metaphysical doctrines of Eckhart and his reply to his critics, Bernard Muller-Thym noticed that his repudiation of pantheism did not lead Eckhart to change his controversial theory of esse. Selection (43) suggests an explanation for this puzzling situation and, in doing so, brings out the contribution which a sustained comparative analysis can make to the understanding of a philosophical text. Eckhart could reaffirm his theism and yet not alter his basic position, because he was applying to the problem of God and the world the principles of solution used by St. Albert the Great to determine the relation between soul and body. The same dualism of aspects which we have already seen to be present in Albert's definition of the soul, now as substance, and now as act of the body, was also employed by Eckhart. If the divine esse can be considered now as absolute or in its own proper being and now as informing the nature of the creature, then there need be no confusion between esse in God and in finite things, any more than there is between the soul in its own substantial being and in the formal powers it confers upon the body. Were this solution evaluated in the light of the Thomistic doctrine on the human composite, it would entail the substantial and essential oneness of God and the world. But in stating that God's relation to the world is one of touching and impenetrating, informing and diffusing, Eckhart was drawing upon the tradition of Proclus, Avicebron, and the school of St. Albert. The controlled use of these historical referents enables Muller-Thym to clarify the mind of Eckhart, in the midst of the controversies and the obscure expressions in the texts.

The library of Cardinal Nicholas Cusanus was well stocked not only with manuscripts of Eckhart but also with many basic Western sources in philosophy and science. With Cusanus, who was both an energetic bishop and a humanistic scholar, the later Middle Ages and the Renaissance achieved a blend and displayed their essential continuity. He was just as convinced as Nicholas of Autrecourt about the probabilist nature of current Aristotelianism, but instead of drawing a skeptical conclusion he looked with Eckhart toward the resources of Christian Platonism. Selection (44) is taken from his chief treatise, Of Learned Ignorance, the major premise of which is that our mind is incommensurable with God, the infinite one or maximum of being. This need not lead to agnosticism, however, since we have the testimony of faith and the aid of mathe-

matical symbols. The choice of a geometrical symbolism not only belongs in the tradition of Boethius and the school of Chartres but also fore-shadows the Cartesian philosophical viewpoint, especially in its stress upon the removal from sensation, the pattern of mathematical certitude, and the mathematical approach to an infinite.

Cusanus symbolized the relation between the universe and God through the relation of geometrical figures to the infinite line. Although accused of pantheism, he was able to reply that this symbolization did not involve any identification between God and the world. For it was his very stress upon the divine transcendence, together with a mensura-tional conception of what genuine knowledge should be, which obliged him to employ symbols in discussing the nature of God and the refer-ence of the world to him. The distinction between the absolute maxi-mum or infinity of divine perfection and the relative or contracted maxi-mum of the universe prevented any confusion of God and the universe, even though it also prevented any cognitive approach to God except through faith and symbolical approximation. From the side of his medi-eval antecedents, two points were emphasized by Cusanus. He agreed with Eckhart and against Avicenna that the immediate term of creation is the universe as a structural whole, rather than a highest intelligence. This enabled him to establish a second position, namely, that indivi-duals are related to God through the universe, and hence that the vener-able relation of microcosm-macrocosm holds between the individual and the universe. This relation was soon to be interpreted in a monistic way by Bruno and theistically by Leibniz.

Our final Selection (45) is a chapter from the treatise on The Analogy of Names, *composed by Thomas de Vio, Cardinal Cajetan. Written just six years after the discovery of America, this work seeks to formalize the doctrine on analogy, distinguish the various types of analogy, and de-termine which kind is most appropriate for metaphysical inquiry. It opens with the remark that "an understanding of this doctrine is so nec-essary that without it no one can study metaphysics, and ignorance of it gives rise to many errors" (Bushenski-Koren translation, p. 9). Relying mainly upon Aristotle, Averroes, and Aquinas, Cajetan reduces all analo-gous terms to analogy of inequality, attribution, and proportionality. Analogy of proper proportionality is accepted as the most adequate one for metaphysics, since it concerns a likeness grounded in the intrinsic per-fection of the analogates. On this basis, Cajetan distinguishes it sharply from Aristotle's* to-one-thing *or* pros-hen *predication, which is a form of*

equivocity, since the perfection is intrinsic to only one analogate. Caje-
tan's theory of analogy is not merely a codification of the Thomistic
doctrine, since he retains his own meaning for esse *and is influenced by*
the Averroistic conception of being. Not only the later Scholastics, how-
ever, but such a modern philosopher as George Berkeley will find a
point of departure for the discussion of analogous predication in Caje-
tan's systematic treatment of the subject.

42

NICHOLAS OF AUTRECOURT'S CRITICISM OF ARISTOTLE [1]

THE correspondence between Nicholas of Autrecourt and Bernard
of Arezzo, together with the condemned articles from the *Satis
Exigit Ordo,* have been for the most part the basis for the studies
on the thought of the former. As they have already been many times utilized, I shall limit this article to an analysis of the treatise entitled
*Tractatus Universalis Magistri Nicholai De Ultricuria Ad Videndum
An Sermones Peripateticorum Fuerint Demonstrativi* or, as it is more
commonly called, the *Exigit Ordo.*

As the full title indicates, it is a critical examination of the teaching
of Aristotle and his disciples, especially Averroes. The conclusion drawn
from this examination is that the Stagirite, when subject to a diligent
logical scrutiny, is found wanting. At best only varying degrees of probability can be assigned to the conclusions of the Peripatetics.

1. THE MOTIVE FOR CRITICISM

It is to be noted from the outset that our author had no apparent
intention of setting up a positive doctrine for its own sake, which he
would accept as a true one, but rather he makes provisory acceptance
of theories, both ancient and contemporary, at variance with the teaching of Aristotle, in order to fulfill his main purpose, the discrediting
of the Aristotelian system. True he will deviate from both the ancients
and contemporaries, if it suits his purpose, yet in his writings many of
the current problems of the history of philosophy are discussed and
utilized. Nicholas was well acquainted with contemporary teaching and
disputations, as well as with the much used method of the *quaestiones*

---

[1] [From J. R. O'Donnell, C.S.B., "The Philosophy of Nicholas of Autrecourt and His
Appraisal of Aristotle," *Mediaeval Studies,* vol. 4 (1942), pp. 97-109. Reprinted by permission. Some paragraphs and the notes are omitted.]

quodlibetales; consequently it will be not without interest to the history of philosophy to draw a portrait of Nicholas of Autrecourt from the *Satis Exigit Ordo,* wherein fourteen century radicalism is given free rein.

The treatise in question was written between the years 1340 and 1345. At the date of composition the author had already fallen into the bad grace of his colleagues and was being subjected to violent attacks. These attacks probably culminated in his citation to the papal court at Avignon by Benedict XII on Nov. 21st, 1340, to answer the charges leveled at him. The condemnation of the articles of the *Satis Exigit Ordo* and Nicholas' retraction took place at Avignon on May 19th, 1346, under Clement V.

What were the motives which inspired Nicholas to write the *Satis Exigit Ordo?* There are two which seem more or less patent. The first, remote, can be attributed to the fact that he had definitely taken sides in the controversy which had grown up around the doctrine of Aristotle, expecially as seen in the so called Latin Averroist school. However he would not only seek to disprove Averroes, but attack the evil in its very root, the doctrine of Aristotle himself. The second and more immediate motive seems to have originated in his dispute with an unidentified Aegidius or Giles, who had written in a letter to Nicholas that it would not be difficult to prove that Aristotle had known a thousand conclusions. Nicholas claims to have examined the writings of Aristotle and found a thousand attempted demonstrations which were in no way cogent, but that on the contrary a probable opinion, if not always a more probable one, could be advanced against each and every one of these demonstrations.

Since the philosophical principles of Aristotle are unsound, to spend the best part of one's life studying them is a criminal waste of time. The duty of each and every one is to teach the Word of God and to live it. If truth is to be had, it should be had quickly. Consequently Nicholas felt conscience-bound to write this treatise in order to awaken from their lethargy and to convert those who had to no avail spent years in studying the teachings of Aristotle and his Commentator Averroes, since they were no closer to the truth at the end of their life than when they began, but rather further from it.

Nicholas of Autrecourt has been variously categorized as skeptic, Ockhamist or Nominalist, religious moralist. However, these three are not so isolated that traces of all cannot be found in the same man; on the contrary there is a very marked relationship between them. Skepticism with its denial of certitude to natural knowledge, Ockhamism with the overstressing of the Divine Omnipotence to the extent that there can be no guarantee of any constancy in nature, and the intrusion of this doctrine into the realm of knowledge, both lead to a distrust and despair of human reason, which in turns brings about the tendency to rely on Revelation alone. The Gospel is primarily a way of life which leads to salvation, and consequently those who cleave to it alone will stress Faith and moral conduct. These were common teachings in the fourteenth century. Such then, I suggest, was the basic motive for the *Satis Exigit Ordo,* namely the discrediting of Aristotle and through him scholastic philosophy, so that positive theology and the study of asceticism might reign supreme. Nicholas was not alone, neither was he born out of due time, but rather one more exponent of a tradition which neither began with him nor ended there.

Although the fact that he used the adversaries' own weapons, formal logic and dialectics, places him somewhat outside the tradition, nonetheless the ends in view were, I think, identical. Moreover from the very beginning of the treatise Nicholas gives clear expression to his intention of writing nothing which would be contrary to the teaching of the Church or of asserting his opinions contumaciously.

2. THE METHOD OF CRITICISM

The method which the author adopts is clearly stated and closely adhered to in the *Exigit Ordo,* namely to examine some of the conclusions of Aristotle to ascertain if they will satisfy the exigencies of dialectical procedure. To do this he takes several of the doctrines which were indubitably taught by Aristotle and attempts to show that they were insufficiently proved. His procedure is to doubt or question these doctrines, rather than to give a clear-cut system of his own. Consequently we cannot hope to find in this treatise a well established doctrine proper to the author, but rather only so much as will be sufficient to suit his purpose, that is, a manifestation of the insufficiency of evidence for the position of Aristotle. For this reason the prologues to the *Exigit Ordo* are the most important part of the treatise. Many of the conclusions which he advances as dialectically probable, he declares to be simply false.

The conclusions or teachings of Aristotle which Nicholas singles out for scrutiny are: (1) generation and corruption—to which he will oppose the principle that all things are eternal; (2) the infinite divisibility of the continuum—Nicholas will try to demonstrate that a continuum is composed of indivisibles, atoms or points; (3) the non-existence of the vacuum—Nicholas will prove both the necessity and possibility of the existence of a void; (4) the distinction between material substance and quantity—our author will claim indistinction; (5) the proofs of Aristotle against Protagoras' contention that everything which was apparent existed, and if apparently true was true, Nicholas answers point by point; (6) the Averroist doctrine of the unity of the intellect he rejects as untenable. The above problems present occasions for the discussion of corollaries, and necessitate further proof of details involved in the establishment of his main thesis, the eternity of things.

We are fortunate that Nicholas has given an outline of his involved method of procedure. The eternity of things based on atomism is the example he takes to show us his method at work. First of all he lays down a general rule which will, if accepted, serve as a demonstration that things are eternal. The principle is this: A perfect whole endowed with every perfection and excluding every imperfection should have the component parts of that whole, in as far as it is possible, possessed of the greatest possible perfection. This postulate seems to stem from the principle of plenitude. Against this general assumption there are objections. According to Averroes, the species, not individuals, contributes to the perfection of the universe. Therefore it might be concluded that since individuals do not contribute to the perfection of the universe, it matters little whether they are eternal or generable and corruptible; therefore it can be concluded that it is not necessary that a perfect whole have its parts perfect; therefore the postulate as enunciated is not true. The next step in the method is to answer the objection. The method to which we are most accustomed is first the stating of the objections, then the setting up of a definite doctrine, from which the answers to the objections flow. However the procedure adopted by Nicholas suits his purpose much better, since he is not as interested in establishing positive doctrine as in disproving and answering objections to opinions which he considers only probable.

His first step in answering this objection is to question the truth of the statement of Averroes. It would seem that, according to the principles laid down by Aristotle, individuals do actually contribute to the perfection of the universe, especially when we consider his doctrine on finality. If in nature, as in art, the details are made to harmonize with the whole, so also must individual things in the universe be considered as belonging to the good order which prevails therein. Again according to authentic Aristotelian doctrine, every being in the universe exists for another, consequently the perfection of any one individual rebounds to the perfection of the whole, of which that individual is a part. Likewise according to Aristotle, nature does nothing in vain. But individuals do exist; therefore they cannot be said to make no contribution to the perfection of the universe. Moreover Aristotle, according to one interpretation at least, taught the eternity of the world. Now if the world is eternal, so should its parts be eternal, and individuals certainly are part of the world. Consequently from the very principles of Aristotle himself, it can be deduced that the eternity of all things can be held.

All the steps of his answer to the objection, Nicholas says, are commonly accepted, but he will use them as probable only, not as certain. Again if we take two extreme positions: (1) never does anything exist; (2) every possible being always exists; midway between these two extremes is the mean that sometimes some things exist, sometimes they do not exist. From the first extreme it follows that, since *ens* and *bonum* are convertible terms, there would be a total defect of the good. If, as the mean allows, sometimes some things exist, sometimes they do not, the universe cannot be continually perfect. Therefore there is one choice left, namely, that every possible being always exists. This position satisfies the intellect; we would always feel pain, when things are said to pass into non-existence, if it were not for the fact that we have become accustomed to the idea of generation and corruption.

Still another phase of his technique is to prove that Aristotle taught doctrines which were undoubtedly condemned in 1277 and, as a consequence, contrary to the teaching of the Church. For example, Aristotle claimed that in a dead man there was neither good nor evil; this theory was, in addition to being condemned in 1277, contrary to the belief in heaven and hell.

The next step is to show that, if the eternity of all things be accepted as probable, all these difficulties will disappear. The eternity of things fits in better with the concept of the good, and is therefore preferable to the notion of generation and corruption. Everything which does not imply a contradiction is possible. When it is objected that the existence of corruptible things entails no contradiction, therefore they are possible, he answers that there is a contradiction contained in the notion of corruption, once we admit that the universe is always equally perfect.

Another argument for eternity is taken from Averroes, according to whom no truth could remain forever hidden from the human intellect. But if things are not eternal, how are we ever going to know why a thing endures only so long and no longer? If we grant eternity, this question cannot even be asked. Again if we pass into non-existence when we die, how can we be expected to give up our life for the common good? Nicholas here seems to indicate that there are no philosophical proofs for immortality. A *sure* answer to this question can be found in the Gospel, or a *probable* one [found in philosophy], if we accept the opinion that all things are eternal.

Nicholas bases his proofs for the eternity of things on a doctrine of atomism. So far he accepted it as a fact, but since Aristotle had already disproved the atomism of the ancients, objections could be raised against such a position and these objections he seeks to forestall. Corruption is, according to Nicholas, only a dispersal of the atoms which constitute a thing. There are those who will not accept such a doctrine, since it is not possible to show these atoms actually in the process of dispersing. This objection could come from one of two sources, either from those that maintain that nothing is in the intellect which was not previously in the senses, or more probably from the empiricists of Nicholas' own day who refused to accept anything that was not observable by the senses. The objection is absurd, says Nicholas, since even those who raise it will admit that the senses can deceive us. Moreover, studying observable phenomena is not the only means of arriving at truth. The remainder of the second part of the first prologue follows the same plan, namely the multiplication of Aristotelian principles opposed to the eternity of things and their refutation one by one; it is the method of the *questiones quodlibetales.*

To summarize: He starts with the concept of the good, which he declares to be fundamental to his system. Next, he proposes a theory which he will defend as probable, just as probable, if not more so than that of Aristotle. He does not claim this theory to be true for two reasons: (1) the dogmas of Faith and Revelation are the only sure norms of truth and real certitude; (2) there is no need to go beyond pure probability in order to find an adequate substitute for the Aristotelian doctrines. He raises and answers objections by proving the objector's position, if not untenable, at least less probable than his own, either because it is contrary to the Faith or because it presents difficulties altogether impossible of solution, which difficulties either do not arise if one accepts the eternity of things, or at least they can easily be solved.

If at times we find Nicholas stressing empiricism, at another time Revelation, at still another rational demonstration, we are not justified in accusing him of inconsistency. His intention is to examine the conclusions of Aristotle and to subject them to a rigorous test from all possible angles. He has chosen a very fundamental doctrine of Aristotle to attack, one from which many of his conclusions follow, namely that of generation and corruption, and which as a consequence offers many opportunities for refuting the doctrine of Aristotle in general. The arguments used to refute the peripatetic doctrine, because he intends to refute rather than to build, need not be drawn from any definite system of philosophy. Consequently, we need not be surprised if we find him using the principles of Ockham, Plato, Averroes or even of Aristotle himself against Aristotelianism. What could suit his purpose better than to manifest contradictions latent in the works of Aristotle? Since he seeks only probability, the manner or argumentation set forth in the *Topics* is sufficient.

If Nicholas of Autrecourt admits only dialectical probability to the system of Aristotle and claims no more for his own (if we may call his own a system), what, may we ask, are his requirements for certitude? Little certitude can be had from things through the natural appearances, and what little certitude can be had, would be had quickly, if men would turn to things rather than to the sayings of Aristotle and his Commentator Averroes. For a real demonstration, it is required that we proceed from things which are *per se nota* from the terms, from principles to which the intellect naturally gives assent, and from those things which we experience in us, e.g. sorrow and joy. In this he is practically quoting William of Ockham. Another source of *philosophical* certitude is the testimony of the senses, a principle which he had already enunciated in disputations at the Sorbonne and which he often reiterates in the *Satis Exigit Ordo*.

Nicholas' return to atomism can have two explanations. First of all, since Aristotle had written long chapters against the ancient atomists, he could find a ready-made system to place in opposition to that of the Stagirite; our author's position differs little from that of Democritus and

Leucippus. A second reason for adopting atomism is that it fits in so well with an anti-philosophical attitude of mind. If the universe is composed of atoms, between which there is no necessary connection, then the world must depend directly on God. It was for this reason that atomism had been adopted by the Arabian theologians. It was a current doctrine at Paris in the thirteenth and fourteenth centuries, and St. Thomas takes pains to refute it at length. No science can result from such a system and probabilism is bound to result. It was no accident that Nicholas chose atomism as the foundation for his doctrine of the eternity of things.

To the Aristotelian system of generation and corruption, then, Nicholas will oppose his hypothesis of the local motion of eternal atoms. Even intellection will be explained by the local motion of atoms. Nicholas claims for himself eternity, in as much as the atoms which compose his present being will at some time be dispersed, again to be assembled elsewhere at another time and so *ad infinitum*. Nicholas in no way believes this speculation, since the Faith, which is his norm of truth, teaches otherwise.

43

MEISTER ECKHART'S THEORY OF GOD AS *ESSE* [1]

THE whole force of the innumerable assertions of Meister Eckhart that God is *esse,* is *ipsum esse,* in virtue of whatever title that *esse* may be considered an absolute, appears to be a desire to show how creatures are contained in *esse* and so are made to be; for in itself the creature and the *quod est* is nothing. It is only then on the condition that creatures are one with *ipsum esse* or with God—for in divine things one can interchange terms freely if it will help the argument—that Eckhart can grant them being; for outside of *esse* there is simply nothing, and what is more, nothing is so nothing as that which is not only beyond *esse* but altogether distinct from it. If we consider the case of *esse,* then, as well as of the other general terms which are convertible with it (*unum, verum, bonum*—, the case is not at all clear for the other transcendentals *res* and *aliquid*), *esse* is simply a first, especially in regard to things that have existence. For *esse* in no wise is such that it can be made to be in something that already has a measure of reality, it can come from no such thing or by the agency of any such thing, but it must

1 [From Bernard Muller-Thym, *The Establishment of the University of Being in the Doctrine of Meister Eckhart of Hochheim* (New York: Sheed and Ward, 1939), pp. 68-73, 83-88. Reprinted by permission. Notes are omitted. The exposition is based primarily upon Eckhart's *Opus Tripartitum,* his commentary on the *Book of Wisdom,* and his *Apology.*]

precede all that is in the finite existent. And so the *esse* which is the *esse* of all things (in a moment we shall see that this manner of speaking is exactly what Eckhart means by the *esse omnium*) must be immediately from the first and universal cause of all things. Therefore, he adds, "from *esse* itself and through it and in it are all things. *Esse* itself is neither in anything nor from anything: for that which is other than *esse* is not or is nothing." The words are hardly more than a paraphrase of St. Paul's *Epistle to the Romans*.

What is more, already we can recognize in this doctrine that all things must be contained in *ipsum esse,* a marked parallel to the Albertine-Eckhartian doctrine that the body and the lower parts of the soul must all be contained and made one in the subsistence, the highest part of the soul. St. Albert had taught as part of a general theory of being that the substantial form contains that matter of the composite and gives it definite perfection, so that, in virtue of that form's being the cause of the *esse* of the whole, it ought to bear the name *principium*. So it is, that all that exists, exists only so far as it is in *esse* and *esse* is in it, for this is the meaning of St. John's *He abides in God, and God in him*. For, as we have just remarked, to be outside of God or of *esse*—it is one and the same thing—is to be nothing; this, again, is what St. John means when he says *sine ipso factum est nihil,* "without God the thing made is nothing." This had been Meister Eckhart's constant reading of the passage of the prologue to the fourth Gospel from the time of writing his *Parisian Questions*. It is not without interest to remark that exactly the same interpretation had been made by that consummate Platonist of the twelfth century, Alan of Lille, and that in Proclus also one can discover passages that suggest the same outlook. The creature, the thing made, then, exists only upon its being in *ipsum esse,* for the whole perfection of secondary and inferior things consists in their assimilation to the higher.

It is thus that the act by which creatures come into existence, so that they have *esse* and not simply that specification of *esse* which is *esse hoc aut illud* (*sosein, dasein*), is the act of creation; for the correlate and contrary of *esse* is nothing, *nihil,* and so the act of giving things existence must be a production from nothingness, that is, creation. This act, all the great doctors of the thirteenth century had taught, is proper to God, so proper even that God cannot delegate it to a creature. Meister Eckhart would shrink from saying anything else; creation is the act of the first cause which in that act produces being simply, necessarily, in accordance with its peculiar possession of and identity with *esse*.

That is standard doctrine, and all the editors have been at pains to refer to the numerous places in which St. Thomas has taught that only God can create, since it demands infinite power to bridge the infinite gap between being and absolute nothingness, and so to make things be where nothing was before. That doctrine could have been found as easily in St. Albert, in St. Bonaventure. Nor ought we forget that the

Liber de Causis, circulated widely in the western world at least after 1187, the year Gerard of Cremona died, a work whose neo-Platonism gives more than one text to Meister Eckhart, had taught that the first cause produces being in the mode of creation.

But the orientation of that commonly received doctrine is quite different in Meister Eckhart. For one thing, he enunciates it to the end that no other being than God can confer *esse,* since *esse* is God. By this *esse* and by no other must all things exist—there is no other *esse*—, as all things that are white must be white by whiteness alone—the comparison already is suggestive of a doctrine of formalities. For another, and more noteworthy thing, Meister Eckhart teaches that doctrine to the end that all things exist in God; for everything that God creates, everything He works or does, He creates, works and does in Himself. Whatever is outside of God or comes into being outside of God, is or comes into being outside of *esse.* But let us be clear: one may say the thing "is" outside of God, if the "is" has a purely copulative sense unrelated to existence. Thus Eckhart says that whatever is outside of *esse* "is" nothing. But one may not say at all that anything comes into being outside of *esse,* of God, for the term of becoming is *esse,* is God.

Eckhart has described *ipsum esse* at two moments in its being, one at which it is present to the creature as touching it, the other at which the same *esse* informs the creature by an act of penetration. Even before we investigate that doctrine further, we cannot help being reminded of the Albertine doctrine of the soul, at one moment substance, at another the form of the body. Moreover, the sense of a distinction at exactly this point in Eckhart's thought is heightened by the distinction Eckhart himself had made, during his *Apology* at Cologne, between *esse absolutum* and *esse formaliter inhaerens,* by virtue of which distinction it is quite clear that he meant to avoid the apparent inconveniences of his doctrine.

In the fourth of the articles of accusation extracted from the *First Commentary on Genesis,* Eckhart had been charged with saying that *esse* is an absolute first, so that the *esse* of all things is immediately from the first and universal cause of all things, that from *esse,* therefore, by it and in it are all things, itself not from any other, that what is other than *esse* simply is not, is nothing. The passage was quite accurately reported, and we have already seen its meaning. To this Eckhart replied that what he had said was true, although a distinction must be made between *esse formaliter inhaerens* and *esse absolutum,* which is God. It must be remarked that he did not qualify the text with which he had been presented—he has left us no rule for telling when *esse* is to be considered *esse formaliter inhaerens,* when it is to be considered *esse absolutum.* He simply says that the distinction is to be made, and that *esse absolutum* is God.

Again, the proposition *Esse est Deus* had been brought against him, with the five reasons he had taught established that proposition. One of them declares that *esse* must be God, for if it were other than God, the thing would have *esse* from something else and not from God. Another affirmed that all things have *esse* from *ipsum esse,* as all white things are white by whiteness. In his *Apology,* Eckhart said that in truth these reasons are such that no answer can be given to them, they cannot be refuted. He also said, however, that the *esse* of the proposition *Esse est Deus* refers to *esse absolutum,* not to *esse formaliter inhaerens.* Now again, what at first appears to be a distinction between two diverse kinds of *esse,* upon a second reading of the text seems to mean nothing more than when we say *Esse est Deus, esse,* which in regard to creatures exercises formal causality, does not exercise that sort of causality in regard to God, which it is.

This reading is consonant with what Eckhart says elsewhere; for he uses the word *formaliter* to signify the sort of activity that form carries on in matter and in the composite. Thus it is that the perfections of the things about us, creatures, are in those things according to the mode of formal causality; those same perfections, however, do not inform God, for they are in God not *formaliter* but *virtute* [or by power]. This, we must say, is more than the traditional Christian teaching of how the perfections of creatures are contained eminently in God. It is another resemblance to the Albertine doctrine according to which the subsistence of the soul, its highest part, contains all inferior perfections *virtute, potestate,* and only by a descent of "forms" do these perfections come to exist *as such,* and inform part by part their respective organs. It is a doctrine of formalities which Eckhart is following, as we may be sure from more than one text.

Finally, when confronted with the very texts we have cited, texts which prove all things must have existence from God, must have that existence immediately from God, who alone is *esse* and outside of whom there is nothing, Meister Eckhart again replied to each charge that that was the true doctrine, although the distinction he had already enunciated between *esse absolutum,* God, and *esse formaliter inhaerens* should be applied in these cases also. Now it was by a restatement of the same argument in the same work that he had added the significant words: "For whatever aspect of any thing is neither immediately touched nor penetratingly informed by *esse* itself, is nothing." There can be no doubt that the two modes of expression deal with one and the same reality. There can also be no doubt that the distinction enunciated in this twofold fashion applies to *esse* conceived as something unique, for we must never forget that Eckhart considers that if he admits a second *esse,* that of creature, distinct as *esse* from the *esse* which is God, he will not be able to hold the immediacy of God to creature.

Within these conditions, we may disengage in brief fashion the import of the distinction:

1. *Esse* itself is an absolute and is God. If we consider that the creature is existing in *esse,* it is contained in *esse,* taken in this manner, *virtute;* also, if we consider that the creature is existing in *esse, esse* (God) is

present to it in a way that may be described as touching it. If we consider this *esse* quite in its absolute character, then the creature is utterly opposed to it and is absolutely nothing, and this for two reasons: because *esse* is the only reality, and otuside of it there is nothing, and because the *quod est* considered in itself is absolutely nothing, as St. Albert had said.

2. This same *esse*, now considered as form and the sort of form that confers being, while it is in fact God, is not God as form. Thus considered, *esse* gives being to creature by an act of penetration. Because it is the same *esse* which is God, *esse* so-considered is equally immediate to creature. The creature is contained in it, as every inferior must be contained in its superior; when the creature is contained in *esse*, the creature is *ens*. And because this very *esse* is God, although it is not considered God in so far as it is form, this *esse*, God, and creature are related to each other respectively as *esse*, the abstract (in the terminology of Gilbert of La Porrée), and *ens*, the concrete, as act and potency, as form and matter. And because *esse*, one in itself, receives number according to the *quod est* in which it is diffused (it is numbered only considered as diffused, it is one considered in itself, even as the soul is utterly one in its subsistence and is as manifold as its powers, having emanated from the unity of that subsistence, are diffused in the man), this *esse* is the one which is in the many and which constitutes the many by its unity.

This explanation, which in no way does violence to the text of Eckhart, but takes all the apparently contrary texts in their literal signification, bears a marked resemblance to the case of the soul. For that reality which we are wont to call the soul—St. Albert and Meister Eckhart are both agreed that "soul" is not its proper name—has two different states of being and so two different considerations. One and the same reality, under one consideration it is an absolute, utterly simple in its subsistence (i.e., in reference to all of which it will be the act) and one. Under another consideration it is form and act, containing the lower powers and the body in itself with the unity of potency and act, matter and form, whose diffusion in the composite is the *esse* of the composite, and whose unity becomes multitude in the composite. We can see how literally Eckhart meant that God is in the world as the soul is in the body.

44

CUSANUS ON MATHEMATICAL SYMBOLS AND THE RELATION BETWEEN GOD AND THE WORLD [1]

ALL our greatest philosophers and theologians unanimously assert that the visible universe is a faithful reflection of the invisible, and that from creatures we can rise to a knowledge of the Creator, "in a mirror and in a dark manner," as it were. The fundamental reason for the use of symbolism in the study of spiritual things, which in themselves are beyond our reach, has already been given [in the doctrine that God is both absolute unity and the cause of the universe]. Though we neither perceive it nor understand it, we know for a fact that all things stand in some sort of relation to one another; that, in virtue of this interrelation, all the individuals constitute one universe, and that in the one Absolute the multiplicity of beings is unity itself. Every image is an approximate reproduction of the exemplar; yet, apart from the Absolute image or the Exemplar itself in unity of nature, no image will so faithfully or precisely reproduce the exemplar, as to rule out the possibility of an infinity of more faithful and precise images, as we have already made clear.

When we use an image and try to reach analogically what is as yet unknown, there must be no doubt at all about the image; for it is only by way of postulates and things certain that we can arrive at the unknown. But in all things sensible, material possibility abounds, which explains their being in a continual state of flux. Our knowledge of things is not acquired by completely disregarding their material conditions, without which no image of them could be formed; nor is it wholly subject to their possible variations; but the more we abstract from sensible conditions, the more certain and solid our knowledge is. Mathematics is an example of such abstract knowledge. That explains why philosophers so readily turned to mathematics for examples of the things which the intellect had to investigate; and none of the masters of old, when solving a difficulty, used other than mathematical illustrations, so that Boethius, the most learned of Romans, went so far as to say that knowledge of things divine was impossible without some knowledge of mathematics.

Following in the way of the Ancients, we are in complete agreement with them in saying that, since there is no other approach to a knowl-

[1] [From Nicholas Cusanus, *Of Learned Ignorance*, translated by G. Heron, O.F.M. (London: Routledge and Kegan Paul, Ltd.; New Haven: Yale University Press, 1954), pp. 25-27, 80-85. Reprinted by permission.]

edge of things divine than that of symbols, we cannot do better than use mathematical signs on account of their indestructible certitude.

It is now evident from what we have said that no object that we know or of which we have any idea, can be the Absolute Maximum; and since it is by way of symbols that we intend to conduct our search of it, we must, therefore, look for something more than a simple comparison. In mathematics, in fact, we are always dealing with finite things, for if they were not finite we could form no idea of them at all. If then we want to reach the Absolute Maximum through the finite, we must, in the first place, study finite, mathematical figures as they are, namely a mixture of potency and act. Then we must attribute the respective perfections to the corresponding infinite figures, and finally we must, in a much more sublime way, attribute the perfections of the infinite figures to the simple Infinite, which cannot possibly be expressed by any figure. Then, whilst we are groping in the dark, our ignorance will enlighten us in an incomprehensible fashion, and enable us to form a more correct and truer notion of the Absolute.

2. THE UNIVERSE AS A LIKENESS OF THE ABSOLUTE

If we simply recall that all things are, or owe their existence to, the Absolute Maximum, we will be able to discover a good deal about the world or universe. For me, the universe is only a restricted form of maximum. It is restricted or concrete, because it holds all its being from the Absolute; and because it is a maximum, it reproduces the Absolute Maximum in the greatest way possible. We may affirm, therefore, that all we learn about the Absolute Maximum as belonging to him without any restriction whatsoever, may be applied in a relative way to the restricted maximum.

Let us take some examples to help the student in his enquiry. God is the Absolute Maximum and absolute unity, and, as such, he forestalls and unites things different and distant; e.g., contradictories, between which there is no mean, are identified in him. In an absolute way he is what all things are; he is the absolute beginning in all, the end of all and the entity of all. Just as the infinite line is all the figures, so the Absolute Maximum, in its infinite simplicity and unity, is all things without plurality. The world or universe is also a maximum, though a limited maximum; it anticipates in its unity limited opposites like contraries; within its limited existence it is what all things are; and in a restricted sense it is the beginning, end and being of things. It is infinity contracted to the relatively infinite; and just as the relative maximum line is relatively all figures, so the limited maximum—the universe—in its relative simplicity and unity is all things without plurality.

All becomes clear, then, once we have a correct idea of this contraction. In fact, the relative infinity or simplicity or unity in the universe comes from, though it is infinitely inferior to, the absolute, with the result that the infinity, eternity and unity of the world bear no comparison with the infinity, eternity and unity of the absolute. On that account, absolute unity admits no plurality, whereas the unity of the universe does; for, though the universe is one and even a maximum from the point of view of unity, it is a relative unity and only a relative maximum. Therefore, maximum unity though it be, its unity is limited by plurality, just as its infinity is by finiteness, its simplicity by composition, its eternity by succession, and so on. It is as if absolute necessity were to communicate itself without fusion to another, and find in that other a term that restricted it; or as if, independently of the intellect's act of abstraction, absolute whiteness were to exist in itself. Any relatively white object would receive its whiteness from it, and an object would be white only in so far as it received whiteness; in other words, in any object, absolute whiteness would find itself limited by non-whiteness.

Much can be deduced from these considerations by the student. For instance, just as God, by reason of his Immensity, is neither in the sun nor the moon, yet in an absolute way he is in them what they are. So the universe is neither in the sun nor in the moon, yet in a restricted fashion it is in them what they are. No distinction can be made between the absolute quiddity of the sun and moon, for it is God himself Who is the absolute entity and quiddity of all. But the restricted quiddity of the sun is distinct from the restricted quiddity of the moon, because the restricted quiddity of a thing is the thing itself, whereas the absolute quiddity is God and not the thing itself. For that reason, it is evident that, in the universe, identity consists in diversity as unity consists in plurality, for the universe is a restricted quiddity, which in the sun is restricted in one way and in the moon in another. The universe, then, is not the sun nor the moon, yet it is the sun in the sun and the moon in the moon; on the other hand, God is not the sun in the sun nor the moon in the moon, but he is without plurality and diversity what the sun and moon are. Universe means universality, i.e., unity of distinct things. Therefore the relationship of the universe to all things is that of humanity to men: humanity is neither Socrates nor Plato, but in Socrates it is Socrates and in Plato it is Plato.

Having established that the universe is only a principle and a maximum in a restricted sense, we can see now that the entire universe was brought into being by a simple emanation of the restricted maximum from the Absolute Maximum. The opinion of Avicenna and other philosophers that intelligences were created first, the spiritual soul next, and then nature, is not acceptable. All the beings which form parts of the universe must have come into being together with the universe, for without them it would be impossible for the universe in its limited nature to be one, entire and perfect. In the artist's mind the whole is conceived before the part, for example the house, before a wall; and so it was with the mind of God, to Whose will all things owe their being. First, then, to be produced was the universe and, as a consequence, all that the existence of the universe and its perfection necessarily demanded. We consider the Absolute Maximum at first in the restricted maximum with a view to finding it afterwards in all the individuals, like the abstract in the concrete; for the Absolute Maximum exists in an absolute way in the universe. In fact, God is the absolute quiddity of the world or universe, whereas it is a restricted quiddity that forms the universe. Contraction means being restricted to some particular thing. The universe, therefore, in a restricted fashion, exists in all the particular beings that form it, whilst God, Who is one, is in the universe as a unity.

In this way we will be able to understand how God, Who is unity in its infinite simplicity, exists in the universe as a unity and, as a consequence, in all things through the intermediary of the universe; how, too, through the universe as a unity the plurality of things is in God.

3. EVERYTHING IN EVERYTHING

From a keen study of what has already been said, we come to understand easily enough, perhaps even more fully than Anaxagoras himself, the depth of the truth he expressed in the words "everything is everything." For we learned that God is in all things in such a way that all things are in him. God is in all things by the medium, as it were, of the universe; so it follows that all is in all, and each in each. As if by nature's order it was that the most perfect—the universe—came into being before all things, so that anything might be in anything. In fact, in every creature the universe is the creature; consequently each creature receives all, so that in any creature, all creatures are found in a relative way. Since all creatures are finite, no creature could be all things in act; but all things are contracted in order to form each creature. If, then, all things are in all, it is clear that all is prior to the individual; and all here does not signify plurality, for prior to the individual there is no plurality. For that reason, all-without-plurality has preceded the individual in the order of nature, with the consequence that in any actual individual there is not more than one: all-without-plurality is that one.

Only by way of contraction is the universe in things; in fact it is restricted by each actually existing thing to be actually what each thing is. Everything actually existing is in God, for He is the act of all. Act means perfection and the realization of what was possible. Since the universe restricted is in each actually existing individual, then evidently God, Who is in the universe, is in every individual and every individual actually existing is, like the universe, immediately in God. To say that "everything is in everything" is the same as saying that God, by the intermediary of the universe, is in all things and that the universe, by the intermediary of all things, is in God. How God is without any diversity in all, since everything is everything, and how all is in God, because all is in all, are truths of a very high order which are clearly understood by keen minds. The universe is in each individual in such a way that each individual is in it, with the result that in each individual the universe is by contraction what the particular individual is. And every individual in the universe is the universe, though the universe is in each individual in a different way, and each thing is in the universe in a different way.

Here is an example: The infinite line is clearly a line, a triangle, a circle and a sphere; but a finite line receives its existence from the infinite line, and the infinite line is all that the finite line is. All, therefore, that is identified with the infinite line—line, triangle and the others—is also found identified with the finite line. Every figure in the finite line is the line itself; but that does not mean that the triangle or circle or sphere is actually present in it. That everything is in everything does not imply actual presence, for the actual unity of the thing would be destroyed by such a plurality; but the triangle in the line is the line, the circle in the line is the line, and so on. To note that a line can only actually exist in a body—a point to be proved elsewhere—helps you to see this more clearly. No one doubts that in a body with length, breadth and depth, all the figures are virtually contained. So in an actual line all the figures are actually the line itself, and in a triangle all are the triangle, and so on. In a stone all is stone, in the vegetative soul all is soul, in life all is life, in one sense power all is that sense, in sight all is sight, in hearing all is hearing, in the imagination all is imagination, in reason all is reason, in the understanding all is understanding, in God all is God. From that you see how the unity of things or the universe exists in plurality, and conversely how plurality exists in unity.

You will also see on closer study how each individual in actual existence is at peace, for all in the individual is the individual and the individual in God is God; and there appears the wonderful unity of things, the admirable equality and the most remarkable connection, by which all is in all. In this we see the one source of the connection and diversity of things. An individual could not be actually all things, for it would be God, and therefore all things would be actualized in it in the way in which they can exist as individual natures. Nor can any two things be absolutely equal, since all things were made in varying degrees of being—like the being which could not possess all at once the perfection of incorruptibility and was made to exist without corruption in temporal succession. Consequently, all things are what they are, because they could not be otherwise nor better.

45

ANALOGY OF PROPORTIONALITY IN CAJETAN [1]

1. NATURE OF ANALOGY OF PROPORTIONALITY

DESCRIPTION. Passing over from what is called incorrectly analogous to analogy in the proper sense, we say that analogous by proportionality are called those things which have a common name, and the notion expressed by this name is proportionally the same. Or to say the same in a different way, analogous by proportionality are called those things which have a common name, and the notion expressed by this name is similar according to a proportion. For instance, to see by corporeal vision and by intellectual vision are indicated by the common term *to see,* because just as *to understand* presents something to the mind, so *to see* presents something to the animated body.

Proportion and Proportionality. The name *proportion* is given to a definite relation of one quantity to another; e.g., we say that four is twice as much in proportion to two. The name *proportionality* is given to a similitude of two proportions; e.g., we say that eight is to four as six is to three, because both are twice as much in proportion, etc. However, philosophers have transferred the term *proportion* [from the sphere of mathematics and use it] to express any relationship of conformity, commensuration, capacity, etc. As a result they have extended the use of the term *proportionality* to every similitude of relationships. It is in this sense that we use the term in the present study.

2. ITS DIVISION

Analogy of proportionality can occur in two ways—namely, metaphorically and properly. It is *metaphorical* when the common term has absolutely one formal meaning, which is realized in one of the analogates and predicated of the other by metaphor. For example, *to smile* has one meaning in itself, but is metaphorically analogous with respect to a true smile and a blooming meadow or good fortune; for thus we indicate that these things are just like a man smiling. Sacred Scripture is full of examples of this sort of analogy, wherever it teaches us about God by means of metaphors.

Analogy of proportionality occurs in the *proper* sense, when the com-

[1] [From Thomas de Vio, Cardinal Cajetan, *The Analogy of Names,* translated by E. A. Bushinski, C.S.Sp., and H. J. Koren, C.S.Sp. (Pittsburgh: Duquesne University Press, 1953), pp. 24-29, with omission of the notes. Reprinted by permission.]